INSTANT POT COOKBOOK

TOP 550 AMAZINGLY TASTY & HEALTHY INSTANT POT RECIPES FOR YOUR HEALTHY FAMILY

By

Mary Grace

Copyright © 2017 by Mary Grace. All legal rights reserved.

ISBN-10: 1975719387
ISBN-13: 978-1975719388

You cannot offer this book for free or sell it. You do not have reselling legal rights to this book. This Book may not be recreated in any file format or physical format without having the expressed written approval of Mary Grace. All Violators will be sued.

While efforts have been made to assess that the information contained in this book is valid, neither the author nor the publisher assumes any accountability for errors, interpretations, omissions or usage of the subject matters herein.

Disclaimer:

The Information presented in this book is Cleated to provide useful information on the subject areas discussed. The publisher and author are not accountable for any particular health or allergic reaction needs that may involve medical supervision and are not liable for any damage or damaging outcomes from any treatment, application or Prep, action, to any person reading or adhering to the Information in this book. References are presented for informational reasons only and do not represent an endorsement of any web sites or other sources. Audience should be informed that the websites mentioned on this book may change.

This publication includes opinions and ideas of its author and is meant for informational purposes only. The author and publisher shall in no event be held liable for any damage or loss sustained from the usage of this publication.

TABLE OF CONTENTS

INTRODUCTION 1

Instant Pot Pressure Cooker 2

Uses of an Electric Pressure Cooker 4

How To Use The Control Panel and Automatic Cooking Programs 5

BREAKFAST RECIPES 7

- 1. Amazingly Delicious Pear Oatmeal 8
- 2. French Style Special Toast 8
- 3. Tasty Mushroom Oatmeal 9
- 4. Delicious Cinnamon Steel Cut Oats 10
- 5. Spinach And Tomato Breakfast 10
- 6. Banana Cake For Breakfast 11
- 7. Yummy Pomegranate Porridge 11
- 8. Tasty Breakfast Cobbler 12
- 9. Appetizing Scotch Eggs 12
- 10. Tasty Poached Eggs 13
- 11. Amazing Pumpkin Oats Granola 14
- 12. Simply Steamed Eggs 14
- 13. Yummy Breakfast Risotto 15
- 14. Appetizing Vanilla Steel Cut Oats 15
- 15. Tasty Egg Muffins 16
- 16. Appetizing Rice Bowl 16
- 17. Delicious Carrot Oatmeal 17
- 18. Yummy Rice Pudding 17
- 19. Delicious Breakfast Millet Pilaf 18
- 20. Simple Breakfast Pudding 18
- 21. Tasty Breakfast Quinoa Salad 19
- 22. Appetizing Millet Pudding 19
- 23. Yummy Breakfast Chia Pudding 20
- 24. Mouthwatering Breakfast Quinoa 20
- 25. Delicious Breakfast Sandwiches 21

26. Breakfast Peppers And Sausages 21
27. Breakfast Tacos 22
28. Yummy Breakfast Hash 22
29. Breakfast Berries Jam 23
30. Amazing Chicken Liver Breakfast Spread 23
31. Appetizing Lemon Marmalade 24
32. Breakfast Blackberry Jam 24
33. Tasty Chickpeas Spread 25
34. Delicious Cheesy Grits 25
35. Amazing Ricotta Cheese Spread 26
36. Yummy Pecan Sweet Potatoes 26
37. Breakfast Pumpkin Butter 27
38. Amazing Breakfast 27
39. Appetizing Mushroom Pate 28
40. Yummy Breakfast Potatoes 28
41. Best BBQ Tofu 29
42. Amazing Tofu Breakfast 29
43. Tasty Tofu Scramble 30
44. Tofu And Potatoes Breakfast 30
45. Amazing Breakfast Salad 31

SIDE DISH RECIPES 32

46. Delicious Farro Pilaf And Wild Rice 33
47. Awesome Mushroom Risotto 33
48. Delicious Almonds And Quinoa Side Dish 34
49. Yummy Quinoa Pilaf 34
50. Tasty Pumpkin Risotto 35
51. Amazing Flavored Mashed Potatoes 35
52. Special Pink Rice 36
53. Rice And Veggies Side Dish 36
54. Saffron Risotto Side Dish 37
55. Delicious Potatoes Side Dish 37
56. Mexican Rice Side dish 38

57. Tasty Herbed Polenta 38
58. Simple Barley And Cauliflower Risotto 39
59. Instant Farro Side Dish 40
60. Goat Cheese And Spinach Risotto 40
61. Artichokes And Rice Side Dish 41
62. Yummy Mashed Squash 41
63. Mouthwatering Lemon Parmesan & Peas Risotto 42
64. Tasty Potato Casserole Side Dish 42
65. Delicious Refried Beans 43
66. Yummy Black Beans 44
67. Rice And Red Beans 44
68. Amazing Side Dish 45
69. Simple Cauliflower And Pineapple Rice 45
70. Delicious Potatoes Gratin 46
71. Triple Beans Mix Side Dish 47
72. Mushrooms And Green Beans Side Dish 47
73. Amazing French Fries 48
74. Yummy Cauliflower Mash Side Dish 48
75. Apple And Butternut Mash 49
76. Delicious Brussels Sprouts Side Dish 49
77. Simple Sweet Carrot Puree Side Dish 50
78. Parmesan Asparagus And Garlic 50
79. Tasty Glazed Carrots 51
80. Poached Fennel Side dish 51
81. Amazing "Drunken "Peas Side Dish 52
82. Yummy Mashed Turnips 52
83. Delicious Broccoli Side Dish 53
84. Healthy Artichokes Side Dish 53
85. Delicious Onions And Parsnips 54
86. Awesome Eggplant Side Dish 54
87. Garlic And Beet Side Dish 55
88. Simple Citrus And Cauliflower Side Dish 55

89. Special Fava Bean Sauté 56

90. Tomato And Calamari Side Dish 56

91. Delicious Veggies Side Dish 57

92. Special Bok Choy Side Dish 57

93. Amazing Green Bean Side Dish 58

94. Israeli Style Couscous Side Dish 58

POULTRY RECIPES 59

95. Special Moroccan Chicken 60

96. BBQ Honey Chicken 60

97. Potatoes And Chicken Dish 61

98. Delicious Turkey Chili 61

99. Tasty Veggies And Duck 62

100. Yummy Chicken And Tomatillo Sauce 62

101. Simple Salsa Chicken Dish 63

102. Mouthwatering Chicken Sandwiches 64

103. Delightful Lemongrass Chicken 64

104. Thai Style Chicken Dish 65

105. Delicious Cacciatore Chicken 65

106. Yummy Turkey Meatballs 66

107. Special Filipino Chicken 67

108. Mashed Potatoes With Turkey Mix 67

109. Easy Chicken Salad 68

110. Tasty Crispy Chicken 69

111. Yummy Braised Quail 69

112. Braised Potatoes And Duck 70

113. Simple Chicken Dish 71

114. Delicious Rice And Chicken 71

115. Tasty Chicken Romano 72

116. Mouthwatering Duck Chili 73

117. Chicken And Coca-Cola 74

118. Tasty Turkey Wings 74

119. Mouthwatering Chicken Curry 75

120. Special Coq Au Vin 75

121. Italian Style Chicken 76

122. Cheering Chicken Gumbo 76

123. Tasty Creamy Chicken 77

124. Yummy Buffalo Chicken 78

125. Delight Chicken... 78

126. Delicious Chicken Curry With Squash And Eggplant.. 79

127. Colombian Style Chicken Dish 79

128. Special Chicken & Lentils Dish... 80

129. Tasty Teriyaki Chicken 81

130. Yummy Chicken & Dumplings 81

131. Tasty Noodles And Chicken 82

132. Simple Sesame Chicken 82

133. Delicious Chicken With Duck Sauce 83

134. Special Chicken Wings 84

135. Chickpea Masala With Chicken 84

136. Indian style Butter Chicken 85

137. Mix Chicken And Corn 86

138. Tasty Goose Dish.. 86

139. Pomegranate And Chicken 87

140. Tasty Shrimp And Chicken 87

141. Delicious Goose With Chili Sauce 88

142. Delicious Cabbage And Chicken 89

143. Yummy Chicken & Broccoli.. 89

MEAT RECIPES 91

144. Easy Corned Beef... 92

145. Tasty Chili Con Carne 92

146. Yummy Beef Stroganoff.. 93

147. Delicious Beef Curry 93

148. Mixed Beans Beef... 94

149. Special Beef Bourguignon.. 95

150. Tasty Beef Pot Roast... 95

151. Korean Style Beef Dish ... 96
152. Best Beef & Pasta Casserole ... 96
153. Appetizing Veal Dish ... 97
154. Tasty Cabbage & Beef ... 98
155. Simple Beef Dish ... 98
156. Delicious Lamb Dish ... 99
157. Tasty Lamb Shanks ... 99
158. Mouthwatering Lamb Dish ... 100
159. Special Lamb Dish ... 101
160. Easy Lamb Ragout ... 101
161. Barley And Lamb Dish ... 102
162. White Beans And Lamb Dish ... 102
163. Mexican Lamb Dish ... 103
164. Yummy Goat Mix ... 104
165. Tasty Lamb Curry ... 104
166. Potatoes And Goat ... 105
167. Broccoli And Beef ... 106
168. Moroccan Style Lamb ... 106
169. Delicious Short Ribs ... 107
170. Tasty Meatloaf ... 108
171. Red Beans And Sausage Dish ... 108
172. Delicious Ribs & Coleslaw ... 109
173. Asian Style Short Ribs Dish ... 110
174. Tomato Sauce And Meatballs ... 110
175. Mouthwatering Meatloaf ... 111

FISH AND SEAFOOD RECIPES ... 113

176. Yummy Salmon Dish ... 114
177. Tasty Steamed Fish ... 114
178. Appetizing Fish With Orange Sauce ... 115
179. Delicious Fish Curry ... 115
180. Poached Yummy Salmon ... 116
181. Special Mediterranean Fish ... 116

- 182. Tasty Veggies And Salmon 117
- 183. Spicy tasty Salmon 117
- 184. Simple Salmon Burger 118
- 185. Yummy Fish Pudding 118
- 186. Raspberry Sauce And Salmon 119
- 187. Peas And Cod 120
- 188. Crispy Tasty Salmon Fillet 120
- 189. Delicious Rice And Salmon 121
- 190. Best Fish Dish 121
- 191. Tasty Cheesy Tuna 122
- 192. Special Jambalaya 122
- 193. Noodle And Tuna Dish 123
- 194. Hot Roasted Mackerel Dish 123
- 195. Pot Steamed Mussels Dish 124
- 196. Sausage With Mussels 124
- 197. Delicious Clams 125
- 198. Yummy Mussels And Spicy Sauce 125
- 199. Tasty Mussels 126
- 200. Mouthwatering Mackerel With Lemon 126
- 201. Special Clams Dish 127
- 202. Delicious Cioppino 127
- 203. Simple Crab Dish 128
- 204. Yummy Shrimp Delight 128
- 205. Mouthwatering Miso Mackerel 129
- 206. Amazing Shrimp Curry 130
- 207. Simple Shrimp Paella 130
- 208. Delicious Shrimp & Dill Sauce 131
- 209. Potatoes And Shrimp Mix 131
- 210. Special Shrimp Creole 132
- 211. Instant Shrimp Boil 132
- 212. Special Shrimp Curry 133
- 213. Quick Shrimp Scampi 134

214. Amazing Shrimp Dish ... 134

215. Shrimp And Fish ... 135

216. Tasty Shrimp Teriyaki Dish ... 135

217. Amazing Shrimp With Risotto & Herbs ... 136

218. Yummy Seafood Gumbo ... 136

219. Potatoes And Octopus ... 137

220. Delicious Octopus Stew ... 137

221. Greek Style Octopus ... 138

222. Masala Squid ... 139

223. Amazing Stuffed Squid ... 139

224. Hot Squid Roast ... 140

225. Special Braised Squid Dish ... 140

VEGETABLE RECIPES ... 142

226. Healthy Artichoke Hearts ... 143

227. Delicious Artichokes With Lemon Sauce ... 143

228. Spinach And Artichokes Dip ... 144

229. Delicious Blue Cheese And Beets ... 144

230. Healthy Artichokes With Tasty Dip ... 145

231. Tasty Beet Salad ... 145

232. Amazing Wrapped Asparagus Canes ... 146

233. Tomato And Beet Salad ... 146

234. Orange And Beet Salad ... 147

235. Shrimp And Asparagus ... 147

236. Pomegranate And Brussels Sprouts ... 148

237. Garlic And Broccoli ... 148

238. Delicious Stuffed Bell Peppers ... 149

239. Simple Stuffed Bell Peppers Dish ... 149

240. Bacon And Brussels Sprouts ... 150

241. Potatoes And Brussels Sprouts ... 150

242. Yummy Brussels Sprouts With Parmesan ... 151

243. Delicious Cabbage Dish ... 151

244. Spicy And Sweet Cabbage ... 152

245. Tasty Sweet Carrots Dish 152

246. Tasty Sausages And Cabbage 153

247. Amazing Maple Glazed Carrots 153

248. Tasty Pasta And Cauliflower 154

249. Special Collard Greens And Bacon 154

250. Yummy Collard Greens Delight 155

251. Special Collard Greens Dish 155

252. Classic Carrots Dish 156

253. Tasty Braised Endives 156

254. Quick Endives Risotto 156

255. Delicious Sautéed Endives 157

256. Smple Eggplant Dish 157

257. Special Babaganoush dish 158

258. Yummy Eggplant Ratatouille 158

259. Braised Fennel 159

260. Surprise Eggplant 160

261. Easy Fennel Risotto 160

262. Kale With Lemon And Garlic 161

263. Bacon And Kale 161

264. Tasty Braised Kale 162

265. Corn And Okra 162

266. Quick Steamed Leeks 163

267. Mouthwatering Crispy Potatoes 163

268. Special Okra Pilaf 163

269. Hot Roasted Potatoes 164

270. Tomatoes And Zucchinis 164

271. Carrots And Turnips 165

272. Tasty And Spicy Turnips 165

273. Delicious Corn Soup 166

274. Yummy Stuffed Tomatoes 167

SOUPS AND STEWS RECIPES 168

275. Yummy Chicken Soup 169

276. Cheese And Potato Soup	169
277. Amazing Split Pea Soup	170
278. Tasty Butternut Squash Soup	171
279. Rice And Beef Soup	171
280. Wild Rice And Chicken Soup	172
281. Chinese Chicken Noodle Soup	172
282. Awesome Zuppa Toscana	173
283. Hot Creamy Tomato Soup	174
284. Special Minestrone Soup	174
285. Special Tomato Soup	175
286. Tasty Carrot Soup	176
287. Healthy Cabbage Soup	176
288. Healthy Cream Of Asparagus	177
289. Amazing Artichoke Soup	177
290. Delicious Beet Soup	178
291. Yummy Cream Of Broccoli	178
292. Tasty Lentils Soup	179
293. Simple Celery Soup	179
294. Delicious Chestnut Soup	180
295. Simple Fennel Soup	180
296. Healthy Cauliflower Soup	181
297. Sweet Potato And Turkey Soup	181
298. Mouthwatering Chicken Meatball Soup	182
299. Healthy Veggie Soup	182
300. Amazing Chicken Chili Soup	183
301. Bacon And Broccoli Soup	184
302. Chorizo, Kale And Chicken Soup	184
303. Tasty Endive Soup	185
304. Special Chicken Enchilada Soup	185
305. Barley And Beef Soup	186
306. Yummy Beef Stew	186
307. Tasty Chicken Stew	187

308. Easy Fish Chowder 188
309. Tasty Quik Bean Stew 188
310. Delicious Sweet Potato Stew 189
311. Healthy Spinach Stew 189
312. Amazing Oxtail Stew 190
313. Tasty Lamb Stew 190
314. Classic Turkey Stew 191
315. Beef And Mushroom Stew 191
316. Root Vegetables And Beef Stew 192
317. Special Lamb Stew 193
318. Amazing German Stew 193
319. Tasty Okra Stew 193
320. Amazing Italian Style Sausage Stew 194

BEANS AND GRAINS RECIPES 195

321. Special Barley Dish 196
322. Tasty Barley Salad 196
323. Mushroom And Barley Risotto 197
324. Veggies And Cracked Wheat 197
325. Yummy Bulgur Salad 198
326. Special Wheat berry Salad 198
327. Delicious Bulgur Pilaf 199
328. Yummy Cracked Wheat Surprise 199
329. Easy Buckwheat Porridge 200
330. Couscous With Veggies And Chicken 200
331. Israeli Style Couscous 201
332. Mouthwatering Millet Dish 201
333. Tasty Veggies And Oats 202
334. Tasty Creamy Millet Dish 202
335. Pasta And Cranberry Beans 203
336. Veggies And Quinoa 204
337. Mexican Style Cranberry Beans 204
338. Amazing Lentils Tacos 205

339. Tomato Sauce And Lentils ... 205
340. Yummy Cranberry Beans Mix ... 206
341. Delicious Cranberry Bean Chili ... 206
342. Italian Style Lentils Dinner ... 207
343. Indian Style Lentils ... 207
344. Tasty Lentils Salad ... 208
345. Amazing Kidney Beans Etouffee ... 208
346. Tasty Kidney Beans Curry ... 209
347. Yummy Chickpeas Curry ... 210
348. Dumplings And Chickpeas ... 210
349. Garlic And Chickpeas ... 211
350. Succulent Chili Lime Black Beans ... 211
351. Pesto And Chickpea Delight ... 212
352. Mouthwatering Marrow Beans And Lemon ... 213
353. Shrimp And White Beans ... 213
354. Different Kidney Beans Dish ... 214
355. Chorizo And Black Beans ... 214
356. Spicy Tasty Black Beans ... 215
357. Tasty Baked Beans ... 215
358. Yummy Creamy White Beans ... 216
359. Mouthwatering Mung Beans Dish ... 216
360. Indian Mung Beans Dish ... 217
361. Cabbage And Navy Beans ... 217
362. Delicious Black Eyed Pea Curry ... 218
363. Yummy Fava Bean Dip ... 218
364. Tasty Fava Bean Puree ... 219
365. Delicious Full Mudammas ... 220
366. Tasty Pineapple And Pea Curry ... 220
367. Simple Split Pea Curry ... 221

SAUCE RECIPES ... 222

368. Amazing Apple sauce ... 223
369. Tasty Ancho Chili Sauce ... 223

370. Delicious Marinara Sauce	224
371. Tasty Giblet Gravy	224
372. Ginger And Orange Sauce	225
373. Tummy Cranberry Sauce	225
374. Special Zucchini Pesto	225
375. Special Sauce	226
376. Easy Spaghetti Sauce	226
377. Tasty Cheese Sauce	227
378. Delicious BBQ Sauce	228
379. Yummy Mushroom Sauce	228
380. Simple Cauliflower Sauce	229
381. Tasty Mango Sauce	229
382. Tasty Tabasco Sauce	230
383. Amazing Strawberry Sauce	230
384. Indian Style Tomato Chutney	231
385. Special Tomato Sauce	231
386. Different Green Tomato Sauce	232
387. Simple Plum Sauce	232
388. Yummy Pineapple Sauce	233
389. Amazing Orange Sauce	233
390. Delicious Bread Sauce	234
391. Easy Onion Sauce	234
392. Simple Chili Jam	235
393. Amazing Clementine Sauce	235
394. Delicious Sriracha Sauce	236
395. Tasty Grapes Sauce	236
396. Simple Mustard Sauce	237
397. Tasty Apricot Sauce	237
398. Easy Eggplant Sauce	238
399. Delicious Pomegranate Sauce	238
400. Yummy Broccoli Sauce	239
401. Tasty Carrot Sauce	239

- 402. Delicious Dates Sauce 240
- 403. Tasty Pear Sauce 240
- 404. Tasty Cherry Sauce 241
- 405. Delicious Guava Sauce 241
- 406. Yummy Melon Sauce 242
- 407. Tasty Fennel Sauce 242
- 408. Special Elderberry Sauce 243
- 409. Simple Peach Sauce 243
- 410. Amazing Peach And Whiskey Sauce 244
- 411. Tasty Corn Sauce 244
- 412. Delicious Leeks Sauce 245
- 413. Yummy Chestnut Sauce 245
- 414. Special Parsley Sauce 246
- 415. Amazing Cilantro Sauce 246
- 416. Simple Quince Sauce 247
- 417. Delicious Rhubarb Sauce 247

DESSERT RECIPES 248

- 418. Tasty Banana Bread 249
- 419. Amazing Apple Bread 249
- 420. Apple Crisp 250
- 421. Delicious Chocolate Cheesecake 250
- 422. Simple Candied Lemon Peel 251
- 423. Yummy Baked Apples 252
- 424. Special Pumpkin Chocolate Cake 252
- 425. Tasty Chocolate Lava Cake 253
- 426. Amazing Chocolate Fondue 253
- 427. Holiday Pudding 254
- 428. Amazing Apple Cake 254
- 429. Yummy Tapioca Pudding 255
- 430. Tasty Pumpkin Pie 255
- 431. Brownie Cake 256
- 432. Special Dulce De Leche 257

433. Tasty Crème Brulee	257
434. Delicious Bread Pudding	258
435. Delicious Rice Pudding	258
436. Ruby Pears	259
437. Tasty Ricotta Cake	259
438. Simple Lemon Marmalade	260
439. Easy Orange Marmalade	260
440. Special Pumpkin Rice Pudding	261
441. Yummy Berry Jam	261
442. Delicious Pears Jam	262
443. Red Tomato Jam	262
444. Yummy Peach Jam	263
445. Tasty Raspberry Curd	263
446. Tasty Berry Compote	263
447. Yummy Key Lime Pie	264
448. Tasty Stuffed Peaches	264
449. Amazing Cobbler	265
450. Yummy Peach Compote	265
451. Easy Carrot Cake	266
452. Amazing Zucchini Nut Bread	266
453. Tasty Samoa Cheesecake	267
454. Special Pina Colada Pudding	268
455. Instant Flan	269
456. Awesome Chocolate Pudding	269
457. Tasty Sticky Pudding	270
458. Easy Chocolate Cake	271
459. Easy Carrot Pudding	271
460. simple Eggnog Cheesecake	272
461. Delicious Rhubarb Compote	272
462. Tasty Corn Pudding	273
463. Amazing Lemon Crème Pots	273
464. Yummy Poached Figs	274

465. Special Sweet Carrots ... 274

466. Ginger And Pineapple Risotto Dessert ... 275

SPECIAL WEIGHT LOSS RECIPES ... 276

"SPECIAL KETOGENIC BREAKFAST RECIPES" ... 277

467. Tasty Keto Coconut Bread ... 277

468. Delicious Keto Cabbage Onspoo Sauté ... 277

469. Yummy Keto Berries And Cream Cake ... 278

470. Easy Cheesy Keto Sausage Rounding ... 278

471. Amazing Keto Coffee Jug Chocolate Cake ... 279

472. Keto Garlic Butter Spread ... 279

473. Delicious Keto Blueberry Muffins ... 280

474. Yummy Keto Cauliflower Muffins ... 280

475. Tasty Keto Banana And Nut Loaf ... 281

476. Amazing Keto Sunny Side Up with Bacon ... 281

477. Tasty Keto Fashioned Scrambled Eggs ... 282

478. Tasty Keto Toast ... 282

479. Delicious Keto Egg Loaf Spread ... 283

480. Yummy Keto Egg Scramble ... 283

481. Awesome Keto Cheesy And Milky Bacon Muffin ... 284

482. Tasty Keto Garlic & Olive Butter Spread ... 285

483. Amazing Keto Pumpkin Spice Almond Cake ... 285

484. Easy Keto Egg Fast ... 286

485. Yummy Keto Egg Spinach Muffins ... 286

486. Delicious Keto Steamed Scallion Omelet ... 287

487. Tasty Keto Coconut Zucchini Muffins ... 287

"SPECIAL KETOGENIC LUNCH RECIPES" ... 289

488. Amazing Keto Cranberry Turkey ... 289

489. Easy Keto Squid Springs Sauté ... 289

490. Tasty Keto Bacon Chicken ... 290

491. Yummy Keto Cheesy Hotdog Huggers ... 290

492. Delicious Keto Taco Beef Frittata ... 291

493. Amazing Keto Provolone Sirloin Steak ... 292

494. Different Keto Chuck Roast 292

495. Surprise Keto Olive Chicken Walnut 293

496. Keto Chicken Green Papaya 294

497. Delicious Keto Smoked Salmon Avocado Caulirolls 294

498. Yummy Keto Smoked Bacon Asparagus Spears 295

499. Tasty Keto Chicken Chorizo Charade 295

500. Tasty Keto Tuna-Bacon & Steamed Egg Spread 296

501. Delicious Keto Spiced Chicken Romaine Wrap 297

"SPECIAL KETOGENIC DINNER RECIPES" 298

502. Tasty Keto Tomato Sauté And Green Beans 298

503. Mouthwatering Keto Chicken Veggies Salad 298

504. Amazing Keto Beef Burgundy Stew 299

505. Tasty Cheesy Keto Hungarian Style Meatballs 299

506. Delicious Keto Cauliflower Pancakes 300

507. Yummy Keto Blue Arugula Toss 300

508. Tasty Keto Tuna Pecan Toss 301

509. Favorite Keto Tuna Belly Adobo 301

510. Delicious Keto Green Beans And Cheesy Beef Casserole 302

511. Amazing Keto Smoke Spice Beef Brisket 303

512. Yummy Keto Sautéed Beef Broccoli Mushroom Ensemble 303

513. Mouthwatering Keto Tuna Egg Salad Sandwich 304

514. Tasty Keto Creamy Spinach Bacon Dish 304

515. Tasty Keto Tomato Base Spicy Beef Stew 305

516. Amazing Keto Salmon Steamed Filet 305

517. Different Keto Green Mango Salmon Strips 306

518. Delicious Keto Chuck Eye Roast Stew 306

519. Yummy Keto Lemon, Honey And Salmon Steamed Filets 307

520. Tasty Keto Creamy Mushroom Sauce With Cod Fish 308

"SPECIAL KETOGENIC SNACKS RECIPES" 309

521. Yummy Keto Razil Nuts Snacks 309

522. Amazing Keto Broccoli And Almond Muffins 309

523. Awesome Keto Banana Nut Muffins 310

524. Amazing Keto Cream Cheese Celery Bacon Dip ... 310
525. Delicious Keto Aruzmat Pizza ... 311
526. Easy Cheesy Keto Bacon Biscuit ... 311
527. Tasty Keto Peanut Butter Coconut Cookies ... 312
528. Different Keto Coconut Bread ... 313
529. Delicious Keto Dark Chocolate Butter Cookies ... 313
530. Yummy Keto Cheese Aubergines Spinach Layers ... 314
531. Amazing Keto Avocado Chocolate Cake ... 315
532. Tasty Keto Mango Macadamia Avocado Toss ... 315
533. Easy Keto Coconut Loco Bread ... 316
534. Tasty Keto White Loaf ... 316
535. Tasty Keto Tuna Toss ... 317
536. Yummy Keto Jamana Grapefruit Avocado Toss ... 318
537. Delicious Keto Creamy Cauliflower Mashed ... 318

"SPECIAL KETOGENIC DESSERT RECIPES" ... 320

538. Awesome Keto Cheesecake With Marmalade ... 320
539. Tasty Keto Frosted Almond Coconut Cupcakes ... 320
540. Yummy Keto Cocoa Macadamia Boosters ... 321
541. Delicious Keto Peanut Butter Cookies ... 321
542. Tasty Keto Torched Creamy Egg Custard ... 322
543. Mouthwatering Keto Caramel Glazed Cheesecake Cups ... 322
544. Amazing Keto Nutty Cheesecake Overload ... 323
545. Yummy Keto Dark Chocolate Brownies ... 324
546. Delicious Keto Coco Walnut Snowball ... 325
547. Tasty Keto Torched Coco Avocado Custard ... 325
548. Yummy Keto Cinnamon Vanilla Cookies ... 326
549. Amazing Keto Butternut Squash Cupcake ... 326
550. Delicious Keto Dark Chocolate Truffles ... 327
551. Mouthwatering Keto Macadamia Laced Cake ... 328

CONCLUSION ... **329**

INTRODUCTION

We know you want to become a master chef in the kitchen! We know you want to impress your guests, your friends and all your loved ones with your cooking skills.

Well, now you can! This magnificent cookbook provides you the tools you were looking for so long! You now know how to make the best dishes in the world in the easiest way possible: using an instant pot.

If you don't have such a wonderful machine yet, it's time to go and purchase one! Then get your hands on this wonderful cooking journal and start making some of the tastiest, unique, rich and flavored dishes ever!

We can assure you that everyone will admire you from now on! Everyone will adore your foods! Your success in the kitchen is guaranteed with just 2 simple tools: this great cookbook and an instant pot!

Have fun!
Enjoy cooking!

INSTANT POT PRESSURE COOKER

Before making any food, spend some time reading your Instant Pot's manual. It'll be worth it, trust us. If you've misplaced the manual, you can easily find an electronic replacement online at InstantPot.com.

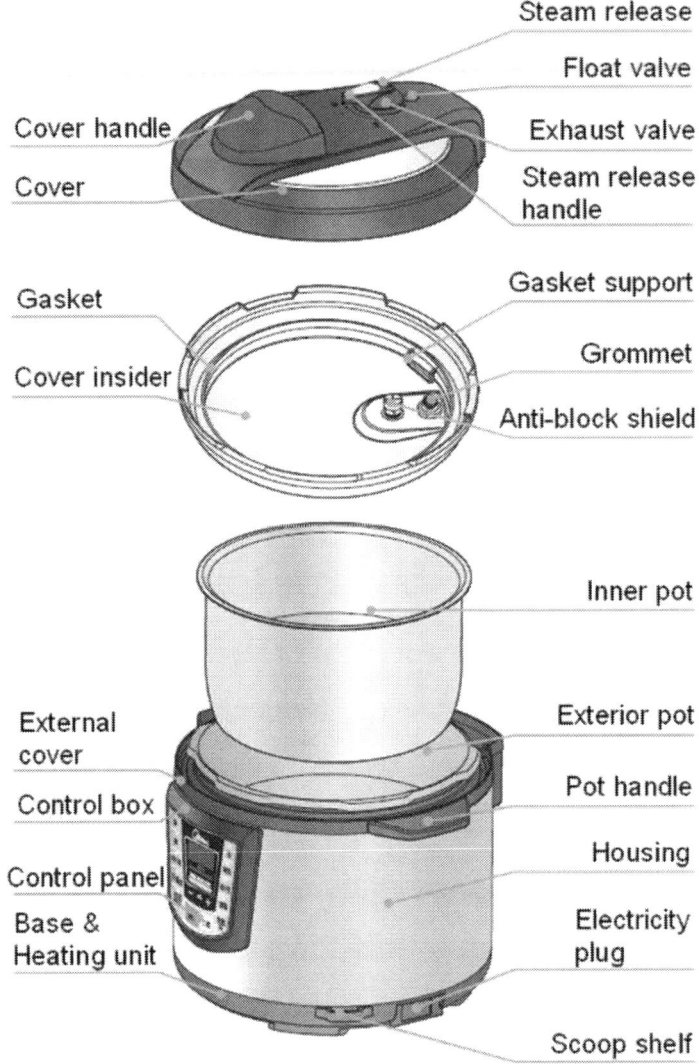

Instant Pot® – Electric Pressure Cooker

What you see is largely what you get with the Instant Pot. The components are the exterior pot, with the heating element, and the exterior control panel.

There's also an interior pot, which sits inside that exterior pot. Then there's the lid, with its steam valve and handle.

You can use the valve to quickly release pressure, but remember to always exercise extreme caution if you do this, to avoid painful burns.

You cannot use the Instant Pot for pressure cooking with the valve open. Right under the lid you have two more valves, one for exhaust, one called a float, and the all-important sealing ring. These elements work together to form a perfect seal that allows pressure cooking to begin.

You can cook a variety of different ways with the Instant Pot. We'll largely be discussing Manual use here, but we encourage you to try other functions too.

The Instant Pot Has Plus {+} and Minus {-}, Adjust buttons, which allow you to control temperature and time.

You also have a pressure button for either low or high pressure cooking of any food with the exception of rice. Most people use the Instant Pot with high pressure.

One occasion in which you might choose low pressure is for seafood. After you finishing inputting your desired cooking and pressure settings, the machine will start to preheat automatically within 10 seconds.

Uses of an Electric Pressure Cooker

The following is a very short list of great reasons to invest in an electric pressure cooker. No doubt, after you start using one regularly, you'll be inventing your own list.

#Fewer Dishes

Throw all your ingredients into the pressure cooker and lock the lid: It's the best version of a one pot meal you've ever made.

When it's finished cooking, the only dishes will be the pot and the plates {which will undoubtedly have been licked clean.}

#Gourmet Fare Is Easy

Unlike the earlier pressure cooker incarnations, electric ones have timers that you can set, for maximum cooking convenience. Beyond basic settings such as high, medium, and low, you don't need to worry about temperature or pressure. Unlike a stove, the pressure cooker does it all for you, and much more safely, too.

Once you've installed your pressure cooker in its designated spot and discovered how useful it is, it's likely that you'll always keep it at the ready for the next quick meal.

#The Faster, The Better

Our lives are busy. No one needs to tell you that. Cooking meals in the oven can take hours and cooking on the stove requires a wary eye to keep dishes from overcooking.

Pressure cookers can reduce cooking times by up to 2/3rds. Where it might have taken 24 hours before to make a pot of beans, a pressure cooker makes the task so time-efficient, you'll no longer have to worry about watching the stove for hours on end.

With the arrival of the electric pressure cooker in your kitchen, the days of burned beans or scorched meats are over.

#Saves Energy

Pressure cookers save you time. They also use energy so efficiently that they more than halve the amount of energy typically used by an oven or stove. Time-friendly, flavor-friendly, and environment-friendly. What more could you ask for?

#Delicious Should Also Always Be Nutritious

Remember the days of boiling food {like beans} for hours on end? Boiling literally washes away key nutrients, whereas pressure cooking locks in all those necessary minerals and vitamins.

HOW TO USE THE CONTROL PANEL AND AUTOMATIC COOKING PROGRAMS.

1. Steam Function

The Instant Pot comes with a rack, or you can use your own steamer basket if it fits in the inner pot. Instant Pot's STEAM function boils water underneath the pot so the food in the rack or basket steams evenly.

2. Manual Function

The Manual function lets you choose your time and pressure, according to your recipe. It's very convenient, which is why we use it the most.

3. Slow Function

Want the experience of coming home to a fully cooked meal? Vent the steam release handle as you activate this function, and you'll have your one pot meal all ready to go when you walk in the door.

4. Keep Hot Function

If your Instant Pot's timer runs out, the KEEP HOT function kicks in to make sure your meal stays Hot.

You can turn this function off by using the CANCEL button. 0nce the dish is finished cooking, turn off the KEEP HOT function and the pressure will be more quickly released.

5. Delayed Cooking Function

This is yet another great Instant Pot setting to put even more cooking and timing control into your hands.

6. Sauté Function

As mentioned before, if you want to tenderize veggies or brown your meat a little bit, this is the function to use with the lid off.

You can also thicken sauces beautifully with the sauté function. Low is good for slow, high is good for getting a good sear, and normal is great for that sautéing and browning.

7. Chicken and Other Poultry

Use the POULTRY function to cook these meats at high pressure. Your manual or the afore-mentioned Electric Pressure Time Cook Chart {easily found online} can give you suggested cooking times.

8. Rice Function

This is a great automatic function to make low pressure rice. The Instant Pot automatically determines how long to cook and at what pressure depending on the quantities of rice and liquid you put in. You can make large quantities, or amounts as small as 1 cup.

9. Soup Function

Never have a pot of soup boil over again! The Instant Pot is wonderful for making all manner of soups.

10. Grains

Want to cook other types of rice? Refer to that Electric Pressure Time Cook Chart so you know how much liquid to use and how long to cook the grains.

11. Bean Function

This works for both dried beans, and bean-heavy dishes like chili. You can choose the time you want the dish to cook, so it's done exactly to your taste.

12. Porridge Function

If you use this function, at the end make sure you use the CANCEL function we described earlier, where pressure is slowly released. Porridge can be cooked on "normal" for rice porridge or "high" for beans or grains.

13. Meat or Stew Function

Choose this function if you want to cook thick, possibly tough meat cuts under high pressure. Your Instant Pot will give you suggested cooking times or you can look up the Electric Pressure Time Cook Chart.

BREAKFAST RECIPES

1. AMAZINGLY DELICIOUS PEAR OATMEAL

Perp time: 5 minutes **Cooking time:** 6 minutes **Servings:** 4

Nutrition Facts:
- Calories: 250
- Fat (In grams): 10
- Fiber (In grams): 11.3
- Carbs (In grams): 14
- Protein (In grams): 7

Ingredients:
- One-cup water
- 2 cups milk
- One-tablespoon soft butter
- A pinch of salt
- 1/4 cups brown Sugar
- Half-teaspoon cinnamon powder
- One-cup rolled oats
- Half-cup walnuts, chopped
- 2 cups pear, peeled and chopped
- Half-cup raisins

Instructions:
1. In a heatproof dish, mix milk with Sugar, butter, salt, oats, cinnamon, raisins, pears and walnuts and stir.
2. Place the dish in the steamer basket of the pot, add One-cup water in the pot, cover and cook at High for 6 minutes.
3. Release the pressure quick, divide oatmeal into bowls and serve.

Bon Appétit!

2. FRENCH STYLE SPECIAL TOAST

Perp time: 10 minutes **Cooking time:** 30 minutes **Servings:** 6

Nutrition Facts:
- Calories: 300
- Fat (In grams): 14
- Fiber (In grams): 2
- Carbs (In grams): 80
- Sugar (In grams): 12
- Protein (In grams): 14

Ingredients:

For the orange sauce:
- 1/4 cup orange juice
- Half-cup Sugar
- 2 cups cranberries
- A pinch of salt
- 1/4 teaspoon cinnamon, ground

For the toast:
- 2 cups milk
- 3 eggs, whisked
- 4 tablespoons melted butter
- Half-cup Sugar
- Zest from 1 orange, grated
- A pinch of salt
- One-teaspoon vanilla extract
- 1 loaf bread, cubed
- One-cup water

Instructions:
1. Heat up a small pot over medium heat, add cranberries, orange juice, 1/4 teaspoon cinnamon, a pinch of salt and Half-cup Sugar, stir well and cook for 5 minutes.

2. Pour this into a greased pan and leave aside for now.
3. In a bowl, mix butter with milk, Half-cup Sugar, eggs, vanilla extract, a pinch of salt and orange zest and stir.
4. Add bread cubes and stir again.
5. Pour this over cranberry, place pan in the steamer basket of your instant pot, add the water on the bottom, cover and cook at High for 25 minutes.
6. Release the pressure, take the pan out, divide the mix among plates and serve.

Bon Appétit!

---

3. TASTY MUSHROOM OATMEAL

Perp time: 10 minutes   **Cooking time:** 15 minutes   **Servings:** 4

Nutrition Facts:
- Calories: 300
- Fat (In grams): 14
- Fiber (In grams): 6.7
- Carbs (In grams): 30.2
- Protein (In grams): 20.5

Ingredients:
- 1 small yellow onion, chopped
- One-cup steel cut oats
- 2 garlic cloves, minced
- 2 tablespoons butter
- Half-cup water
- 14 ounces canned chicken stock
- 3 thyme springs, chopped
- 2 tablespoons extra virgin olive oil
- Half-cup gouda, grated
- 8 ounces mushroom, sliced
- Salt and black pepper to the taste

Instructions:
1. Select Sauté mode on your instant pot, add butter and melt it.
2. Add onions, stir and cook for 3 minutes.
3. Add garlic, stir and cook for 1 minute more.
4. Add oats, stir and cook for 1 minute.
5. Add water, salt, pepper, stock, and thyme, cover the pot and cook at High for 10 minutes.
6. Release the pressure and leave the pot aside.
7. Meanwhile, heat up a pan with the olive oil over medium heat, add mushrooms and cook them for 3 minutes.
8. Add them to the instant pot, also add more salt and pepper to the taste and the gouda, stir and divide among plates.

4. DELICIOUS CINNAMON STEEL CUT OATS

Perp time: 10 minutes   **Cooking time:** 13 minutes   **Servings:** 4

Nutrition Facts:
- Calories: 140
- Fat (In grams): 3
- Fiber (In grams): 3
- Carbs (In grams): 26
- Sugar (In grams): 4
- Protein (In grams): 4

Ingredients:
- One-cup steel oats
- 3 ½-cups water
- A pinch of salt
- One-tablespoon butter
- 3/4 cup raisins
- One-teaspoon cinnamon
- 1/4 cup brown Sugar
- 2 tablespoons white Sugar
- 2 ounces cream cheese, soft
- One-teaspoon milk

Instructions:
1. Select Sauté mode on your instant pot, add butter and melt it.
2. Add oats, stir and toast for 3 minutes.
3. Add a pinch of salt and the water, cover the pot and cook at High for 10 minutes.
4. Release the pressure naturally for 5 minutes and uncover the pot.
5. Add raisins, stir and leave aside for now.
6. Meanwhile, in a bowl, mix cinnamon with brown Sugar and stir.
7. In another bowl, mix white Sugar with cream cheese and milk and stir well.
8. Transfer oats mix to breakfast bowls and top each with cinnamon mix and cream cheese one.

Bon Appétit!

5. SPINACH AND TOMATO BREAKFAST

Perp time: 10 minutes   **Cooking time:** 20 minutes   **Servings:** 6

Nutrition Facts:
- Calories: 200
- Fat (In grams): 10.1
- Fiber (In grams): 1.8
- Carbs (In grams): 16
- Sugar (In grams): 1
- Protein (In grams): 10

Ingredients:
- Half-cup milk
- Salt and black pepper to the taste
- 12 eggs
- 3 cups baby spinach, chopped
- 3 green onions, sliced
- One-cup tomato, diced
- 4 tomato sliced
- 1/4 cup parmesan, grated
- 1 ½ cups water

Instructions:
1. Put the water in your instant pot.
2. In a bowl, mix the eggs with salt, pepper and milk and stir well.
3. Put diced tomato, spinach and green onions in a baking dish and stir them.
4. Pour the eggs mix over veggies, spread tomato slices on top and sprinkle parmesan at the end.

5. Arrange this in the steamer basket of your instant pot, cover and cook everything at High for 20 minutes.
6. Release the pressure, open the pot and introduce the baking dish in preheated broiler until the mixture is brown on top.
7. Divide among plates and serve.

Bon Appétit!

---

6. BANANA CAKE FOR BREAKFAST

Perp time: 10 minutes **Cooking time:** 55 minutes **Servings:** 5

Nutrition Facts:
- Calories: 326
- Fat (In grams): 11
- Fiber (In grams): 1.1
- Carbs (In grams): 55
- Protein (In grams): 4.3

Ingredients:
- One-cup water
- 1 ½ cups Sugar
- 2 cups flour
- 3 bananas, peeled and mashed
- 2 eggs
- 1 stick butter, soft
- 2 teaspoon baking powder
- A pinch of salt
- One-teaspoon cinnamon
- One-teaspoon nutmeg

Instructions:
1. In a bowl, mix eggs with butter and Sugar and stir very well.
2. Add salt, baking powder, cinnamon and nutmeg and stir well again.
3. Add bananas and flour and stir again.
4. Grease a spring form pan with some butter, pour the batter in it and cover the pan with a paper towel and tin foil
5. Add One-cup water to your instant pot, place the pan in the pot, cover and cook at High for 55 minutes.
6. Release the pressure quickly, remove the pan, leave banana breakfast cake to cool down, cut and serve it.

Bon Appétit!

---

7. YUMMY POMEGRANATE PORRIDGE

Perp time: 5 minutes **Cooking time:** 2 minutes **Servings:** 2

Nutrition Facts:
- Calories: 200
- Fat (In grams): 2.8
- Fiber (In grams): 4.4
- Carbs (In grams): 40
- Protein (In grams): 7.3

Ingredients:
- One-cup porridge oats
- A pinch of salt
- One-cup water
- 3/4 cup pomegranate juice
- Seeds from 1 pomegranate

Instructions:
1. Put oats in your instant pot.
2. Add water, a pinch of salt and pomegranate juice, stir, cover the pot and cook at High for 2 minutes.
3. Release the pressure quick, add pomegranate seeds, stir well, divide into bowls and serve.

Bon Appétit!

---

8. TASTY BREAKFAST COBBLER

Perp time: 10 minutes   **Cooking time:** 15 minutes   **Servings:** 4

Nutrition Facts:
- Calories: 150
- Fat (In grams): 7
- Fiber (In grams): 3
- Carbs (In grams): 12
- Sugar (In grams): 7
- Protein (In grams): 6

Ingredients:
- 1 plum, chopped
- 1 pear, chopped
- 1 apple chopped
- 2 tablespoons honey
- Half-teaspoon cinnamon, ground
- 3 tablespoons coconut oil
- 1/4 cup pecans, chopped
- 1/4 cup coconut, shredded
- 2 tablespoons sunflower seeds

Instructions:
1. Put all fruits in a heatproof dish, add coconut oil, cinnamon and honey and toss to coat.
2. Place the dish in the steamer basket of your instant pot, cover and cook at High for 10 minutes.
3. Release the pressure naturally, take out the dish and transfer all fruits to a bowl.
4. In the same baking dish, mix coconut with sunflower seeds and pecans and stir.
5. Transfer these to your instant pot, set it on Sauté mode and toast them for 5 minutes.
6. Add these to fruits in the bowl, toss to coat and serve.

Bon Appétit!

---

9. APPETIZING SCOTCH EGGS

Perp time: 10 minutes   **Cooking time:** 15 minutes   **Servings:** 4

Nutrition Facts:
- Calories: 300
- Fat (In grams): 21
- Fiber (In grams): 0
- Carbs (In grams): 16
- Protein (In grams): 12

Ingredients:
- 1-pound sausage, ground
- One-tablespoon vegetable oil
- 4 eggs
- 2 cups water

Instructions:
1. Put the eggs in the instant pot, add One-cup water, cover the pot and cook at High for 6 minutes.
2. Release the pressure for 6 minutes, uncover the pot, remove the eggs and put them in a bowl filled with ice water.

3. Peel the eggs and place them on a working surface.
4. Divide sausage mix into 4 balls, flatten them, place 1 egg in the center of each sausage piece, wrap meat around each egg and put them all on a plate.
5. Set your instant pot on Sauté mode, add the oil and heat it up.
6. Add scotch eggs, brown them on each side and transfer them to a plate.
7. Add the rest of the water to your instant pot, arrange the eggs in the steamer basket of the pot, cover and cook at High for 6 minutes more.
8. Release the pressure quick, divide the eggs among plates and serve.

Bon Appétit!

---

10. TASTY POACHED EGGS

Perp time: 10 minutes **Cooking time:** 10 minutes **Servings:** 2

Nutrition Facts:
- Calories: 129
- Fat (In grams): 8
- Fiber (In grams): 1
- Carbs (In grams): 9
- Protein (In grams): 12

Ingredients:
- 1 bunch rucola leaves
- 2 eggs
- 2 bell peppers, ends cut off
- 2 slices mozzarella cheese
- 2 slices whole wheat bread, toasted
- One-cup water

For the sauce:
- 1 ½ teaspoons mustard
- 2/3 cup homemade mayonnaise
- Salt to the taste
- One-teaspoon turmeric powder
- One-teaspoon lemon juice
- 3 tablespoons orange juice
- One-tablespoon white wine vinegar

Instructions:
1. In a bowl, mix mayo with salt, turmeric, mustard, lemon juice, orange juice and vinegar, stir well, cover the bowl and keep in the fridge for now.
2. Break an egg in each bell pepper, place them in the steamer basket of your instant pot, cover the basket with tin foil, add the water to the pot and cook on Low for 5 minutes.
3. Release the pressure naturally and uncover the pot.
4. Divide toasted bread into 2 plates, add cheese on each, some rucola leaves and top with pepper cups.
5. Drizzle the sauce all over and serve.

Bon Appétit!

11. AMAZING PUMPKIN OATS GRANOLA

Perp time: 20 minutes   **Cooking time:** 15 minutes   **Servings:** 6

Nutrition Facts:
- Calories: 200
- Fat (In grams): 7
- Fiber (In grams): 3
- Carbs (In grams): 33
- Sugar (In grams): 14
- Protein (In grams): 5

Ingredients:
- 3 cups water
- One-tablespoon soft butter
- One-cup pumpkin puree
- One-cup steel cut oats
- 1/4 cup maple syrup
- 2 teaspoons cinnamon
- One-teaspoon pumpkin pie spice
- A pinch of salt

Instructions:
1. Select Sauté mode on your instant pot, add butter and melt it.
2. Add oats, stir and cook for 3 minutes.
3. Add pumpkin puree, water, cinnamon, salt, maple syrup and pumpkin spice, stir, cover the pot and cook at High for 10 minutes.
4. Release the pressure naturally for 10 minutes, stir oats granola, leave it aside for 10 minutes, divide it and serve.

Bon Appétit!

12. SIMPLY STEAMED EGGS

Perp time: 10 minutes   **Cooking time:** 5 minutes   **Servings:** 2

Nutrition Facts:
- Calories: 230
- Fat (In grams): 13
- Fiber (In grams): 3
- Sugar (In grams): 1
- Protein (In grams): 21

Ingredients:
- 1 and 1/3 cup water
- 2 eggs
- Salt and black pepper to the taste
- A pinch of garlic powder
- A pinch of sesame seeds
- 2 scallions, finely chopped
- Hot rice for serving

Instructions:
1. In a bowl, mix the eggs with 1/3 cup water and whisk well.
2. Strain this into a heat proof dish.
3. Add salt, pepper to the taste, sesame seeds, garlic powder and scallions and whisk very well.
4. Put One-cup water in your instant pot, place the dish in the steamer basket, cover the pot and cook at High for 5 minutes.
5. Release the pressure, uncover the pot, divide the rice among plates and add eggs mix on the side.

Bon Appétit!

13. YUMMY BREAKFAST RISOTTO

Perp time: 10 minutes **Cooking time:** 12 minutes **Servings:** 4

Nutrition Facts:
- Calories: 160
- Fat (In grams): 16
- Fiber (In grams): 3
- Carbs (In grams): 30
- Sugar (In grams): 1
- Protein (In grams): 11

Ingredients:
- 1 ½ cups Arborio rice
- 1 ½ teaspoons cinnamon powder
- 1/3 cup brown Sugar
- A pinch of salt
- 2 tablespoons butter
- 2 apples, cored and sliced
- One-cup apple juice
- 3 cups milk
- Half-cup cherries, dried

Instructions:
1. Set your instant pot on Sauté mode, add butter and melt it.
2. Add rice, stir and cook for 5 minutes.
3. Add Sugar, apples, apple juice, milk, a pinch of salt and cinnamon, stir, cover and cook at High for 6 minutes.
4. Release the pressure naturally for 6 minutes, uncover the pot, add cherries, stir, cover and leave aside for 5 more minutes.
5. Divide into breakfast bowls and serve right away.

Bon Appétit!

14. APPETIZING VANILLA STEEL CUT OATS

Perp time: 10 minutes **Cooking time:** 10 minutes **Servings:** 4

Nutrition Facts:
- Calories: 250
- Fat (In grams): 3.1
- Fiber (In grams): 5.4
- Carbs (In grams): 43
- Sugar (In grams): 4
- Protein (In grams): 5

Ingredients:
- One-cup milk
- One-cup steel cut oats
- 2 ½-cups water
- 2 tablespoons Sugar
- A pinch of salt
- One-teaspoon espresso powder
- 2 teaspoons vanilla extract
- Whipped cream for serving
- Grated chocolate for serving

Instructions:
1. In your instant pot, mix oats with water, Sugar, milk, salt and espresso powder and stir.
2. Cover the pot and cook at High for 10 minutes.
3. Release the pressure for 10 minutes, take the lid off, add vanilla extract, stir and leave everything aside for 5 minutes.
4. Divide into bowls and serve with whipped cream and grated chocolate.

Bon Appétit!

15. TASTY EGG MUFFINS

Perp time: 10 minutes　　**Cooking time:** 10 minutes　　**Servings:** 4

Nutrition Facts:
- Calories: 70
- Fat (In grams): 2.4
- Fiber (In grams): 1
- Carbs (In grams): 1.5
- Protein (In grams): 4.6

Ingredients:
- 1 ½ cups water
- 1 green onion, chopped
- 4 bacon slices, cooked and crumbled
- 4 tablespoons cheddar cheese, shredded
- 1/4 teaspoon lemon pepper
- 4 eggs
- A pinch of salt

Instructions:
1. In a bowl, mix eggs with a pinch of salt and lemon pepper and whisk well.
2. Divide green onion, bacon and cheese into muffin cups.
3. Add eggs and stir a bit.
4. Put the water in your instant pot, add muffin cups in the steamer basket, cover the pot and cook at High for 10 minutes.
5. Release the pressure quick, divide the egg muffins among plates and serve them right away.

Bon Appétit!

16. APPETIZING RICE BOWL

Perp time: 5 minutes　　**Cooking time:** 7 minutes　　**Servings:** 4

Nutrition Facts:
- Calories: 240
- Fat (In grams): 7
- Fiber (In grams): 9.5
- Carbs (In grams): 45
- Sugar (In grams): 13
- Protein (In grams): 13

Ingredients:
- One-cup brown rice
- Half-cup coconut chips
- One-cup coconut milk
- 2 cups water
- Half-cup maple syrup
- 1/4 cup raisins
- 1/4 cup almonds
- A pinch of cinnamon powder
- A pinch of salt

Instructions:
1. Put the rice in a pot, add the water, place on stove over medium high heat, cook according to instructions, drain and transfer it to your instant pot.
2. Add milk, coconut chips, almonds, raisins, salt, cinnamon and maple syrup, stir well, cover the pot and cook at High for 5 minutes.
3. Release pressure quick, transfer rice to breakfast bowls and serve right away.

Bon Appétit!

17. DELICIOUS CARROT OATMEAL

Perp time: 20 minutes **Cooking time:** 13 minutes **Servings:** 6

Nutrition Facts:
- Calories: 145
- Fat (In grams): 3
- Fiber (In grams): 1.3
- Carbs (In grams): 25
- Protein (In grams): 3.5
- Sugar (In grams): 11

Ingredients:
- One-cup steel cut oats
- 4 cups water
- One-tablespoon butter
- 3 tablespoons maple syrup
- A pinch of salt
- 2 teaspoons cinnamon
- One-teaspoon pie spice
- One-cup grated carrots
- 1/4 cup chia seeds
- 3/4 cup raisins

Instructions:
1. Select the Sauté mode on your instant pot, add butter and melt it.
2. Add oats, stir and toast for 3 minutes.
3. Add carrots, water, maple syrup, cinnamon, spice and a pinch of salt, stir, cover the pot and cook at High for 10 minutes.
4. Release the pressure naturally for 10 minutes, add raisins and chia seeds, stir, leave oatmeal aside for 10 minutes, divide it between bowls and serve right away.

Bon Appétit!

18. YUMMY RICE PUDDING

Perp time: 10 minutes **Cooking time:** 35 minutes **Servings:** 4

Nutrition Facts:
- Calories: 118
- Fat (In grams): 1
- Fiber (In grams): 1
- Carbs (In grams): 21
- Protein (In grams): 8

Ingredients:
- 6 and Half-cups water
- 3/4 cup Sugar
- 2 cups black rice, washed and rinsed
- 2 cinnamon sticks
- A pinch of salt
- 5 cardamom pods, crushed
- 3 cloves
- Half-cup coconut, grated
- Chopped mango for serving

Instructions:
1. Put the rice in your instant pot, add a pinch of salt and the water and stir.
2. In a cheesecloth bag, mix cardamom with cinnamon and cloves and tie it.
3. Place this in the pot with the rice, cover and cook on Low for 35 minutes.
4. Release the pressure naturally, uncover the pot, stir the rice, add coconut and set your pot to sauté mode.
5. Cook for 10 minutes, discard spices bag, transfer to breakfast bowls and serve with chopped mango on top.

Bon Appétit!

19. Delicious Breakfast Millet Pilaf

Perp time: 10 minutes **Cooking time:** 10 minutes **Servings:** 4

Nutrition Facts:
- Calories: 100
- Fat (In grams): 3.1
- Fiber (In grams): 1.3
- Carbs (In grams): 16
- Protein (In grams): 2.5

Ingredients:
- One-tablespoon ghee
- One-teaspoon cardamom, crushed
- 3 teaspoons cumin seeds
- 1 bay leaf
- 1-inch cinnamon stick
- 2 cups organic millet
- 1 white onion, chopped
- Salt to the taste
- 3 cups water

Instructions:
1. Set your instant pot on sauté mode, add ghee and heat it up.
2. Add cumin, cinnamon, cardamom and bay leaf, stir and cook for 1 minute.
3. Add onion, stir and cook for 4 minutes.
4. Add millet, salt and water, stir, cover the pot and cook at High for 1 minute.
5. Release the pressure naturally, fluff the mix with a fork, transfer to bowls and serve.

Bon Appétit!

20. Simple Breakfast Pudding

Perp time: 5 minutes **Cooking time:** 10 minutes **Servings:** 4

Nutrition Facts:
- Calories: 122
- Fat (In grams): 2
- Fiber (In grams): 0
- Carbs (In grams): 21
- Sugar (In grams): 6
- Protein (In grams): 5

Ingredients:
- 1 ½ cups water
- 1/3 cup tapioca pearls
- 1 and 1/4 cup whole milk
- Zest from ½ lemon
- Half-cup Sugar

Instructions:
1. Put One-cup water in your instant pot.
2. Put tapioca pearls in a heat proof bowl add milk, Half-cup water, lemon zest and Sugar.
3. Stir everything, place the bowl in the steamer basket of the pot, cover and cook at High for 10 minutes.
4. Release the pressure, transfer pudding to cups and serve.

Bon Appétit!

21. TASTY BREAKFAST QUINOA SALAD

Perp time: 10 minutes **Cooking time:** 15 minutes **Servings:** 8

Nutrition Facts:
- Calories: 239
- Fat (In grams): 6.4
- Fiber (In grams): 7.7
- Carbs (In grams): 39
- Protein (In grams): 9

Ingredients:
- 2 garlic cloves, minced
- 2 and 1/4 cups water
- 1 ½ cups quinoa, rinsed
- A pinch of salt
- 2 tomatoes, chopped
- 1 cucumber, chopped
- 1 jalapeno pepper, chopped
- One-cup corn, already cooked
- Half-cup scallions, finely chopped
- 1 ½ cups chickpeas, already cooked
- 2/3 cup parsley leaves, finely chopped
- 1/3 cup mint leaves, chopped
- 1 avocado, pitted, peeled and diced
- 3 tablespoons veggie stock
- 1/4 cup lime juice
- Black pepper to the taste
- Half-teaspoon chipotle chili pepper

Instructions:
1. In your pressure cooker, mix quinoa with 1 garlic clove, a pinch of salt and the water, stir, cover and cook at High for 1 minute.
2. Release the pressure, uncover the instant pot, fluff quinoa with a fork and leave it to cool down.
3. Transfer quinoa to a bowl, add tomatoes, cucumber, jalapeno pepper, corn, scallions, chickpeas, parsley, mint, and avocado.
4. In a bowl, mix veggie stock with black pepper to the taste, 1 garlic clove, lime juice and chipotle chili pepper and stir very well.
5. Pour this over salad, toss to coat and serve.

Bon Appétit!

22. APPETIZING MILLET PUDDING

Perp time: 10 minutes **Cooking time:** 10 minutes **Servings:** 4

Nutrition Facts:
- Calories: 240
- Fat (In grams): 2
- Fiber (In grams): 2.6
- Carbs (In grams): 25
- Sugar (In grams): 33
- Protein (In grams): 8

Ingredients:
- 14 ounces coconut milk
- 7 ounces water
- 2/3 cup millet
- A pinch of salt
- 4 dates, pitted
- Honey for serving

Instructions:
1. Put the millet in your instant pot.
2. Add milk, dates and a pinch of salt and stir.
3. Add the water, stir again, cover the pot and cook at High for 10 minutes.
4. Release the pressure naturally, uncover the pot, divide the pudding into bowls, top with honey and serve.

23. YUMMY BREAKFAST CHIA PUDDING

Perp time: 2 hours   **Cooking time:** 3 minutes   **Servings:** 4

Nutrition Facts:
- Calories: 130
- Fat (In grams): 12
- Fiber (In grams): 22
- Carbs (In grams): 2
- Protein (In grams): 14

Ingredients:
- Half-cup chia seeds
- 2 cups almond milk
- 1/4 cup almonds
- 1/4 cup coconut, shredded
- 4 teaspoons Sugar

Instructions:
1. Put chia seeds in your instant pot.
2. Add milk, almonds and coconut flakes, stir, cover and cook at High for 3 minutes.
3. Release the pressure quick, divide the pudding between bowls, top each with a teaspoon of Sugar and serve.

Bon Appetit.

24. MOUTHWATERING BREAKFAST QUINOA

Perp time: 10 minutes   **Cooking time:** 10 minutes   **Servings:** 6

Nutrition Facts:
- Calories: 100
- Fat (In grams): 3
- Fiber (In grams): 1
- Carbs (In grams): 4
- Sugar (In grams): 3
- Protein (In grams): 2

Ingredients:
- 2 and 1/4 cups water
- 1 ½ cups quinoa, rinsed
- 2 tablespoon maple syrup
- A pinch of salt
- 1/4 teaspoon cinnamon powder
- Half-teaspoon vanilla extract
- Fresh berries for serving
- Milk for serving
- Almonds, sliced for serving

Instructions:
1. In your instant pot, add water, quinoa, vanilla, cinnamon, salt and maple syrup.
2. Stir, cover the pot and cook at High for 10 minutes.
3. Release the pressure naturally, fluff quinoa with a fork, divide it into breakfast bowls, add milk and stir.
4. Top with almonds and berries and serve.

Bon Appétit!

25. DELICIOUS BREAKFAST SANDWICHES

Perp time: 10 minutes **Cooking time:** 40 minutes **Servings:** 8

Nutrition Facts:
- Calories: 340
- Fat (In grams): 21
- Fiber (In grams): 2
- Carbs (In grams): 12
- Protein (In grams): 34

Ingredients:
- 2 tablespoons brown Sugar
- 4-pound beef roast, cut into small chunks
- Salt and black pepper to the taste
- 2 teaspoons paprika
- 2 ½-teaspoons garlic powder
- 2 teaspoons mustard powder
- 2 teaspoons onion flakes
- 3 cups beef stock
- One-tablespoon balsamic vinegar
- 2 tablespoon Worcestershire sauce
- 4 tablespoons butter, soft
- 8 hoagie rolls
- 8 slices provolone cheese

Instructions:
1. Put the meat in your instant pot.
2. Add salt, pepper, paprika, 2 teaspoons garlic powder, mustard powder, onion flakes, stock, vinegar and Worcestershire sauce, stir well, cover the pot and cook at High for 40 minutes.
3. Release the pressure quick, transfer meat to a cutting board, strain the liquid and keep it in a bowl.
4. Shred meat and divide among rolls after you've buttered them.
5. Add provolone cheese on top, introduce sandwiches in preheated broiler and broil until cheese melts.
6. Dip sandwiches in the sauce from the pot and serve them.

Bon Appétit!

26. BREAKFAST PEPPERS AND SAUSAGES

Perp time: 10 minutes **Cooking time:** 25 minutes **Servings:** 5

Nutrition Facts:
- Calories: 400
- Fat (In grams): 31
- Fiber (In grams): 1
- Carbs (In grams): 8
- Protein (In grams): 23

Ingredients:
- 15 ounces tomato sauce
- 28 ounces canned tomatoes, diced
- 10 Italian sausages
- 4 green bell peppers, cut into thin strips
- One-cup water
- 4 garlic cloves, minced
- One-tablespoon basil, dried
- One-tablespoon Italian seasoning

Instructions:
1. Put tomatoes, tomato sauce, basil, water, garlic, sausages, bell peppers and Italian seasoning in your instant pot and stir gently.

2. Cover the pot and cook at High for 25 minutes.
3. Release the pressure quick, divide the mix between plates and serve.

Bon Appétit!

27. Breakfast Tacos

Perp time: 10 minutes **Cooking time:** 5 minutes **Servings:** 4

Nutrition Facts:
- Calories: 240
- Fat (In grams): 11.5
- Fiber (In grams): 1
- Carbs (In grams): 3.4
- Protein (In grams): 31.1

Ingredients:
- 1 pound turkey meat, ground
- One-tablespoon Worcestershire sauce
- One-tablespoon extra virgin olive oil
- 1 and 1/4 cups beef stock
- 2 teaspoons corn flour
- 1 ½ teaspoons cumin, ground
- One-tablespoon chili powder
- 1/4 teaspoon onion powder
- 1/4 teaspoon garlic powder
- 1/4 teaspoon dried onions
- Half-teaspoon paprika
- 1/4 teaspoon oregano, dried
- A pinch of cayenne pepper
- Salt and black pepper to the taste
- Tacos shells for serving

Instructions:
1. Set your instant pot on Sauté mode, add oil and heat it up.
2. Add meat and Half-cup stock, stir and brown for a few minutes.
3. Discard excess fat, add the rest of the stock, Worcestershire sauce, flour, cumin, chili powder, garlic and onion powder, dried onions, paprika, oregano, salt, pepper and cayenne pepper, stir, cover the pot and cook at High for 5 minutes.
4. Release the pressure naturally, uncover the pot, stir meat mix and divide it in taco shells.

Serve right away.

Bon Appétit!

28. Yummy Breakfast Hash

Perp time: 10 minutes **Cooking time:** 7 minutes **Servings:** 4

Nutrition Facts:
- Calories: 300
- Fat (In grams): 16
- Fiber (In grams): 4
- Carbs (In grams): 30
- Protein (In grams): 17

Ingredients:
- 8 ounces sausage, ground
- 1 package hash browns, frozen
- 1/3 cup water
- 1 yellow onion, chopped
- 1 green bell pepper, chopped
- One-cup cheddar cheese, grated
- Salt and black pepper to the taste
- 4 eggs, whisked
- Salsa for serving

Instructions:
1. Set your instant pot on Sauté mode, add sausage, stir and cook for 2 minutes.
2. Drain excess fat, add bell pepper and onion, stir and cook for 2 more minutes.
3. Add hash browns, water, eggs, salt and cheese, stir, cover and cook on Low for 4 minutes.
4. Release the pressure quick, divide hash among plates and serve with salsa.

Bon Appétit!

29. BREAKFAST BERRIES JAM

Perp time: 20 minutes   **Cooking time:** 1 hour and 15 minutes   **Servings:** 12

Nutrition Facts:
- Calories: 60
- Fat (In grams): 0
- Fiber (In grams): 0
- Carbs (In grams): 12
- Protein (In grams): 1
- Sugar (In grams): 12

Ingredients:
- 16 ounces cranberries
- 16 ounces strawberries, chopped
- Zest from 1 lemon
- 4 ounces raisins
- A pinch of salt
- 3 ounces water
- 2 ½ pounds Sugar

Instructions:
1. In your instant pot, mix strawberries with cranberries, lemon zest, and raisins.
2. Add Sugar, stir and leave pot aside to 1 hour.
3. Add water and a pinch of salt, cover the pot and cook at High for 15 minutes.
4. Release the pressure, leave jam aside for 5 minutes, stir, pour into small jars and Bon Appétit!
5. Serve with toasted bread slices!

30. AMAZING CHICKEN LIVER BREAKFAST SPREAD

Perp time: 5 minutes   **Cooking time:** 15 minutes   **Servings:** 8

Nutrition Facts:
- Calories: 150
- Fat (In grams): 12
- Fiber (In grams): 0
- Carbs (In grams): 5
- Sugar (In grams): 2
- Protein (In grams): 4

Ingredients:
- One-teaspoon extra virgin olive oil
- 3/4 pound chicken liver
- 1 yellow onion, roughly chopped
- 1 bay leaf
- 1/4 cup red wine
- 2 anchovies
- One-tablespoons capers, drained and chopped
- One-tablespoon butter
- Salt and black pepper to the taste

Instructions:
1. Put the olive oil in your instant pot, add onion, salt, pepper, chicken liver, bay leaf and wine.
2. Stir, cover the pot and cook at High for 10 minutes.
3. Release the pressure quick, add anchovies, capers, and butter.

4. Stir, transfer to kitchen blender and pulse very well everything
5. Add salt and pepper to the taste, blend again, transfer to a bowl and serve with toasted bread slices!

Bon Appétit!

---

31. APPETIZING LEMON MARMALADE

Perp time: 10 minutes **Cooking time:** 15 minutes **Servings:** 8

Nutrition Facts:
- Calories: 60
- Fat (In grams): 1
- Fiber (In grams): 0
- Carbs (In grams): 12
- Sugar (In grams): 13

Ingredients:
- 2 pounds lemons, washed and sliced with a mandolin
- 4 pounds Sugar
- One-tablespoon vinegar

Instructions:
1. Put lemon slices in your instant pot.
2. Cover the pot and cook the marmalade at High for 10 minutes.
3. Release the pressure, add the Sugar, cover the pot again and cook at High for 4 more minutes.
4. Release the pressure again, stir your marmalade, pour it into jars and refrigerate until your serve it.

Bon Appétit!

---

32. BREAKFAST BLACKBERRY JAM

Perp time: 10 minutes **Cooking time:** 20 minutes **Servings:** 4

Nutrition Facts:
- Calories: 63
- Fat (In grams): 6
- Fiber (In grams): 7.6
- Carbs (In grams): 12
- Protein (In grams): 2
- Sugar (In grams): 7

Ingredients:
- 4 pints blackberries
- Juice of 1 small lemon
- 5 cups Sugar
- 3 tablespoons pectin powder

Instructions:
1. Put the blackberries in your instant pot.
2. Add the Sugar, stir, select sauté mode and cook for 3 minutes.
3. Transfer the jam to clean jars, close them and place them in the steamer basket of your instant pot.
4. Add water to cover the jars halfway, select Canning mode on your pot, cover and leave them for 20 minutes.

5. Remove jars after 20 minutes, leave them to cool down and keep your jam in the fridge until you serve it in the morning with some toasted bread and some butter.

Bon Appétit!

---

33. TASTY CHICKPEAS SPREAD

Perp time: 5 minutes **Cooking time:** 20 minutes **Servings:** 8

Nutrition Facts:
- Calories: 270
- Fat (In grams): 19
- Fiber (In grams): 5.1
- Carbs (In grams): 21.5
- Protein (In grams): 6.8

Ingredients:
- One-cup chickpeas soaked and drained
- 6 cups water
- 1 bay leaf
- 4 garlic cloves crushed
- 2 tablespoons tahini paste
- Juice of 1 lemon
- 1/4 teaspoon cumin
- Salt to the taste
- 1/4 cup chopped parsley
- A pinch of paprika
- Extra virgin olive oil

Instructions:
1. Put chickpeas and water in your instant pot.
2. Add bay leaf, 2 garlic cloves, cover the pot and cook at High for 18 minutes
3. Release the pressure, discard excess liquid and bay leaf and reserve some of the cooking liquid.
4. Add tahini paste, the cooking liquid you've reserved, lemon juice, cumin, the rest of the garlic and salt to the taste.
5. Transfer everything to your food processor and pulse well.
6. Transfer your chickpeas spread in a serving bowl, sprinkle olive oil and paprika on top and Bon Appétit!

---

34. DELICIOUS CHEESY GRITS

Perp time: 10 minutes **Cooking time:** 10 minutes **Servings:** 4

Nutrition Facts:
- Calories: 280
- Fat (In grams): 13
- Fiber (In grams): 1
- Carbs (In grams): 26
- Sugar (In grams): 2
- Protein (In grams): 13.2

Ingredients:
- 2 tablespoons coconut oil
- 1 and 3/4 cup half and half
- One-cup stone ground grits
- 3 cups water
- 2 teaspoons salt
- 3 tablespoons butter
- 4 ounces cheddar cheese, grated
- Butter for serving

Instructions:
1. Set your instant pot on sauté mode, add grits, stir and toast them for 3 minutes.

2. Add oil, half, and half, water, salt, butter and cheese, stir, cover and cook on High for 10 minutes.
   3. Release the pressure naturally, leave cheesy grits aside for 15 minutes, transfer to breakfast bowls, add butter on top and serve.

Bon Appétit!

35. AMAZING RICOTTA CHEESE SPREAD

Perp time: 10 minutes **Cooking time:** 5 minutes **Servings:** 4

Nutrition Facts:
- Calories: 294
- Fat (In grams): 18
- Fiber (In grams): 1
- Carbs (In grams): 4
- Protein (In grams): 7

Ingredients:
- 10 ounces canned tomatoes and green chilies, chopped
- 1 and 3/4 cups Italian sausage, ground
- 4 cups processed cheese, cut into chunks
- 4 tablespoons water

Instructions:
1. In your instant pot, mix tomatoes and chilies with water, ground sausage, and cheese.
2. Stir, cover and cook at High for 5 minutes.
3. Release the pressure naturally for 5 minutes, uncover the pot, stir spread, transfer to a bowl and serve it.

Bon Appétit!

36. YUMMY PECAN SWEET POTATOES

Perp time: 10 minutes **Cooking time:** 10 minutes **Servings:** 8

Nutrition Facts:
- Calories: 230
- Fat (In grams): 13
- Fiber (In grams): 4
- Carbs (In grams): 15
- Protein (In grams): 6

Ingredients:
- One-cup water
- One-tablespoon lemon peel
- Half-cup brown Sugar
- 1/4 teaspoon salt
- 3 sweet potatoes peeled and sliced
- 1/4 cup butter
- 1/4 cup maple syrup
- One-cup pecans chopped
- One-tablespoon cornstarch
- Whole pecans for garnish

Instructions:
1. Put the water in your instant pot, add lemon peel, brown Sugar and salt and stir.
2. Add potatoes, cover the pot and cook at High for 15 minutes.
3. Release the pressure and transfer the potatoes to a serving plate.
4. Select sauté mode on your instant pot, add the butter and melt it.

5. Add pecans, maple syrup, cornstarch and stir very well.
6. Pour this over the potatoes, garnish with whole pecans and serve!

Bon Appétit!

---

37. BREAKFAST PUMPKIN BUTTER

Perp time: 15 minutes   **Cooking time:** 10 minutes   **Servings:** 18

Nutrition Facts:
- Calories: 50
- Fat (In grams): 1
- Fiber (In grams): 0
- Carbs (In grams): 10
- Sugar (In grams): 9
- Protein (In grams): 1

Ingredients:
- 30 ounces pumpkin puree
- 3 apples, peeled, cored and chopped
- One-tablespoon pumpkin spice
- One-cup Sugar
- A pinch of salt
- 12 ounces apple cider
- Half-cup honey

Instructions:
1. In your instant pot, mix pumpkin puree with pumpkin spice, apple pieces, Sugar, honey, cider and a pinch of salt,
2. Stir well, cover the pot and cook at High for 10 minutes.
3. Release the pressure naturally for 15 minutes, transfer the butter to small jars and keep it in the fridge until you serve it.

Bon Appétit!

---

38. AMAZING BREAKFAST

Perp time: 10 minutes   **Cooking time:** 25 minutes   **Servings:** 4

Nutrition Facts:
- Calories: 140
- Fat (In grams): 1.2
- Fiber (In grams): 8.4
- Carbs (In grams): 35
- Sugar (In grams): 14
- Protein (In grams): 5

Ingredients:
- 3 cups rooibos tea
- One-tablespoon cinnamon, ground
- One-cup red lentils, soaked for 4 hours and drained
- 2 apples, diced
- One-teaspoon cloves, ground
- One-teaspoon turmeric, ground
- Maple syrup to the taste
- Coconut milk for serving

Instructions:
1. Put lentils in your instant pot, add tea, stir, cover and cook at High for 15 minutes.
2. Release pressure, uncover the pot, add cinnamon, apples, turmeric, and cloves, stir, cover and cook at High for 15 more minutes.
3. Release pressure quick, divide lentils between bowls, add maple syrup to the taste and coconut milk

Bon Appétit!

39. APPETIZING MUSHROOM PATE

Perp time: 6 minutes   **Cooking time:** 18 minutes   **Servings:** 6

Nutrition Facts:
- Calories: 220
- Fat (In grams): 15
- Fiber (In grams): 0
- Carbs (In grams): 15
- Sugar (In grams): 3
- Protein (In grams): 5

Ingredients:
- 1-ounce dry porcini mushrooms
- 1 pound button mushrooms sliced
- One-cup boiled water
- One-tablespoon butter
- One-tablespoon extra virgin olive oil
- 1 shallot finely chopped
- 1/4 cup white wine
- Salt and pepper to the taste
- 1 bay leaf
- One-tablespoon truffle oil
- 3 tablespoons grated parmesan cheese

Instructions:
1. Put dry mushrooms in a bowl, add One-cup boiling water over them and leave them aside for now.
2. Set your instant pot on sauté mode, add butter and the olive oil and heat them up.
3. Add the shallot, stir and cook for 2 minutes
4. Add dry mushrooms and their liquid, fresh mushrooms, wine, salt, pepper, and bay leaf.
5. Stir, cover the pot and cook at High for 16 minutes.
6. Release the pressure, discard bay leaf and some of the liquid, transfer everything to your blender and pulse until you obtain a creamy spread.
7. Add truffle oil and grated parmesan cheese, blend again, transfer to a bowl and serve.

Bon Appétit!

40. YUMMY BREAKFAST POTATOES

Perp time: 5 minutes   **Cooking time:** 7 minutes   **Servings:** 2

Nutrition Facts:
- Calories: 90
- Fat (In grams): 3
- Fiber (In grams): 1
- Carbs (In grams): 11
- Protein (In grams): 1

Ingredients:
- 4 gold potatoes, washed
- 2 teaspoons Italian seasoning
- One-tablespoon bacon Fat
- One-cup chives, chopped for serving.
- Water
- Salt and pepper to the taste

Instructions:
1. Put potatoes in your instant pot, add water to cover them, cover the pot and cook at High for 10 minutes.
2. Release the pressure naturally, transfer potatoes to a working surface and leave them to cool down.
3. Peel potatoes, transfer them to a bowl and mash them a bit with a fork.
4. Set your instant pot on sauté mode, add bacon Fat and heat up.

5. Add potatoes, seasoning, salt and pepper to the taste, stir, cover the pot and cook at High for 1 minute.
6. Release the pressure quickly, stir potatoes again, divide them between plates and serve with chives sprinkled on top.

Bon Appétit!

---

41. BEST BBQ TOFU

Perp time: 10 minutes   **Cooking time:** 10 minutes   **Servings:** 6

Nutrition Facts:
- Calories: 200
- Fat (In grams): 11
- Fiber (In grams): 3
- Carbs (In grams): 14.1
- Protein (In grams): 14.4

Ingredients:
- 28 ounces firm tofu, cubed
- 12 ounces bbq sauce
- 2 tablespoons extra virgin olive oil
- 4 garlic cloves, minced
- 1 yellow onion, chopped
- 1 celery stalk, chopped
- 1 red bell pepper, chopped
- 1 green bell pepper, chopped
- Salt to the taste
- A pinch of curry powder

Instructions:
1. Set your instant pot on Sauté mode, add the oil and heat it up.
2. Add bell peppers, garlic, onion and celery and stir.
3. Add salt and curry powder, stir and cook for 2 minutes.
4. Add tofu, stir and cook 4 minutes more.
5. Add bbq sauce, stir, cover the pot and cook at High for 5 minutes.
6. Release the pressure, uncover the pot, transfer to plates and serve.

Bon Appétit!

---

42. AMAZING TOFU BREAKFAST

Perp time: 10 minutes   **Cooking time:** 7 minutes   **Servings:** 4

Nutrition Facts:
- Calories: 170
- Fat (In grams): 12
- Fiber (In grams): 7
- Carbs (In grams): 18
- Protein (In grams): 16

Ingredients:
- 1 bunch kale leaves, chopped
- 1 leek, cut into halves lengthwise and thinly sliced
- One-teaspoon paprika
- One-tablespoon olive oil
- Half-cup water
- Sat to the taste
- A pinch of cayenne pepper
- 2 teaspoons sherry vinegar
- 3 ounces tofu, cubed and baked
- 1/4 cup almonds, chopped

Instructions:
1. Set your instant pot on Sauté mode, add oil and heat it up.
2. Add leeks, stir and sauté them for 5 minutes.
3. Add paprika, stir and cook for 1 minute.
4. Add water, kale, salt and cayenne, cover the pot and cook at High for 2 minutes.
5. Release the pressure quick, add tofu and vinegar and more salt if needed, stir and transfer to plates.
6. Sprinkle almonds on top and serve right away.

Bon Appétit!

43. TASTY TOFU SCRAMBLE

Perp time: 10 minutes   **Cooking time:** 7 minutes   **Servings:** 4

Nutrition Facts:
- Calories: 144
- Fat (In grams): 5.7
- Fiber (In grams): 3.1
- Carbs (In grams): 11.8
- Protein (In grams): 13

Ingredients:
- 1 yellow onion, thinly sliced
- One-teaspoon walnut oil
- 3 garlic cloves, minced
- 1/4 cup veggie stock
- One-cup carrot, chopped
- 1 block firm tofu, drained
- 12 ounces canned tomatoes, diced
- One-teaspoon cumin
- 2 tablespoons red pepper, chopped
- One-tablespoon Italian seasoning
- One-teaspoon nutritional yeast
- Salt and black pepper to the taste

Instructions:
1. Set your instant pot on Sauté mode, add oil and heat it up.
2. Add onion, carrot and garlic, stir and cook for 3 minutes.
3. Crumble tofu, add it to pot and stir.
4. Add stock, red pepper, tomatoes, cumin, Italian seasoning, salt and pepper, stir, cover the pot and cook at High for 4 minutes.
5. Release the pressure quick, transfer to bowls and serve with nutritional yeast on top.

Bon Appétit!

44. TOFU AND POTATOES BREAKFAST

Perp time: 10 minutes   **Cooking time:** 4 minutes   **Servings:** 4

Nutrition Facts:
- Calories: 156
- Fat (In grams): 10
- Fiber (In grams): 3
- Carbs (In grams): 11.4
- Protein (In grams): 13

Ingredients:
- 3 purple potatoes, cubed
- 1 yellow onion, chopped
- 2 garlic cloves, minced
- 1 carrot, chopped

- 1 ginger root, grated
- ½ pound firm tofu, cubed
- 3 tablespoons water
- One-tablespoon tamari
- Mexican spice blend to the taste
- 1 ½ cups Brussels sprouts

Instructions:
1. Set your instant pot on sauté mode, add onion and brown it for 1 minute.
2. Add potatoes, ginger, garlic, tofu, carrots, tamari, spices, Brussels sprouts and water, cover and cook at High for 2 minutes.
3. Release the pressure, uncover the pot, uncover the pot, transfer to plates and serve.

Bon Appétit!

---

45. Amazing Breakfast Salad

Perp time: 10 minutes **Cooking time:** 4 minutes **Servings:** 4

Nutrition Facts:
- Calories: 150
- Fat (In grams): 8
- Fiber (In grams): 1.3
- Carbs (In grams): 11
- Protein (In grams): 3

Ingredients:
- 6 potatoes, peeled and cubed
- 4 eggs
- 1 ½ cups water
- One-cup homemade mayonnaise
- 1/4 cup onion, finely chopped
- One-tablespoon dill pickle juice
- 2 tablespoons parsley, finely chopped
- One-tablespoon mustard
- Salt and black pepper to the taste

Instructions:
1. Put potatoes, eggs and the water in the steamer basket of your instant pot, cover and cook on High for 4 minutes.
2. Release the pressure quick, transfer eggs to a bowl filled with ice water and leave them to cool down.
3. In a bowl, mix mayo with pickle juice, onion, parsley and mustard and stir well.
4. Add potatoes and toss to coat.
5. Peel eggs, chop them, add them to salad and toss again.
6. Add salt and pepper to the taste, stir and serve your salad with toasted bread slices.

Bon Appétit!

SIDE DISH RECIPES

46. DELICIOUS FARRO PILAF AND WILD RICE

Perp time: 10 minutes **Cooking time:** 35 minutes **Servings:** 12

Nutrition Facts:
- Calories: 120
- Fat (In grams): 1
- Fiber (In grams): 1.5
- Carbs (In grams): 21
- Protein (In grams): 4.5

Ingredients:
- 1 shallot, finely chopped
- One-teaspoon garlic, minced
- A drizzle of extra virgin olive oil
- 1 ½ cups whole grain faro
- 3/4 cup wild rice
- 6 cups chicken stock
- Salt and black pepper to the taste
- One-tablespoons parsley and sage, finely chopped
- Half-cup hazelnuts, toasted and chopped
- 3/4 cup cherries, dried
- Some chopped chives for serving

Instructions:
1. Set your instant pot on Sauté mode, add a drizzle of oil and heat it up.
2. Add onion and garlic, stir and cook for 2-3 minutes.
3. Add farro, rice, salt, pepper, stock and One-tablespoon mixed sage and parsley, stir, cover the pot and cook on High for 25 minutes.
4. Meanwhile, put cherries in a pot, add hot water to cover, leave aside for 10 minutes and drain them.
5. Release the pressure from the pot for 5 minutes, drain excess liquid, add hazelnuts and cherries, stir gently, divide among plates and garnish with chopped chives.

Bon Appétit!

47. AWESOME MUSHROOM RISOTTO

Perp time: 10 minutes **Cooking time:** 15 minutes **Servings:** 4

Nutrition Facts:
- Calories: 340
- Fat (In grams): 1
- Fiber (In grams): 1
- Carbs (In grams): 15
- Protein (In grams): 4

Ingredients:
- 2 cups risotto rice
- 4 cups chicken stock
- 2 garlic cloves, crushed
- 2 ounces extra virgin olive oil
- 1 yellow onion, chopped
- 8 ounces mushrooms, sliced
- 4 ounces heavy cream
- 4 ounces sherry vinegar
- 2 tablespoons parmesan cheese, grated
- 1-ounce basil, finely chopped

Instructions:
1. Set your instant pot on Sauté mode, add the oil and heat it up.
2. Add onions, garlic and mushrooms, stir and cook for 3 minutes.
3. Add rice, stock and vinegar, stir, cover the pot and cook at High for 10 minutes.

4. Release the pressure, uncover the pot, add cream and parmesan and stir
   5. Divide among plates, sprinkle basil and serve.

Bon Appétit!

48. DELICIOUS ALMONDS AND QUINOA SIDE DISH

Perp time: 10 minutes   **Cooking time:** 11 minutes   **Servings:** 4

Nutrition Facts:
- Calories: 140
- Fat (In grams): 3
- Fiber (In grams): 2
- Carbs (In grams): 12
- Protein (In grams): 12.4

Ingredients:
- Half-cup yellow onion, finely chopped
- One-tablespoon butter
- 1 celery stalk, chopped
- 1 ½ cups quinoa, rinsed
- 14 ounces chicken stock
- Salt and black pepper to the taste
- 1/4 cup water
- Half-cup almonds, toasted and sliced
- 2 tablespoons parsley, chopped

Instructions:
1. Set your instant pot on Sauté mode, add butter and melt it.
2. Add onion and celery, stir and cook for 5 minutes.
3. Add quinoa, water, stock, salt and pepper, stir, cover and cook at High for 3 minutes.
4. Release the pressure for 5 minutes, uncover, fluff with a fork, add almonds and parsley, stir, divide among plates and serve as a side dish.

Bon Appétit!

49. YUMMY QUINOA PILAF

Perp time: 10 minutes   **Cooking time:** 2 minutes   **Servings:** 4

Nutrition Facts:
- Calories: 130
- Fat (In grams): 0.9
- Fiber (In grams): 3.2
- Carbs (In grams): 12
- Protein (In grams): 6.9

Ingredients:
- 2 cups quinoa
- 2 garlic cloves, minced
- 2 tablespoons extra virgin olive oil
- Salt to the taste
- 2 teaspoons turmeric
- 3 cups water
- 1 handful parsley, chopped
- 2 teaspoons cumin, ground

Instructions:
1. Set your instant pot on Sauté mode, add oil and heat it up.
2. Add garlic, stir and cook for 30 seconds.
3. Add water, quinoa, cumin, turmeric and salt, stir, cover and cook at High for 1 minute.
4. Release the pressure naturally for 10 minutes, fluff quinoa with a fork, transfer to plates, season with more salt if needed, sprinkle parsley on top and serve as a side dish.

50. Tasty Pumpkin Risotto

Perp time: 5 minutes **Cooking time:** 10 minutes **Servings:** 4

Nutrition Facts:
- Calories: 263
- Fat (In grams): 5
- Fiber (In grams): 2
- Carbs (In grams): 37
- Protein (In grams): 6

Ingredients:
- 2 ounces extra virgin olive oil
- 1 small yellow onion, chopped
- 2 garlic cloves, minced
- 12 ounces risotto rice
- 4 cups chicken stock
- 6 ounces pumpkin puree
- Half-teaspoon nutmeg
- One-teaspoon thyme, chopped
- Half-teaspoon ginger, grated
- Half-teaspoon cinnamon
- Half-teaspoon allspice
- 4 ounces heavy cream

Instructions:
1. Set your instant pot on Sauté mode, add oil and heat it up.
2. Add onion and garlic, stir and cook for 1-2 minutes.
3. Also add risotto, chicken stock, pumpkin puree, thyme, nutmeg, cinnamon, ginger and allspice and stir.
4. Cover the pot and cook at High for 10 minutes
5. Release the pressure, add cream, stir very well and serve as a side dish.

Bon Appétit!

51. Amazing Flavored Mashed Potatoes

Perp time: 10 minutes **Cooking time:** 9 minutes **Servings:** 8

Nutrition Facts:
- Calories: 240
- Fat (In grams): 1
- Fiber (In grams): 8.2
- Carbs (In grams): 34
- Protein (In grams): 4.5

Ingredients:
- 2 garlic cloves
- 3 pounds sweet potatoes, peeled and chopped
- Salt and black pepper to the taste
- Half-teaspoon parsley, dried
- 1/4 teaspoon sage, dried
- Half-teaspoon rosemary, dried
- Half-teaspoon thyme dried
- 1 ½ cups water
- 1/4 cup milk
- Half-cup parmesan, grated
- 2 tablespoon butter

Instructions:
1. Put potatoes and garlic in the steamer basket of your instant pot, add 1 ½ cups water in the pot, cover and cook at High for 10 minutes.
2. Release the pressure quick, drain water, transfer the potatoes and garlic to a bowl and mash them using your kitchen mixer.

3. Add butter, parmesan, milk, salt, pepper, parsley, sage, rosemary and thyme and blend everything well.
4. Divide among plates and serve.

Bon Appétit!

52. SPECIAL PINK RICE

Perp time: 10 minutes **Cooking time:** 5 minutes **Servings:** 8

Nutrition Facts:
- Calories: 114
- Fat (In grams): 1
- Fiber (In grams): 2
- Carbs (In grams): 13
- Protein (In grams): 4

Ingredients:
- One-teaspoon salt
- 2 ½-cups water
- 2 cups pink rice

Instructions:
1. Put the rice in your instant pot.
2. Add the water and salt, stir, cover and cook at High for 5 minutes.
3. Release the pressure naturally for 10 minutes, uncover the pot, fluff rice with a fork, divide among plates and serve.

Bon Appétit!

53. RICE AND VEGGIES SIDE DISH

Perp time: 6 minutes **Cooking time:** 15 minutes **Servings:** 4

Nutrition Facts:
- Calories: 340
- Fat (In grams): 6
- Fiber (In grams): 5.5
- Carbs (In grams): 40
- Protein (In grams): 14.2

Ingredients:
- 2 cups basmati rice
- One-cup mixed frozen carrots, peas, corn, green beans
- 2 cups water
- Half-teaspoon green chili, minced
- Half-teaspoon ginger, grated
- 3 garlic cloves, minced
- 2 tablespoons butter
- 1 cinnamon stick
- One-tablespoon cumin seeds
- 2 bay leaves
- 3 whole cloves
- 5 black peppercorns
- 2 whole cardamoms
- One-tablespoon Sugar
- Salt to the taste

Instructions:
1. Put the water in your instant pot.
2. Add rice, mixed frozen veggies, green chili, grated ginger, garlic cloves, cinnamon stick, whole cloves and butter.

3. Also add cumin seeds, bay leaves, cardamoms, black peppercorns, salt and Sugar.
4. Stir, cover and cook at High for 15 minutes
5. Release the pressure, divide among plates and serve with your favorite steaks.

Bon Appétit!

---

54. SAFFRON RISOTTO SIDE DISH

Perp time: 10 minutes   **Cooking time:** 10 minutes   **Servings:** 10

Nutrition Facts:
- Calories: 260
- Fat (In grams): 7
- Fiber (In grams): 2
- Carbs (In grams): 41
- Sugar (In grams): 1.5
- Protein (In grams): 3.9

Ingredients:
- 2 tablespoons extra virgin olive oil
- Half-teaspoon saffron threads, crushed
- Half-cup onion, chopped
- 2 tablespoons hot milk
- 1 ½ cups Arborio rice
- 3 ½-cups veggie stock
- A pinch of salt
- One-tablespoon honey
- 1 cinnamon stick
- 1/3 cup almonds, chopped
- 1/3 cup currants, dried

Instructions:
1. In a bowl, mix hot milk with saffron, stir and leave aside.
2. Set your instant pot on Sauté mode, add oil and heat it up.
3. Add onions, stir and cook for 5 minutes.
4. Add rice, veggie stock, saffron and milk, honey, salt, almonds, cinnamon stick and currants.
5. Stir, cover the pot and cook at High for 5 minutes.
6. Release the pressure quick, fluff the rice a bit, discard cinnamon, divide it among plates and serve.

Bon Appétit!

---

55. DELICIOUS POTATOES SIDE DISH

Perp time: 10 minutes   **Cooking time:** 6 minutes   **Servings:** 4

Nutrition Facts:
- Calories: 94
- Fat (In grams): 1
- Fiber (In grams): 2.2
- Carbs (In grams): 21
- Protein (In grams): 2.5

Ingredients:
- 1 pound new potatoes, peeled and thinly sliced
- One-cup water
- Salt and black pepper to the taste
- 1/4 teaspoon rosemary, dried
- One-tablespoon extra virgin olive oil
- 2 garlic cloves, minced

Instructions:

1. Put the potatoes and the water in the steamer basket of your instant pot, cover and cook at High for 4 minutes.
2. In a heat proof dish, mix rosemary with oil and garlic, cover and microwave for 1 minute.
3. Release the pressure fro the pot, drain potatoes and spread them on a lined baking sheet.
4. Add heated oil mix, salt and pepper to the taste, toss to coat, divide among plates and serve as a side dish.

Bon Appétit!

56. MEXICAN RICE SIDE DISH

Perp time: 10 minutes **Cooking time:** 4 minutes **Servings:** 8

Nutrition Facts:
- Calories: 100
- Fat (In grams): 2
- Fiber (In grams): 1
- Carbs (In grams): 18
- Protein (In grams): 2

Ingredients:
- One-cup long grain rice
- 1 and 1/4 cups veggie stock
- Half-cup cilantro, chopped
- ½ avocado, pitted, peeled and chopped
- Salt and black pepper to the taste
- 1/4 cup green hot sauce

Instructions:
1. Put the rice in your instant pot, add stock, stir, cover and cook at High for 4 minutes.
2. Release the pressure naturally for 10 minutes, uncover the pot, fluff it with a fork and transfer to a bowl.
3. Meanwhile, in your food processor, mix avocado with hot sauce and cilantro and blend well.
4. Pour this over rice, stir well, add salt and pepper to the taste, stir again, divide among plates and serve.

Bon Appétit!

57. TASTY HERBED POLENTA

Perp time: 15 minutes **Cooking time:** 6 minutes **Servings:** 6

Nutrition Facts:
- Calories: 150
- Fat (In grams): 1.6
- Fiber (In grams): 3.6
- Carbs (In grams): 35
- Protein (In grams): 3.7

Ingredients:
- 4 cups veggie stock
- 2 tablespoons extra virgin olive oil
- 2 teaspoons garlic, minced
- Half-cup yellow onion, chopped
- 1/3 cup sun-dried tomatoes, chopped
- Salt to the taste
- One-cup polenta
- 1 bay leaf
- 2 teaspoons oregano, finely chopped
- 3 tablespoons basil, finely chopped
- One-teaspoon rosemary, finely chopped
- 2 tablespoons parsley, finely chopped

Instructions:
1. Set your instant pot on sauté mode, add the oil and heat it up.
2. Add onion, stir and cook for 1 minute.
3. Add garlic, stir again and cook for 1 minute.
4. Add stock, salt, tomatoes, bay leaf, rosemary, oregano, half of the basil, half of the parsley and polenta.
5. Do not stir, cover the pot, cook at High for 5 minutes and release pressure naturally for 10 minutes.
6. Uncover the pot, discard bay leaf, stir polenta gently, add the rest of the parsley, basil and more salt, stir, divide among plates and serve.

Bon Appétit!

58. SIMPLE BARLEY AND CAULIFLOWER RISOTTO

Perp time: 10 minutes **Cooking time:** 1 hour **Servings:** 4

Nutrition Facts:
- Calories: 350
- Fat (In grams): 16
- Fiber (In grams): 10
- Carbs (In grams): 25
- Protein (In grams): 14.6

Ingredients:
- 4 tablespoons extra virgin olive oil
- Salt and black pepper to the taste
- 1 cauliflower head, florets separated
- Half-cup parmesan, grated
- 2 garlic cloves, minced
- One-cup pearl barley
- 1 yellow onion, chopped
- 3 cups chicken stock
- 2 thyme springs
- 2 tablespoons parsley, chopped
- One-tablespoon butter

Instructions:
1. Spread cauliflower florets on a lined baking dish, add 3 tablespoons oil, salt and pepper, toss to coat, introduce in the oven at 425 degrees F and bake for 20 minutes, turning them every 10 minutes.
2. Take cauliflower out of the oven, sprinkle 1/4 cup parmesan and bake for 5 minutes more.
3. Meanwhile, set your instant pot on Sauté mode, add One-tablespoon oil and heat it up.
4. Add onion, stir and cook for 5 minutes.
5. Add garlic, stir and cook for 1 minute.
6. Add stock, thyme, and barley, stir, cover the pot and cook at High for 25 minutes.
7. Release the pressure quickly, uncover, the pot, stir the barley, discard thyme, add butter, the rest of the parmesan, roasted cauliflower, salt, pepper to the taste and parsley.
8. Stir the risotto well, divide among plates and serve.

59. INSTANT FARRO SIDE DISH

Perp time: 10 minutes **Cooking time:** 40 minutes **Servings:** 6

Nutrition Facts:
- Calories: 160
- Fat (In grams): 1
- Fiber (In grams): 2
- Carbs (In grams): 12
- Protein (In grams): 4

Ingredients:
- One-tablespoon apple cider vinegar
- One-cup whole grain farro
- One-teaspoon lemon juice
- Salt to the taste
- 3 cups water
- One-tablespoon extra virgin olive oil
- Half-cup cherries, dried and chopped
- 1/4 cup green onions, chopped
- 10 mint leaves, chopped
- 2 cups cherries, pitted and cut into halves

Instructions:
1. Put the water in your instant pot, add rinsed farro, stir, cover and cook at High for 40 minutes.
2. Release the pressure quick, drain farro, transfer to a bowl and mix with salt, oil, lemon juice, vinegar, dried cherries, fresh cherries, green onions, and mint.
3. Stir well, divide among plates and serve,

Bon Appétit!

60. GOAT CHEESE AND SPINACH RISOTTO

Perp time: 10 minutes **Cooking time:** 10 minutes **Servings:** 6

Nutrition Facts:
- Calories: 340
- Fat (In grams): 23
- Fiber (In grams): 4.5
- Carbs (In grams): 24
- Protein (In grams): 18.9

Ingredients:
- 2 garlic cloves, minced
- 2 tablespoons extra virgin olive oil
- 3/4 cup yellow onion, chopped
- 1 ½ cups Arborio rice
- Half-cup white wine
- 12 ounces spinach, chopped
- 3 ½-cups hot veggie stock
- Salt and black pepper to the taste
- 4 ounces goat cheese, soft and crumbled
- 2 tablespoons lemon juice
- 1/3 cup pecans, toasted and chopped

Instructions:
1. Set your instant pot on sauté mode, add the oil and heat it up.
2. Add garlic and onions, stir and cook for 5 minutes.
3. Add rice, stir and cook for 1 minute more.
4. Add wine, stir and cook until it's absorbed.
5. Add 3 cups stock, cover the pot and cook at High for 4 minutes.
6. Release the pressure quickly, uncover the pot, add spinach, stir and cook on Simmer mode for 3 minutes.

7. Add salt, pepper, the rest of the stock, lemon juice and goat cheese and stir.
8. Divide among plates, garnish with pecans and serve.

Bon Appétit!

---

61. ARTICHOKES AND RICE SIDE DISH

Perp time: 10 minutes **Cooking time:** 20 minutes **Servings:** 4

Nutrition Facts:
- Calories: 240
- Fat (In grams): 7.2
- Fiber (In grams): 5.1
- Carbs (In grams): 34
- Protein (In grams): 6

Ingredients:
- One-tablespoon extra virgin olive oil
- 5 ounces Arborio rice
- 2 garlic cloves crushed
- 1 and 1/4 cups chicken broth
- One-tablespoon white wine
- 6 ounces graham cracker crumbs
- 1 and 1/4 cups water
- 15 ounces canned artichoke hearts chopped
- 16 ounces cream cheese
- One-tablespoon grated parmesan cheese
- 1 ½ tablespoons thyme chopped
- Salt and black pepper to the taste

Instructions:
1. Set your instant pot on Sauté mode, add the oil, heat up, add rice and cook for 2 minutes.
2. Add garlic, stir and cook for 1 minute.
3. Transfer this to a heat proof dish.
4. Add stock, crumbs, salt, pepper and wine, stir and cover the with tin foil.
5. Place the dish in the steamer basket of the pot, add water, cover and cook at High for 8 minutes
6. Release the pressure, take the dish out, uncover, add cream cheese, parmesan, artichoke hearts, and thyme.
7. Mix well and serve while it's hot!

Bon Appétit!

---

62. YUMMY MASHED SQUASH

Perp time: 10 minutes **Cooking time:** 20 minutes **Servings:** 4

Nutrition Facts:
- Calories: 140
- Fat (In grams): 1
- Fiber (In grams): 0.5
- Carbs (In grams): 10.5
- Protein (In grams): 1.7

Ingredients:
- Half-cup water
- 2 acorn squash, cut into halves and seeded
- Salt and black pepper to the taste
- 1/4 teaspoon baking soda
- 2 tablespoons butter
- Half-teaspoon nutmeg, grated
- 2 tablespoons brown Sugar

Instructions:
1. Sprinkle squash halves with salt, pepper and baking soda and place them in the steamer basket of your instant pot.
2. Add Half-cup water to the pot, cover and cook at High for 20 minutes.
3. Release the pressure quickly, take squash and leave aside on a plate to cool down.
4. Scrape flesh from the squash and put in a bowl.
5. Add salt, pepper to the taste, butter, Sugar and nutmeg and mash everything with a potato mashes.
6. Stir well and serve.

Bon Appétit!

63. MOUTHWATERING LEMON PARMESAN & PEAS RISOTTO

Perp time: 10 minutes   **Cooking time:** 17 minutes   **Servings:** 6

Nutrition Facts:
- Calories: 140
- Fat (In grams): 1.5
- Fiber (In grams): 1
- Carbs (In grams): 27
- Protein (In grams): 5

Ingredients:
- 1 ½cup rice
- 2 tablespoons butter
- 1 yellow onion, chopped
- One-tablespoon extra virgin olive oil
- 2 tablespoons lemon juice
- One-teaspoon lemon zest, grated
- 3 ½-cups chicken stock
- 2 tablespoons parsley, finely chopped
- Salt and black pepper to the taste
- 1 ½cup peas
- 2 tablespoons parmesan, finely grated

Instructions:
1. Set your instant pot on sauté mode, add One-tablespoon butter and the oil and heat them up.
2. Add onions, stir and cook for 5 minutes.
3. Add rice, stir and cook for 3 more minutes.
4. Add 3 cups stock and the lemon juice, stir, cover and cook at High for 5 minutes.
5. Release the pressure quickly, set the pot on Simmer, add peas and the rest of the stock, stir and cook for 2 minutes.
6. Add parmesan, parsley, the rest of the butter, lemon zest, salt and pepper to the taste and stir.
7. Divide among plates and serve.

Bon Appétit!

64. TASTY POTATO CASSEROLE SIDE DISH

Perp time: 15 minutes   **Cooking time:** 10 minutes   **Servings:** 4

Nutrition Facts:
- Calories: 150
- Fat (In grams): 9
- Fiber (In grams): 3
- Carbs (In grams): 25
- Sugar (In grams): 10
- Protein (In grams): 4

Ingredients:
- 3 pounds sweet potatoes, scrubbed
- One-cup water
- 1/4 cup coconut milk
- 1/3 cup palm Sugar
- Half-teaspoon nutmeg, ground
- 2 tablespoons coconut flour
- One-teaspoon cinnamon
- 1/4 teaspoon allspice
- Salt to the taste

For the topping:
- Half-cup almond flour
- Half-cup walnuts, soaked, drained and ground
- 1/4 cup pecans, soaked, drained and ground
- 1/4 cup shredded coconut
- One-tablespoon chia seeds
- 1/4 cup palm Sugar
- A pinch of salt
- One-teaspoon cinnamon, ground
- 5 tablespoons salted butter

Instructions:
1. Prick potatoes with a fork, place them in the steamer basket of your instant pot, add One-cup water to the pot, cover and cook at High for 20 minutes.
2. Meanwhile, in a bowl, mix almond flour with pecans, walnuts, 1/4 cup coconut, 1/4 cup palm Sugar, chia seeds, One-teaspoon cinnamon, a pinch of salt and the butter and stir everything.
3. Release the pressure naturally from the pot, take potatoes and peel them and add Half-cup water to the pot.
4. Chop potatoes and place them in a baking dish.
5. Add crumble mix you've made, stir everything, spread evenly in the dish, cover, place in the steamer basket, cover the pot again and cook at High for 10 minutes.
6. Release the pressure quickly, take the dish out of the pot, uncover, leave it to cool down, cut and serve as a side dish.

Bon Appétit!

---

65. DELICIOUS REFRIED BEANS

Perp time: 10 minutes **Cooking time:** 20 minutes **Servings:** 4

Nutrition Facts:
- Calories: 100
- Fat (In grams): 2
- Fiber (In grams): 5
- Carbs (In grams): 15
- Protein (In grams): 6

Ingredients:
- 3 cups pinto beans, soaked for 4 hours and drained
- 1 yellow onion, cut into halves
- 1 jalapeno, chopped
- 2 tablespoons garlic, minced
- Salt and black pepper to the taste
- 9 cups vegetable stock
- 1/8 teaspoon cumin, ground

Instructions:
1. In your instant pot, mix beans with salt, pepper, stock, onion, jalapeno, garlic and cumin.
2. Stir, cover and cook at High for 20 minutes.

3. Release the pressure naturally, discard onion halves, strain beans, transfer them to your blender and reserve cooking liquid.
4. Blend very well adding some of the liquid, transfer to a bowl and serve them as a side dish.

Bon Appétit!

---

66. YUMMY BLACK BEANS

Perp time: 10 minutes   **Cooking time:** 5 minutes   **Servings:** 8

Nutrition Facts:
- Calories: 330
- Fat (In grams): 1
- Fiber (In grams): 16
- Carbs (In grams): 23
- Protein (In grams): 21

Ingredients:
- One-cup black beans, soaked overnight, drained and rinsed
- 1 piece kombu seaweed
- 2/3 cup water
- Salt to the taste
- 1 spring epazote
- 2 garlic cloves, minced
- Half-teaspoon cumin seeds

Instructions:
1. In your instant pot, mix beans with kombu, water, garlic, epazote, and cumin.
2. Stir, cover the pot and cook at High for 5 minutes.
3. Release the pressure quickly, discard kombu and epazote, divide beans among plates, season with salt and serve.

Bon Appétit!

---

67. RICE AND RED BEANS

Perp time: 20 minutes   **Cooking time:** 25 minutes   **Servings:** 6

Nutrition Facts:
- Calories: 160
- Fat (In grams): 3.8
- Fiber (In grams): 3.4
- Carbs (In grams): 24
- Protein (In grams): 4.6

Ingredients:
- 1 pound red kidney beans, soaked overnight and drained
- Salt to the taste
- One-teaspoon vegetable oil
- 1 pound smoked sausage, cut into wedges
- 1 yellow onion, chopped
- 1 celery stalk, chopped
- 4 garlic cloves, chopped
- 1 green bell pepper, chopped
- One-teaspoon thyme, dried
- 2 bay leaves
- 5 cups water
- Long grain rice already cooked
- 2 green onions, minced for serving
- 2 tablespoons parsley, minced for serving
- Hot sauce for serving

Instructions:
1. Set your instant pot on Sauté mode, add the oil and heat it up.

2. Add sausage, onion, bell pepper, celery, garlic, thyme and salt to the taste, stir and cook for 8 minutes.
3. Add beans, bay leaves and the water, stir, cover the pot and cook at High for 15 minutes.
4. Release the pressure naturally for 20 minutes, discard bay leaves and put 2 cups of beans and some liquid in your blender.
5. Pulse them well and return to pot.
6. Divide the rice among plates, add beans, sausage, and veggies on top, sprinkle green onions and parsley and serve with hot sauce on top.

Bon Appétit!

68. AMAZING SIDE DISH

Perp time: 10 minutes **Cooking time:** 20 minutes **Servings:** 4

Nutrition Facts:
- Calories: 230
- Fat (In grams): 3.4
- Fiber (In grams): 3.2
- Carbs (In grams): 23
- Protein (In grams): 11

Ingredients:
- 1 ½ cups water
- Half-cup butter
- 1 and 1/4 cup turkey stock
- 1 bread loaf, cubed and toasted
- One-cup celery, chopped
- 1 yellow onion, chopped
- Salt and black pepper to the taste
- One-teaspoon sage
- One-teaspoon poultry seasoning

Instructions:
1. Set your instant pot on Sauté mode, add butter and melt it.
2. Add stock, onion, celery, salt, pepper, sage and poultry seasoning and stir well.
3. Add bread cubes, stir and cook for 1 minute.
4. Transfer this to a Bundt pan and cover it with tin foil.
5. Clean your instant pot, add the water and place the pan in the steamer basket, cover the pot and cook at High for 15 minutes.
6. Release the pressure quickly, uncover the pan, introduce it in the oven at 350 degrees F and bake for 5 minutes.

Serve hot.

Bon Appétit!

69. SIMPLE CAULIFLOWER AND PINEAPPLE RICE

Perp time: 10 minutes **Cooking time:** 20 minutes **Servings:** 6

Nutrition Facts:
- Calories: 100
- Fat (In grams): 2.7
- Fiber (In grams): 2.9
- Carbs (In grams): 12
- Protein (In grams): 4.9

Ingredients:
- 2 cups rice
- 4 cups water
- 1 cauliflower, florets separated and chopped
- ½ pineapple, peeled and chopped
- Salt and black pepper to the taste
- 2 teaspoons extra virgin olive oil

Instructions:
1. In your instant pot, mix rice with pineapple, cauliflower, water, oil, salt and pepper, stir, cover and cook for 20 minutes on Low.
2. Release the pressure naturally for 10 minutes, uncover the pot, fluff with a fork, add more salt and pepper to the taste, divide among plates and serve.

Bon Appétit!

70. Delicious Potatoes Gratin

Perp time: 10 minutes   **Cooking time:** 17 minutes   **Servings:** 6

Nutrition Facts:
- Calories: 340
- Fat (In grams): 22
- Fiber (In grams): 2
- Carbs (In grams): 32
- Protein (In grams): 11

Ingredients:
- One-cup chicken stock
- Half-cup yellow onion, chopped
- 2 tablespoons butter
- 6 potatoes, peeled and sliced
- Salt and black pepper to the taste
- Half-cup sour cream
- One-cup Monterey jack cheese, shredded

For the topping:
- 3 tablespoons melted butter
- One-cup bread crumbs

Instructions:
1. Set your instant pot on Sauté mode, add butter and melt it.
2. Add onion, stir and cook for 5 minutes.
3. Add stock, salt, pepper and put the steamer basket in the pot as well.
4. Add potatoes, cover the pot and cook at High for 5 minutes.
5. In a bowl, mix 3 tablespoons butter with bread crumbs and stir well.
6. Release pressure from the pot fast, take the steamer basket out and transfer potatoes to a baking dish.
7. Pour cream and cheese into instant pot and stir.
8. Add potatoes and stir gently.
9. Spread bread crumbs mix all over, introduce in preheated broiler and broil for 7 minutes.
10. Serve right away!

Bon Appétit!

71. TRIPLE BEANS MIX SIDE DISH

Perp time: 10 minutes **Cooking time:** 15 minutes **Servings:** 4

Nutrition Facts:
- Calories: 200
- Fat (In grams): 1
- Fiber (In grams): 6
- Carbs (In grams): 45
- Protein (In grams): 4

Ingredients:
- One-cup garbanzo beans, soaked overnight and drained
- One-cup cranberry beans, soaked overnight and drained
- 1 ½ cups green beans
- 4 cups water
- 1 garlic clove, crushed
- 1 bay leaf
- 2 celery stalks, chopped
- 1 bunch parsley, chopped
- 1 small red onion, chopped
- One-tablespoon Sugar
- 5 tablespoons apple cider vinegar
- 4 tablespoons extra virgin olive oil
- Salt and black pepper to the taste

Instructions:
1. Put the water in your instant pot.
2. Add bay leaf, garlic and garbanzo beans.
3. Put the steamer basket in your pot as well and put cranberry beans in it.
4. Wrap green beans in tin foil and also place in the steamer basket.
5. Cover the pot and cook at High for 15 minutes.
6. Release the pressure naturally for 10 minutes, uncover the pot, drain beans, unwrap green beans and put them all in a bowl.
7. In another bowl, mix onion with vinegar and Sugar, stir well and leave aside for a few minutes.
8. Add onions to beans and toss to coat.
9. Also add celery, olive oil, salt, pepper to the taste and parsley, toss to coat and divide among plates.
10. Serve right away as a side dish.

Bon Appétit!

72. MUSHROOMS AND GREEN BEANS SIDE DISH

Perp time: 10 minutes **Cooking time:** 6 minutes **Servings:** 4

Nutrition Facts:
- Calories: 120
- Fat (In grams): 3.7
- Fiber (In grams): 3.3
- Carbs (In grams): 7.5
- Protein (In grams): 2.4

Ingredients:
- 1 pound fresh green beans, trimmed
- 1 small yellow onion, chopped
- 6 ounces bacon, chopped
- 1 garlic clove, minced
- 8 ounces mushrooms, sliced
- Salt and black pepper to the taste
- A splash of balsamic vinegar

Instructions:
1. Put the beans in your instant pot, add water to cover them, cover the pot and cook at High for 3 minutes.
2. Release the pressure naturally, drain beans and leave them aside for now.
3. Set your instant pot on Sauté mode, add bacon and brown it for 1 or 2 minutes stirring often.
4. Add garlic and onion, stir and cook 2 more minutes.
5. Add mushrooms, stir and cook until they are soft.
6. Add drained beans, salt, pepper and a splash of vinegar, stir, take off heat, divide among plates and serve.

Bon Appétit!

---

73. AMAZING FRENCH FRIES

Perp time: 10 minutes   **Cooking time:** 10 minutes   **Servings:** 4

Nutrition Facts:
- Calories: 300
- Fat (In grams): 10
- Fiber (In grams): 3.7
- Carbs (In grams): 41
- Protein (In grams): 3.4

Ingredients:
- 8 medium potatoes, peeled, cut into medium matchsticks and pat dried
- One-cup water
- Salt to the taste
- 1/4 teaspoon baking soda
- Oil for frying

Instructions:
1. Put the water in your instant pot, add salt and the baking soda and stir.
2. Put potatoes in the steamer basket and introduce it in the pot.
3. Cover and cook at High for 3 minutes.
4. Release the pressure naturally, take fries out of the pot and put them in a bowl.
5. Heat up a pan with enough oil over medium high heat, add fries, spread them and cook until they become golden.
6. Transfer fries to paper towels to drain excess grease and then put them in a bowl.
7. Add salt, toss to coat and serve.

Bon Appétit!

---

74. YUMMY CAULIFLOWER MASH SIDE DISH

Perp time: 10 minutes   **Cooking time:** 6 minutes   **Servings:** 4

Nutrition Facts:
- Calories: 70
- Fat (In grams): 5
- Fiber (In grams): 2
- Carbs (In grams): 5
- Protein (In grams): 2

Ingredients:
- 1 cauliflower, florets separated
- Salt and black pepper to the taste
- 1 ½ cups water
- Half-teaspoon turmeric
- One-tablespoon butter
- 3 chives, finely chopped

Instructions:
1. Put the water in your instant pot, place cauliflower in the steamer basket, cover the pot and cook at High for 6 minutes.
2. Release the pressure naturally for 2 minutes and then release the rest quick.
3. Transfer cauliflower to a bowl and mash it with a potato masher.
4. Add salt, pepper, butter and turmeric, stir, transfer to a blender and pulse well.
5. Serve with chives sprinkled on top.

Bon Appétit!

---

75. APPLE AND BUTTERNUT MASH

Perp time: 10 minutes **Cooking time:** 15 minutes **Servings:** 4

Nutrition Facts:
- Calories: 140
- Fat (In grams): 2.3
- Fiber (In grams): 6.5
- Carbs (In grams): 24
- Protein (In grams): 2.5

Ingredients:
- One-cup water
- 1 butternut squash, peeled and cut into medium chunks
- 2 apples, sliced
- 2 tablespoons brown butter
- 1 yellow onion, thinly sliced
- Half-teaspoon apple pie spice
- Salt to the taste

Instructions:
1. Put squash, onion and apple pieces in the steamer basket of your instant pot, put the water in the pot, cover and cook at High for 8 minutes.
2. Release the pressure quickly and transfer squash, onion and apple pieces to a bowl.
3. Mash using a potato masher, add salt, apple pie spice and brown butter, stir well and serve warm.

Bon Appétit!

---

76. DELICIOUS BRUSSELS SPROUTS SIDE DISH

Perp time: 10 minutes **Cooking time:** 4 minutes **Servings:** 8

Nutrition Facts:
- Calories: 65
- Fat (In grams): 2
- Fiber (In grams): 3
- Carbs (In grams): 12
- Protein (In grams): 3

Ingredients:
- 2 pounds Brussels sprouts
- Salt and black pepper to the taste
- 1/4 cup orange juice
- One-teaspoon orange zest, grated

- One-tablespoon buttery spread
- 2 tablespoons maple syrup

Instructions:
1. In your instant pot, mix Brussels sprouts with orange juice, orange zest, buttery spread, maple syrup, salt and pepper to the taste, stir, cover and cook at High for 4 minutes.
2. Release the pressure naturally, transfer sprouts mix to plates and serve them.

Bon Appétit!

77. Simple Sweet Carrot Puree Side Dish

Perp time: 5 minutes **Cooking time:** 5 minutes **Servings:** 4

Nutrition Facts:
- Calories: 50
- Fat (In grams): 1
- Fiber (In grams): 3
- Carbs (In grams): 11
- Protein (In grams): 1

Ingredients:
- 1 ½ pounds carrots, peeled and chopped
- One-tablespoon soft butter
- Salt to the taste
- One-cup water
- One-tablespoon honey
- One-teaspoon brown Sugar

Instructions:
1. Put carrots in your instant pot, add the water, cover and cook at High for 4 minutes.
2. Release the pressure naturally, drain carrots and place them in a bowl.
3. Mash them using a hand blender, add butter salt and honey.
4. Blend again well, add Sugaron top and serve right away.

Bon Appétit!

78. Parmesan Asparagus And Garlic

Perp time: 5 minutes **Cooking time:** 8 minutes **Servings:** 4

Nutrition Facts:
- Calories: 70
- Fat (In grams): 5.2
- Fiber (In grams): 1.8
- Carbs (In grams): 3.8
- Protein (In grams): 4

Ingredients:
- 3 garlic cloves, minced
- 1 bunch asparagus, trimmed
- One-cup water
- 3 tablespoons butter
- 3 tablespoons parmesan cheese, grated

Instructions:
1. Put the water in your instant pot.
2. Place asparagus on a tin foil, add garlic and butter and curve the edges of the foil.
3. Place this in your pot, cover it and cook at High for 8 minutes.
4. Release the pressure quickly, arrange asparagus on plates, sprinkle parmesan and serve.

79. TASTY GLAZED CARROTS

Perp time: 10 minutes **Cooking time;** 6 minutes **Servings:** 4

Nutrition Facts:
- Calories: 200
- Fat (In grams): 11
- Fiber (In grams): 4
- Carbs (In grams): 12
- Protein (In grams): 1.4

Ingredients:
- Half-cup water
- 1-pound baby carrots
- Half-cup honey
- One-teaspoon thyme, dried
- One-teaspoon dill, dried
- Salt to the taste
- 2 tablespoons butter

Instructions:
1. Put the water in your instant pot, place carrots in the steamer basket, cover and cook at High for 3 minutes.
2. Release the pressure, drain carrots and put them in a bowl.
3. Set your instant pot on Sauté mode, add butter and melt it.
4. Add dill, thyme, honey and salt and stir well.
5. Add carrots, toss to coat, cook for 1 minute, transfer them to plates and serve hot as a side dish.

Bon Appétit!

80. POACHED FENNEL SIDE DISH

Perp time: 5 minutes **Cooking time:** 6 minutes **Servings:** 3

Nutrition Facts:
- Calories: 140
- Fat (In grams): 5
- Fiber (In grams): 4.7
- Carbs (In grams): 12
- Protein (In grams): 4.4

Ingredients:
- 2 big fennel bulbs, sliced
- 2 tablespoons butter
- One-tablespoon white flour
- 2 cups milk
- A pinch of nutmeg, ground
- Salt to the taste

Instructions:
1. Set your instant pot on Sauté mode, add butter and melt it.
2. Add fennel slices, stir and cook until they brown a bit.
3. Add flour, salt, pepper, nutmeg and milk, stir, cover and cook on Low for 6 minutes.
4. Release pressure quick, transfer fennel to plates and serve.

Bon Appétit!

81. Amazing "Drunken" Peas Side Dish

Perp time: 10 minutes   **Cooking time:** 7 minutes   **Servings:** 4

Nutrition Facts:
- Calories: 134
- Fat (In grams): 2
- Fiber (In grams): 2.5
- Carbs (In grams): 10
- Protein (In grams): 4.3

Ingredients:
- 4 ounces smoked pancetta, chopped
- 1 pound fresh peas
- 1 green onion, sliced
- One-tablespoon mint, chopped
- 1/4 cup beer
- One-tablespoon butter
- Salt and black pepper to the taste
- 2 cups water

Instructions:
1. Put the water in your instant pot, place the steamer basket inside as well and leave aside.
2. In a heat proof pan, mix pancetta with half of the onion and spread on the bottom.
3. Heat this up on the stove over medium high heat for 3 minutes, add beer, peas, and salt, stir and take off heat.
4. Cover this pan with some tin foil, place in the steamer basket, cover the pot and cook at High for 1 minute.
5. Release the pressure quickly, uncover the pan, add more salt, pepper, mint and butter, stir, divide among plates and serve with the rest of the onions sprinkled on top.

Bon Appétit!

82. Yummy Mashed Turnips

Perp time: 10 minutes   **Cooking time:** 5 minutes   **Servings:** 4

Nutrition Facts:
- Calories: 70
- Fat (In grams): 1
- Fiber (In grams): 4.6
- Carbs (In grams): 11.2
- Protein (In grams): 1.6

Ingredients:
- 4 turnips, peeled and chopped
- Salt and black pepper to the taste
- 1 yellow onion, chopped
- 1/4 cup sour cream
- Half-cup chicken stock

Instructions:
1. In your instant pot, mix turnips with stock and onion.
2. Stir, cover and cook at High for 5 minutes.
3. Release the pressure naturally, drain turnips and transfer them to a bowl.
4. Puree them using your mixer and add salt, pepper to the taste and sour cream.
5. Blend again and serve right away.

Bon Appétit!

83. Delicious Broccoli Side Dish

Perp time: 5 minutes   **Cooking time:** 15 minutes   **Servings:** 6

Nutrition Facts:
- Calories: 55
- Fat (In grams): 0.5
- Fiber (In grams): 5
- Carbs (In grams): 11
- Protein (In grams): 3.4

Ingredients:
- 31 oz broccoli, florets separated
- One-cup water
- 5 lemon slices
- Salt and black pepper to the taste

Instructions:
1. Pour the water in your instant pot
2. Season broccoli with salt and pepper to the taste and add it to the pot
3. Also, add lemon slices and stir gently.
4. Cover the pot and cook at High for 15 minutes.
5. Release the pressure and divide broccoli among plates.
6. Serve with a tasty meat-based the main course!

Bon Appétit!

84. Healthy Artichokes Side Dish

Perp time: 10 minutes   **Cooking time:** 25 minutes   **Servings:** 4

Nutrition Facts:
- Calories: 78
- Fat (In grams): 0.4
- Fiber (In grams): 3
- Carbs (In grams): 2
- Protein (In grams): 4

Ingredients:
- One-cup water
- 2 medium artichokes, trimmed
- 1 lemon wedges
- Salt to the taste

Instructions:
1. Rub artichokes with the lemon wedges, place them in the steamer basket of your instant pot, add the water in the pot, cover and cook at High for 20 minutes.
2. Release the pressure for 10 minutes, divide artichokes among plates add salt on top and serve them with a dipping sauce and with a steak on the side.

Bon Appétit!

85. Delicious Onions And Parsnips

Perp time: 10 minutes　　**Cooking time:** 30 minutes　　**Servings:** 4

Nutrition Facts:
- Calories: 130
- Fat (In grams): 2
- Fiber (In grams): 3
- Carbs (In grams): 6.7
- Protein (In grams): 10.1

Ingredients:
- 2 ½ pounds parsnips, chopped
- 4 tablespoons pastured lard
- Salt and black pepper to the taste
- 1 ½ cups beef stock
- 1 thyme spring
- 1 yellow onion, thinly sliced

Instructions:
1. Set your instant pot on Sauté mode, add 3 tablespoons lard and heat it up.
2. Add parsnips, stir and cook for 15 minutes.
3. Add stock and thyme, stir, cover and cook at High for 3 minutes.
4. Release the pressure, transfer the parsnips mix to your blender, add salt and pepper to the taste and pulse very well.
5. Set the pot on Sauté mode again, add the rest of the lard and heat it up.
6. Add onion, stir and cook for 10 minutes.
7. Transfer blended parsnips to plates, top with sautéed onions and serve.

Bon Appétit!

86. Awesome Eggplant Side Dish

Perp time: 10 minutes　　**Cooking time:** 13 minutes　　**Servings:** 4

Nutrition Facts:
- Calories: 130
- Fat (In grams): 5
- Fiber (In grams): 10
- Carbs (In grams): 12
- Protein (In grams): 15

Ingredients:
- 2 eggplants, cubed
- Salt and black pepper to the taste
- 2 tablespoons extra virgin olive oil
- 1 garlic clove, crushed
- A pinch of hot pepper flakes
- 1 bunch oregano, chopped
- Half-cup water
- 2 anchovies, chopped

Instructions:
1. Sprinkle eggplant pieces with salt, place them in a strainer, press them with a plate and then drain them.
2. Set your instant pot on Sauté mode, add the oil and the garlic and heat it up.
3. Add anchovies, oregano and pepper flakes, stir and cook for 5 minutes.
4. Discard the garlic, add eggplants, salt and pepper, toss to coat and cook for 5 minutes.
5. Add the water, stir, cover the pot and cook at High for 3 minutes.
6. Release the pressure quick, transfer eggplant mix to plates and serve.

Bon Appétit!

87. GARLIC AND BEET SIDE DISH

Perp time: 10 minutes **Cooking time:** 15 minutes **Servings:** 4

Nutrition Facts:
- Calories: 70
- Fat (In grams): 1
- Fiber (In grams): 3.8
- Carbs (In grams): 13
- Protein (In grams): 2.2

Ingredients:
- 3 beets, greens cut off and washed
- Water to cover
- One-tablespoon extra virgin olive oil
- Salt to the taste
- 2 garlic cloves, minced
- One-teaspoon lemon juice

Instructions:
1. Put beets in your instant pot, add water to cover, also add salt to the taste, cover the pot and cook at High for 15 minutes.
2. Release the pressure naturally for 10 minutes, strain beets, peel them and roughly chop.
3. Heat up a pan with the oil over medium high heat, add beets, stir and cook for 3 minutes.
4. Add garlic, lemon juice, and more salt, stir, take off heat and divide among plates.

Bon Appétit!

88. SIMPLE CITRUS AND CAULIFLOWER SIDE DISH

Perp time: 10 minutes **Cooking time:** 6 minutes **Servings:** 4

Nutrition Facts:
- Calories: 260
- Fat (In grams): 2.9
- Fiber (In grams): 6.5
- Carbs (In grams): 33
- Protein (In grams): 4.2

Ingredients:
- 1 cauliflower, florets separated
- 1 pound broccoli, florets separated
- 1 romanesco cauliflower, florets separated
- 2 oranges, peeled and sliced
- Zest from 1 orange
- One-cup water
- Juice from 1 orange
- A pinch of hot pepper flakes
- 4 anchovies
- One-tablespoon capers, chopped
- Salt and black pepper to the taste
- 4 tablespoons extra virgin olive oil

Instructions:
1. In a bowl, mix orange zest with orange juice, pepper flakes, anchovies, capers salt, pepper and olive oil, stir well and leave aside for now.
2. Place cauliflower and broccoli florets in the steamer basket of you instant pot, add One-cup water to the pot, cover and cook on Low for 6 minutes.
3. Release the pressure quickly, uncover the pot, transfer florets to a bowl and mix with orange slices.
4. Add the orange vinaigrette you've made earlier, toss to coat and divide among plates.
5. Serve with some chicken!

89. Special Fava Bean Sauté

Perp time: 10 minutes **Cooking time:** 7 minutes **Servings:** 4

Nutrition Facts:
- Calories: 140
- Fat (In grams): 3
- Fiber (In grams): 1
- Carbs (In grams): 23
- Protein (In grams): 13

Ingredients:
- 3 pounds fava beans, shelled
- One-teaspoon extra virgin olive oil
- Salt and black pepper to the taste
- 4 ounces bacon, chopped
- Half-cup white wine
- 3 parsley springs, chopped
- 3/4 cup water

Instructions:
1. Set your instant pot on Sauté mode, add the oil and heat up.
2. Add bacon, stir and cook until it browns.
3. Add wine, stir and cook for 2 minutes.
4. Add water and fava beans, stir, cover and cook at High for 7 minutes.
5. Release pressure quick, transfer beans to plates, add parsley, salt and pepper, stir and serve.

Bon Appétit!

90. Tomato And Calamari Side Dish

Perp time: 10 minutes **Cooking time:** 32 minutes **Servings:** 4

Nutrition Facts:
- Calories: 230
- Fat (In grams): 6.5
- Fiber (In grams): 1.2
- Carbs (In grams): 11
- Protein (In grams): 24

Ingredients:
- 1 ½ pounds calamari, washed, tentacles separated and cut into strips
- Salt and black pepper to the taste
- 14 ounces canned tomatoes, chopped
- 1 bunch parsley, chopped
- 1 garlic clove, crushed
- Half-cup white wine
- One-cup water
- 2 anchovies
- Juice of 1 lemon
- 2 tablespoons extra virgin olive oil
- A pinch of red pepper flakes

Instructions:
1. Set your instant pot on Sauté mode, add oil, pepper flakes, garlic and anchovies, stir and cook for 3 minutes.
2. Add calamari, stir and cook for 5 minutes.
3. Add wine, stir and cook 3 minutes.
4. Add tomatoes, One-cup water, half of the parsley, salt, and pepper.
5. Stir, cover the pot and cook at High for 20 minutes.
6. Release the pressure quick, add the rest of the parsley, the lemon juice, salt, and pepper, stir, divide among plates and serve with rice.

91. DELICIOUS VEGGIES SIDE DISH

Perp time: 10 minutes **Cooking time:** 6 minutes **Servings:** 4

Nutrition Facts:
- Calories: 146
- Fat (In grams): 2.2
- Fiber (In grams): 8.1
- Carbs (In grams): 28.1
- Protein (In grams): 4.5

Ingredients:
- 2 yellow bell peppers, thinly sliced
- 1 green bell pepper, thinly sliced
- 2 red bell peppers, thinly sliced
- 2 tomatoes, chopped
- 2 garlic cloves, minced
- 1 red onion, thinly sliced
- Salt and black pepper to the taste
- 1 bunch parsley, finely chopped
- A drizzle of extra virgin olive oil

Instructions:
1. Set your instant pot on Sauté mode, add a drizzle of oil and heat it up.
2. Add onions, stir and cook for 3 minutes.
3. Add red, yellow and green peppers, stir and cook for 5 minutes.
4. Add tomatoes, salt and pepper, stir, cover and cook at High for 6 minutes.
5. Release the pressure quickly, uncover the pot, transfer peppers and tomatoes to a bowl, add more salt and pepper if needed, chopped garlic, parsley and a drizzle of oil.
6. Toss to coat and serve as a side dish!

Bon Appétit!

92. SPECIAL BOK CHOY SIDE DISH

Perp time: 10 minutes **Cooking time:** 10 minutes **Servings:** 4

Nutrition Facts:
- Calories: 60
- Fat (In grams): 0.4
- Fiber (In grams): 1.3
- Carbs (In grams): 6.5
- Protein (In grams): 2.4

Ingredients:
- 5 bok choy bunches, end cut off
- 5 cups water
- 2 garlic cloves, minced
- One-teaspoon ginger, grated
- One-tablespoon coconut oil
- Salt to the taste

Instructions:
1. Put bok choy in your instant pot, add the water, cover the pot and cook at High for 7 minutes.
2. Release the pressure, drain bok choy, chop it and put them in a bowl.
3. Heat up a pan with the oil over medium heat, add bok choy, stir and cook for 3 minutes.
4. Add more salt to the taste, garlic and ginger, stir and cook for 2 more minutes.
5. Divide among plates and serve with your favorite meat.

Bon Appétit!

93. AMAZING GREEN BEAN SIDE DISH

Perp time: 10 minutes **Cooking time:** 5 minutes **Servings:** 4

Nutrition Facts:
- Calories: 55
- Fat (In grams): 3.2
- Fiber (In grams): 2.6
- Carbs (In grams): 1.6
- Protein (In grams): 1.6

Ingredients:
- 2 cups tomatoes, chopped
- One-tablespoon extra virgin olive oil
- 1 garlic clove crushed
- 1 pound green beans, trimmed
- One-teaspoon extra virgin olive oil
- Salt to the taste
- 1 basil spring

Instructions:
1. Set your instant pot on Sauté mode, add One-tablespoon oil and heat it up.
2. Add garlic, stir and cook for 1 minute.
3. Add tomatoes, stir and cook for 1minute.
4. Place green beans in the steamer basket and introduce it in the pot.
5. Add salt to the taste, cover the pot and cook at High for 5 minutes.
6. Release the pressure quick, transfer green beans from the basket into the pot and toss to coat.
7. Transfer to plates, sprinkle with basil and drizzle One-teaspoon oil over them.

Bon Appétit!

94. ISRAELI STYLE COUSCOUS SIDE DISH

Perp time: 10 minutes **Cooking time:** 5 minutes **Servings:** 10

Nutrition Facts:
- Calories: 190
- Fat (In grams): 1
- Fiber (In grams): 2
- Carbs (In grams): 34
- Protein (In grams): 6

Ingredients:
- 16 ounces harvest grains blend
- Salt and black pepper to the taste
- 2 ½-cups chicken stock
- 2 tablespoons butter
- Parsley leaves, chopped for serving

Instructions:
1. Set your instant pot on Sauté mode, add butter and melt it.
2. Add grains and stock and stir.
3. Cover the pot and cook at High for 5 minutes.
4. Release pressure quick, fluff couscous with a fork, season with salt and pepper to the taste, divide among plates, sprinkle parsley on top and serve.

POULTRY RECIPES

95. SPECIAL MOROCCAN CHICKEN

Perp time: 10 minutes   **Cooking time:** 25 minutes   **Servings:** 4

Nutrition Facts:
- Calories: 381
- Fat (In grams): 10.2
- Fiber (In grams): 7.8
- Carbs (In grams): 4
- Fiber (In grams): 32.2

Ingredients:
- 6 chicken thighs
- 2 tablespoons extra virgin olive oil
- 10 cardamom pods
- 2 bay leaves
- Half-teaspoon coriander
- One-teaspoon cloves
- Half-teaspoon cumin
- Half-teaspoon ginger
- Half-teaspoon turmeric
- Half-teaspoon cinnamon, ground
- One-teaspoon paprika
- 2 yellow onions, chopped
- 2 tablespoons tomato paste
- 5 garlic cloves, chopped
- 1/4 cup white wine
- One-cup green olives
- One-cup chicken stock
- 1/4 cup cranberries, dried
- Juice of 1 lemon
- Half-cup parsley, finely chopped

Instructions:
1. In a bowl, mix bay leaf with cardamom, cloves, coriander, ginger, cumin, cinnamon, turmeric and paprika and stir.
2. Set your instant pot on Sauté mode, add the oil and heat up.
3. Add chicken thighs, brown for a few minutes and transfer to a plate.
4. Add onion to the pot, stir and cook for 4 minutes.
5. Add garlic, stir and cook for 1 minute.
6. Add wine, tomato paste, spices from the bowl, stock and chicken.
7. Stir, cover and cook at High for 15 minutes.
8. Release the pressure quick, discard bay leaf, cardamom, and cloves, add olives, cranberries, lemon juice and parsley, stir, divide chicken mix among plates and serve.

Bon Appétit!

96. BBQ HONEY CHICKEN

Perp time: 10 minutes   **Cooking time:** 25 minutes   **Servings:** 4

Nutrition Facts:
- Calories: 147.5
- Fat (In grams): 2.2
- Fiber (In grams): 1
- Carbs (In grams): 8
- Protein (In grams): 21.8

Ingredients:
- 2 pounds chicken wings
- Salt and black pepper to the taste
- 3/4 cup honey Bbq sauce
- A pinch of cayenne pepper
- Half-cup apple juice
- One-teaspoon red pepper, crushed

- 2 teaspoons paprika
- Half-cup water
- Half-teaspoon basil, dried
- Half-cup brown Sugar

Instructions:
1. Put chicken wings in your instant pot.
2. Add BBQ sauce, apple juice, salt, pepper, red pepper, paprika, basil, Sugar, and water.
3. Stir, cover and cook at High for 10 minutes.
4. Release the pressure quickly, uncover the pot, transfer chicken to a baking sheet, add sauce all over, introduce in preheated broiler, broil for 7 minutes, flip chicken wings, broil for 7 more minutes, divide among plates and serve.

Bon Appétit!

97. POTATOES AND CHICKEN DISH

Perp time: 15 minutes **Cooking time:** 15 minutes **Servings:** 4

Nutrition Facts:
- Calories: 190
- Fat (In grams): 6
- Fiber (In grams): 3.3
- Carbs (In grams): 23
- Protein (In grams): 18

Ingredients:
- 2 tablespoons extra virgin olive oil
- 2 pounds chicken thighs, skinless and boneless
- 3/4 cup chicken stock
- 1/4 cup lemon juice
- 2 pounds red potatoes, peeled and cut into quarters
- 3 tablespoons Dijon mustard
- 2 tablespoons Italian seasoning
- Salt and black pepper to the taste

Instructions:
1. Set your instant pot on sauté mode, add the oil and heat it up.
2. Add chicken thighs, salt, and pepper, stir and brown for 2 minutes.
3. In a bowl, mix stock with mustard, Italian seasoning, and lemon juice and stir well.
4. Pour this over chicken, add potatoes, stir, cover the pot and cook at High for 15 minutes.
5. Release the pressure quickly, uncover the pot, stir chicken, divide among plates and serve.

Bon Appétit!

98. DELICIOUS TURKEY CHILI

Perp time: 10 minutes **Cooking time:** 10 minutes **Servings:** 4

Nutrition Facts:
- Calories: 224
- Fat (In grams): 7.7
- Fiber (In grams): 6.1
- Carbs (In grams): 18
- Protein (In grams): 19.7

Ingredients:
- 1 pound turkey meat, ground
- Salt and black pepper to the taste
- 5 ounces water
- 15 ounces chickpeas, already cooked
- 1 yellow onion, chopped
- 1 yellow bell pepper, chopped

- 3 garlic cloves, chopped
- 2 ½-tablespoons chili powder
- 1 ½ teaspoons cumin
- A pinch of cayenne pepper
- 12 ounces veggies stock

Instructions:
1. Put turkey meat in your instant pot.
2. Add water, stir, cover and cook at High for 5 minutes.
3. Release the pressure quickly, uncover the pot and add chickpeas, bell pepper, onion, garlic, chili powder, cumin, salt, pepper, cayenne and veggie stock.
4. Stir, cover the pot and cook at High for 5 minutes.
5. Release the pressure for 10 minutes, uncover the pot again, stir chili, divide it among plates and serve.

Bon Appétit!

99. Tasty Veggies And Duck

Perp time: 10 minutes **Cooking time:** 40 minutes **Servings:** 8

Nutrition Facts:
- Calories: 189
- Fat (In grams): 2
- Fiber (In grams): 1
- Carbs (In grams): 4
- Protein (In grams): 22

Ingredients:
- 1 duck, chopped into medium pieces
- 1 cucumber, chopped
- One-tablespoon wine
- 2 carrots, chopped
- 2 cups water
- Salt and black pepper to the taste
- 1 inch ginger pieces, chopped

Instructions:
1. Put duck pieces in your instant pot.
2. Add cucumber, carrots, wine, water, ginger, salt and pepper, stir, cover and cook on Poultry mode for 40 minutes.
3. Release the pressure, divide the mix among plates and serve.

Bon Appétit!

100. Yummy Chicken And Tomatillo Sauce

Perp time: 10 minutes **Cooking time:** 15 minutes **Servings:** 6

Nutrition Facts:
- Calories: 245
- Fat (In grams): 11.4
- Fiber (In grams): 1.3
- Carbs (In grams): 14.2
- Protein (In grams): 20

Ingredients:
- 1 pound chicken thighs, skinless and boneless
- 2 tablespoons extra virgin olive oil
- 1 yellow onion, thinly sliced
- 1 garlic clove, crushed
- 4 ounces canned green chilies, chopped

- 1 handful cilantro, finely chopped
- Salt and black pepper to the taste
- 15 ounces canned tomatillos, chopped
- 5 ounces canned garbanzo beans, drained
- 15 ounces rice, already cooked
- 5 ounces tomatoes, chopped
- 15 ounces cheddar cheese, grated
- 4 ounces black olives, pitted and chopped

Instructions:
1. Set your instant pot on Sauté mode, add oil and heat it up.
2. Add onions, stir and cook for 5 minutes.
3. Add garlic, stir and cook 15 more seconds.
4. Add chicken, chilies, salt, pepper, cilantro, and tomatillos, stir, cover the pot and cook on Poultry mode for 8 minutes.
5. Release the pressure quickly, uncover the pot, take the chicken out and shred it.
6. Return chicken to pot, add rice, beans, set the instant pot on Sauté mode again and cook for 1 minute.
7. Add cheese, tomatoes, and olives, stir, cook for 2 minutes more, divide among plates and serve.

Bon Appétit!

101. SIMPLE SALSA CHICKEN DISH

Perp time: 10 minutes **Cooking time:** 25 minutes **Servings:** 5

Nutrition Facts:
- Calories: 125
- Fat (In grams): 3
- Fiber (In grams): 1
- Carbs (In grams): 3
- Protein (In grams): 22

Ingredients:
- 1 pound chicken breast, skinless and boneless
- 3/4 teaspoon cumin
- Salt and black pepper to the taste
- A pinch of oregano
- One-cup chunky salsa

Instructions:
1. Season chicken with salt and pepper to the taste and add it to your instant pot.
2. Add oregano, cumin and the chunky salsa, stir, cover, set the pot on "poultry" mode and cook for 25 minutes.
3. Release the pressure quick, transfer chicken and salsa to a bowl, shred meat with a fork and serve with some tortillas on the side.

Bon Appétit!

102. MOUTHWATERING CHICKEN SANDWICHES

Perp time: 10 minutes   **Cooking time:** 15 minutes   **Servings:** 8

Nutrition Facts:
- Calories: 240
- Fat (In grams): 4.6
- Fiber (In grams): 4
- Carbs (In grams): 21
- Protein (In grams): 14

Ingredients:
- 6 chicken breasts, skinless and boneless
- 12 ounces canned orange juice
- 2 tablespoons lemon juice
- 15 ounces canned peaches and their juice
- One-teaspoon soy sauce
- 20 ounces canned pineapple and its juice, chopped
- One-tablespoon cornstarch
- 1/4 cup brown Sugar
- 8 hamburger buns
- 8 grilled pineapple slices, for serving

Instructions:
1. In a bowl, mix orange juice with soy sauce, lemon juice, canned pineapples pieces, peaches and Sugar and stir well.
2. Pour half of this mix in your instant pot, add chicken and pour the rest of the sauce over meat.
3. Cover the pot and cook at High for 12 minutes.
4. Release the pressure quick, take the chicken and put on a cutting board.
5. Shred meat and leave aside for now.
6. In a bowl, mix cornstarch with One-tablespoon cooking juice and stir well.
7. Transfer the sauce to a pot, add cornstarch mix and chicken, stir and cook for a few more minutes.
8. Divide this chicken mix on hamburger buns, top with grilled pineapple pieces and serve.

Bon Appétit!

103. DELIGHTFUL LEMONGRASS CHICKEN

Perp time: 10 minutes   **Cooking time:** 20 minutes   **Servings:** 5

Nutrition Facts:
- Calories: 400
- Fat (In grams): 18
- Fiber (In grams): 2
- Carbs (In grams): 6
- Protein (In grams): 20

Ingredients:
- 1 bunch lemongrass, rough bottom removed and trimmed
- 1 inch piece ginger root, chopped
- 4 garlic cloves, crushed
- 2 tablespoons fish sauce
- 3 tablespoons coconut aminos
- One-teaspoon Chinese five spice
- 10 chicken drumsticks
- One-cup coconut milk
- Salt and black pepper to the taste
- One-teaspoon ghee
- 1/4 cup cilantro, finely chopped
- 1 yellow onion, chopped
- One-tablespoon lime juice

Instructions:
1. In your food processor, mix lemongrass with ginger, garlic, aminos, fish sauce and five spice and pulse well.
2. Add coconut milk and pulse again.
3. Set your instant pot on Sauté mode, add ghee and melt it.
4. Add onion, stir and cook for 5 minutes.
5. Add chicken pieces, salt and pepper, stir and cook for 1 minute.
6. Add coconut milk and lemongrass mix, stir, cover, set "poultry" mode and cook for 15 minutes sat High.
7. Release the pressure quickly, uncover, add more salt and pepper and lime juice, stir, divide among plates and serve with cilantro sprinkled on top.

Bon Appétit!

104. THAI STYLE CHICKEN DISH

Perp time: 10 minutes **Cooking time:** 10 minutes **Servings:** 4

Nutrition Facts:
- Calories: 300
- Fat (In grams): 5
- Fiber (In grams): 4
- Carbs (In grams): 23
- Protein (In grams): 32

Ingredients:
- 2 pounds chicken thighs, boneless and skinless
- Half-cup fish sauce
- One-cup lime juice
- 2 tablespoons coconut nectar
- 1/4 cup extra virgin olive oil
- One-teaspoon ginger, grated
- 2 teaspoons cilantro, finely chopped
- One-teaspoon mint, chopped

Instructions:
1. Put chicken thighs in your instant pot.
2. In a bowl, mix lime juice with fish sauce, olive oil, coconut nectar, ginger, mint and cilantro and whisk well.
3. Pour this over chicken, cover the pot and cook at High for 10 minutes.
4. Release the pressure quick, divide Thai chicken among plates and serve.

Bon Appétit!

105. DELICIOUS CACCIATORE CHICKEN

Perp time: 10 minutes **Cooking time:** 15 minutes **Servings:** 4

Nutrition Facts:
- Calories: 210
- Fat (In grams): 2.9
- Fiber (In grams): 2.4
- Carbs (In grams): 9.5
- Protein (In grams): 25.9

Ingredients:
- One-cup chicken stock
- Salt to the taste

- 8 chicken drumsticks, bone-in
- 1 bay leaf
- One-teaspoon garlic powder
- 1 yellow onion, chopped
- 28 ounces canned tomatoes and juice, crushed
- One-teaspoon oregano, dried
- Half-cup black olives, pitted and sliced

Instructions:
1. Set your instant pot on Sauté mode, add stock, bay leaf and salt and stir.
2. Add chicken, garlic powder, onion, oregano, and tomatoes, stir, cover the pot and cook at High for 15 minutes.
3. Release the pressure naturally, uncover the pot, discard bay leaf, divide cacciatore chicken among plates, drizzle cooking liquid all over, sprinkle olives and serve.

Bon Appétit!

---

106. YUMMY TURKEY MEATBALLS

Perp time: 10 minutes   **Cooking time:** 40 minutes   **Servings:** 8

Nutrition Facts:
- Calories: 330
- Fat (In grams): 16
- Fiber (In grams): 3
- Carbs (In grams): 21
- Protein (In grams): 28

Ingredients:
- 1 pound turkey meat, ground
- 1 yellow onion, minced
- 1/4 cup parmesan cheese, grated
- Half-cup panko bread crumbs
- 4 garlic cloves, minced
- 1/4 cup parsley, chopped
- Salt and black pepper to the taste
- One-teaspoon oregano, dried
- 1 egg, whisked
- 1/4 cup milk
- 2 teaspoons soy sauce
- One-teaspoon fish sauce
- 12 cremini mushrooms, chopped
- 3 dried shiitake mushrooms, soaked in water, drained and chopped
- One-cup chicken stock
- 2 tablespoons extra virgin olive oil
- 2 tablespoons butter
- A splash of sherry wine
- 2 tablespoons cornstarch mixed with 2 tablespoons water

Instructions:
1. In a bowl, mix turkey meat with parmesan cheese, salt, pepper to the taste, yellow onion, garlic, bread crumbs, parsley, oregano, egg, milk, One-teaspoon soy sauce and One-teaspoon fish sauce, stir very well and shape 16 meatballs.
2. Heat up a pan with One-tablespoon oil over medium high heat, add meatballs, brown them for 1 minutes on each side and transfer them to a plate.
3. Pour chicken stock into the pan, stir and take off heat.
4. Set your instant pot on Sauté mode, add One-tablespoon oil and 2 tablespoons butter and heat them up.
5. Add cremini mushrooms, salt, and pepper, stir and cook for 10 minutes.
6. Add dried mushrooms, sherry wine and the rest of the soy sauce and stir well.

7. Add meatballs, cover the pot and cook at High for 6 minutes.
8. Release the pressure quickly, uncover the pot, add cornstarch mix, stir well, divide everything between plates and serve.

Bon Appétit!

---

107. SPECIAL FILIPINO CHICKEN

Perp time: 10 minutes   **Cooking time:** 15 minutes   **Servings:** 4

Nutrition Facts:
- Calories: 430
- Fat (In grams): 19.2
- Fiber (In grams): 1
- Carbs (In grams): 2.4
- Protein (In grams): 76

Ingredients:
- 5 pounds chicken thighs
- Salt and black pepper to the taste
- Half-cup white vinegar
- One-teaspoon black peppercorns
- 4 garlic cloves, minced
- 3 bay leaves
- Half-cup soy sauce

Instructions:
1. Set your instant pot on Poultry mode, add chicken, vinegar, soy sauce, salt, pepper, garlic, peppercorns and bay leaves, stir, cover and cook for 15 minutes.
2. Release the pressure for 10 minutes, uncover the pot, discard bay leaves, stir, divide chicken between plates and serve.

Bon Appétit!

---

108. MASHED POTATOES WITH TURKEY MIX

Perp time: 10 minutes   **Cooking time:** 50 minutes   **Servings:** 3

Nutrition Facts:
- Calories: 200
- Fat (In grams): 5
- Fiber (In grams): 4
- Carbs (In grams): 19
- Protein (In grams): 18

Ingredients:
- 2 turkey quarters
- 1 yellow onion, chopped
- 1 carrot, chopped
- 3 garlic cloves, minced
- 1 celery stalk, chopped
- One-cup chicken stock
- Salt and black pepper to the taste
- A splash of white wine
- 2 tablespoons extra virgin olive oil
- A pinch of rosemary, dried
- 2 bay leaves
- A pinch of sage, dried
- A pinch of thyme, dried
- 3 tablespoons cornstarch mixed with 2 tablespoons water
- 5 gold potatoes, cut into halves
- 2 tablespoons parmesan cheese, grated
- 2 tablespoons butter

Instructions:
1. Season turkey with salt and pepper.

2. Put One-tablespoon oil in your instant pot, set the pot on Sauté mode and heat it up.
3. Add turkey, brown pieces for 4 minutes, transfer them to a plate and leave aside for now.
4. Add Half-cup stock to the pot and stir well.
5. Add One-tablespoon oil and heat it up.
6. Add onion, stir and cook for 1 minute.
7. Add garlic, stir and cook for 20 seconds.
8. Add salt and pepper, carrot and celery, stir and cook for 7 minutes.
9. Add 2 bay leaves, thyme, sage, and rosemary, stir and cook everything 1 minute.
10. Add wine, turkey and the rest of the stock.
11. Put potatoes in the steamer basket and also introduce it in the pot, cover and cook for 20 minutes at High.
12. Release the pressure for 10 minutes, uncover the pot, transfer potatoes to a bowl and mash them.
13. Add salt, pepper, butter, parmesan and cream and stir well.
14. Divide turkey quarters to plates and set your instant pot on Sauté mode again.
15. Add cornstarch mix to pot, stir well and cook for 2-3 minutes.
16. Drizzle sauce over turkey, add mashed potatoes on the side and serve.

109. EASY CHICKEN SALAD

Perp time: 55 minutes   **Cooking time:** 10 minutes   **Servings:** 2

Nutrition Facts:
- Calories: 140
- Fat (In grams): 2.5
- Fiber (In grams): 4
- Carbs (In grams): 11
- Protein (In grams): 19

Ingredients:
- 1 chicken breast, skinless and boneless
- 3 cups water
- Salt and black pepper to the taste
- One-tablespoon mustard
- 3 garlic cloves, minced
- One-tablespoon balsamic vinegar
- One-tablespoon honey
- 3 tablespoons extra virgin olive oil
- Mixed salad greens
- A handful cherry tomatoes, cut into halves

Instructions:
1. In a bowl, mix 2 cups water with salt to the taste.
2. Add chicken to this mix, stir and keep in the fridge for 45 minutes.
3. Add One-cup water to your instant pot, place chicken breast in the steamer basket of the pot, cover and cook at High for 5 minutes.
4. Release the pressure naturally, leave chicken breast on a plate for 8 minutes and cut into thin strips.
5. In a bowl, mix garlic with salt and pepper to the taste, mustard, honey, vinegar and olive oil and whisk very well.
6. In a salad bowl, mix chicken strips with salad greens and tomatoes.
7. Drizzle the vinaigrette on top and serve.

110. TASTY CRISPY CHICKEN

Perp time: 10 minutes **Cooking time:** 40 minutes **Servings:** 4

Nutrition Facts:
- Calories: 360
- Fat (In grams): 7
- Fiber (In grams): 4
- Carbs (In grams): 18
- Protein (In grams): 15

Ingredients:
- 4 garlic cloves, chopped
- 6 chicken thighs
- 1 yellow onion, thinly sliced
- A pinch of rosemary, dried
- One-cup cold water
- One-tablespoon soy sauce
- Salt and black pepper to the taste
- 2 tablespoons cornstarch mixed with 2 ½-tablespoons water
- 1 ½ cups panko breadcrumbs
- 2 tablespoons extra virgin olive oil
- 2 tablespoons butter
- One-cup white flour
- 2 eggs, whisked

Instructions:
1. In your instant pot, mix garlic with onion, rosemary and One-cup water.
2. Place chicken things in the steamer basket and introduce in the pot.
3. Cover and cook at High for 9 minutes.
4. Release the pressure naturally for 10 minutes and uncover the pot.
5. Heat up a pan with the butter and oil over medium high heat.
6. Add 1 ½ cups breadcrumbs, stir, toast them and take them off heat.
7. Remove chicken thighs from the pot; pat dry them, season with salt and pepper to the taste, coat them with the flour, dip them in whisked egg and then coat them in toasted breadcrumbs.
8. Place chicken thighs on a lined baking sheet, introduce in the oven at 300 degrees F and bake for 10 minutes.
9. Meanwhile, set your instant pot on Sauté mode and heat up the cooking liquid.
10. Add One-tablespoon soy sauce, salt, pepper and cornstarch, stir and transfer to a bowl.
11. Take chicken thighs out of the oven, divide them between plates and serve with the sauce from the pot on the side.

Bon Appétit!

111. YUMMY BRAISED QUAIL

Perp time: 10 minutes **Cooking time:** 15 minutes **Servings:** 2

Nutrition Facts:
- Calories: 300
- Fat (In grams): 17
- Fiber (In grams): 0.2
- Carbs (In grams): 0.2
- Protein (In grams): 40

Ingredients:
- 2 quails, cleaned and emptied
- 3.5 ounces smoked pancetta, chopped
- Half-cup champagne
- 2 scallions, chopped
- ½ bunch thyme, chopped
- ½ bunch thyme

- 1 bay leaf
- Salt and black pepper to the taste
- ½ bunch rosemary, chopped
- ½ bunch rosemary
- ½ fennel bulb, cut into matchsticks
- 4 carrots, cut into thin matchsticks
- A handful arugula
- Lemon juice of 1 lemon
- A drizzle of olive oil

Instructions:
1. Put fennel and carrot in the steamer basket of your instant pot, add 2 cups water to the pot, cover, cook at High for 1 minute, release the pressure, rinse veggies with cold water, transfer them to a bowl and also keep the cooking liquid in a separate bowl.
2. Set your instant pot on Sauté mode, add shallots, pancetta, chopped rosemary, chopped thyme and bay leaf, salt and pepper, stir and cook for 4 minutes.
3. Stuff quail with whole rosemary and thyme and add to pot.
4. Brown on all sides, add champagne, stir and cook for 2 minutes.
5. Add cooking liquid from veggies, stir, cover and cook at High for 9 minutes.
6. Release the pressure, take quail out of the pot and leave aside.
7. Strain liquid from the pot into a pan, heat up over medium heat and simmer until it reduces to half.
8. Arrange arugula on a platter, add steamed fennel and carrots, a drizzle of oil, lemon juice and top with quail.
9. Drizzle the sauce from the pan all over and serve.

112. BRAISED POTATOES AND DUCK

Perp time: 10 minutes **Cooking time:** 20 minutes **Servings:** 4

Nutrition Facts:
- Calories: 238
- Fat (In grams): 18
- Fiber (In grams): 0
- Carbs (In grams): 1
- Protein (In grams): 19

Ingredients:
- 1 duck, cut into small chunks
- Black pepper to the taste
- 1 potato, cut into cubes
- 1 inch ginger root, sliced
- 4 garlic cloves, minced
- 4 tablespoons Sugar
- 4 tablespoons soy sauce
- 2 green onions, roughly chopped
- 4 tablespoons sherry wine
- A pinch of salt
- 1/4 cup water

Instructions:
1. Set your instant pot on Sauté mode, add duck pieces, stir and brown them for a few minutes.
2. Add garlic, ginger, green onions, soy sauce, Sugar, wine, a pinch of salt, black pepper and water, stir, cover, set the pot to Poultry mode and cook for 18 minutes.
3. Release the pressure quickly, uncover the pot, add potatoes, stir, cover and cook at High for 5 minutes.
4. Release the pressure quick, divide braised duck among plates and serve.

113. SIMPLE CHICKEN DISH

Perp time: 10 minutes **Cooking time:** 35 minutes **Servings:** 8

Nutrition Facts:
- Calories: 260
- Fat (In grams): 3.1
- Fiber (In grams): 1
- Carbs (In grams): 4
- Protein (In grams): 26.7

Ingredients:
- 1 whole chicken
- One-tablespoon extra virgin olive oil
- 1 ½tablespoons lemon zest
- One-cup chicken stock
- One-tablespoon thyme leaves
- Half-teaspoon cinnamon powder
- Salt and black pepper to the taste
- One-tablespoon cumin powder
- 2 teaspoons garlic powder
- One-tablespoon coriander powder

Instructions:
1. In a bowl, mix cinnamon with cumin, garlic, coriander, salt, pepper and lemon zest and stir well.
2. Rub chicken with half of the oil, then rub it inside and out with spices mix.
3. Set your instant pot on Sauté mode, add the rest of the oil and heat it up.
4. Add chicken and brown it on all sides for 5 minutes.
5. Add stock and thyme, stir, cover and cook at High for 25 minutes.
6. Release the pressure naturally and transfer chicken to a platter.
7. Add cooking liquid over it and serve.

Bon Appétit!

114. DELICIOUS RICE AND CHICKEN

Perp time: 15 minutes **Cooking time:** 35 minutes **Servings:** 2

Nutrition Facts:
- Calories: 200
- Fat (In grams): 9
- Fiber (In grams): 1
- Carbs (In grams): 22
- Protein (In grams): 26

Ingredients:
- 3 chicken quarters cut into small pieces
- 2 carrots, cut into chunks
- 2 potatoes, cut into quarters
- 1 shallot, sliced
- 1 yellow onion, sliced
- 3 garlic cloves, minced
- Salt and black pepper to the taste
- 1 green bell pepper, chopped
- 7 ounces coconut milk
- 2 bay leaves
- One-tablespoon soy sauce
- One-tablespoon peanut oil
- 1 ½teaspoon turmeric powder
- One-teaspoon cumin, ground
- 1 ½tablespoons cornstarch mixed with 2 tablespoons water

For the marinade:
- One-tablespoon soy sauce
- Half-teaspoon Sugar

- One-tablespoon white wine
- A pinch of white pepper
- 1 ½ cups water
- 1 ½ cups rice

Instructions:
1. In a bowl, mix chicken with Sugar, white pepper, One-tablespoon soy sauce and One-tablespoon white wine, stir and keep in the fridge for 20 minutes.
2. Set your instant pot on Sauté mode, add peanut oil and heat it up.
3. Add onion and shallot, stir and cook for 3 minutes.
4. Add garlic, salt, and pepper, stir and cook for 2 minutes more.
5. Add chicken, stir and brown for 2 minutes.
6. Add turmeric and cumin, stir and cook for 1 minute.
7. Add bay leaves, carrots, potatoes, bell pepper, coconut milk and One-tablespoon soy sauce.
8. Stir everything, place steamer basket in the pot, place the rice in a bowl and the basket,
9. Add 1 ½ cups water in the bowl, cover the pot and cook at High for 4 minutes.
10. Release the pressure naturally, take the rice out of the pot and divide among plates, add cornstarch to pot and stir.
11. Add chicken next to rice and serve.

Bon Appétit!

---

115. Tasty Chicken Romano

Perp time: 10 minutes **Cooking time:** 15 minutes **Servings:** 4

Nutrition Facts:
- Calories: 450
- Fat (In grams): 11
- Fiber (In grams): 1
- Carbs (In grams): 24.2
- Protein (In grams): 61.2

Ingredients:
- 6 chicken things, boneless and skinless and cut into medium chunks
- Salt and black pepper to the taste
- Half-cup white flour
- 2 tablespoons vegetable oil
- 10 ounces tomato sauce
- One-teaspoon white wine vinegar
- 4 ounces mushrooms, sliced
- One-tablespoon Sugar
- One-tablespoon oregano, dried
- One-teaspoon garlic, minced
- One-teaspoon basil, dried
- One-teaspoon chicken bouillon granules
- 1 yellow onion, chopped
- One-cup Romano cheese, grated

Instructions:
1. Set your instant pot on Sauté mode, add oil and heat it up.
2. Add chicken pieces, stir and brown them for 2 minutes.
3. Add onion and garlic, stir and cook for 3 minutes more.
4. Add salt, pepper, flour and stir very well.
5. Add tomato sauce, vinegar, mushrooms, Sugar, oregano, basil and bouillon granules, stir cover and cook at High for 10 minutes.

6. Release the pressure for 10 minutes, uncover the pot, add cheese, stir, divide among plates and serve.

Bon Appétit!

---

116. Mouthwatering Duck Chili

Perp time: 10 minutes **Cooking time:** 1 hour **Servings:** 4

Nutrition Facts:
- Calories: 270
- Fat (In grams): 13
- Fiber (In grams): 26
- Carbs (In grams): 15
- Protein (In grams): 25

Ingredients:
- 1 pound northern beans, soaked and rinsed
- 1 yellow onion, cut into half
- 1 garlic heat, top trimmed off

For the duck:
- 1 pound duck, ground
- One-tablespoon vegetable oil
- 1 yellow onion, minced
- 2 carrots, chopped
- Salt and black pepper to the taste
- Salt to the taste
- 2 cloves
- 1 bay leaf
- 6 cups water
- 4 ounces canned green chilies and their juice
- One-teaspoon brown Sugar
- 15 ounces canned tomatoes and their juices, chopped
- A handful cilantro, chopped

Instructions:
1. Put the beans in your instant pot.
2. Add whole onion, garlic head, cloves, bay leaf, the water and salt to the taste, stir, cover and cook at High for 25 minutes.
3. Release the pressure, uncover the pot, discard solids and transfer beans to a bowl.
4. Heat up a pan with the oil over medium high heat, add carrots and chopped onion, season with salt and pepper to the taste, stir and cook for 5 minuets.
5. Add duck, stir and cook for 5 minutes.
6. Add chilies and tomatoes, bring to a simmer and take off heat.
7. Pour this into your instant pot, cover and cook at High for 5 minutes.
8. Release pressure naturally for 15 minutes, uncover the pot, add more salt and pepper, beans and brown Sugar, stir and divide among plates.
9. Serve with cilantro on top.

Bon Appétit!

117. CHICKEN AND COCA-COLA

Perp time: 10 minutes **Cooking time:** 10 minutes **Servings:** 4

Nutrition Facts:
- Calories: 410
- Fat (In grams): 23
- Fiber (In grams): 1
- Carbs (In grams): 24
- Sugar (In grams): 21
- Protein (In grams): 27

Ingredients:
- 1 yellow onion, minced
- 4 chicken drumsticks
- One-tablespoon balsamic vinegar
- 1 chili pepper, chopped
- 15 ounces coca cola
- Salt and black pepper to the taste
- 2 tablespoons extra virgin olive oil

Instructions:
1. Set your instant pot on Sauté mode, add the oil and heat it up.
2. Add chicken pieces, stir and brown them on all sides and then transfer them to a plate.
3. Add vinegar, coca cola and chili to the pot, stir and simmer for 2 minutes.
4. Return chicken, add salt and pepper to the taste, stir, cover and cook at High for 10 minutes.
5. Release the pressure quickly, uncover the pot, divide chicken among plates and serve.

Bon Appétit!

118. TASTY TURKEY WINGS

Perp time: 10 minutes **Cooking time:** 20 minutes **Servings:** 4

Nutrition Facts:
- Calories: 320
- Fat (In grams): 15.3
- Fiber (In grams): 2.1
- Carbs (In grams): 16.4
- Protein (In grams): 29

Ingredients:
- 4 turkey wings
- 2 tablespoons butter
- 2 tablespoons vegetable oil
- 1 ½ cups cranberries
- Salt and black pepper to the taste
- 1 yellow onions, sliced
- One-cup walnuts
- One-cup orange juice
- 1 bunch thyme, roughly chopped

Instructions:
1. Set your instant pot on Sauté mode, add butter and oil and heat up.
2. Add turkey wings, salt and pepper and brown them on all sides.
3. Take wings out of the pot, add onion, walnuts, cranberries and thyme, stir and cook for 2 minutes.
4. Add orange juice and return turkey wings to pot, stir, cover and cook at High for 20 minutes.
5. Release the pressure naturally, uncover the pot and divide turkey wings among plates.
6. Transfer cranberry mix to a pan, heat up over medium heat and simmer for 5 minutes.
7. Drizzle sauce over turkey wings and serve.

Bon Appétit!

119. MOUTHWATERING CHICKEN CURRY

Perp time: 10 minutes **Cooking time:** 20 minutes **Servings:** 4

Nutrition Facts:

- Calories: 120
- Fat (In grams): 8.6
- Fiber (In grams): 1.2
- Carbs (In grams): 6.11
- Protein (In grams): 14.8

Ingredients:

- 15 ounces chicken breast, chopped
- One-tablespoon extra virgin olive oil
- 1 yellow onion, thinly sliced
- 6 potatoes, cut into halves
- 5 ounces canned coconut cream
- 1 bag chicken curry base
- ½ bunch coriander, chopped

Instructions:

1. Set your instant pot on Sauté mode, add the oil and heat it up.
2. Add chicken, stir and brown for 2 minutes.
3. Add onion, stir and cook for 1 minute.
4. In a bowl, mix curry base with coconut cream and stir.
5. Pour this over chicken, also add potatoes, stir, cover and cook at High for 15 minutes.
6. Release pressure fast, uncover the pot, divide curry among plates and serve with chopped coriander on top.

Bon Appétit!

120. SPECIAL COQ AU VIN

Perp time: 10 minutes **Cooking time:** 50 minutes **Servings:** 4

Nutrition Facts:

- Calories: 281
- Fat (In grams): 12.4
- Fiber (In grams): 2.2
- Carbs (In grams): 15
- Protein (In grams): 23

Ingredients:

- 2 pounds chicken pieces
- 4 ounces bacon, chopped
- 1/4 cup peanut oil
- 2 brown onions, sliced
- 2 garlic cloves, crushed
- 14 ounces red wine
- 1 bay leaf
- 2 tablespoons flour
- 7 ounces white mushrooms, sliced
- One-cup parsley, finely chopped
- Salt and black pepper to the taste
- 12 small potatoes, cut into halves
- 2 tablespoons cognac

Instructions:

1. Set your instant pot on Sauté mode, add the oil and heat it up.
2. Add chicken pieces, brown them on all sides and transfer them to a bowl.
3. Add bacon and onions to the pot, stir and cook for 5 minutes.
4. Add garlic, stir and cook for 1 minute
5. Return chicken to pot, add flour and cognac, stir and cook for 1 minute.

6. Add salt, pepper, bay leaf and red wine, stir, bring to a boil, cover pot and cook at High for 30 minutes.
7. Release the pressure quick, add mushrooms to the pot, add potatoes in the steamer basket, cover the pot again and cook everything for 15 minutes.
8. Release the pressure again, take potatoes and divide them among plates.
9. Add chicken on top, sprinkle parsley and serve.

Bon Appétit!

121. ITALIAN STYLE CHICKEN

Perp time: 10 minutes **Cooking time:** 20 minutes **Servings:** 6

Nutrition Facts:
- Calories: 340
- Fat (In grams): 15
- Fiber (In grams): 3.5
- Carbs (In grams): 10.1
- Protein (In grams): 34

Ingredients:
- One-tablespoon extra virgin olive oil
- 2 pounds chicken breasts, skinless and boneless
- Salt and black pepper to the taste
- 3/4 cup yellow onion, diced
- Half-cup green bell pepper, chopped
- Half-cup red bell pepper, chopped
- 3/4 cup marinara sauce
- 2 tablespoons pesto
- 3/4 cup mushrooms, sliced
- Cheddar cheese, shredded for serving

Instructions:
1. Set your instant pot on Sauté mode, add the oil and heat it up.
2. Add onion, red and green bell pepper, salt and pepper to the taste, stir and cook for 4 minutes.
3. Add pesto, marinara sauce and chicken, stir, cover and cook at High for 12 minutes.
4. Release the pressure, uncover the pot, remove chicken, place on a cutting board and shred,
5. Discard 2/3 cup cooking liquid, add mushrooms to the pot, set it on Sauté mode again and cook them for 3 minutes.
6. Return chicken, stir, divide among plates and serve with shredded cheese on top.

Bon Appétit!

122. CHEERING CHICKEN GUMBO

Perp time: 10 minutes **Cooking time:** 45 minutes **Servings:** 4

Nutrition Facts:
- Calories: 208
- Fat (In grams): 15
- Fiber (In grams): 1
- Carbs (In grams): 8
- Protein (In grams): 10

Ingredients:
- 1 pound smoky sausage, sliced
- One-tablespoon vegetable oil
- 1 pound chicken thighs, cut into halves
- Salt and black pepper to the taste

For the roux:

- Half-cup flour
- 1/4 cup vegetable oil
- One-teaspoon Cajun spice

Aromatics:
- 1 bell pepper, chopped
- 1 yellow onion, chopped
- 1 celery stalk, chopped
- Salt to the taste
- 4 garlic cloves, minced
- 2 quarts chicken stock
- 15 ounces canned tomatoes, chopped
- ½ pound okra
- A dash of Tabasco sauce

For serving:
- White rice, already cooked
- Half-cup parsley, chopped

Instructions:
1. Set your instant pot on Sauté mode, add One-tablespoon oil and heat it up.
2. Add sausage, stir, brown for 4 minutes and transfer to a plate.
3. Add chicken pieces, stir, brown for 6 minutes and transfer next to the sausage.
4. Add 1/4 cup vegetable oil to your pot and heat it up.
5. Add Cajun spice, stir and cook for 5 minutes.
6. Add bell pepper, onion, garlic, celery, salt and pepper, stir and cook for 5 minutes more.
7. Return chicken and sausage to the pot and stir.
8. Add stock, tomatoes and stir everything.
9. Cover the pot and cook at High for 10 minutes.
10. Release the pressure naturally for 15 minutes, uncover the pot, add okra, set the pot to Simmer mode and cook for 10 minutes.
11. Add more salt and pepper and the Tabasco sauce, stir and divide gumbo among plates.
12. Serve with rice on the side and with parsley sprinkled on top.

Bon Appétit!

123. TASTY CREAMY CHICKEN

Perp time: 10 minutes **Cooking time:** 20 minutes **Servings:** 6

Nutrition Facts:
- Calories: 300
- Fat (In grams): 7
- Fiber (In grams): 3
- Carbs (In grams): 23
- Protein (In grams): 22

Ingredients:
- 2 slices bacon, chopped
- One-cup chicken stock
- 4 ounces cream cheese
- 1 ounce ranch seasoning
- 2 pounds chicken breasts, skinless and boneless
- Green onions, chopped for serving

Instructions:

1. Set your instant pot on Sauté mode, add bacon and cook for 4 minutes.
2. Add chicken, stock and seasoning, stir, cover and cook at High for 12 minutes.
3. Release the pressure, uncover the pot, transfer chicken to a cutting board and shred it.
4. Remove 2/3 cup liquid from the pot, add cream cheese, set the pot to Sauté mode again and cook for 3 minutes.
5. Return chicken to pot, stir, add green onions, divide among plates and serve.

Bon Appétit!

124. Yummy Buffalo Chicken

Perp time: 10 minutes   **Cooking time:** 15 minutes   **Servings:** 6

Nutrition Facts:
- Calories: 190
- Fat (In grams): 9
- Fiber (In grams): 1
- Carbs (In grams): 20
- Protein (In grams): 14

Ingredients:
- 2 pounds chicken breasts, skinless, boneless and cut into thin strips
- Half-cup celery, chopped
- 1 small yellow onion, chopped
- Half-cup buffalo sauce
- Half-cup chicken stock
- 1/4 cup bleu cheese, crumbled

Instructions:
1. In your instant pot, mix onion with celery, buffalo sauce, stock and chicken, stir, cover and cook at High for 12 minutes.
2. Release the pressure, uncover the pot, discard 2/3 cup of cooking liquid, add crumbled cheese, stir very well, divide among plates and serve.

Bon Appétit!

125. Delight Chicken

Perp time: 10 minutes   **Cooking time:** 37 minutes   **Servings:** 4

Nutrition Facts:
- Calories: 237
- Fat (In grams): 12
- Fiber (In grams): 0
- Carbs (In grams): 1
- Protein (In grams): 30

Ingredients:
- 6 chicken thighs
- One-teaspoon vegetable oil
- Salt and black pepper to the taste
- 1 yellow onion, chopped
- 1 celery stalk, chopped
- 1/4 pound baby carrots, cut into halves
- Half-teaspoon thyme, dried
- 2 tablespoons tomato paste
- Half-cup white wine
- 15 ounces canned tomatoes, chopped
- 2 cups chicken stock
- 1 ½ pounds potatoes, chopped

Instructions:
1. Set your instant pot on Sauté mode, add oil and heat it up.

2. Add chicken pieces, salt and pepper to the taste and brown them for 4 minutes on each side.
3. Take chicken out of the pot and leave on a plate for now.
4. Add onion, carrots, celery, thyme and tomato paste to the pot, stir and cook for 5 minutes.
5. Add white wine and salt, stir and cook for 3 minutes.
6. Add chicken stock, chicken pieces and chopped tomatoes and stir.
7. Place the steamer basket in the pot, add potatoes in it, cover the pot and cook at High for 30 minutes.
8. Release the pressure, take potatoes out of the pot and also take chicken pieces out.
9. Shred chicken meat and return to pot.
10. Also return potatoes, more salt and pepper, stir, divide among plates and serve.

Bon Appétit!

126. Delicious Chicken Curry With Squash And Eggplant

Perp time: 10 minutes **Cooking time:** 25 minutes **Servings:** 4

Nutrition Facts:
- Calories: 160
- Fat (In grams): 8.2
- Fiber (In grams): 4.1
- Carbs (In grams): 13.2
- Protein (In grams): 6

Ingredients:
- 3 garlic cloves, crushed
- 2 tablespoons vegetable oil
- 3 bird's eye chilies, cut into halves
- 1 inch piece ginger, sliced
- 2 tablespoons green curry paste
- 1/8 teaspoon cumin, ground
- 1/4 teaspoon coriander, ground
- 14 ounces canned coconut milk
- 6 cups quash, cubed
- 8 chicken pieces
- 1 eggplant, cubed
- Salt and black pepper to the taste
- One-tablespoon fish sauce
- 4 cups spinach, chopped
- Half-cup cilantro, chopped
- Half-cup basil, chopped
- Cooked barley for serving
- Lime wedges, for serving

Instructions:
1. Set your instant pot on Sauté mode, add oil and heat it up.
2. Add garlic, ginger, chilies, cumin and coriander, stir and cook for 1 minute.
3. Add curry paste, stir and cook 3 minutes.
4. Add coconut milk, stir and simmer for 1 minute.
5. Add chicken, squash, eggplant, salt, and pepper, stir, cover and cook at High for 20 minutes.
6. Release the pressure, uncover the pot, add spinach, fish sauce, more salt and pepper, basil and cilantro, stir and divide among plates.
7. Serve with cooked barley on the side and lime wedges.

Bon Appétit!

127. Colombian Style Chicken Dish

Perp time: 10 minutes **Cooking time:** 25 minutes **Servings:** 4

Nutrition Facts:
- Calories: 270
- Fat (In grams): 12
- Fiber (In grams): 1
- Carbs (In grams): 23
- Protein (In grams): 14

Ingredients:
- 4 gold potatoes, cut into medium chunks
- 1 yellow onion, thinly sliced
- 4 big tomatoes, cut into medium chunks
- 1 chicken, cut into 8 pieces
- Salt and black pepper to the taste
- 2 bay leaves
- Salt and black pepper to the taste

Instructions:
1. In your instant pot, mix potatoes with onion, chicken, tomato, bay leaves, salt, and pepper, stir well, cover and cook at High for 25 minutes.
2. Release the pressure naturally, uncover the pot, add more salt and pepper, discard bay leaves, divide chicken among plates and serve.

Bon Appétit!

---

128. SPECIAL CHICKEN & LENTILS DISH

Perp time: 10 minutes **Cooking time:** 25 minutes **Servings:** 4

Nutrition Facts:
- Calories: 340
- Fat (In grams): 3.3
- Fiber (In grams): 23
- Carbs (In grams): 30
- Protein (In grams): 29

Ingredients:
- 8 ounces bacon, chopped
- 2 tablespoons extra virgin olive oil
- A drizzle of olive oil for serving
- One-cup yellow onion, chopped
- 8 ounces lentils, dried
- 2 carrots, chopped
- 12 parsley springs, chopped
- Salt and black pepper to the taste
- 2 bay leaves
- 2 ½ pounds chicken pieces
- 1-quart chicken stock
- 2 teaspoons sherry vinegar

Instructions:
1. Set your instant pot on Sauté mode, add the oil and heat it up.
2. Add bacon, stir and cook for 1 minute.
3. Add onions, stir and cook 2 minutes.
4. Add lentils, carrots, chicken pieces, parsley, bay leaves, stock, salt and pepper to the taste, stir, cover and cook at High for 20 minutes.
5. Release pressure, take chicken pieces and place them on a cutting board.
6. Discard skin and bones, shred chicken and return to pot.
7. Set the pot on Sauté mode again and cook everything for 7 minutes.
8. Add more salt and pepper and the vinegar, stir and divide among plates.
9. Drizzle some olive oil over the whole mix and serve.

Bon Appétit!

129. Tasty Teriyaki Chicken

Perp time: 10 minutes **Cooking time:** 12 minutes **Servings:** 6

Nutrition Facts:
- Calories: 240
- Fat (In grams): 13
- Fiber (In grams): 1
- Carbs (In grams): 8
- Protein (In grams): 34

Ingredients:
- 2 pounds chicken breasts, skinless and boneless
- 2/3 cup teriyaki sauce
- One-tablespoon honey
- Half-cup chicken stock
- Salt and black pepper to the taste
- A handful green onions, chopped

Instructions:
1. Set your instant pot on Sauté mode, add teriyaki sauce and honey, stir and simmer for 1 minute.
2. Add stock, chicken, salt and pepper, stir, cover and cook at High for 12 minutes.
3. Release the pressure quick, take chicken breasts, place them on a cutting board and shred with 2 forks.
4. Remove Half-cup of cooking liquid, return shredded chicken to pot, add green onions, stir, divide among plates and serve.

Bon Appétit!

130. Yummy Chicken & Dumplings

Perp time: 10 minutes **Cooking time:** 20 minutes **Servings:** 6

Nutrition Facts:
- Calories: 380
- Fat (In grams): 4.2
- Fiber (In grams): 2.9
- Carbs (In grams): 40
- Protein (In grams): 43

Ingredients:
- 2 pounds chicken breasts, skinless and bone-in
- 4 carrots, chopped
- 1 yellow onion, chopped
- 3 celery stalks, chopped
- 3/4 cup chicken stock
- Salt and black pepper to the taste
- Half-teaspoon thyme, dried
- 2 eggs
- 2/3 cup milk
- One-tablespoon baking powder
- 2 cups flour
- One-tablespoon chives

Instructions:
1. In your instant pot, add chicken, onion, carrots, celery, stock, thyme, salt and pepper, stir, cover and cook on Low for 15 minutes.
2. Release the pressure quick, transfer chicken to a bowl and keep warm for now.
3. In a bowl, mix eggs with salt, milk and baking powder and stir.

4. Add flour gradually and stir very well.
5. Set instant pot to Simmer mode and bring the liquid inside to a boil.
6. Shape dumplings from eggs mix, drop them into stock, cover the pot and cook at High for 7 minutes.
7. Shred chicken and add to the pot after you've released the pressure, stir, divide everything among plates and serve with chives sprinkled on top.

Bon Appétit!

131. TASTY NOODLES AND CHICKEN

Perp time: 10 minutes   **Cooking time:** 20 minutes   **Servings:** 6

Nutrition Facts:
- Calories: 560
- Fat (In grams): 11.2
- Fiber (In grams): 5.2
- Carbs (In grams): 77
- Protein (In grams): 39

Ingredients:
- 8 chicken thighs, skinless and boneless
- 3 carrots, chopped
- 2 garlic cloves, minced
- 1 yellow onion, chopped
- 3 celery stalks, chopped
- 6 cups chicken stock
- 1 bay leaf
- 2 sage springs
- 1 rosemary spring
- 5 thyme springs
- Salt and black pepper to the taste
- One-teaspoon chicken seasoning
- 1 pound egg noodles
- 2 tablespoons cornstarch
- 3 tablespoons water
- One-cup peas, frozen
- Juice of 1 lemon
- 1/4 cup parsley, chopped

Instructions:
1. Set your instant pot on Sauté mode, add onion, garlic, and celery, stir and brown for 4 minutes.
2. Add carrot, chicken, stock, bay leaf, thyme, rosemary, sage, chicken seasoning, salt and pepper to the taste, stir, cover the pot and cook on Low for 10 minutes.
3. Release the pressure naturally, uncover the pot, add egg noodles, cornstarch mixed with water, peas, lemon juice, parsley and more salt and pepper if needed.
4. Discard herbs springs, stir everything, divide among plates and serve.

Bon Appétit!

132. SIMPLE SESAME CHICKEN

Perp time: 10 minutes   **Cooking time:** 8 minutes   **Servings:** 4

Nutrition Facts:
- Calories: 170
- Fat (In grams): 3.5
- Fiber (In grams): 2.9
- Carbs (In grams): 16
- Protein (In grams): 7

Ingredients:

- 2 pounds chicken breasts, skinless, boneless and chopped
- Half-cup yellow onion, chopped
- Salt and black pepper to the taste
- One-tablespoon vegetable oil
- 2 garlic cloves, minced
- Half-cup soy sauce
- 1/4 cup ketchup
- 2 teaspoons sesame oil
- Half-cup honey
- 2 tablespoons cornstarch
- 1/4 teaspoon red pepper flakes
- 3 tablespoons water
- 2 green onions, chopped
- One-tablespoons sesame seeds, toasted

Instructions:
1. Set your instant pot on Sauté mode, add the oil and heat it up.
2. Add garlic, onion, chicken, salt and pepper, stir and cook for 3 minutes.
3. Add pepper flakes, soy sauce and ketchup, stir, cover and cook at High for 3 minutes.
4. Release pressure quick, uncover the pot, add sesame oil and honey and stir.
5. In a bowl, mix cornstarch with water and stir well.
6. Add this to the pot, also add green onions and sesame seeds, stir well, divide among plates and serve.

Bon Appétit!

---

133. DELICIOUS CHICKEN WITH DUCK SAUCE

Perp time: 10 minutes **Cooking time:** 20 minutes **Servings:** 4

Nutrition Facts:
- Calories: 170
- Fat (In grams): 4
- Fiber (In grams): 3
- Carbs (In grams): 9
- Protein (In grams): 23

Ingredients:
- 1 chicken, cut into medium pieces
- Salt and black pepper to the taste
- One-tablespoon extra virgin olive oil
- Half-teaspoon paprika
- 1/4 cup white wine
- Half-teaspoon marjoram, dried
- 1/4 cup chicken stock

For the duck sauce:
- 2 tablespoons white vinegar
- 1/4 cup apricot preserves
- 1 ½ teaspoon ginger root, grated
- 2 tablespoons honey

Instructions:
1. Set your instant pot on Sauté mode, add oil and heat it up.
2. Add chicken pieces, brown them on all sides and transfer to a bowl.
3. Season them with salt, pepper, marjoram and paprika and toss to coat.
4. Drain Fat from pot, add stock and wine, stir and simmer for 2 minutes.
5. Return chicken, cover the pot and cook at High for 9 minutes.
6. Release the pressure, transfer chicken to servings dishes and leave aside for now.
7. Add apricot preserves to pot, ginger, vinegar, and honey, set pot to Sauté mode again, stir and simmer sauce for 10 minutes.
8. Drizzle over chicken and serve.

Bon Appétit!

134. SPECIAL CHICKEN WINGS

Perp time: 10 minutes **Cooking time:** 25 minutes **Servings:** 6

Nutrition Facts:
- Calories: 300
- Fat (In grams): 3.1
- Fiber (In grams): 2
- Carbs (In grams): 14
- Protein (In grams): 33

Ingredients:
- 12 chicken wings, cut into 24 pieces
- 1 pound celery, cut into thin matchsticks
- 1/4 cup honey
- 4 tablespoons hot sauce
- Salt to the taste
- One-cup water
- 1/4 cup tomato puree
- One-cup yogurt
- One-tablespoon parsley, finely chopped

Instructions:
1. Put One-cup water into your instant pot.
2. Place chicken wings in the steamer basket of your pot, cover and cook at High for 19 minutes.
3. Meanwhile, in a bowl, mix tomato puree with hot sauce, salt and honey and stir very well.
4. Release the pressure from the pot, add chicken wings to honey mix and toss them to coat.
5. Arrange chicken wings on a lined baking sheet and introduce in preheated broiler for 5 minutes.
6. Arrange celery sticks on a platter and add chicken wings next to it.
7. In a bowl, mix yogurt with parsley, stir well and place next to the platter.
8. Serve right away.

Bon Appétit!

135. CHICKPEA MASALA WITH CHICKEN

Perp time: 10 minutes **Cooking time:** 25 minutes **Servings:** 4

Nutrition Facts:
- Calories: 270
- Fat (In grams): 8
- Fiber (In grams): 7.6
- Carbs (In grams): 30
- Protein (In grams): 31

Ingredients:
- 1 yellow onion, finely chopped
- 2 tablespoons butter
- 4 garlic cloves, minced
- One-tablespoon ginger, grated
- 1 ½ teaspoon paprika
- One-tablespoon cumin, ground
- 1 ½ teaspoons coriander, ground
- One-teaspoon turmeric, ground
- Salt and black pepper to the taste
- A pinch of cayenne pepper
- 15 ounces canned tomatoes, crushed
- 1/4 cup lemon juice
- 1 pound spinach, chopped
- 3 pounds chicken drumsticks and thighs
- Half-cup cilantro, chopped

- Half-cup chicken stock
- 15 ounces canned chickpeas, drained
- Half-cup heavy cream

Instructions:
1. Set your instant pot on Sauté mode, add butter and melt it.
2. Add ginger, onion, and garlic, stir and cook for 5 minutes.
3. Add paprika, cumin, coriander, cayenne, turmeric, salt, and pepper, stir and cook for 30 seconds.
4. Add tomatoes and spinach, stir and cook for 2 minutes.
5. Add half of the cilantro, chicken pieces, and stock, stir, cover the pot and cook at High for 15 minutes.
6. Release the pressure, uncover the pot, add heavy cream, chickpeas, lemon juice, more salt, and pepper, stir, set the pot on Sauté mode again and simmer for 3 minutes.
7. Sprinkle the rest of the cilantro on top, stir, divide among plates and serve.

Bon Appétit!

136. INDIAN STYLE BUTTER CHICKEN

Perp time: 10 minutes **Cooking time:** 15 minutes **Servings:** 6

Nutrition Facts:
- Calories: 380
- Fat (In grams): 29
- Fiber (In grams): 2
- Carbs (In grams): 8
- Sugar (In grams): 2
- Protein (In grams): 24

Ingredients:
- 10 chicken thighs, skinless and boneless
- 2 jalapeno peppers, chopped
- 28 ounces canned tomatoes and their juice, chopped
- 2 teaspoons cumin, ground
- 2 tablespoons ginger, chopped
- Half-cup butter
- Salt and black pepper to the taste
- 3/4 cup heavy cream
- 2 teaspoons garam masala
- 3/4 cup Greek yogurt
- 2 teaspoons cumin seeds, toasted and ground
- 2 tablespoons cornstarch
- 2 tablespoons water
- 1/4 cup cilantro, chopped

Instructions:
1. In your food processor, mix tomatoes with ginger and jalapenos and blend well.
2. Set your instant pot on Sauté mode, add butter and melt it.
3. Add chicken, stir and brown for 3 minutes on each side.
4. Transfer chicken pieces to a bowl and leave aside.
5. Add paprika and ground cumin to your pot, stir and cook for 10 seconds.
6. Add tomato mix, salt, pepper, yogurt, heavy cream and chicken pieces, stir, cover and cook at High for 5 minutes.
7. Release the pressure naturally for 15 minutes, uncover the pot, add cornstarch mixed with the water, garam masala and cumin seeds and stir well.
8. Add cilantro, stir, divide among plates and serve with naan bread.

137. MIX CHICKEN AND CORN

Perp time: 10 minutes   **Cooking time:** 25 minutes   **Servings:** 4

Nutrition Facts:
- Calories: 320
- Fat (In grams): 10
- Fiber (In grams): 3
- Carbs (In grams): 18
- Protein (In grams): 42

Ingredients:
- 8 chicken drumsticks
- Salt and black pepper to the taste
- One-teaspoon extra virgin olive oil
- Half-teaspoon garlic powder
- 3 scallions, chopped
- ½ yellow onion, chopped
- 1 tomato, chopped
- 1/4 cup cilantro, chopped
- 1 garlic clove, minced
- 2 cups water
- 8 ounces tomato sauce
- One-tablespoon chicken bouillon
- 2 corn on the cob, husked and cut into halves
- Half-teaspoon cumin, ground

Instructions:
1. Set your instant pot on Sauté mode, add oil and heat up.
2. Add onions, tomato, scallions, and garlic, stir and cook for 3 minutes.
3. Add cilantro, stir and cook for 1 minute.
4. Add tomato sauce, water, bouillon, cumin, garlic powder, chicken, salt, pepper and top with the corn.
5. Cover the pot and cook at High for 20 minutes.
6. Release the pressure quickly, uncover the pot, add more salt and pepper if needed, divide chicken and corn among plates and serve.

Bon Appétit!

138. TASTY GOOSE DISH

Perp time: 10 minutes   **Cooking time:** 1 hour   **Servings:** 5

Nutrition Facts:
- Calories: 345
- Fat (In grams): 7.8
- Fiber (In grams): 1
- Carbs (In grams): 1
- Protein (In grams): 28.4

Ingredients:
- 1 goose breast, Fat trimmed off and cut into pieces
- 1 goose leg, skinless
- 1 goose thigh, skinless
- Salt and black pepper to the taste
- 3 ½-cups water
- 2 teaspoons garlic, minced
- 1 yellow onion, chopped
- 12 ounces canned mushroom cream

Instructions:
1. Put goose meat in your instant pot.
2. Add onion, salt, pepper, water and garlic, stir, cover and cook on Low for 1 hour.

3. Release the pressure, uncover the pot, add mushroom cream, set the pot on Simmer mode and cook everything for 5 minutes.
4. Divide into bowls and serve with toasted bread on the side.

Bon Appétit!

139. POMEGRANATE AND CHICKEN

Perp time: 10 minutes   **Cooking time:** 15 minutes   **Servings:** 6

Nutrition Facts:
- Calories: 200
- Fat (In grams): 1
- Fiber (In grams): 4
- Carbs (In grams): 27
- Protein (In grams): 17

Ingredients:
- 10 chicken pieces
- 2 cups walnuts
- Salt and black pepper to the taste
- 3 tablespoons extra virgin olive oil
- 1 yellow onion, chopped
- 1/4 teaspoon cardamom, ground
- Half-teaspoon cinnamon, ground
- 2/3 cup pomegranate molasses
- 3/4 cup water
- 2 tablespoons Sugar
- Juice of ½ lemon
- Pomegranate seeds for serving

Instructions:
1. Heat up a pan over medium high heat, add walnuts, stir and toast for 5 minutes.
2. Transfer them to your food processor, blend well, transfer to a bowl and leave aside.
3. Set your instant pot on Sauté mode, add 2 tablespoons oil and heat it up.
4. Add chicken pieces, salt and pepper, brown them on all sides and transfer them to a plate.
5. Add the rest of the oil to the pot, add onion, stir and cook for 3 minutes.
6. Add cardamom and cinnamon, stir and cook for 1 minute.
7. Add ground walnuts, pomegranate molasses, lemon juice, chicken and Sugar, stir, cover and cook at High for 7 minutes.
8. Release the pressure, uncover the pot, add more salt and pepper, stir, divide among plates and serve with the sauce from the pot and with pomegranate seeds on top.

Bon Appétit!

140. TASTY SHRIMP AND CHICKEN

Perp time: 10 minutes   **Cooking time:** 15 minutes   **Servings:** 4

Nutrition Facts:
- Calories: 269
- Fat (In grams): 5.9
- Fiber (In grams): 2.4
- Carbs (In grams): 23.5
- Protein (In grams): 28.4

Ingredients:
- 8 ounces shrimp, peeled and deveined
- 8 ounces sausages, sliced
- 8 ounces chicken breasts, skinless, boneless and chopped
- 2 tablespoons extra virgin olive oil

- One-teaspoon Creole seasoning
- 2 teaspoons thyme, dried
- A pinch of cayenne pepper
- 2 teaspoons Worcestershire sauce
- 1 dash Tabasco sauce
- 3 garlic cloves, minced
- 1 yellow onion, chopped
- 1 green bell pepper, chopped
- 3 celery stalks, chopped
- One-cup white rice
- One-cup chicken stock
- 2 cups canned tomatoes, chopped
- 3 tablespoons parsley, chopped

Instructions:
1. In a bowl, mix Creole seasoning with thyme and cayenne and stir.
2. Set your instant pot on Sauté mode, add the oil and heat it up.
3. Add chicken and brown for a few minutes.
4. Add sausage slices, stir and cook for 3 minutes.
5. Add shrimp and half of the seasoning mix, stir and cook for 2 minutes.
6. Transfer everything to a bowl and leave aside for now.
7. Add garlic, onions, celery and bell peppers to your instant pot.
8. Add the rest of the seasoning mix, stir and cook for 10 minutes.
9. Add rice, stock, tomatoes, Tabasco sauce and Worcestershire sauce, stir, cover and cook on High for 8 minutes.
10. Release the pressure, return chicken, sausage and shrimp, stir, cover and leave instant pot aside for 5 minutes.
11. Divide everything among plates and serve.

Bon Appétit!

---

141. DELICIOUS GOOSE WITH CHILI SAUCE

Perp time: 10 minutes **Cooking time:** 15 minutes **Servings:** 4

Nutrition Facts:
- Calories: 190
- Fat (In grams): 8
- Fiber (In grams): 1
- Carbs (In grams): 1
- Protein (In grams): 29

Ingredients:
- 1 goose breast half, skinless, boneless and cut into thin slices
- 1/4 cup extra virgin olive oil
- 1 sweet onion, chopped
- 2 teaspoons garlic, chopped
- Salt and black pepper to the taste
- 1/4 cup sweet chili sauce

Instructions:
1. Set your instant pot on Sauté mode, add the oil and heat it up.
2. Add onion and garlic, stir and cook for 2 minutes.
3. Add goose breast slices, salt and pepper to the taste, stir and cook for 2 minutes on each side.
4. Add chili sauce, stir, cover and cook at High for 5 minutes.
5. Release pressure quick, divide among plates and serve.

Bon Appétit!

142. Delicious Cabbage And Chicken

Perp time: 10 minutes   **Cooking time:** 30 minutes   **Servings:** 3

Nutrition Facts:
- Calories: 260
- Fat (In grams): 5.5
- Fiber (In grams): 4.9
- Carbs (In grams): 15.2
- Protein (In grams): 30.2

Ingredients:
- 1 ½ pounds chicken thighs, boneless
- 1 green cabbage, roughly chopped
- One-tablespoon vegetable oil
- Salt and black pepper to the taste
- 2 chili peppers, chopped
- 1 yellow onion, chopped
- 4 garlic cloves, chopped
- 3 tablespoons curry paste
- A pinch of cayenne pepper
- Half-cup white wine
- 10 ounces coconut milk
- One-tablespoon fish sauce

Instructions:
1. Set your instant pot on Sauté mode, add oil and heat it up.
2. Add chicken, season with salt and pepper, stir, brown for a few minutes and transfer to a bowl.
3. Add garlic, chili peppers and onions to the pot, stir and cook for 4 minutes.
4. Add curry paste, stir and cook for 2 minutes more.
5. Add wine, cabbage, coconut milk, cayenne, fish sauce, chicken pieces, salt and pepper, stir, cover and cook at High for 20 minutes.
6. Release the pressure naturally, uncover the pot, stir your mix, divide it among plates and serve.

Bon Appétit!

143. Yummy Chicken & Broccoli

Perp time: 10 minutes   **Cooking time:** 15 minutes   **Servings:** 6

Nutrition Facts:
- Calories: 280
- Fat (In grams): 13
- Fiber (In grams): 4
- Carbs (In grams): 23
- Protein (In grams): 30

Ingredients:
- 2 chicken breasts, skinless and boneless
- One-tablespoon butter
- One-tablespoon extra virgin olive oil
- Half-cup yellow onion, chopped
- 14 ounces canned chicken stock
- Salt and black pepper to the taste
- A pinch of red pepper flakes
- One-tablespoon parsley, dried
- 2 tablespoons water
- 2 tablespoons cornstarch
- 3 cups broccoli, steamed and chopped
- One-cup cheddar cheese, shredded
- 4 ounces cream cheese, cubed

Instructions:
1. Set your instant pot on Sauté mode, add butter and oil and heat up.
2. Add chicken breasts, salt and pepper, brown on all sides and transfer to a bowl.
3. Add onion to the pot, stir and cook for 5 minutes.

4. Add more salt, pepper, stock, parsley, pepper flakes and return chicken breasts as well.
5. Stir, cover the pot and cook at High for 5 minutes.
6. Release the pressure quick, transfer chicken to a cutting board, chop it and return to pot.
7. Add cornstarch mixed with the water, shredded cheese and cream cheese and stir until all cheese dissolves.
8. Add broccoli, stir, set the pot on Simmer mode and cook for 5 minutes.
9. Divide among plates and serve.

MEAT RECIPES

144. Easy Corned Beef

Perp time: 10 minutes **Cooking time:** 60 minutes **Servings:** 6

Nutrition Facts:
- Calories: 251
- Fat (In grams): 3.14
- Fiber (In grams): 0
- Carbs (In grams): 1
- Protein (In grams): 7

Ingredients:
- 4 pounds beef brisket
- 2 oranges, sliced
- 2 garlic cloves, minced
- 2 yellow onions, thinly sliced
- 11 ounces celery, thinly sliced
- One-tablespoon dill, dried
- 3 bay leaves
- 4 cinnamon sticks, cut into halves
- Salt and black pepper to the taste
- 17 ounces water

Instructions:
1. Put the beef in a bowl, add some water to cover, leave aside to soak for a few hours, drain and transfer to your instant pot.
2. Add celery, orange slices, onions, garlic, bay leaves, dill, cinnamon, dill, salt and pepper and 17 ounces water.
3. Stir, cover the pot and cook at High for 50 minutes.
4. Release the pressure, leave beef aside to cool down for 5 minutes, transfer to a cutting board, slice and divide among plates.
5. Drizzle the juice and veggies from the pot over beef and serve.

Bon Appétit!

145. Tasty Chili Con Carne

Perp time: 10 minutes **Cooking time:** 30 minutes **Servings:** 4

Nutrition Facts:
- Calories: 256
- Fat (In grams): 8
- Fiber (In grams): 1
- Carbs (In grams): 22
- Protein (In grams): 25

Ingredients:
- 1 pound beef, ground
- 1 yellow onion, chopped
- 4 tablespoons extra virgin olive oil
- Salt and black pepper to the taste
- 2 garlic cloves, minced
- 1 bay leaf
- 4 ounces kidney beans, soaked overnight and drained
- One-teaspoon tomato paste
- 8 ounces canned tomatoes, chopped
- One-tablespoon chili powder
- Half-teaspoon cumin, ground
- 5 ounces water

Instructions:
1. Set your instant pot on Sauté mode, add One-tablespoon oil and heat it up.
2. Add meat, brown for a few minutes and transfer to a bowl.
3. Add the rest of the oil to the pot and also heat it up.

4. Add onion and garlic, stir and cook for 3 minutes.
5. Return beef to pot, add bay leaf, beans, tomato paste, tomatoes, chili powder, cumin, salt, pepper and water, stir, cover and cook on High for 18 minutes.
6. Release the pressure, uncover the pot, discard bay leaf, divide chili among bowls and serve.

Bon Appétit!

---

146. YUMMY BEEF STROGANOFF

Perp time: 10 minutes   **Cooking time:** 25 minutes   **Servings:** 4

Nutrition Facts:
- Calories: 335
- Fat (In grams): 18.4
- Fiber (In grams): 1.3
- Carbs (In grams): 22.5
- Protein (In grams): 20.1

Ingredients:
- 10 pounds beef, cut into small cubes
- 1 yellow onion, chopped
- 2 ½-tablespoons vegetable oil
- 1 ½tablespoons white flour
- 2 garlic cloves, minced
- 4 ounces mushrooms, sliced
- 1 ½tablespoon tomato paste
- Salt and black pepper to the taste
- 3 tablespoons Worcestershire sauce
- 13 ounces beef stock
- 8 ounces sour cream
- Egg noodles, already cooked for serving

Instructions:
1. Put beef, salt, pepper and flour in a bowl and toss to coat.
2. Set your instant pot on Sauté mode, add oil and heat it up.
3. Add meat and brown it on all sides.
4. Add onion, garlic, mushrooms, Worcestershire sauce, stock and tomato paste, stir well, cover the pot and cook at High for 20 minutes.
5. Release the pressure, uncover the pot, add sour cream, more salt and pepper, stir well and divide among plates on top of egg noodles.

Bon Appétit!

---

147. DELICIOUS BEEF CURRY

Perp time: 10 minutes   **Cooking time:** 20 minutes   **Servings:** 4

Nutrition Facts:
- Calories: 434
- Fat (In grams): 20
- Fiber (In grams): 2.9
- Carbs (In grams): 14
- Protein (In grams): 27.5

Ingredients:
- 2 pounds beef steak, cubed
- 2 tablespoons extra virgin olive oil
- 3 potatoes, diced
- One-tablespoon wine mustard
- 2 ½-tablespoons curry powder
- 2 yellow onions, chopped
- 2 garlic cloves, minced
- 10 ounces canned coconut milk
- 2 tablespoons tomato sauce
- Salt and black pepper to the taste

Instructions:
1. Set your instant pot on Sauté mode, add the oil and heat it up.
2. Add onions and garlic, stir and cook for 4 minutes.
3. Add potatoes and mustard, stir and cook for 1 minute.
4. Add beef, stir and brown on all sides.
5. Add curry powder, salt and pepper, stir and cook for 2 minutes.
6. Add coconut milk and tomato sauce, stir, cover the pot and cook at High for 10 minutes.
7. Release the pressure, uncover the pot, divide curry among plates and serve.

Bon Appétit!

148. Mixed Beans Beef

Perp time: 10 minutes   **Cooking time:** 40 minutes   **Servings:** 6

Nutrition Facts:
- Calories: 272
- Fat (In grams): 5
- Fiber (In grams): 0
- Carbs (In grams): 32
- Protein (In grams): 25

Ingredients:
- 1 ½ pounds beef, ground
- 1 sweet onion, chopped
- Salt and black pepper to the taste
- 16 ounces mixed beans, soaked overnight and drained
- 28 ounces canned tomatoes, chopped
- 17 ounces beef stock
- 12 ounces pale ale
- 6 garlic cloves, chopped
- 7 jalapeno peppers, diced
- 2 tablespoons vegetable oil
- 4 carrots, chopped
- 3 tablespoons chili powder
- 1 bay leaf
- One-teaspoon chipotle powder

Instructions:
1. Set your instant pot on Sauté mode, add half of the oil and heat it up.
2. Add beef, stir, brown for 8 minutes and transfer to a bowl.
3. Add the rest of the oil to the pot and heat it up.
4. Add carrots, onion, jalapenos and garlic, stir and sauté for 4 minutes.
5. Add ale and tomatoes and stir.
6. Also add beans, bay leaf, stock, chili powder, chipotle powder, salt and pepper and the beef, stir, cover and cook at High for 25 minutes.
7. Release the pressure naturally, uncover the pot, stir chili, transfer to bowls and serve.

Bon Appétit!

149. Special Beef Bourguignon

Perp time: 15 minutes **Cooking time:** 30 minutes **Servings:** 6

Nutrition Facts:
- Calories: 442
- Fat (In grams): 17.2
- Fiber (In grams): 3
- Carbs (In grams): 16
- Protein (In grams): 39

Ingredients:
- 10 pounds round steak, cut into small cubes
- 2 carrots, sliced
- Half-cup beef stock
- One-cup dry red wine
- 3 bacon slices, chopped
- 8 ounces mushrooms, cut into quarters
- 2 tablespoons white flour
- 12 pearl onions
- 2 garlic cloves, minced
- 1/4 teaspoon basil, dried
- Salt and black pepper to the taste

Instructions:
1. Set your instant pot on Sauté mode, add bacon and brown it for 2 minutes.
2. Add beef pieces, stir and brown for 5 minutes.
3. Add flour and stir very well.
4. Add salt, pepper, wine, stock, onions, garlic and basil, stir, cover and cook at High for 20 minutes.
5. Release the pressure quickly, uncover your pot, add mushrooms and carrots, cover the pot again and cook at High for 5 minutes more.
6. Release the pressure again, divide beef bourguignon among plates and serve.

Bon Appétit!

150. Tasty Beef Pot Roast

Perp time: 10 minutes **Cooking time:** 1 hour **Servings:** 6

Nutrition Facts:
- Calories: 290
- Fat (In grams): 20
- Fiber (In grams): 0
- Carbs (In grams): 2
- Protein (In grams): 25

Ingredients:
- 3 pounds beef roast
- Salt and black pepper to the taste
- 17 ounces beef stock
- 3 ounces red wine
- Half-teaspoon chicken salt
- Half-teaspoon smoked paprika
- 1 yellow onion, chopped
- 4 garlic cloves, minced
- 3 carrots, chopped
- 5 potatoes, chopped

Instructions:
1. In a bowl, mix salt, pepper, chicken salt and paprika and stir.
2. Rub beef with this mix and put it in your instant pot.
3. Add onion, garlic, stock, and wine, toss to coat, cover the pot and cook on High for 50 minutes.

4. Release the pressure quickly, uncover the pot, add carrots and potatoes, cover again and cook at High for 10 minutes.
5. Release the pressure again, uncover the pot, transfer roast to a platter, drizzle cooking juices all over and serve with veggies on the side.

Bon Appétit!

---

151. KOREAN STYLE BEEF DISH

Perp time: 10 minutes **Cooking time:** 25 minutes **Servings:** 6

Nutrition Facts:
- Calories: 310
- Fat (In grams): 9.3
- Fiber (In grams): 0.2
- Carbs (In grams): 18.4
- Protein (In grams): 35.3

Ingredients:
- 1/4 cup Korean soybean paste
- One-cup chicken stock
- 2 pounds beefsteak, cut into thin strips
- 1/4 teaspoon red pepper flakes
- Salt and black pepper to the taste
- 1 yellow onion, thinly sliced
- 1 zucchini, cubed
- 1-ounce shiitake mushroom caps, cut into quarters
- 12 ounces extra firm tofu, cubed
- 1 chili pepper, sliced
- 1 scallion, chopped

Instructions:
1. Set your instant pot on Sauté mode, add stock and soybean paste, stir and simmer for 2 minutes.
2. Add beef, salt, pepper, and pepper flakes stir, cover the pot and cook at High for 15 minutes.
3. Release the pressure quickly, add tofu, onion, zucchini and mushrooms, stir, bring to a boil, cover the pot and cook at High for 4 minutes more.
4. Release the pressure again, uncover the pot, add more salt and pepper to the taste, add chili and scallion, stir, divide into bowls and serve.

Bon Appétit!

---

152. BEST BEEF & PASTA CASSEROLE

Perp time: 10 minutes **Cooking time:** 20 minutes **Servings:** 4

Nutrition Facts:
- Calories: 182
- Fat (In grams): 1
- Fiber (In grams): 1.4
- Carbs (In grams): 31
- Protein (In grams): 12

Ingredients:
- 17 ounces pasta
- 1 pound beef, ground
- 13 ounces mozzarella cheese, shredded
- 16 ounces tomato puree
- 1 celery stalk, chopped
- 1 yellow onion, chopped
- 1 carrot, chopped
- One-tablespoon red wine
- 2 tablespoons butter
- Salt and black pepper to the taste

Instructions:
1. Set your instant pot on Sauté mode, add the butter and melt it.
2. Add carrot, onion, and celery, stir and cook for 5 minutes.
3. Add beef, salt and pepper and cook for 10 minutes.
4. Add wine, stir and cook for 1 minute more.
5. Add pasta, tomato puree and water to cover pasta, stir, cover and cook at High for 6 minutes.
6. Release the pressure, uncover the pot, add cheese, stir, divide everything among plates and serve.

Bon Appétit!

---

153. APPETIZING VEAL DISH

Perp time: 10 minutes **Cooking time:** 35 minutes **Servings:** 4

Nutrition Facts:
- Calories: 395
- Fat (In grams): 18
- Fiber (In grams): 1.4
- Carbs (In grams): 7.1
- Protein (In grams): 47.8

Ingredients:
- 3.5 ounces button mushrooms, sliced
- 3.5 ounces shiitake mushrooms, sliced
- 2 pounds veal shoulder, cut into medium chunks
- 17 ounces potatoes, chopped
- 16 ounces shallots, chopped
- 9 ounces beef stock
- 2 ounces white wine
- One-tablespoon white flour
- 2 garlic cloves, minced
- 2 tablespoons chives, chopped
- One-teaspoon sage, dried
- 1/8 teaspoon thyme, dried
- Salt and black pepper to the taste
- 3 ½-tablespoons extra virgin olive oil

Instructions:
1. Set your instant pot on Sauté mode, add 1 ½ tablespoons oil and heat it up.
2. Add veal, season with salt and pepper, stir, brown for 5 minutes and transfer to a bowl.
3. Add the rest of the oil to the pot and heat it up.
4. Add all mushrooms, stir and cook for 3 minutes.
5. Add garlic, stir, cook for 1 minute and transfer everything to a bowl.
6. Add wine and flour to the pot, stir and cook for 1 minute.
7. Add stock, sage, thyme and return meat to pot as well.
8. Stir, cover and cook at High for 20 minutes.
9. Release pressure, uncover the pot, return mushrooms and garlic and stir.
10. Also add potatoes and shallots, stir, cover and cook at High for 4 minutes.
11. 1Release the pressure again, uncover your instant pot, add more salt and pepper if needed, also add chives, stir, divide among bowls and serve.

Bon Appétit!

154. Tasty Cabbage & Beef

Perp time: 10 minutes **Cooking time:** 1 hour and 20 minutes **Servings:** 6

Nutrition Facts:
- Calories: 340
- Fat (In grams): 24
- Fiber (In grams): 1
- Carbs (In grams): 14
- Protein (In grams): 26

Ingredients:
- 2 ½ pounds beef brisket
- 4 cups water
- 2 bay leaves
- 3 garlic cloves, chopped
- 4 carrots, chopped
- 1 cabbage heat, cut into 6 wedges
- 6 potatoes, cut into quarters
- Salt and black pepper to the taste
- 3 turnips, cut into quarters
- Horseradish sauce for serving

Instructions:
1. Put beef brisket and water in your instant pot, add salt, pepper, garlic and bay leaves, cover the pot and cook at High for 1 hour and 15 minutes.
2. Release the pressure quickly, uncover the pot, add carrots, cabbage, potatoes, and turnips, stir, cover the pot again and cook at High for 6 minutes.
3. Release the pressure naturally, uncover your pot again, divide among plates and serve with horseradish sauce on top.

Bon Appétit!

155. Simple Beef Dish

Perp time: 10 minutes **Cooking time:** 30 minutes **Servings:** 4

Nutrition Facts:
- Calories: 221
- Fat (In grams): 5.3
- Fiber (In grams): 1
- Carbs (In grams): 20.2
- Protein (In grams): 22.7

Ingredients:
- 2 tablespoons extra virgin olive oil
- 1 ½ pounds beef stew meat, cubed
- 4 tablespoons white flour
- 1 yellow onion, chopped
- 2 tablespoons red wine
- 2 garlic cloves, minced
- 2 cups water
- 2 cups beef stock
- Salt and black pepper to the taste
- 1 bay leaf
- Half-teaspoon thyme, dried
- 2 celery stalks, chopped
- 2 carrots, chopped
- 4 potatoes, chopped
- ½ bunch parsley, chopped

Instructions:
1. Season beef with salt and pepper and mix with half of the flour.
2. Set your instant pot on Sauté mode, add oil and heat it up.

3. Add beef, brown for 2 minutes and transfer to a bowl.
4. Add onion to your pot, stir and cook for 3 minutes.
5. Add garlic, stir and cook for 1 minute.
6. Add wine, stir well and cook for 15 seconds.
7. Add the rest of the flour and stir well for 2 minutes.
8. Return meat to pot, add stock, water, bay leaf and thyme, stir, cover and cook on High for 12 minutes.
9. Release the pressure quickly, uncover your pot, add carrots, celery and potatoes, stir, cover pot again and cook at High for 5 minutes.
10. Release the pressure naturally for 10 minutes, uncover the pot, divide among plates and serve with parsley sprinkled on top.

Bon Appétit!

156. DELICIOUS LAMB DISH

Perp time: 15 minutes **Cooking time:** 20 minutes **Servings:** 8

Nutrition Facts:
- Calories: 234
- Fat (In grams): 8.4
- Fiber (In grams): 1
- Carbs (In grams): 3
- Protein (In grams): 35

Ingredients:
- 8 lamb ribs
- 4 garlic cloves, minced
- 2 carrots, chopped
- 13 ounces veggie stock
- 4 rosemary springs
- 2 tablespoons extra virgin olive oil
- Salt and black pepper to the taste
- 3 tablespoons white flour

Instructions:
1. Set your instant pot on Sauté mode, add the oil and heat it up.
2. Add lamb, garlic, salt and pepper and brown it on all sides.
3. Add flour, stock, rosemary and carrots, stir well, cover the pot and cook at High for 20 minutes.
4. Release pressure quickly, uncover the pot, discard rosemary, divide lamb on plates and serve with the cooking liquid drizzled on top.

Bon Appétit!

157. TASTY LAMB SHANKS

Perp time: 10 minutes **Cooking time:** 45 minutes **Servings:** 4

Nutrition Facts:
- Calories: 430
- Fat (In grams): 17
- Fiber (In grams): 2.5
- Carbs (In grams): 11.3
- Protein (In grams): 50

Ingredients:
- 4 lamb shanks
- 2 tablespoons extra virgin olive oil
- 2 tablespoons white flour
- 1 yellow onion, finely chopped

- 3 carrots, roughly chopped
- 2 garlic cloves, minced
- 2 tablespoons tomato paste
- One-teaspoon oregano, dried
- 1 tomato, roughly chopped
- 2 tablespoons water
- 4 ounces red wine
- Salt and black pepper to the taste
- 1 beef bouillon cube

Instructions:
1. In a bowl, mix flour with salt and pepper.
2. Add lamb shanks and toss to coat.
3. Set your instant pot on Sauté mode, add oil and heat it up.
4. Add lamb, brown on all sides and transfer to a bowl.
5. Add onion, oregano, carrots and garlic to the pot, stir and cook for 5 minutes.
6. Add tomato, tomato paste, water, wine and bouillon cube, stir and bring to a boil.
7. Return lamb to pot, stir, cover and cook on High for 25 minutes.
8. Release the pressure, uncover the pot, divide lamb among plates, pour cooking sauce all over and serve.

Bon Appétit!

158. Mouthwatering Lamb Dish

Perp time: 15 minutes **Cooking time:** 60 minutes **Servings:** 4

Nutrition Facts:
- Calories: 238
- Fat (In grams): 5
- Fiber (In grams): 4
- Carbs (In grams): 17
- Protein (In grams): 7.3

Ingredients:
- 6-pound lamb leg, boneless
- 2 tablespoons extra virgin olive oil
- Salt and black pepper to the taste
- 1 bay leaf
- One-teaspoon marjoram
- One-teaspoon sage, dried
- One-teaspoon ginger, grated
- 3 garlic cloves, minced
- One-teaspoon thyme, dried
- 2 cups veggie stock
- 3 pounds potatoes, chopped
- 3 tablespoons arrowroot powder mixed with 1/3 cup water

Instructions:
1. Set your instant pot on Sauté mode, add the oil and heat it up.
2. Add lamb leg and brown on all sides.
3. Add salt, pepper, bay leaf, marjoram, sage, ginger, garlic, thyme and stock, stir, cover the pot and cook at High for 50 minutes.
4. Release the pressure quickly, add potatoes, arrowroot mix, more salt and pepper if needed, stir, cover again and cook on High for 10 minutes.
5. Release the pressure again, uncover the pot, divide Mediterranean lamb among plates and serve.

Bon Appétit!

159. SPECIAL LAMB DISH

Perp time: 15 minutes **Cooking time:** 35 minutes **Servings:** 6

Nutrition Facts:
- Calories: 435
- Fat (In grams): 31
- Fiber (In grams): 4
- Carbs (In grams): 6
- Protein (In grams): 22

Ingredients:
- 3 pounds lamb chops
- Salt and black pepper to the taste
- 2 tablespoons flour
- 2 tablespoons extra virgin olive oil
- 2 yellow onions, chopped
- 3 ounces red wine
- 2 garlic cloves, crushed
- 2 carrots, sliced
- 2 celery sticks, chopped
- 2 tablespoons tomato sauce
- 2 bay leaves
- One-cup green peas
- 14 ounces canned tomatoes, chopped
- 4 ounces green beans
- 2 tablespoons parsley, finely chopped
- Beef stock for the pot

Instructions:
1. Put flour in a bowl and mix with salt and pepper.
2. Add lamb chops and toss to coat.
3. Set your instant pot on Sauté mode, add the oil and heat it up.
4. Add lamb, stir, brown for 3 minutes on all sides and transfer to a plate.
5. Add garlic and onion to the taste, stir and cook for 2 minutes.
6. Add wine and cook for 2 minutes.
7. Add bay leaves, carrots, celery and return lamb to pot.
8. Also add tomato sauce, tomatoes, green beans and peas and stir.
9. Add stock to cover everything, cover the pot and cook at High for 20 minutes.
10. Release the pressure, uncover the pot, add parsley, more salt and pepper if needed, divide among plates and serve.

Bon Appétit!

160. EASY LAMB RAGOUT

Perp time: 15 minutes **Cooking time:** 1 hour **Servings:** 8

Nutrition Facts:
- Calories: 360
- Fat (In grams): 14
- Fiber (In grams): 3
- Carbs (In grams): 15.1
- Protein (In grams): 30

Ingredients:
- 1 ½ pounds mutton, bone-in
- 2 carrots, sliced
- ½ pounds mushrooms, sliced
- 4 tomatoes, chopped
- 1 small yellow onion, chopped
- 6 garlic cloves, minced
- 2 tablespoons tomato paste
- One-teaspoon vegetable oil

- Salt and black pepper to the taste
- One-teaspoon oregano, dried
- A handful parsley, finely chopped

Instructions:
1. Set your instant pot on Sauté mode, add oil and heat it up.
2. Add meat and brown it on all sides.
3. Add tomato paste, tomatoes, onion, garlic, mushrooms, oregano, carrots and water to cover everything.
4. Add salt, pepper, stir, cover the pot and cook at High for 1 hour.
5. Release the pressure, take meat out of the pot, discard bones and shred it.
6. Return meat to pot, add parsley and stir.
7. Add more salt and pepper if needed and serve right away.

Bon Appétit!

161. BARLEY AND LAMB DISH

Perp time: 15 minutes **Cooking time:** 45 minutes **Servings:** 4

Nutrition Facts:
- Calories: 324
- Fat (In grams): 9
- Fiber (In grams): 4
- Carbs (In grams): 21
- Protein (In grams): 15

Ingredients:
- 6 ounces barley
- 5 ounces peas
- 1 lamb leg, already cooked, boneless and chopped
- 3 yellow onions, chopped
- 5 carrots, chopped
- 6 ounces beef stock
- 12 ounces water
- Salt and black pepper to the taste

Instructions:
1. In your instant pot, mix stock with water and barley, cover and cook at High for 20 minutes.
2. Release the pressure, uncover the pot, add onions, peas and carrots, stir, cover again and cook at High for 10 minutes.
3. Release the pressure again, add meat, salt and pepper to the taste, stir, divide into bowls and serve.

Bon Appétit!

162. WHITE BEANS AND LAMB DISH

Perp time: 10 minutes **Cooking time:** 40 minutes **Servings:** 4

Nutrition Facts:
- Calories: 520
- Fat (In grams): 17
- Fiber (In grams): 7
- Carbs (In grams): 35
- Protein (In grams): 56

Ingredients:
- 4 lamb chops

- 1 ½ cups white beans, soaked overnight and drained
- One-cup onion, chopped
- 2 cups canned tomatoes, chopped
- One-cup leek, chopped
- 2 tablespoons garlic, minced
- One-teaspoon herbs de Provence
- Salt and black pepper to the taste
- 3 cups water
- 2 teaspoons Worcestershire sauce

Instructions:
1. Put lamb chops in your instant pot.
2. Add beans, onion, tomatoes, leek, garlic, salt, pepper, herbs de Provence, Worcestershire sauce and water.
3. Stir, cover and cook at High for 40 minutes.
4. Release the pressure, uncover the pot, divide among plates and serve.

Bon Appétit!

---

163. MEXICAN LAMB DISH

Perp time: 10 minutes **Cooking time:** 50 minutes **Servings:** 4

Nutrition Facts:
- Calories: 484
- Fat (In grams): 19
- Fiber (In grams): 9
- Carbs (In grams): 28
- Protein (In grams): 44

Ingredients:
- 3 pounds lamb shoulder, cubed
- 19 ounces enchilada sauce
- 3 garlic cloves, minced
- 1 yellow onion, chopped
- 2 tablespoons extra virgin olive oil
- Salt to the taste
- ½ bunch cilantro, finely chopped
- corn tortillas, warm for serving
- lime wedges for serving
- refried beans for serving

Instructions:
1. Put enchilada sauce in a bowl, add lamb meat and marinade for 24 hours.
2. Set your instant pot on Sauté mode, add the oil and heat it up.
3. Add onions and garlic, stir and cook for 5 minutes.
4. Add lamb, salt and its marinade, stir, bring to a boil, cover the pot and cook at High for 45 minutes.
5. Release the pressure, take meat and put on a cutting board and leave aside to cool down for a few minutes.
6. Shred meat and put in a bowl.
7. Add cooking sauce to it and stir.
8. Divide meat on tortillas, sprinkle cilantro on each, add beans, squeeze lime juice, roll and serve.

Bon Appétit!

164. Yummy Goat Mix

Perp time: 10 minutes **Cooking time:** 60 minutes **Servings:** 4

Nutrition Facts:
- Calories: 340
- Fat (In grams): 3.8
- Fiber (In grams): 4.1
- Carbs (In grams): 30
- Protein (In grams): 12.6

Ingredients:
- 17 ounces goat meat, cubed
- 1 carrot, chopped
- 1 celery rib, chopped
- 4 ounces tomato paste
- 1 yellow onion, chopped
- 3 garlic cloves, crushed
- A dash of sherry wine
- Half-cup water
- Salt and black pepper to the taste
- One-cup chicken stock
- 2 tablespoons extra virgin olive oil
- One-tablespoon cumin seeds, ground
- A pinch of rosemary, dried
- 2 roasted tomatoes, chopped

Instructions:
1. Set your instant pot on Sauté mode, add One-tablespoon oil and heat it up.
2. Add goat meat, salt and pepper and brown for a few minutes on each side.
3. Add cumin seeds, rosemary, stir, cook for 2 minutes and transfer to a bowl.
4. Add the rest of the oil to the pot and heat it up.
5. Add onion, garlic, salt and pepper, stir and cook for 1 minute.
6. Add carrot and celery, stir and cook 2 minutes.
7. Add sherry wine, stock, water, goat meat, tomato paste, more salt and pepper, stir, cover and cook on High for 40 minutes.
8. Release the pressure naturally, uncover the pot, add tomatoes, stir, divide among plates and serve.

Bon Appétit!

165. Tasty Lamb Curry

Perp time: 10 minutes **Cooking time:** 25 minutes **Servings:** 6

Nutrition Facts:
- Calories: 378
- Fat (In grams): 8
- Fiber (In grams): 3
- Carbs (In grams): 18
- Protein (In grams): 22

Ingredients:
- 1 ½ pounds lamb shoulder, cut into medium chunks
- 2 ounces coconut milk
- 3 ounces dry white wine
- 3 tablespoons pure cream
- 3 tablespoons curry powder
- 2 tablespoons vegetable oil
- 3 tablespoons water
- 1 yellow onion, chopped
- One-tablespoon parsley, chopped
- Salt and black pepper to the taste

Instructions:
1. In a bowl, mix half of the curry powder with salt, pepper and coconut milk and stir well.
2. Set your instant pot on Sauté mode, add oil and heat it up.
3. Add onion, stir and cook for 4 minutes.
4. Add the rest of the curry powder, stir and cook for 1 minute.
5. Add lamb pieces, brown them for 3 minutes and mix with water, salt, pepper and wine.
6. Stir, cover the pot and cook at High for 20 minutes.
7. Release the pressure quickly, set the pot to Simmer mode, add coconut milk mix, stir and boil for 5 minutes.
8. Divide among plates, sprinkle parsley on top and serve.

Bon Appétit!

166. POTATOES AND GOAT

Perp time: 10 minutes   **Cooking time:** 50 minutes   **Servings:** 5

Nutrition Facts:
- Calories: 300
- Fat (In grams): 17
- Fiber (In grams): 1
- Carbs (In grams): 5
- Protein (In grams): 30

Ingredients:
- 2 ½ pounds goat meat, cut into small cubes
- Salt and black pepper to the taste
- 5 tablespoons vegetable oil
- 3 teaspoons turmeric powder
- 3 potatoes, cut into halves
- One-teaspoon Sugar
- 4 cloves
- 3 cardamom pods
- 3 onions, chopped
- 2-inch cinnamon stick
- A small piece of ginger, grated
- 2 tomatoes, chopped
- 4 garlic cloves, minced
- 2 green chilies, chopped
- 3/4 teaspoon chili powder
- 2 ½-cups water
- One-teaspoon coriander, chopped

Instructions:
1. Put goat cubes in a bowl, add salt, pepper and turmeric, toss to coat and leave aside for 10 minutes.
2. Set your instant pot on Sauté mode, add the oil and half of the Sugar, stir and heat up.
3. Add potatoes, fry them a bit and transfer to a bowl.
4. Add cloves, cinnamon stick and cardamom to pot and stir.
5. Also add ginger, onion, chilies and garlic, stir and cook for 3 minutes.
6. Add tomatoes and chili powder, stir and cook for 5 minutes.
7. Add meat, stir and cook for 10 minutes.
8. Add 2 cups water, stir, cover and cook at High for 15 minutes.
9. Release the pressure, uncover the pot, add more salt and pepper, the rest of the Sugar, potatoes and Half-cup water, cover and cook at High for 5 minutes.

10. Release the pressure again, uncover the pot, divide among plates, sprinkle coriander on top and serve.

Bon Appétit!

167. BROCCOLI AND BEEF

Perp time: 10 minutes   **Cooking time:** 10 minutes   **Servings:** 4

Nutrition Facts:
- Calories: 338
- Fat (In grams): 18
- Fiber (In grams): 5
- Carbs (In grams): 50
- Protein : 20 g

Ingredients:
- 3 pounds chuck roast, cut into thin strips
- One-tablespoon peanut oil
- 1 yellow onion, chopped
- Half-cup beef stock
- 1 pound broccoli florets
- 2 teaspoons toasted sesame oil
- 2 tablespoons potato starch

For the marinade:
- Half-cup soy sauce
- Half-cup black soy sauce
- One-tablespoon sesame oil
- 2 tablespoons fish sauce
- 5 garlic cloves, minced
- 3 red peppers, dried and crushed
- Half-teaspoon Chinese five spice
- White rice, already cooked for servings
- Toasted sesame seeds for serving

Instructions:
1. In a bowl, mix black soy sauce with soy sauce, fish sauce, One-tablespoon sesame oil, 5 garlic cloves, five spice and crushed red peppers and stir well.
2. Add beef strips, toss to coat and leave aside for 10 minutes.
3. Set your instant pot on Sauté mode, add peanut oil and heat it up.
4. Add onions, stir and cook for 4 minutes.
5. Add beef and marinade, stir and cook for 2 minutes.
6. Add stock, stir, cover the pot and cook at High for 5 minutes.
7. Release the pressure naturally for 10 minutes, uncover the pot, add cornstarch after you've mixed it with 1/4 cup liquid from the pot, add broccoli to the steamer basket, cover pot again and cook for 3 minutes at High.
8. Release the pressure again, uncover the pot, divide beef into bowls on top of rice, add broccoli on the side, drizzle toasted sesame oil, sprinkle sesame seeds and serve.

Bon Appétit!

168. MOROCCAN STYLE LAMB

Perp time: 10 minutes   **Cooking time:** 25 minutes   **Servings:** 8

Nutrition Facts:
- Calories: 434
- Fat (In grams): 21
- Fiber (In grams): 4
- Carbs (In grams): 41
- Protein (In grams): 20
- Sugar (In grams): 9

Ingredients:
- 2 ½ pounds lamb shoulder, chopped
- 3 tablespoons honey
- 3 ounces almonds, peeled and chopped
- 9 ounces prunes, pitted
- 8 ounces vegetable stock
- 2 yellow onions, chopped
- 2 garlic cloves, minced
- 1 bay leaf
- Salt and black pepper to the tastes
- 1 cinnamon stick
- One-teaspoon cumin powder
- One-teaspoon turmeric powder
- One-teaspoon ginger powder
- One-teaspoon cinnamon powder
- Sesame seeds for servings
- 3 tablespoons extra virgin olive oil

Instructions:
1. In a bowl, mix the cinnamon powder with ginger, cumin, turmeric, garlic and 2 tablespoons olive oil and stir well.
2. Add meat and toss to coat.
3. Put prunes in a bowl, cover them with hot water and leave aside.
4. Set your instant pot on Sauté mode, add the rest of the oil and heat it up.
5. Add onions, stir, cook for 3 minutes, transfer to a bowl and leave aside.
6. Add meat to your pot and brown it for 10 minutes.
7. Add stock, cinnamon stick, bay leaf and return onions, stir, cover the pot and cook at High for 25 minutes.
8. Release the pressure naturally, uncover the pot, add drained prunes, salt, pepper, honey and stir.
9. Set the pot on Simmer mode, cook everything for 5 minutes and discard bay leaf and cinnamon stick.
10. Divide among plates and serve with almonds and sesame seeds on top.

Bon Appétit!

169. DELICIOUS SHORT RIBS

Perp time: 15 minutes **Cooking time:** 60 minutes **Servings:** 6

Nutrition Facts:
- Calories: 240
- Fat (In grams): 8.1
- Fiber (In grams): 1
- Carbs (In grams): 11
- Protein (In grams): 24

Ingredients:
- 4 pounds short ribs, cut into small pieces
- One-teaspoon vegetable oil
- 1 yellow onion, chopped
- Salt and black pepper to the taste
- 1/4 cup tomato paste
- One-cup dark beer
- One-cup chicken stock
- 1 bay leaf
- 6 thyme springs
- 1 Portobello mushroom, dried

Instructions:
1. Set your instant pot on Sauté mode, add the oil and heat it up.
2. Add ribs, salt, and pepper, brown for 3 minutes on each side and transfer to a bowl.

3. Add tomato paste and onion to the pot, stir and cook for 5 minutes.
4. Add stock and beer, stir and cook 30 seconds more.
5. Add mushroom, bay leaves, thyme, and ribs, stir, cover the pot and cook at High for 35 minutes.
6. Release the pressure naturally for 15 minutes, uncover the pot, discard thyme, mushroom and bay leaves and strain sauce.
7. Divide ribs among plates and serve with beer sauce drizzled all over.

Bon Appétit!

170. TASTY MEATLOAF

Perp time: 10 minutes **Cooking time:** 40 minutes **Servings:** 6

Nutrition Facts:
- Calories: 300
- Fat (In grams): 18
- Fiber (In grams): 1
- Carbs (In grams): 10
- Protein: 24 g

Ingredients:
- 1/3 cup milk
- Half-cup panko breadcrumbs
- 1 yellow onion, grated
- Salt and black pepper to the taste
- 2 eggs, whisked
- 2 pounds ground meat
- 2 cups water
- 1/4 cup ketchup

Instructions:
1. In a bowl, mix breadcrumbs with milk, stir and leave aside for 5 minutes.
2. Add onion, salt, pepper and eggs and stir.
3. Add ground meat and stir very well again.
4. Place this on a greased tin foil and shape a loaf.
5. Add ketchup on top.
6. Put the water in your instant pot, arrange meatloaf in the steamer basket of the pot, cover and cook at High for 35 minutes.
7. Release the pressure for 10 minutes, uncover, take meatloaf out, leave it to cool down for 5 minutes, slices and serve it.

Bon Appétit!

171. RED BEANS AND SAUSAGE DISH

Perp time: 15 minutes **Cooking time:** 30 minutes **Servings:** 8

Nutrition Facts:
- Calories: 248
- Fat (In grams): 5
- Fiber (In grams): 12.3
- Carbs (In grams): 40
- Protein (In grams): 15.4

Ingredients:

- 1 pound smoked sausage, sliced
- 1 pound red beans, dried, soaked overnight and drained
- 1 bay leaf
- 2 tablespoons Cajun seasoning
- 1 celery stalk, chopped
- Salt and black pepper to the taste
- ½ green bell pepper, chopped
- One-teaspoon parsley, dried
- 5 cups water
- 1/4 teaspoon cumin, ground
- 1 garlic clove, chopped
- 1 small yellow onion, chopped

Instructions:
1. In your instant pot, mix beans with sausage, bay leaf, Cajun seasoning, celery, salt, pepper, bell pepper, parsley, cumin, garlic, onion and water, stir, cover and cook at High for 30 minutes.
2. Release the pressure, uncover the pot, divide mix into bowls and serve.

Bon Appétit!

---

172. DELICIOUS RIBS & COLESLAW

Perp time: 15 minutes **Cooking time:** 35 minutes **Servings:** 4

Nutrition Facts:
- Calories: 360
- Fat (In grams): 15
- Fiber (In grams): 1
- Carbs (In grams): 4
- Sugar (In grams): 3
- Protein : 17 g

Ingredients:
- 2 ½ pounds baby back ribs
- Salt and black pepper to the taste
- One-teaspoon onion powder
- Half-teaspoon paprika
- Half-teaspoon dry mustard
- Half-teaspoon chili powder
- Half-teaspoon garlic powder

For the sauce:
- 1 small yellow onion, chopped
- 2 bacon slices, chopped
- 6 ounces tomato paste
- 3/4 cup tomato sauce
- 2 garlic cloves, minced
- Salt and black pepper to the taste
- 1/4 cup coconut aminos
- Half-teaspoon smoked paprika
- A pinch of cayenne pepper
- 1/3 cup apple cider vinegar
- One-tablespoon cooking Fat
- Half-cup apple juice

For the coleslaw:
- One-cup red cabbage, shredded
- 3 cups green cabbage, shredded
- One-cup raisins
- 2 ½-teaspoons caraway seeds
- 1/4 cup apple cider vinegar
- 3/4 cup mayonnaise
- Salt and black pepper to the taste
- 2 carrots, grated
- 2 green onions,, chopped

Instructions:
1. In a salad bowl, mix red and green cabbage with green onions, carrots, and raisins.
2. In a small bowl, mix caraway seeds with mayo, salt, pepper and 1/4 cup vinegar and stir well.
3. Pour this over salad, toss to coat and keep in the fridge until you serve it.

4. In a bowl, mix onion powder with paprika, salt, pepper, dry mustard, garlic powder, chili powder.
5. Rub ribs with this mix and place them in your instant pot, add some water, cover the pot and cook at High for 15 minutes.
6. Meanwhile, heat up a pan with cooking Fat over medium heat, add bacon and cook for 2 minutes.
7. Add onion and garlic, stir and cook for 5 minutes.
8. Add tomato sauce and tomato paste, apple juice, coconut aminos, 1/3 cup vinegar, smoked paprika, a pinch of cayenne pepper, salt and pepper to the taste, stir and cook for 10 minutes.
9. Release the pressure from the pot, uncover and transfer ribs to a plate.
10. Add some of the sauce on the bottom of the pot, add a layer of ribs, then a layer of sauce, then another layer of ribs and so on.
11. 1Cover the pot again and cook at High for 10 minutes.
12. 1Release the pressure again, divide ribs and sauce among plates and serve with the coleslaw you've made at the beginning.

Bon Appétit!

---

173. ASIAN STYLE SHORT RIBS DISH

Perp time: 10 minutes **Cooking time:** 60 minutes **Servings:** 4

Nutrition Facts:
- Calories: 300
- Fat (In grams): 11
- Fiber (In grams): 1
- Carbs (In grams): 5
- Protein (In grams): 10

Ingredients:
- 2 green onions, chopped
- One-teaspoon vegetable oil
- 3 garlic cloves, minced
- 3 ginger slices
- 4 pounds short ribs
- Half-cup water
- Half-cup soy sauce
- 1/4 cup rice wine
- 1/4 cup pear juice
- 2 teaspoons sesame oil

Instructions:
1. Set your instant pot on Sauté mode, add the oil and heat it up.
2. Add green onions, ginger and garlic, stir and cook for 1 minute.
3. Add ribs, water, wine, soy sauce, sesame oil and pear juice, stir and cook for 2-3 minutes.
4. Cover the pot and cook at High for 45 minutes.
5. Release the pressure naturally for 15 minutes, uncover the pot and transfer the ribs to a plate.
6. Strain liquid from the pot, divide ribs among plates and drizzle the sauce all over.

Bon Appétit!

---

174. TOMATO SAUCE AND MEATBALLS

Perp time: 10 minutes **Cooking time:** 10 minutes **Servings:** 6

Nutrition Facts:
- Calories: 150
- Fat (In grams): 3

- Fiber (In grams): 1
- Carbs (In grams): 4
- Protein (In grams): 8

Ingredients:
- 1 onion, chopped
- 1/3 cup parmesan, grated
- Half-cup bread crumbs
- Half-teaspoon oregano, dried
- Salt and black pepper to the taste
- Half-cup milk
- 1 pound ground meat
- One-tablespoon extra virgin olive oil
- 1 egg, whisked
- 1 carrot, chopped
- ½ celery stalk, chopped
- 2 and 3/4 cups tomato puree
- 2 cups water

Instructions:
1. In a bowl, mix bread crumbs with cheese, half of the onion, oregano, salt and pepper and stir.
2. Add milk and meat and stir well.
3. Add the egg and stir well again.
4. Set your instant pot on Sauté mode, add oil and heat it up.
5. Add onion, stir and cook for 3 minutes.
6. Add celery and carrot, tomato puree, water and salt and stir again.
7. Shape meatballs and add them to the pot, toss them to coat, cover and cook at High for 5 minutes.
8. Release the pressure naturally for 10 minutes and serve with your favorite spaghetti.

Bon Appétit!

175. MOUTHWATERING MEATLOAF

Perp time: 10 minutes   **Cooking time:** 25 minutes   **Servings:** 8

Nutrition Facts:
- Calories: 227
- Fat (In grams): 14.5
- Fiber (In grams): 1
- Carbs (In grams): 8.8
- Protein (In grams): 15

Ingredients:
- 2 pounds ground beef
- 3 bread slices
- Half-cup milk
- 3/4 cup parmesan, grated
- Salt and black pepper to the taste
- 2 tablespoons parsley, dried
- 2 cups water
- 8 bacon slices
- 3 eggs, whisked
- Half-cup BBQ sauce

Instructions:
1. In a bowl, mix bread slices with milk and leave aside for 5 minutes.
2. Add meat, cheese, salt, pepper, eggs and parsley and stir well.
3. Shape a loaf, place on a tin foil, arrange bacon slices on top, tuck them underneath and spread half of the BBQ sauce all over.
4. Put 2 cups water in the instant pot, place meatloaf in the steamer basket of the pot, cover and cook on High for 20 minutes.

5. Release the pressure, uncover the pot, transfer meat loaf to a pan and spread the rest of the BBQ sauce over it.
6. Introduce in preheated broiler for 5 minutes, transfer to a platter and slice.

Bon Appétit!

FISH AND SEAFOOD RECIPES

176. Yummy Salmon Dish

Perp time: 10 minutes **Cooking time:** 15 minutes **Servings:** 4

Nutrition Facts:
- Calories: 180
- Fat (In grams): 5
- Fiber (In grams): 1
- Carbs (In grams): 0
- Protein: 31

Ingredients:
- 4 salmon fillets
- 1 lemon, sliced
- 1 white onion, chopped
- 3 tomatoes, sliced
- 4 thyme springs
- 4 parsley springs
- 3 tablespoons extra virgin olive oil
- Salt and black pepper to the taste
- 2 cups water

Instructions:
1. Drizzle the oil on a parchment paper.
2. Add a layer of tomatoes, salt and pepper.
3. Drizzle some oil again, add fish and season them with salt and pepper.
4. Drizzle some more oil, add thyme and parsley springs, onions, lemon slices, salt and pepper.
5. Fold and wrap packet, place in the steamer basket of your instant pot.
6. Add 2 cups water to the pot, cover and cook on Low for 15 minutes.
7. Release the pressure, uncover the pot, open packet, divide fish mix among plates and serve.

Bon Appétit!

177. Tasty Steamed Fish

Perp time: 10 minutes **Cooking time:** 10 minutes **Servings:** 4

Nutrition Facts:
- Calories: 157
- Fat (In grams): 3.2
- Fiber (In grams): 0
- Carbs (In grams): 0
- Protein: 29

Ingredients:
- 4 white fish fillets
- One-cup olives, pitted and chopped
- 1 pound cherry tomatoes, cut into halves
- A pinch of thyme, dried
- 1 garlic clove, minced
- A drizzle of olive oil
- Salt and black pepper to the taste
- One-cup water

Instructions:
1. Put the water in your instant pot.
2. Put fish fillets in the steamer basket of the pot.
3. Add tomatoes and olives on top.
4. Also add garlic, thyme, oil, salt and pepper.
5. Cover the pot and cook on Low for 10 minutes.

6. Release the pressure, uncover the pot, divide fish, olives and tomatoes mix among plates and serve.

Bon Appétit!

178. APPETIZING FISH WITH ORANGE SAUCE

Perp time: 10 minutes **Cooking time:** 7 minutes **Servings:** 4

Nutrition Facts:
- Calories: 170
- Fat (In grams): 2
- Fiber (In grams): 0.4
- Carbs (In grams): 10
- Protein : 23 g

Ingredients:
- 4 white fish fillets
- 4 spring onions, chopped
- A drizzle of extra virgin olive oil
- A small piece of ginger, chopped
- Salt and black pepper to the taste
- Juice and zest from 1 orange
- One-cup fish stock

Instructions:
1. Pat dry fish fillets, season with salt, pepper and rub them with the olive oil.
2. Put stock, ginger, orange juice, orange zest and onions in your instant pot.
3. Put fish fillets in the steamer basket, cover the pot and cook at High for 7 minutes.
4. Release the pressure, divide fish among plates and drizzle the orange sauce on top.

Bon Appétit!

179. DELICIOUS FISH CURRY

Perp time: 10 minutes **Cooking time:** 15 minutes **Servings:** 6

Nutrition Facts:
- Calories: 230
- Fat (In grams): 10
- Fiber (In grams): 3
- Carbs (In grams): 12
- Protein: 23

Ingredients:
- 6 fish fillets, cut into medium pieces
- 1 tomato, chopped
- 14 ounces coconut milk
- 2 onions, sliced
- 2 capsicums, cut into strips
- 2 garlic cloves, minced
- 6 curry leaves
- One-tablespoons coriander, ground
- One-tablespoon ginger, finely grated
- Half-teaspoon turmeric, ground
- 2 teaspoons cumin, ground
- Salt and black pepper to the taste
- Half-teaspoon fenugreek, ground
- One-teaspoon hot pepper flakes
- 2 tablespoons lemon juice

Instructions:
1. Set your instant pot on Sauté mode, add oil and curry leaves and fry for 1 minute.
2. Add ginger, onion and garlic, stir and cook for 2 minutes.
3. Add coriander, turmeric, cumin, fenugreek and hot pepper, stir and cook 2 minutes.

4. Add coconut milk, tomatoes, fish and capsicum, stir, cover and cook on Low for 5 minutes.
5. Release the pressure naturally, add salt and pepper to the taste, stir and divide into bowls.
6. Serve with lemon juice on top.

Bon Appétit!

---

180. POACHED YUMMY SALMON

Perp time: 10 minutes **Cooking time:** 5 minutes **Servings:** 4

Nutrition Facts:
- Calories: 140
- Fat (In grams): 4
- Fiber (In grams): 0
- Carbs (In grams): 2
- Protein: 23

Ingredients:
- 16 ounces salmon fillet, skin on
- Zest from 1 lemon
- 4 scallions, chopped
- 3 black peppercorns
- Half-teaspoon fennel seeds
- 1 bay leaf
- One-teaspoon white wine vinegar
- 2 cups chicken stock
- Half-cup dry white wine
- 1/4 cup dill, chopped
- Salt and black pepper to the taste

Instructions:
1. Put salmon in the steamer basket of your instant pot and season with salt and pepper.
2. Add stock, scallions, lemon zest, peppercorns, fennel, vinegar, bay leaf, wine, stock and dill to your pot.
3. Cover and cook at High for 5 minutes.
4. Release the pressure, uncover pot and divide salmon among plates.
5. Set the pot on Simmer mode and cook the liquid for a few minutes more.
6. Drizzle over salmon and serve.

Bon Appétit!

---

181. SPECIAL MEDITERRANEAN FISH

Perp time: 10 minutes **Cooking time:** 10 minutes **Servings:** 4

Nutrition Facts:
- Calories: 170
- Fat (In grams): 9
- Fiber (In grams): 1
- Carbs (In grams): 4
- Protein : 23 g

Ingredients:
- 4 cod fillets
- 17 ounces tomatoes, cut into halves
- 1 garlic clove, crushed
- One-cup olives, pitted and chopped
- 2 tablespoons capers, drained and chopped
- Salt and black pepper to the taste
- One-tablespoon parsley, chopped
- One-tablespoon extra virgin olive oil

Instructions:

1. Put tomatoes on the bottom of a heat proof bowl.
2. Add parsley, salt and pepper and toss to coat.
3. Place fish fillets on top, add olive oil, salt, pepper, garlic, olives and capers.
4. Place the bowl in the steamer basket of the pot, cover and cook at High for 5 minutes.
5. Release the pressure naturally, divide among plates and serve.

Bon Appétit!

---

182. TASTY VEGGIES AND SALMON

Perp time: 10 minutes **Cooking time:** 10 minutes **Servings:** 2

Nutrition Facts:
- Calories: 170
- Fat (In grams): 4.5
- Fiber (In grams): 3.7
- Carbs (In grams): 13
- Protein: 17

Ingredients:
- 2 salmon fillets, skin on
- 1 bay leaf
- One-cup water
- 1 cinnamon stick
- 3 cloves
- One-tablespoon canola oil
- One-cup baby carrots
- 2 cups broccoli florets
- Salt and black pepper to the taste
- Lime wedges for serving

Instructions:
1. Put the water in your instant pot.
2. Add bay leaf, cinnamon stick and cloves.
3. Place salmon fillets in the steamer basket of your pot after you've brushed them with canola oil.
4. Season with salt and pepper, add broccoli and carrots, cover the pot and cook at High for 6 minutes.
5. Release the pressure for 4 minutes, uncover the pot, divide salmon and veggies among plates.
6. Drizzle the sauce from the pot after you've discarded cinnamon, cloves and bay leaf and serve with lime wedges on the side.

Bon Appétit!

---

183. SPICY TASTY SALMON

Perp time: 10 minutes **Cooking time:** 5 minutes **Servings:** 4

Nutrition Facts:
- Calories: 120
- Fat (In grams): 2
- Fiber (In grams): 0.5
- Carbs (In grams): 13
- Protein: 5

Ingredients:
- 4 salmon fillets
- 2 tablespoons assorted chili pepper
- Juice of 1 lemon
- 1 lemon, sliced
- One-cup water
- Salt and black pepper to the taste

Instructions:
1. Place salmon fillets in the steamer basket of your pot, add salt, pepper, lemon juice, lemon slices and chili pepper.
2. Add One-cup water to the pot, cover and cook at High for 5 minutes.
3. Release the pressure, divide salmon and lemon slices among plates and serve.

Bon Appétit!

---

184. SIMPLE SALMON BURGER

Perp time: 10 minutes   **Cooking time:** 10 minutes   **Servings:** 4

Nutrition Facts:
- Calories: 170
- Fat (In grams): 9
- Fiber (In grams): 0
- Carbs (In grams): 1
- Protein : 22 g

Ingredients:
- One-teaspoon extra virgin olive oil
- Half-cup panko
- 1 pound salmon meat, minced
- 2 tablespoons lemon zest
- Salt and black pepper to the taste
- Mustard for serving
- Tomatoes slices for serving
- Arugula leaves for serving

Instructions:
1. Put salmon in your food processor and blend it.
2. Transfer to a bowl, add panko, salt, pepper and lemon zest and stir well.
3. Shape 4 patties and place them on a working surface.
4. Set your instant pot on Sauté mode, add oil and heat it up.
5. Add patties, cook for 3 minutes on each side and divide them on buns.
6. Serve with tomatoes, arugula and mustard.

Bon Appétit!

---

185. YUMMY FISH PUDDING

Perp time: 10 minutes   **Cooking time:** 20 minutes   **Servings:** 4

Nutrition Facts:
- Calories: 200
- Fat (In grams): 3
- Fiber (In grams): 1
- Carbs (In grams): 8
- Protein : 9 g

Ingredients:
- 1 pound cod fillets, cut into medium pieces
- 2 tablespoons parsley, chopped
- 4 ounces bread crumbs
- 2 teaspoons lemon juice
- 2 eggs, whisked
- 2 ounces butter
- ½ pint milk
- ½ pint shrimp sauce
- Salt and black pepper to the taste
- ½ pint water

Instructions:
1. In a bowl, mix fish with crumbs, lemon juice, parsley, salt and pepper and stir.
2. Heat up a pan with the butter over medium high heat.

3. Put milk in a pot and bring to a boil over medium high heat.
4. Pour butter and milk over the egg and stir well.
5. Add this to fish and leave aside for 3 minutes.
6. Pour everything into a greased pudding dish and place in the steamer basket of your pot.
7. Add ½ pint water to the pot, cover and cook at High for 15 minutes.
8. Release the pressure, uncover, divide among plates and serve with shrimp sauce.

Bon Appétit!

---

186. RASPBERRY SAUCE AND SALMON

Perp time: 2 hours   **Cooking time:** 5 minutes   **Servings:** 6

Nutrition Facts:
- Calories: 670
- Fat (In grams): 46
- Fiber (In grams): 1
- Carbs (In grams): 18
- Protein : 81 g

Ingredients:
- 6 salmon steaks
- 2 tablespoons extra virgin olive oil
- 4 leeks, sliced
- 2 garlic cloves, minced
- 2 tablespoons parsley, chopped
- One-cup clam juice
- 2 tablespoons lemon juice
- Salt and white pepper to the taste
- One-teaspoon sherry
- 1/3 cup dill, finely chopped
- Raspberries for serving

For the raspberry vinegar:
- 2 pints red raspberries
- 1-pint cider vinegar

Instructions:
1. Mix red raspberries with vinegar and stir well.
2. Add salmon steaks and leave aside in the fridge for 2 hours.
3. Set your instant pot on Sauté mode, add oil and heat it up.
4. Add parsley, leeks and garlic, stir and cook for 2 minutes.
5. Add clam and lemon juice, sherry, salt, pepper and dill and stir.
6. Add salmon steaks, cover and cook at High for 3 minutes.
7. Release pressure, uncover pot, divide salmon among plates and serve with leeks and fresh raspberries.

Bon Appétit!

187. Peas And Cod

Perp time: 15 minutes **Cooking time:** 5 **Servings:** 4

Nutrition Facts:
- Calories: 200
- Fat (In grams): 2
- Fiber (In grams): 2
- Carbs (In grams): 10
- Protein : 20 g

Ingredients:
- 16 ounces cod fillets
- One-tablespoon parsley, chopped
- 10 ounces peas
- 9 ounces wine
- Half-teaspoon oregano, dried
- Half-teaspoon paprika
- 2 garlic cloves, chopped
- Salt and pepper to the taste

Instructions:
1. In your food processor mix garlic with parsley, oregano and paprika and blend well.
2. Add wine, blend again and leave aside for now.
3. Place fish fillets in the steamer basket of your instant pot, add salt and pepper, cover and cook at High for 2 minutes.
4. Release the pressure and divide fish among plates.
5. Add peas to the steamer basket, cover the pot again and cook at High for 2 minutes.
6. Release the pressure again and arrange peas next to fish fillets.
7. Serve with herbs dressing on top.

Bon Appétit!

188. Crispy Tasty Salmon Fillet

Perp time: 5 minutes **Cooking time:** 10 minutes **Servings:** 2

Nutrition Facts:
- Calories: 230
- Fat (In grams): 12
- Fiber (In grams): 1
- Carbs (In grams): 0
- Protein : 29 g

Ingredients:
- 2 salmon fillets, frozen
- One-cup water
- Salt and black pepper to the taste
- 2 tablespoons extra virgin olive oil

Instructions:
1. Put the water in your instant pot.
2. Place salmon in the steamer basket, cover and cook on Low for 3 minutes.
3. Release pressure quick, transfer salmon to paper towels and pat dry them.
4. Heat up a pan with the oil over medium high heat, add salmon fillets skin side down, season with salt and pepper to the taste and cook for 2 minutes.
5. Divide among plates and serve with your favorite salad on the side.

Bon Appétit!

189. Delicious Rice And Salmon

Perp time: 5 minutes **Cooking time:** 5 minutes **Servings:** 2

Nutrition Facts:
- Calories: 300
- Fat (In grams): 8
- Fiber (In grams): 0.5
- Carbs (In grams): 30
- Protein : 25 g

Ingredients:
- 2 wild salmon fillets, frozen
- Salt and black pepper to the taste
- Half-cup jasmine rice
- One-cup chicken stock
- 1/4 cup vegetable soup mix, dried
- One-tablespoon butter
- A pinch of saffron

Instructions:
1. In your instant pot, mix stock with rice, soup mix, butter and saffron and stir.
2. Season salmon with salt and pepper, place in the steamer basket of your pot, cover and cook on High for 5 minutes.
3. Release the pressure, divide salmon among plates, add rice mix on the side and serve.

Bon Appétit!

190. Best Fish Dish

Perp time: 10 minutes **Cooking time:** 25 minutes **Servings:** 6

Nutrition Facts:
- Calories: 194
- Fat (In grams): 4.4
- Fiber (In grams): 2
- Carbs (In grams): 21
- Protein :17 g

Ingredients:
- 17 ounces white fish, cut into medium chunks
- 1 yellow onion, chopped
- 13 ounces potatoes, peeled and cut into chunks
- 13 ounces milk
- Salt and black pepper to the taste
- 14 ounces chicken stock
- 14 ounces water
- 14 ounces half and half

Instructions:
1. In your instant pot mix fish with onion, potatoes, water, milk and stock.
2. Cover and cook at High for 10 minutes.
3. Release the pressure, uncover and set the pot on Simmer mode.
4. Add salt, pepper, half and half, stir and cook for 10 minutes.
5. Divide among bowls and serve.

Bon Appétit!

191. Tasty Cheesy Tuna

Perp time: 5 minutes **Cooking time:** 5 minutes **Servings:** 4

Nutrition Facts:
- Calories: 270
- Fat (In grams): 12
- Fiber (In grams): 0.5
- Carbs (In grams): 20
- Protein: 15 g

Ingredients:
- 14 ounces canned tuna, drained
- 16 ounces egg noodles
- 28 ounces cream of mushroom
- One-cup peas, frozen
- 3 cups water
- 4 ounces cheddar cheese, grated
- 1/4 cup breadcrumbs

Instructions:
1. Add pasta and water to your instant pot.
2. Also add tuna, peas and cream, stir, cover, cook at High for 4 minutes and release pressure.
3. Add cheese and stir.
4. Transfer everything to a baking dish, spread breadcrumbs all over and introduce in preheated broiler for 3 minutes.
5. Divide among plates and serve.

Bon Appétit!

192. Special Jambalaya

Perp time: 10 minutes **Cooking time:** 4 minutes **Servings:** 8

Nutrition Facts:
- Calories: 250
- Fat (In grams): 13
- Fiber (In grams): 1
- Carbs (In grams): 22
- Protein : 27 g

Ingredients:
- 1 pound chicken breast, chopped
- 1 pound shrimp, peeled and deveined
- 2 tablespoons extra virgin olive oil
- 1 pound sausage, already cooked and chopped
- 2 cups onions, chopped
- 1 ½ cups rice
- 2 tablespoons garlic, chopped
- 2 cups green, yellow and red bell peppers, chopped
- 3 ½-cups chicken stock
- One-tablespoon Creole seasoning
- One-tablespoon Worcestershire sauce
- One-cup tomatoes, crushed

Instructions:
1. Set your instant pot on Sauté mode, add chicken and Creole seasoning, stir, brown on all sides and transfer to a bowl.
2. Add oil and heat it up.
3. Add peppers, onions and garlic, stir and cook for 2 minutes.
4. Add rice, stir and cook for 2 minutes.
5. Add tomato puree, stock, Worcestershire sauce and return chicken, stir, cover and cook for 10 minutes.

6. Release the pressure, add sausage and shrimp, stir, cover and cook at High for 2 minutes.
7. Release the pressure, uncover, divide among plates and serve.

Bon Appétit!

193. NOODLE AND TUNA DISH

Perp time: 10 minutes **Cooking time:** 15 minutes **Servings:** 4

Nutrition Facts:
- Calories: 300
- Fat (In grams): 4
- Fiber (In grams): 9
- Carbs (In grams): 23
- Protein: 29

Ingredients:
- 8 ounces egg noodles
- Half-cup red onion, chopped
- One-tablespoon extra virgin olive oil
- 1 and 1/4 cups water
- 14 ounces canned tomatoes, chopped and mixed with oregano, basil and garlic
- Salt and black pepper to the taste
- 14 ounces canned tuna, drained
- 8 ounces artichoke hearts, drained and chopped
- One-tablespoon parsley, chopped
- Crumbled feta cheese

Instructions:
1. Set your instant pot on Sauté mode, add oil and heat it up.
2. Add onion, stir and cook for 2 minutes.
3. Add tomatoes, noodles, salt, pepper and water, set the pot on Simmer and cook for 10 minutes.
4. Add tuna and artichokes, stir, cover and cook at High for 5 minutes.
5. Release pressure, divide tuna and noodles among plates, sprinkle cheese and parsley on top and serve.

Bon Appétit!

194. HOT ROASTED MACKEREL DISH

Perp time: 10 minutes **Cooking time:** 6 minutes **Servings:** 4

Nutrition Facts:
- Calories: 189
- Fat (In grams): 11
- Fiber (In grams): 0
- Carbs (In grams): 1
- Protein: 20 g

Ingredients:
- 18 ounces mackerel, cut into pieces
- 3 garlic cloves, minced
- 8 shallots, chopped
- One-teaspoon dried shrimp powder
- One-teaspoon turmeric powder
- One-tablespoon chili paste
- 2 lemongrass sticks, cut into halves
- 1 small piece of ginger, chopped
- 6 stalks laska leaves
- 3 ½ ounces water
- 5 tablespoons vegetable oil
- 1 and 1/3 tablespoons tamarind paste mixed with 3 ½ ounces water
- Salt to the taste
- One-tablespoon Sugar

Instructions:
1. In your blender, mix garlic with shallots, chili paste, turmeric powder and shrimp powder and blend well.
2. Set your instant pot on Sauté mode, add oil and heat it up.
3. Add fish pieces; spices paste, ginger, lemongrass and laska leaves and cook for 1 minute.
4. Add tamarind mix, water, salt and Sugar, stir, cover and cook at High for 5 minutes.
5. Release the pressure, uncover the pot, divide among plates and serve.

Bon Appétit!

195. POT STEAMED MUSSELS DISH

Perp time: 10 minutes **Cooking time:** 5 minutes **Servings:** 4

Nutrition Facts:
- Calories: 50
- Fat (In grams): 1
- Fiber (In grams): 1
- Carbs (In grams): 0.3
- Protein: 1.1 g

Ingredients:
- 2 pounds mussels, cleaned and scrubbed
- 1 radicchio, cut into thin strips
- 1 white onion, chopped
- 1 pound baby spinach
- Half-cup dry white wine
- 1 garlic clove, crushed
- Half-cup water
- A drizzle of extra virgin olive oil

Instructions:
1. Arrange baby spinach and radicchio on appetizer plates.
2. Set instant pot on Sauté mode, add oil and heat it up.
3. Add garlic and onion, stir and cook for 4 minutes.
4. Add wine, stir and cook for 1 minute.
5. Place mussels in the steamer basket of the pot, cover and cook on Low for 1 minute.
6. Release the pressure and divide mussels on top of spinach and radicchio.
7. Add cooking liquid all over and serve.

196. SAUSAGE WITH MUSSELS

Perp time: 5 minutes **Cooking time:** 5 minutes **Servings:** 4

Nutrition Facts:
- Calories: 100
- Fat (In grams): 4
- Fiber (In grams): 1
- Carbs (In grams): 3
- Protein: 14 g

Ingredients:
- 2 pounds mussels, scrubbed and debearded
- 12 ounces amber beer
- One-tablespoon extra virgin olive oil
- 1 yellow onion, chopped
- 8 ounces spicy sausage
- One-tablespoon paprika

Instructions:
1. Set your instant pot on Sauté mode, add oil and heat it up.
2. Add onion, stir and cook for 2 minutes.
3. Add sausages and cook for 4 minutes.
4. Add paprika, beer and mussels, stir, cover and cook on Low for 2 minutes.
5. Release the pressure, uncover, discard unopened mussels, transfer to bowls and serve.

Bon Appétit!

197. DELICIOUS CLAMS

Perp time: 10 minutes **Cooking time:** 5 minutes **Servings:** 4

Nutrition Facts:
- Calories: 80
- Fat (In grams): 5
- Fiber (In grams): 0
- Carbs (In grams): 6
- Protein: 3 g

Ingredients:
- 24 clams, shucked
- 3 garlic cloves, minced
- 4 tablespoons butter
- 1/4 cup parsley, chopped
- 1/4 cup parmesan cheese, grated
- One-teaspoon oregano, dried
- One-cup breadcrumbs
- 2 cups water
- Lemon wedges

Instructions:
1. In a bowl, mix breadcrumbs with parmesan, oregano, parsley, butter and garlic and stir.
2. Place One-tablespoon of this mix in exposed clams.
3. Place the clams in the steamer basket of the pot, add 2 cups water to the pot, cover and cook at High for 4 minutes.
4. Release the pressure, uncover, divide among plates and serve with lemon wedges.

Bon Appétit!

198. YUMMY MUSSELS AND SPICY SAUCE

Perp time: 10 minutes **Cooking time:** 4 minutes **Servings:** 4

Nutrition Facts:
- Calories: 60
- Fat (In grams): 0.2
- Fiber (In grams): 0.2
- Carbs (In grams): 1
- Protein: 1.3 g

Ingredients:
- 2 pounds mussels, scrubbed and debearded
- 2 tablespoons extra virgin olive oil
- 1 yellow onion, chopped
- Half-teaspoon red pepper flakes
- 14 ounces tomatoes, chopped
- 2 teaspoons garlic, minced
- Half-cup chicken stock
- 2 teaspoons oregano, dried

Instructions:
1. Set your instant pot on Sauté mode, add oil and heat it up.

2. Add onions, stir and cook for 3 minutes.
3. Add pepper flakes and garlic, stir and cook for 1 minute.
4. Add stock, oregano and tomatoes and stir well.
5. Add mussels, stir, cover and cook on Low for 2 minutes.
6. Release the pressure quickly, discard unopened mussels, divide among bowls and serve.

Bon Appétit!

199. TASTY MUSSELS

Perp time: 10 minutes **Cooking time:** 5 minutes **Servings:** 3

Nutrition Facts:
- Calories: 50
- Fat (In grams): 0.2
- Fiber (In grams): 0.2
- Carbs (In grams): 1
- Protein: 1.5 g

Ingredients:
- 28 ounces canned tomatoes, crushed
- Half-cup white onion, chopped
- 2 jalapeno peppers, chopped
- 1/4 cup dry white wine
- 1/4 cup extra virgin olive oil
- 1/4 cup balsamic vinegar
- 2 pounds mussels, cleaned and scrubbed
- 2 tablespoons red pepper flakes
- 2 garlic cloves, minced
- Salt to the taste
- Half-cup basil, chopped
- Lemon wedges for serving

Instructions:
1. Set your instant pot on Sauté mode, add tomatoes, onion, jalapenos, wine, oil, vinegar, garlic and pepper flakes, stir and bring to a boil.
2. Add mussels, stir, cover and cook on Low for 4 minutes.
3. Release pressure, uncover, discard unopened mussels, add salt and basil, stir, divide among bowls and serve with lemon wedges.

200. MOUTHWATERING MACKEREL WITH LEMON

Perp time: 10 minutes **Cooking time:** 10 minutes **Servings:** 4

Nutrition Facts:
- Calories: 140
- Fat (In grams): 7.8
- Fiber (In grams): 0
- Carbs (In grams): 1
- Protein: 13 g

Ingredients:
- 4 mackerels
- 3 ounces breadcrumbs
- Juice and rind of 1 lemon
- One-tablespoon chives, finely chopped
- Salt and black pepper to the taste
- 1 egg, whisked
- One-tablespoon butter
- One-tablespoon vegetable oil
- 2 tablespoons margarine
- 10 ounces water
- 3 lemon wedges

Instructions:

1. In a bowl, mix breadcrumbs with lemon juice, lemon rind, salt, pepper, egg and chives and stir very well.
2. Coat mackerel with this mix.
3. Set your instant pot on Sauté mode, add oil and butter and heat up.
4. Add fish, brown on all sides and transfer to a plate.
5. Clean the pot and add the water.
6. Grease a heat proof dish with the margarine and introduce in the pot.
7. Add fish, cover the pot and cook at High for 6 minutes.
8. Release the pressure. Divide mackerel among plates and serve with lemon wedges.

Bon Appétit!

201. Special Clams Dish

Perp time: 10 minutes **Cooking time:** 15 minutes **Servings:** 4

Nutrition Facts:
- Calories: 203
- Fat (In grams): 3
- Fiber (In grams): 8
- Carbs (In grams): 10
- Protein: 20 g

Ingredients:
- 15 small clams
- 30 mussels, scrubbed and debearded
- 2 chorizo links, sliced
- 1 pound baby red potatoes
- 1 yellow onion, chopped
- 10 ounces beer
- 2 tablespoons parsley, chopped
- One-teaspoon extra virgin olive oil
- Lemon wedges for serving

Instructions:
1. Set your instant pot on Sauté mode, add oil and heat it up.
2. Add chorizo and onions, stir and cook for 4 minutes.
3. Add clams, mussels, potatoes and beer, stir, cover and cook at High for 10 minutes.
4. Release the pressure, uncover, add parsley, stir, divide among bowls and serve with lemon wedges on the side.

Bon Appétit!

202. Delicious Cioppino

Perp time: 10 minutes **Cooking time:** 15 minutes **Servings:** 4

Nutrition Facts:
- Calories: 300
- Fat (In grams): 12
- Fiber (In grams): 12
- Carbs (In grams): 10
- Protein: 20 g

Ingredients:
- 12 shell clams
- 12 mussels
- 1 ½ pounds big shrimp, peeled and deveined
- 1 ½ pounds fish fillets, cut into medium pieces
- One-cup butter
- 2 yellow onions, chopped

- 3 garlic cloves, minced
- Half-cup parsley, chopped
- 20 ounces canned tomatoes, chopped
- 8 ounces clam juice
- 1 ½ cups white wine
- 2 bay leaves
- Half-teaspoon marjoram, dried
- One-tablespoon basil, dried
- Salt and black pepper to the taste

Instructions:
1. Set your instant pot on Sauté mode, add butter and melt it.
2. Add onion and garlic, stir and cook for 2 minutes.
3. Add clam juice, tomatoes, wine, parsley, basil, bay leaves, marjoram, salt and pepper, stir, cover and cook at High for 10 minutes.
4. Release the pressure and switch pot to Sauté mode again.
5. Add clams and mussels, stir and cook for 8 minutes.
6. Discard unopened mussels and clams, add fish and shrimp, stir and cook for 4 minutes.
7. Divide among bowls and serve.

Bon Appétit!

203. SIMPLE CRAB DISH

Perp time: 5 minutes **Cooking time:** 3 minutes **Servings:** 4

Nutrition Facts:
- Calories: 50
- Fat (In grams): 0.2
- Fiber (In grams): 0.2
- Carbs (In grams): 0
- Protein: 7 g

Ingredients:
- 4 pounds king crab legs, broken in half
- 3 lemon wedges
- 1/4 cup butter
- One-cup water

Instructions:
1. Put crab legs in the steamer basket of the pot.
2. Add water to the pot, cover and cook at High for 3 minutes.
3. Release the pressure, uncover, transfer crab legs to a bowl and butter and serve with lemon wedges on the side.

Bon Appétit!

204. YUMMY SHRIMP DELIGHT

Perp time: 10 minutes **Cooking time:** 5 minutes **Servings:** 4

Nutrition Facts:
- Calories: 566
- Fat (In grams): 20
- Fiber (In grams): 8
- Carbs (In grams): 30
- Protein: 40 g

Ingredients:
- 1 ½ pounds shrimp, peeled and deveined
- 2 tablespoons extra virgin olive oil
- One-cup yellow onion, chopped
- 2 tablespoons parsley, chopped
- 4 garlic cloves, minced

- 2 teaspoons hot paprika
- Half-cup fish stock
- 1/4 cup dry white wine
- One-cup tomato sauce
- A pinch of saffron
- A pinch of Sugar
- One-teaspoon hot pepper, crushed
- 1/4 teaspoon thyme dried
- 1 bay leaf
- Salt and black pepper to the taste

Instructions:
1. Set your instant pot on Sauté mode, add oil and heat up.
2. Add shrimp, cook for 1 minute and transfer to a platter.
3. Add onion, stir and cook for 2 minutes.
4. Add parsley, garlic, paprika and wine, stir and cook for 2 minutes.
5. Add stock, tomato sauce, red pepper, Sugar, saffron, thyme, bay leaf, salt and pepper.
6. Cover and cook at High for 4 minutes.
7. Release the pressure, uncover, add shrimp, cover again and cook at High for 2 minutes.
8. Release pressure, again, uncover, divide shrimp mix among plates and serve.

Bon Appétit!

---

205. MOUTHWATERING MISO MACKEREL

Perp time: 10 minutes **Cooking time:** 50 minutes **Servings:** 4

Nutrition Facts:
- Calories: 290
- Fat (In grams): 13
- Fiber (In grams): 0
- Carbs (In grams): 15
- Protein: 24 g

Ingredients:
- 2 pounds mackerel, cut into big pieces
- One-cup water
- 1 garlic clove, crushed
- 1 shallot, sliced
- 1 inch ginger piece, chopped
- 1/3 cup sake
- 1/3 cup mirin
- 1/4 cup miso
- 1 sweet onion, thinly sliced
- 2 celery stalks, sliced
- One-tablespoon rice vinegar
- One-teaspoon Japanese hot mustard
- Salt to the taste
- One-teaspoon Sugar

Instructions:
1. Set your instant pot on Sauté mode, add mirin, sake, ginger, garlic and shallot, stir and boil for 2 minutes.
2. Add miso and water and stir.
3. Add mackerel, cover the pot and cook at High for 45 minutes.
4. Meanwhile, put onion and celery in a bowl and cover with ice water.
5. In another bowl, mix vinegar with salt, Sugar and mustard and stir well.
6. Release the pressure from the pot naturally for 10 minutes and divide mackerel among plates.
7. Drain onion and celery well and mix with mustard dressing.
8. Divide along mackerel and serve.

Bon Appétit!

206. Amazing Shrimp Curry

Perp time: 10 minutes   **Cooking time:** 30 minutes   **Servings:** 4

Nutrition Facts:
- Calories: 299
- Fat (In grams): 9
- Fiber (In grams): 3
- Carbs (In grams): 26
- Protein: 27 g

Ingredients:
- 1 pound big shrimp, peeled and deveined
- 1/3 cup butter
- 2 bay leaves
- 1 cinnamon stick
- 10 cloves
- 3 cardamom pods
- 2 red onions, chopped
- 14 red chilies, dried
- 3 green chilies, chopped
- Half-cup cashews
- One-tablespoon garlic paste
- One-tablespoon ginger paste
- 4 tomatoes, chopped
- Salt to the taste
- One-teaspoon Sugar
- One-teaspoon fenugreek leaves, dried
- Half-cup cream

Instructions:
1. Set your instant pot on Sauté mode, add butter and melt it.
2. Add bay leaves, cardamom, cinnamon stick and onion, stir and cook for 3 minutes.
3. Add red chilies, green chilies, cashews, tomatoes, garlic paste and ginger paste and stir.
4. Add salt, stir, cover and cook at High for 15 minutes.
5. Release the pressure, transfer everything to your blender and pulse well.
6. Strain into a pan and heat it up over medium high heat.
7. Add shrimp, stir, cover and cook for 12 minutes.
8. Add fenugreek, cream and Sugar, stir, cook for 2 minutes, take off heat and divide among plates.

Bon Appétit!

207. Simple Shrimp Paella

Perp time: 10 minutes   **Cooking time:** 5 minutes   **Servings:** 4

Nutrition Facts:
- Calories: 320
- Fat (In grams): 4
- Fiber (In grams): 1.4
- Carbs (In grams): 12
- Protein: 22 g

Ingredients:
- 20 shrimp, deveined
- One-cup jasmine rice
- 1/4 cup butter
- Salt and black pepper to the taste
- 1/4 cup parsley, chopped
- A pinch of red pepper, crushed
- A pinch of saffron
- Juice of 1 lemon
- 1 ½ cups water
- 4 garlic cloves, minced
- Melted butter for serving
- Hard cheese, grated for serving
- Parsley, chopped for serving

Instructions:
1. Put shrimp in your instant pot.
2. Add rice, butter, salt, pepper, parsley, red pepper, saffron, lemon juice, water and garlic.
3. Stir, cover and cook at High for 5 minutes.
4. Release pressure, uncover pot, takes shrimps and peel them
5. Return to pot, stir well and divide into bowls.
6. Add melted butter, cheese and parsley on top and serve.

Bon Appétit!

208. DELICIOUS SHRIMP & DILL SAUCE

Perp time: 10 minutes   **Cooking time:** 10 minutes   **Servings:** 4

Nutrition Facts:
- Calories: 300
- Fat (In grams): 10
- Fiber (In grams): 0
- Carbs (In grams): 7
- Protein: 10 g

Ingredients:
- 1 pound shrimp, peeled and deveined
- 2 tablespoons shortening
- One-tablespoon yellow onion, chopped
- One-cup white wine
- 2 tablespoons cornstarch
- 3/4 cup milk
- One-teaspoon dill weed

Instructions:
1. Set your instant pot on Sauté mode, add shortening and heat it up.
2. Add onion, stir and cook for 2 minutes.
3. Add shrimp and wine, stir, cover and cook at High for 2 minutes.
4. Release the pressure, uncover pot and set it on Simmer mode.
5. In a bowl, mix cornstarch with milk and stir.
6. Add this to shrimp and stir until it thickens.
7. Add dill weed, stir, simmer for 5 minutes, divide among bowls and serve.

Bon Appétit!

209. POTATOES AND SHRIMP MIX

Perp time: 10 minutes   **Cooking time:** 15 minutes   **Servings:** 4

Nutrition Facts:
- Calories: 140
- Fat (In grams): 2
- Fiber (In grams): 0
- Carbs (In grams): 5
- Protein: 19 g

Ingredients:
- 2 pounds shrimp, peeled and deveined
- 1 pound tomatoes, peeled and chopped
- 8 potatoes, cut into quarters
- Salt to the taste
- 4 tablespoons extra virgin olive oil
- 4 onions, chopped
- One-teaspoon coriander, ground
- One-teaspoon curry powder
- Juice of 1 lemon
- One-tablespoon watercress

Instructions:
1. Put potatoes in the steamer basket of the pot, add some water to the pot, cover and cook at High for 10 minutes.
2. Release the pressure, transfer potatoes to a bowl and clean up your pot.
3. Set the pot on Sauté mode, add oil and heat it up.
4. Add onions, stir and cook for 5 minutes.
5. Add salt, coriander and curry, stir and cook for 5 minutes.
6. Add tomatoes, shrimp, lemon juice and return potatoes as well.
7. Stir, cover and cook at High for 3 minuets.
8. Release the pressure again, divide among bowls and serve with watercress on top.

Bon Appétit!

210. SPECIAL SHRIMP CREOLE

Perp time: 10 minutes **Cooking time:** 5 minutes **Servings:** 4

Nutrition Facts:
- Calories: 294
- Fat (In grams): 9
- Fiber (In grams): 1.5
- Carbs (In grams): 27
- Protein: 24

Ingredients:
- One-cup already cooked shrimp
- 1 ½ cups already cooked, rice
- Half-teaspoon Sugar
- 2 teaspoons vinegar
- One-cup tomato juice
- Salt to the taste
- One-teaspoons chili powder
- 1 yellow onion, chopped
- One-cup celery, chopped
- 2 tablespoons shortening

Instructions:
1. Set the pot on Sauté mode, add shortening and heat it up.
2. Add onion and celery, stir and cook for 2 minutes.
3. Add salt, chili powder, tomato juice, vinegar, Sugar, shrimp and rice.
4. Stir, cover and cook at High for 3 minutes.
5. Release the pressure, uncover pot, divide among plates and serve.

Bon Appétit!

211. INSTANT SHRIMP BOIL

Perp time: 10 minutes **Cooking time:** 5 minutes **Servings:** 4

Nutrition Facts:
- Calories: 360
- Fat (In grams): 10
- Fiber (In grams): 9
- Carbs (In grams): 41
- Protein: 30 g

Ingredients:
- 1 ½ pounds shrimp, head removed
- 12 ounces Andouille sausage, already cooked and chopped

- 4 ears of corn, each cut into 3 pieces
- One-tablespoon old bay seasoning
- 16 ounces beer
- Salt and black pepper to the taste
- One-teaspoon red pepper flakes, crushed
- 2 sweet onions, cut into wedges
- 1 pound potatoes, cut into medium chunks
- 8 garlic cloves, crushed
- French baguettes for serving

Instructions:
1. In your instant pot, mix beer with old bay seasoning, red pepper flakes, salt, black pepper, onions, garlic, potatoes, corn, sausage pieces and shrimp.
2. Cover the pot and cook at High for 5 minutes.
3. Release the pressure, uncover the pot, divide shrimp boil into bowls and serve with French baguettes on the side.

Bon Appétit!

---

212. SPECIAL SHRIMP CURRY

Perp time: 10 minutes   **Cooking time:** 6 minutes   **Servings:** 4

Nutrition Facts:
- Calories: 300
- Fat (In grams): 7
- Fiber (In grams): 2.5
- Carbs (In grams): 34
- Protein: 29

Ingredients:
- 1 pound shrimp, peeled and deveined
- One-cup bouillon
- 4 lemon slices
- Salt and black pepper to the taste
- Half-teaspoon curry powder
- 1/4 cup mushrooms, sliced
- 1/4 cup yellow onion, chopped
- 2 tablespoons shortening
- Half-cup raisins
- 3 tablespoons flour
- One-cup milk

Instructions:
1. Set your instant pot on Sauté mode, add shortenings and heat up.
2. Add onion and mushroom, stir and cook for 2 minutes.
3. Add salt, pepper, curry powder, lemon, bouillon, raisins and shrimp.
4. Stir, cover and cook at High for 2 minutes.
5. Meanwhile, in a bowl mix flour with milk and whisk well.
6. Release the pressure from the pot, uncover, add flour and milk mix, stir well and cook until curry thickens on Simmer mode.
7. Divide among bowls and serve.

Bon Appétit!

213. Quick Shrimp Scampi

Perp time: 10 minutes **Cooking time:** 4 minutes **Servings:** 4

Nutrition Facts:
- Calories: 288
- Fat (In grams): 20
- Fiber (In grams): 0
- Carbs (In grams): 0.01
- Protein: 23

Ingredients:
- 1 pound shrimp, cooked, peeled and deveined
- 2 tablespoons extra virgin olive oil
- 1 garlic clove, minced
- 10 ounces canned tomatoes, chopped
- 1/3 cup tomato paste
- 1/4 teaspoon oregano, dried
- One-tablespoon parsley, finely chopped
- 1/3 cup water
- One-cup parmesan, grated
- Already cooked spaghetti for serving

Instructions:
1. Set your instant pot on Sauté mode, add oil and heat up.
2. Add garlic, stir and brown for 2 minutes.
3. Add shrimp, tomato paste, tomatoes, water, oregano and parsley, stir, cover and cook at High for 3 minutes.
4. Release pressure, divide among plates and serve with your favorite spaghetti.
5. Sprinkle parmesan at the end.

Bon Appétit!

214. Amazing Shrimp Dish

Perp time: 20 minutes **Cooking time:** 10 minutes **Servings:** 4

Nutrition Facts:
- Calories: 200
- Fat (In grams): 2
- Fiber (In grams): 1
- Carbs (In grams): 7
- Protein: 11 g

Ingredients:
- 18 ounces shrimp, peeled and deveined
- Salt to the taste
- Half-tablespoon mustard seeds
- 3 ounces mustard oil
- One-teaspoon turmeric powder
- 2 green chilies, cut into halves lengthwise
- 2 onions, finely chopped
- 4 ounces curd, beaten
- 1 inch ginger, chopped
- Already cooker rice for serving

Instructions:
1. Put mustard seeds in a bowl, add water to cover, leave aside for 10 minutes, drain and grind very well.
2. Put shrimp in a bowl, add mustard oil, turmeric, mustard paste, salt, onions, chilies, curd and ginger, toss to coat and leave aside for 10 minutes.
3. Transfer everything to your instant pot, cover and cook on Low for 10 minutes.
4. Release the pressure, divide among plates and serve with boiled rice.

215. Shrimp And Fish

Perp time: 10 minutes	**Cooking time:** 10 minutes	**Servings:** 4

Nutrition Facts:
- Calories: 200
- Fat (In grams): 0.2
- Fiber (In grams): 0.2
- Carbs (In grams): 1
- Protein: 12 g

Ingredients:
- 2 pounds flounder
- Half-cup water
- ½ pound shrimp, cooked, peeled and deveined
- 2 tablespoons butter
- Salt and black pepper to the taste
- 4 lemon wedges

Instructions:
1. Season fish with salt and pepper and place in the steamer basket of the pot.
2. Add water to the pot, cover and cook at High for 10 minutes.
3. Release the pressure uncover the pot, transfer fish to plates and leave aside.
4. Discard water, clean pot and set on Sauté mode.
5. Add butter and melt it.
6. Add shrimp, salt and pepper, stir and divide among plates on top of fish and serve with lemon wedges on the side.

Bon Appétit!

216. Tasty Shrimp Teriyaki Dish

Perp time: 10 minutes	**Cooking time:** 4 minutes	**Servings:** 4

Nutrition Facts:
- Calories: 200
- Fat (In grams): 4.2
- Fiber (In grams): 0.7
- Carbs (In grams): 13
- Protein: 38 g

Ingredients:
- 1 pounds shrimp, peeled and deveined
- 2 tablespoons soy sauce
- ½ pound pea pods
- 3 tablespoons vinegar
- 3/4 cup pineapple juice
- One-cup chicken stock
- 3 tablespoons Sugar

Instructions:
1. Put shrimp and pea pods in your instant pot.
2. In a bowl, mix soy sauce with vinegar, pineapple juice, stock and Sugar and stir well.
3. Pour this into the pot, stir, cover and cook at High for 3 minutes.
4. Release the pressure, uncover, divide among plates and serve.

Bon Appétit!

217. Amazing Shrimp With Risotto & Herbs

Perp time: 10 minutes   **Cooking time:** 20 minutes   **Servings:** 4

Nutrition Facts:
- Calories: 400
- Fat (In grams): 8
- Fiber (In grams): 4
- Carbs (In grams): 15
- Protein: 29 g

Ingredients:
- 4 tablespoons butter
- 2 garlic cloves, minced
- 1 yellow onion, chopped
- 1 ½ cups Arborio rice
- 2 tablespoons dry white wine
- 4 and Half-cups chicken stock
- Salt and black pepper to the taste
- 1 pound shrimp, peeled and deveined
- 3/4 cup parmesan, grated
- 1/4 cup tarragon and parsley, chopped

Instructions:
1. Set your instant pot on Sauté mode, add 2 tablespoons butter and melt.
2. Add garlic and onion, stir and cook for 4 minutes.
3. Add rice, stir and cook for 1 minute.
4. Add wine, stir and cook 30 seconds more.
5. Add 3 cups stock, salt, and pepper, stir, cover and cook at High for 9 minutes.
6. Release the pressure, uncover the pot, add shrimp, the rest of the stock, set the pot on Sauté mode again and cook for 5 minutes stirring from time to time.
7. Add cheese, the rest of the butter, tarragon and parsley, stir, divide among plates and serve.

Bon Appétit!

218. Yummy Seafood Gumbo

Perp time: 10 minutes   **Cooking time:** 25 minutes   **Servings:** 10

Nutrition Facts:
- Calories: 800
- Fat (In grams): 58
- Fiber (In grams): 3
- Carbs (In grams): 35
- Protein: 36 g

Ingredients:
- 3/4 cup vegetable oil
- 1 and 1/4 cups flour
- One-cup white onions, chopped
- Half-cup celery, chopped
- One-cup green bell pepper, chopped
- 4 garlic cloves, chopped
- 2 tablespoons peanut oil
- 6 plum tomatoes, chopped
- A pinch of cayenne pepper
- 3 bay leaves
- Half-teaspoon onion powder
- Half-teaspoon garlic powder
- One-teaspoon thyme, dried
- One-teaspoon celery seeds
- One-teaspoon sweet paprika
- 1 pound sausage, sliced
- 2 quarts chicken stock
- 24 shrimp, peeled and deveined
- 24 crawfish tails
- 24 oysters
- ½ pound crab meat
- Salt and black pepper to the taste

Instructions:
1. Heat up a pan with the vegetable oil over medium heat, add flour and stir for 3-4 minutes.
2. Set your instant pot on Sauté mode, add peanut oil and heat it up.
3. Add celery, peppers, onions and garlic, stir and cook for 10 minutes.
4. Add sausage, tomatoes, stock, bay leaves, cayenne, onion and garlic powder, thyme, paprika and celery seeds, stir and cook for 3 minutes.
5. Add flour mix you've made earlier, stir until it combines.
6. Add shrimp, crawfish, crab, oysters, salt and pepper, stir, cover and cook at High for 15 minutes.
7. Release the pressure, uncover, divide gumbo among bowls and serve.

Bon Appétit!

---

219. POTATOES AND OCTOPUS

Perp time: 10 minutes   **Cooking time:** 35 minutes   **Servings:** 6

Nutrition Facts:
- Calories: 300
- Fat (In grams): 12
- Fiber (In grams): 2
- Carbs (In grams): 14
- Protein: 20 g

Ingredients:
- 2 pounds octopus, cleaned, head removed, emptied, tentacles separated
- 2 pounds potatoes.
- Water
- 3 garlic cloves, crushed
- Half-teaspoon peppercorns
- 1 bay leaf
- 2 tablespoons parsley, finely chopped
- 5 tablespoons vinegar
- Salt and black pepper salad
- 2 tablespoons extra virgin olive oil

Instructions:
1. Put potatoes in your instant pot, add water to cover them, salt and pepper, cover the pot and cook at High for 15 minutes.
2. Release the pressure, transfer potatoes to a bowl, peeled and chopped.
3. Put octopus in your instant pot, add more water, bay leaf, 1 garlic clove, peppercorns and more salt.
4. Stir, cover and cook at High for 20 minutes.
5. Release the pressure, drain octopus, chop it and add to potatoes.
6. In a bowl, mix olive oil with vinegar, 2 garlic cloves, salt and pepper and stir very well.
7. Add this to octopus salad, also add parsley, toss to coat and serve.

Bon Appétit!

---

220. DELICIOUS OCTOPUS STEW

Perp time: 1 day   **Cooking time:** 8 minutes   **Servings:** 4

Nutrition Facts:
- Calories: 210
- Fat (In grams): 9
- Fiber (In grams): 0
- Carbs (In grams): 4
- Protein: 32 g

Ingredients:
- 1 octopus, already prepared
- One-cup red wine
- One-cup white wine
- One-cup water
- Half-cup vegetable oil
- Half-cup extra virgin olive oil
- 2 teaspoons pepper sauce
- One-tablespoon hot sauce
- One-tablespoon paprika
- One-tablespoon tomato sauce
- Salt and black pepper to the taste
- ½ bunch parsley, chopped
- 2 garlic cloves, minced
- 1 yellow onion, chopped
- 4 potatoes, cut into quarters.

Instructions:
1. Put octopus in a bowl and add white wine, red wine, water, vegetable oil, pepper sauce, hot sauce, paprika, tomato paste, salt, pepper and parsley.
2. Toss to coat, cover and keep in a cold place for 1 day.
3. Set your instant pot on Sauté mode, add olive oil and heat it up.
4. Add onions and potatoes, stir and cook for 3 minutes.
5. Add octopus and its marinade, stir, cover and cook at High for 8 minutes.
6. Release the pressure, uncover the pot, divide stew among bowls and serve.

Bon Appétit!

---

221. GREEK STYLE OCTOPUS

Perp time: 10 minutes **Cooking time:** 16 minutes **Servings:** 6

Nutrition Facts:
- Calories: 161
- Fat (In grams): 1
- Fiber (In grams): 0
- Carbs (In grams): 1
- Protein: 9 g

Ingredients:
- 1 octopus, cleaned and prepared
- 2 rosemary springs
- 2 teaspoons oregano, dried
- ½ yellow onion, roughly chopped
- 4 thyme springs
- ½ lemon
- One-teaspoon black peppercorns
- 3 tablespoons extra virgin olive oil

For the marinade:
- 1/4 cup extra virgin olive oil
- Juice of ½ lemon
- 4 garlic cloves, minced
- 2 thyme springs
- 1 rosemary spring
- Salt and black pepper to the taste

Instructions:
1. Put the octopus in your instant pot.
2. Add oregano, 2 rosemary springs, 4 thyme springs, onion, lemon, 3 tablespoons olive oil, peppercorns and salt.
3. Stir, cover and cook on Low for 10 minutes.
4. Release the pressure, uncover the pot, transfer octopus on a cutting board, cut tentacles and place them in a bowl.

5. Add 1/4 cup olive oil, lemon juice, garlic, 1 rosemary springs, 2 thyme springs, salt and pepper, toss to coat and leave aside for 1 hour.
6. Heat up your grill over medium heat, add octopus, grill for 3 minutes on each side and divide among plates.
7. Drizzle the marinade over octopus and serve.

Bon Appétit!

---

222. MASALA SQUID

Perp time: 10 minutes **Cooking time:** 15 minutes **Servings:** 4

Nutrition Facts:
- Calories: 255
- Fat (In grams): 0
- Fiber (In grams): 1
- Carbs (In grams): 7
- Protein: 9 g

Ingredients:
- 17 ounces squids
- 1 ½ tablespoons red chili powder
- Salt and black pepper to the taste
- 1/4 teaspoon turmeric powder
- 2 cups water
- 5 pieces coconut
- 4 garlic cloves, minced
- Half-teaspoons cumin seeds
- 3 tablespoons extra virgin olive oil
- 1/4 teaspoon mustard seeds
- 1 inch ginger pieces, chopped

Instructions:
1. Put squids in your instant pot.
2. Add chili powder, turmeric, salt, pepper and water, stir, cover and cook on High for 15 minutes.
3. Meanwhile, in your blender, mix coconut with ginger, garlic and cumin and blend well.
4. Heat up a pan with the oil over medium high heat, add mustard seeds and toast for 2-3 minutes.
5. Release the pressure from the pot and transfer squid and water to the pan.
6. Stir and mix with coconut blend.
7. Cook until everything thickens, divide among plates and serve.

Bon Appétit!

---

223. AMAZING STUFFED SQUID

Perp time: 10 minutes **Cooking time:** 20 minutes **Servings:** 4

Nutrition Facts:
- Calories: 148
- Fat (In grams): 2.4
- Fiber (In grams): 1.1
- Carbs (In grams): 7
- Protein: 11 g

Ingredients:
- 4 squid
- One-cup sticky rice
- 14 ounces dashi stock
- 2 tablespoons sake
- 4 tablespoons soy sauce
- One-tablespoon mirin
- 2 tablespoons Sugar

Instructions:
1. Chop tentacles from 1 squid and mix with the rice.
2. Fill each squid with rice and seal ends with toothpicks.
3. Place squid in your instant pot, add stock, soy sauce, sake, Sugar and mirin.
4. Cover and cook at High for 15 minutes.
5. Release the pressure, uncover the pot, divide stuffed squid among plates and serve.

Bon Appétit!

224. HOT SQUID ROAST

Perp time: 10 minutes **Cooking time:** 25 minutes **Servings:** 4

Nutrition Facts:
- Calories: 209
- Fat (In grams): 10
- Fiber (In grams): 0.5
- Carbs (In grams): 9.3
- Protein: 20 g

Ingredients:
- 1 pound squid, cleaned and cut into small pieces
- 10 garlic cloves, minced
- 2-inch ginger piece, grated
- 2 green chilies, chopped
- 2 yellow onions, chopped
- 1 curry leaf
- Half-tablespoon lemon juice
- 1/4 cup coconut, sliced
- One-tablespoon coriander powder
- 3/4 tablespoon chili powder
- One-teaspoon garam masala
- Salt and black pepper to the taste
- A pinch of turmeric
- One-teaspoon mustard seeds
- 3/4 cup water
- 3 tablespoons vegetable oil

Instructions:
1. Set your instant pot on Sauté mode, add oil and heat it up.
2. Add mustard seeds and fry for 1 minute.
3. Add coconut and cook 2 minutes.
4. Add ginger, onions, garlic and chilies, stir and cook 30 seconds.
5. Add salt, pepper, curry leaf, coriander powder, chili powder, garam masala, turmeric, water, lemon juice, and squid.
6. Stir, cover and cook on Low for 25 minutes.
7. Release pressure, uncover, divide among plates and serve.

Bon Appétit!

225. SPECIAL BRAISED SQUID DISH

Perp time: 10 minutes **Cooking time:** 20 minutes **Servings:** 4

Nutrition Facts:
- Calories: 145
- Fat (In grams): 1
- Fiber (In grams): 0
- Carbs (In grams): 7
- Protein: 12 g

Ingredients:
- 1 pound squid, cleaned and cut
- 1 pound fresh peas
- ½ pounds canned tomatoes, crushed
- 1 yellow onion, chopped
- A splash of white wine
- A drizzle of olive oil
- Salt and black pepper to the taste

Instructions:
1. Set your instant pot on Sauté mode, add some oil and heat it up.
2. Add onion, stir and cook for 3 minutes.
3. Add squid, stir and cook for 3 more minutes.
4. Add wine, tomatoes and peas, stir, cover and cook for 20 minutes.
5. Release the pressure, uncover the pot, add salt and pepper to the taste, stir, divide among plates and serve.

Bon Appétit!

VEGETABLE RECIPES

226. HEALTHY ARTICHOKE HEARTS

Perp time: 10 minutes   **Cooking time:** 40 minutes   **Servings:** 4

Nutrition Facts:
- Calories: 120
- Fat (In grams): 2
- Fiber (In grams): 1
- Carbs (In grams): 1
- Protein: 4 g

Ingredients:
- 4 big artichokes, washed, stems and petal tips cut off
- Salt and black pepper to the taste
- 2 tablespoons lemon juice
- 1/4 cup extra virgin olive oil
- 2 teaspoons balsamic vinegar
- One-teaspoon oregano
- 2 cups water
- 2 garlic cloves, minced

Instructions:
1. Put artichokes in the steamer basket of your instant pot.
2. Add 2 cups water to the pot, cover and steam them for 8 minutes.
3. Meanwhile, in a bowl, mix lemon juice with vinegar, oil, salt, pepper, garlic and oregano and stir very well.
4. Release the pressure from the pot, transfer artichokes to a plate, cut them into halves, take out the hearts and arrange them on a platter.
5. Drizzle the vinaigrette over artichokes and leave them aside for 30 minutes.
6. Heat up your kitchen grill over medium heat, add artichokes and cook for 3 minutes on each side.
7. Serve them warm.

Bon Appétit!

227. DELICIOUS ARTICHOKES WITH LEMON SAUCE

Perp time: 10 minutes   **Cooking time:** 20 minutes   **Servings:** 4

Nutrition Facts:
- Calories: 200
- Fat (In grams): 12
- Fiber (In grams): 9
- Carbs (In grams): 20
- Protein: 6 g

Ingredients:
- 4 artichokes
- One-tablespoon tarragon, chopped
- 2 cups chicken stock
- 2 lemons
- 1 celery stalk, chopped
- Half-cup extra virgin olive oil
- Salt to the taste

Instructions:
1. Discard stems and petal tips from artichokes.
2. Zest lemons, cut into 4 slices and place them in your instant pot.
3. Place an artichoke on each lemon slices, add stock, cover pot and cook at High for 20 minutes.
4. Release the pressure fast, uncover the pot and transfer artichokes to a platter.

5. Meanwhile, In your food processor, mix tarragon with lemon zest, with the pulp from the second lemon, celery, salt and olive oil and pulse very well.
6. Drizzle this over artichokes and serve.

Bon Appétit!

---

228. SPINACH AND ARTICHOKES DIP

Perp time: 10 minutes   **Cooking time:** 5 minutes   **Servings:** 6

Nutrition Facts:
- Calories: 288
- Fat (In grams): 20
- Fiber (In grams): 0
- Carbs (In grams): 8
- Protein: 15 g

Ingredients:
- 14 ounces canned artichoke hearts
- 8 ounces cream cheese
- 16 ounces parmesan cheese, grated
- 10 ounces spinach
- Half-cup chicken stock
- 8 ounces mozzarella, shredded
- Half-cup sour cream
- 3 garlic cloves, minced
- Half-cup mayonnaise
- One-teaspoon onion powder

Instructions:
1. In your instant pot, mix artichokes with stock, garlic, spinach, cream cheese, sour cream, onion powder and mayo, stir, cover and cook at High for 5 minutes.
2. Release the pressure fast, uncover the pot, add, mozzarella and parmesan, stir well and transfer to a bowl.
3. Serve with corn chips on the side.

Bon Appétit!

---

229. DELICIOUS BLUE CHEESE AND BEETS

Perp time: 10 minutes   **Cooking time:** 20 minutes   **Servings:** 6

Nutrition Facts:
- Calories: 160
- Fat (In grams): 1
- Fiber (In grams): 5
- Carbs (In grams): 10
- Protein: 7 g

Ingredients:
- 6 beets
- Salt and black pepper to the taste
- 1/4 cup blue cheese, crumbled
- One-cup water

Instructions:
1. Put the beets in the steamer basket of your instant pot, add One-cup water to the pot, cover and cook at High for 20 minutes.
2. Release the pressure naturally, uncover the pot, transfer beets to a cutting board, leave aside to cool down, peel and cut them into quarters.
3. Put beets in a bowl, add blue cheese, salt and pepper to the taste, stir and serve.

230. HEALTHY ARTICHOKES WITH TASTY DIP

Perp time: 10 minutes **Cooking time:** 22 minutes **Servings:** 2

Nutrition Facts:
- Calories: 300
- Fat (In grams): 14
- Fiber (In grams): 9
- Carbs (In grams): 45
- Protein: 15 g

Ingredients:
- 2 artichokes, washed, stems and petal tips cut off
- 1 bay leaf
- One-cup water
- 2 garlic cloves, chopped
- 1 lemon cut into halves

For the sauce:
- 1/4 cup coconut oil
- 1/4 cup extra virgin olive oil
- 3 anchovy fillets
- 3 garlic cloves

Instructions:
1. Put artichokes in the steamer basket of the instant pot, add water in the pot, lemon halves, 2 garlic cloves and bay leaf, cover and cook at High for 20 minutes.
2. Release the pressure naturally for 10 minutes, uncover the pot and divide artichokes among plates.
3. In your food processor, mix coconut oil with anchovy, 3 garlic cloves and olive oil and blend very well.
4. Pour this into a bowl and serve your artichokes with this dip.

Bon Appétit!

231. TASTY BEET SALAD

Perp time: 10 minutes **Cooking time:** 30 minutes **Servings:** 4

Nutrition Facts:
- Calories: 44
- Fat (In grams): 2.4
- Fiber (In grams): 1
- Carbs (In grams): 0
- Protein: 1 g

Ingredients:
- 4 beets
- One-cup water
- 2 tablespoons balsamic vinegar
- A bunch of parsley, chopped
- Salt and black pepper to the taste
- One-tablespoon extra virgin olive oil
- 1 garlic clove, chopped
- 2 tablespoons capers

Instructions:
1. Put the beets in the steamer basket of your instant pot, add One-cup water to the pot, cover and cook for 20 minutes at High.
2. Meanwhile, in a bowl, mix parsley with garlic, salt, pepper, olive oil and capers and stir very well.
3. Release the pressure from the pot, uncover, transfer beets to a cutting board, leave them to cool down, peel them, slice them and arrange them on a platter.
4. Add vinegar over them and drizzle the parsley dressing at the end.

232. Amazing Wrapped Asparagus Canes

Perp time: 5 minutes **Cooking time:** 4 minutes **Servings:** 4

Nutrition Facts:
- Calories: 60
- Fat (In grams): 3
- Fiber (In grams): 1
- Carbs (In grams): 3
- Protein: 4 g

Ingredients:
- 1 pound asparagus, trimmed
- 8 ounces prosciutto slices
- 2 cups water
- A pinch of salt

Instructions:
1. Wrap asparagus spears in prosciutto slices and place them on the bottom of the steamer basket in your instant pot.
2. Add 2 cups water to the pot, add a pinch of salt, cover and cook at High for 4 minutes.
3. Release the pressure naturally, uncover, transfer asparagus canes on a platter and serve at room temperature.

Bon Appétit!

233. Tomato And Beet Salad

Perp time: 30 minutes **Cooking time:** 30 minutes **Servings:** 8

Nutrition Facts:
- Calories: 163
- Fat (In grams): 8
- Fiber (In grams): 4
- Carbs (In grams): 12
- Protein: 4.5 g

Ingredients:
- 1 ½ cups water
- 8 small beets, trimmed
- 1 red onion, sliced
- 4 ounces goat cheese
- One-cup apple cider vinegar
- One-cup water
- 2 teaspoons pickling juice
- Salt and black pepper to the taste
- 2 tablespoons Sugar
- 1 pint mixed cherry tomatoes, cut into halves
- 2 ounces pecans
- 2 tablespoons extra virgin olive oil

Instructions:
1. Put beets in the steamer basket of your instant pot, add 1 ½ cups water, cover and cook at High for 20 minutes.
2. Release the pressure, uncover the pot, transfer beets to a cutting board, leave them to cool down, peel and chop them and put them in a bowl.
3. Clean your instant pot, add One-cup water, vinegar, Sugar, pickling juice and salt to the taste, stir, cover and cook at High for 2 minutes.
4. Release the pressure, strain liquid into a bowl, add onions, stir and leave aside for 10 minutes.
5. Add tomatoes over beets and onions and stir.
6. In a bowl, mix 4 tablespoons of liquid from the onions with 2 tablespoons olive oil, salt and pepper and stir.

7. Add this to beets salad and stir.
8. Also, add goat cheese and pecans, toss to coat and serve.

Bon Appétit!

234. ORANGE AND BEET SALAD

Perp time: 10 minutes **Cooking time:** 10 minutes **Servings:** 4

Nutrition Facts:
- Calories: 140
- Fat (In grams): 6
- Fiber (In grams): 3.1
- Carbs (In grams): 11
- Protein: 4 g

Ingredients:
- 1 ½ pounds beets
- 2 teaspoons orange zest, grated
- 3 strips orange peel
- 2 tablespoons cider vinegar
- Half-cup orange juice
- 2 tablespoons brown Sugar
- 2 scallions, chopped
- 2 teaspoons mustard
- 2 cups arugula and mustard greens

Instructions:
1. Scrub beets well cut them in halves and put them in a bowl.
2. In your instant pot, mix orange peel strips with vinegar and orange juice and stir.
3. Add beets, cover the pot, cook at High for 7 minutes and release the pressure naturally.
4. Uncover, pot, take beets and transfer them to a bowl.
5. Discard peel strips from the pot, add mustard and Sugar and stir well.
6. Add scallions and grated orange zest to beets and toss them.
7. Add liquid from the pot over beets, toss to coat and serve on plates on top of mixed salad greens.

Bon Appétit!

235. SHRIMP AND ASPARAGUS

Perp time: 4 minutes **Cooking time:** 3 minutes **Servings:** 4

Nutrition Facts:
- Calories: 150
- Fat (In grams): 1.4
- Fiber (In grams): 4
- Carbs (In grams): 15
- Protein: 23 g

Ingredients:
- One-cup water
- 1 pound shrimp, peeled and deveined
- One-teaspoon extra virgin olive oil
- 1 bunch asparagus, trimmed
- Half-tablespoon Cajun seasoning

Instructions:
1. Put the water in your instant pot.
2. Put asparagus in the steamer basket of the pot and add shrimp on top.
3. Drizzle olive oil, sprinkle Cajun seasoning, stir, cover and cook on Low for 2 minutes.
4. Release the pressure naturally, transfer asparagus and shrimp to plates and serve.

236. POMEGRANATE AND BRUSSELS SPROUTS

Perp time: 5 minutes **Cooking time:** 10 minutes **Servings:** 4

Nutrition Facts:
- Calories: 100
- Fat (In grams): 1
- Fiber (In grams): 4
- Carbs (In grams): 11
- Protein: 4 g

Ingredients:
- 1 pound Brussels sprouts
- Salt and black pepper to the taste
- 1 pomegranate, seeds separated
- 1/4 cup pine nuts, toasted
- A drizzle of extra virgin olive oil
- One-cup water

Instructions:
1. Put Brussels sprouts in the pressure cooker of your instant pot, add One-cup water to the pot, cover and cook at High for 4 minutes.
2. Release the pressure, uncover your pot and transfer sprouts to a bowl.
3. Add salt, pepper, pine nuts, pomegranate seeds and pine nuts and stir.
4. Add olive oil, toss to coat and serve.

Bon Appétit!

237. GARLIC AND BROCCOLI

Perp time: 10 minutes **Cooking time:** 12 minutes **Servings:** 4

Nutrition Facts:
- Calories: 100
- Fat (In grams): 1
- Fiber (In grams): 0
- Carbs (In grams): 3
- Protein: 6 g

Ingredients:
- 1 broccoli head, cut into 4 pieces
- Half-cup water
- One-tablespoon peanut oil
- 6 garlic cloves, minced
- One-tablespoon Chinese rice wine
- Salt to the taste

Instructions:
1. Put broccoli in the steamer basket of you instant pot, add Half-cup water to the pot, cover and cook on Low for 12 minutes.
2. Release the pressure, transfer broccoli to a bowl filled with cold water, drain and place it in a bowl.
3. Heat up a pan with the oil over medium high heat, add garlic, stir and cook for 3 minutes.
4. Add broccoli and rice wine, stir and cook for 1 minute more.
5. Add salt, stir and cook 30 seconds.
6. Transfer to plates and serve.

Bon Appétit!

238. DELICIOUS STUFFED BELL PEPPERS

Perp time: 15 minutes **Cooking time:** 15 minutes **Servings:** 4

Nutrition Facts:
- Calories: 177
- Fat (In grams): 5
- Fiber (In grams): 3.3
- Carbs (In grams): 22
- Protein: 13 g

Ingredients:
- 1 pound turkey meat, ground
- One-cup water
- 2 green onions, chopped
- 5 ounces canned green chilies, chopped
- 1 jalapeno pepper, chopped
- 2 teaspoons chili powder
- Half-cup whole wheat panko
- One-teaspoon garlic powder
- One-teaspoon cumin, ground
- Salt to the taste
- 4 bell peppers, tops, and seeds discarded
- 4 pepper jack cheese slices
- 1 avocado, chopped
- Crushed tortilla chips
- Pico de gallo

For the chipotle sauce:
- Zest from 1 lime
- Juice from 1 lime
- Half-cup sour cream
- 2 tablespoons chipotle in adobo sauce
- 1/8 teaspoon garlic powder

Instructions:
1. In a bowl, mix sour cream with chipotle in adobo sauce, lime zest and lime juice and garlic powder, stir well and keep in the fridge until you serve it.
2. In a bowl, mix turkey meat with green onions, green chilies, bread crumbs, jalapeno, cumin, salt, chili powder and garlic powder, stir very well and stuff your peppers with this mix.
3. Add One-cup water to your instant pot, add peppers in the steamer basket, cover and cook at High for 15 minutes.
4. Release the pressure naturally for 10 minutes, transfer bell peppers to a pan, add cheese on top, introduce in preheated broiler and broil until cheese is browned.
5. Divide bell peppers on plates, top with the chipotle sauce you've made earlier and serve.

Bon Appétit!

239. SIMPLE STUFFED BELL PEPPERS DISH

Perp time: 10 minutes **Cooking time:** 15 minutes **Servings:** 4

Nutrition Facts:
- Calories: 200
- Fat (In grams): 12
- Fiber (In grams): 1.5
- Carbs (In grams): 13
- Protein: 12 g

Ingredients:
- 4 bell peppers, tops and seeds removed
- Salt and black pepper to the taste
- 16 ounces beef meat, ground
- One-cup white rice, already cooked
- 1 egg
- Half-cup milk
- 2 onions, chopped
- 8 ounces water

- 10 ounces canned tomato soup

Instructions:
1. Put some water in a pot, bring to a boil over medium heat, add bell peppers, blanch them for 3 minutes, drain and transfer them to a working surface.
2. In a bowl, mix beef with rice, salt, pepper, egg, milk and onions and stir very well.
3. Stuff bell peppers with this mix and place them in your instant pot.
4. Add tomato soup mixed with water, cover pot and cook at High for 12 minutes.
5. Release the pressure fast, divide bell peppers among plates, drizzle tomato sauce on top and serve.

Bon Appétit!

240. Bacon And Brussels Sprouts

Perp time: 4 minutes   **Cooking time:** 6 minutes   **Servings:** 4

Nutrition Facts:
- Calories: 175
- Fat (In grams): 11
- Fiber (In grams): 5.6
- Carbs (In grams): 14
- Protein: 6.6

Ingredients:
- 1 pound Brussels sprouts, trimmed and cut into halves
- Salt and black pepper to the taste
- Half-cup bacon, chopped
- One-tablespoon mustard
- One-cup chicken stock
- One-tablespoon butter
- 2 tablespoons dill, finely chopped

Instructions:
1. Set your instant pot on Sauté mode, add bacon and cook it until it's crispy.
2. Add sprouts, stir and cook for 2 minutes.
3. Add stock, mustard, salt and pepper, stir, cover and cook at High for 4 minutes.
4. Release pressure, uncover the pot, add butter and dill, set the pot on Sauté mode again, stir and divide among serving plates.

Bon Appétit!

241. Potatoes And Brussels Sprouts

Perp time: 10 minutes   **Cooking time:** 5 minutes   **Servings:** 4

Nutrition Facts:
- Calories: 100
- Fat (In grams): 2.5
- Fiber (In grams): 4.6
- Carbs (In grams): 18
- Protein: 4 g

Ingredients:
- 1 ½ pounds Brussels sprouts, washed and trimmed
- One-cup new potatoes, chopped
- 1 ½ tablespoons bread crumbs
- Half-cup beef stock
- Salt and black pepper to the taste
- 1 ½ tablespoons butter

Instructions:

1. Put sprouts and potatoes in your instant pot.
2. Add stock, salt and pepper, cover and cook at High for 5 minutes.
3. Release the pressure, uncover pot, set on Sauté mode, add butter and bread crumbs, toss to coat well, divide among plates and serve.

Bon Appétit!

242. Yummy Brussels Sprouts With Parmesan

Perp time: 10 minutes   **Cooking time:** 6 minutes   **Servings:** 4

Nutrition Facts:
- Calories: 160
- Fat (In grams): 2
- Fiber (In grams): 1
- Carbs (In grams): 7
- Protein: 12 g

Ingredients:
- 1 pound Brussels sprouts, washed
- Juice of 1 lemon
- Salt and black pepper to the taste
- 2 tablespoons butter
- One-cup water
- 3 tablespoons parmesan, grated

Instructions:
1. Put sprouts in your instant pot, add salt, pepper and water, stir, cover and cook at High for 3 minutes.
2. Release the pressure, transfer sprouts to a bowl, discard water and clean your pot.
3. Set your pot on Sauté mode, add butter and melt it.
4. Add lemon juice and stir well.
5. Add sprouts, stir and transfer to plates.
6. Add more salt and pepper if needed and parmesan cheese on top.

Bon Appétit!

243. Delicious Cabbage Dish

Perp time: 10 minutes   **Cooking time:** 8 minutes   **Servings:** 8

Nutrition Facts:
- Calories: 100
- Fat (In grams): 4
- Fiber (In grams): 3
- Carbs (In grams): 7
- Protein: 2 g

Ingredients:
- 1 green cabbage head, chopped
- 1/4 cup butter
- 2 cups chicken stock
- 3 bacon slices, chopped
- Salt and black pepper to the taste

Instructions:
1. Set your instant pot on Sauté mode, add bacon, stir and cook for 4 minutes.
2. Add butter and stir until it melts.
3. Add cabbage, stock, salt and pepper, stir, cover and cook at High for 3 minutes.
4. Release the pressure, uncover, transfer cabbage to plates and serve.

Bon Appétit!

244. Spicy And Sweet Cabbage

Perp time: 10 minutes **Cooking time:** 8 minutes **Servings:** 4

Nutrition Facts:
- Calories: 90
- Fat (In grams): 4.5
- Fiber (In grams): 2.1
- Carbs (In grams): 11
- Protein: 1 g

Ingredients:
- 1 cabbage, cut into 8 wedges
- One-tablespoon sesame seed oil
- 1 carrots, grated
- 1/4 cup apple cider vinegar
- 1 and 1/4 cups apple+2 teaspoons water
- One-teaspoon raw Sugar
- Half-teaspoon cayenne pepper
- Half-teaspoon red pepper flakes
- 2 teaspoons cornstarch

Instructions:
1. Set your instant pot on Sauté mode, add oil and heat it up.
2. Add cabbage, stir and cook for 3 minutes.
3. Add carrots, 1 and 1/4 cups water, Sugar, vinegar, cayenne and pepper flakes, stir, cover and cook at High for 5 minutes.
4. Release the pressure, uncover the pot and divide cabbage and carrots mix among plates.
5. Add cornstarch mixed with 2 teaspoons water to the pot, set the pot on Simmer mode, stir very well and bring to a boil.
6. Drizzle over cabbage and serve.

Bon Appétit!

245. Tasty Sweet Carrots Dish

Perp time: 10 minutes **Cooking time:** 15 minutes **Servings:** 4

Nutrition Facts:
- Calories: 60
- Fat (In grams): 0.1
- Fiber (In grams): 1
- Carbs (In grams): 4
- Protein: 1 g

Ingredients:
- 2 cups baby carrots
- A pinch of salt
- One-tablespoon brown Sugar
- Half-tablespoon butter
- Half-cup water

Instructions:
1. In your instant pot, mix butter with water, salt and Sugar and stir well.
2. Set the pot on Sauté mode and cook everything for 30 seconds.
3. Add carrots, stir, cover and cook at High for 15 minutes.
4. Release the pressure, uncover the pot, set it on Sauté mode again and cook everything for 1 more minute.
5. Serve hot.

Bon Appétit!

246. TASTY SAUSAGES AND CABBAGE

Perp time: 10 minutes   **Cooking time:** 5 minutes   **Servings:** 4

Nutrition Facts:
- Calories: 140
- Fat (In grams): 6
- Fiber (In grams): 4
- Carbs (In grams): 11
- Protein: 10 g

Ingredients:
- 3 tablespoons butter
- 1 green cabbage head, chopped
- Salt and black pepper to the taste
- 1 pound sausage links, sliced
- 15 ounces canned tomatoes, chopped
- Half-cup yellow onion, chopped
- 2 teaspoons turmeric

Instructions:
1. Set your instant pot on Sauté mode, add sausage slices, stir and cook until they brown.
2. Drain excess grease, add butter, cabbage, tomatoes salt, pepper, onion and turmeric, stir, cover and cook at High for 2 minutes.
3. Release the pressure fast, uncover, divide cabbage and sausages among plates and serve.

Bon Appétit!

247. AMAZING MAPLE GLAZED CARROTS

Perp time: 10 minutes   **Cooking time:** 4 minutes   **Servings:** 4

Nutrition Facts:
- Calories: 60
- Fat (In grams): 1.1
- Fiber (In grams): 2.6
- Carbs (In grams): 12
- Protein: 1 g

Ingredients:
- 2 pounds carrots, peeled and sliced on the diagonal
- One-tablespoon maple syrup
- Black pepper to the taste
- One-tablespoon butter
- One-cup water
- 1/4 cup raisins

Instructions:
1. Put carrots in your instant pot.
2. Add water and raisins, cover and cook at High for 4 minutes.
3. Release the pressure, uncover, add butter and maple syrup, stir, divide carrots among plates and sprinkle black pepper before serving them.

Bon Appétit!

248. Tasty Pasta And Cauliflower

Perp time: 10 minutes **Cooking time:** 10 minutes **Servings:** 4

Nutrition Facts:
- Calories: 160
- Fat (In grams): 5
- Fiber (In grams): 3
- Carbs (In grams): 23
- Protein: 13 g

Ingredients:
- 2 tablespoons butter
- 8 cups cauliflower florets
- 2 garlic cloves, minced
- One-cup chicken stock
- Salt to the taste
- 2 cups spinach, chopped
- 1 pound fettuccine paste
- 2 green onions, chopped
- One-tablespoon gorgonzola cheese, grated
- 3 sun-dried tomatoes, chopped
- A splash of balsamic vinegar

Instructions:
1. Set your instant pot on Sauté mode, add butter and melt it.
2. Add garlic, stir and cook for 2 minutes.
3. Add stock, salt and cauliflower, stir, cover and cook at High for 6 minutes.
4. Release the pressure for 10 minutes, transfer cauliflower to your blender and pulse well.
5. Add spinach and green onions and stir gently.
6. Heat up a pot with some water and a pinch of salt over medium high heat, bring to a boil, add pasta, cook according to instructions, drain and divide among plates.
7. Add cauliflower sauce, gorgonzola, sun-dried tomatoes and a splash of vinegar on top, toss to coat and serve.

Bon Appétit!

249. Special Collard Greens And Bacon

Perp time: 10 minutes **Cooking time:** 26 minutes **Servings:** 6

Nutrition Facts:
- Calories: 130
- Fat (In grams): 8
- Fiber (In grams): 2
- Carbs (In grams): 4
- Protein: 6 g

Ingredients:
- 1 pound collard greens, trimmed
- 1/4 pound bacon, chopped
- Salt and black pepper to the taste
- Half-cup water

Instructions:
1. Set your instant pot on Sauté mode, add bacon, stir and cook for 5 minutes.
2. Add collard greens, salt, pepper and water, stir, cover and cook at High for 20 minutes.
3. Release the pressure, uncover, divide mix among plates and serve.

Bon Appétit!

250. YUMMY COLLARD GREENS DELIGHT

Perp time: 10 minutes **Cooking time:** 20 minutes **Servings:** 4

Nutrition Facts:
- Calories: 130
- Fat (In grams): 7
- Fiber (In grams): 4.5
- Carbs (In grams): 12
- Protein: 4 g
- Sugar (In grams): 4

Ingredients:
- 1 bunch collard greens, trimmed
- 2 tablespoons extra virgin olive oil
- Half-cup chicken stock
- 2 tablespoons tomato puree
- 1 yellow onion, chopped
- 3 garlic cloves, minced
- Salt and black pepper to the taste
- One-tablespoon balsamic vinegar
- One-teaspoon Sugar

Instructions:
1. In your instant pot, mix stock with oil, garlic, vinegar, onion and tomato puree and stir.
2. Add collard greens after you've rolled them in cigar-shaped bundles.
3. Add salt, pepper and Sugar, cover and cook at High for 20 minutes.
4. Release the pressure fast, uncover pot, divide collard greens among plates and serve.

Bon Appétit!

251. SPECIAL COLLARD GREENS DISH

Perp time: 10 minutes **Cooking time:** 25 minutes **Servings:** 8

Nutrition Facts:
- Calories: 100
- Fat (In grams): 1.4
- Fiber (In grams): 1.7
- Carbs (In grams): 4
- Protein: 6 g

Ingredients:
- 1 sweet onion, chopped
- 2 tablespoons extra virgin olive oil
- 3 garlic cloves, crushed
- 2 ½ pounds collard greens, chopped
- Salt and black pepper to the taste
- 2 cups chicken stock
- 2 tablespoons apple cider vinegar
- One-tablespoon brown Sugar
- Half-teaspoon crushed red pepper
- 2 smoked turkey wings

Instructions:
1. Set your instant pot on Sauté mode, add oil and heat it up.
2. Add onions, stir and cook for 2 minutes.
3. Add garlic, stir and cook for 1 minute.
4. Add stock, greens, vinegar, salt, pepper, crushed red pepper and Sugar and stir gently.
5. Add smoked turkey, cover and cook at High for 20 minutes.
6. Release the pressure fast, uncover, divide greens and turkey among plates and serve.

Bon Appétit!

252. Classic Carrots Dish

Perp time: 10 minutes **Cooking time:** 2 minutes **Servings:** 4

Nutrition Facts:
- Calories: 60
- Fat (In grams): 1
- Fiber (In grams): 2
- Carbs (In grams): 4
- Protein: 3 g

Ingredients:
- 16 ounces baby carrots
- Salt and black pepper to the taste
- 2 tablespoons butter
- 4 ounces molasses
- 2 ounces water
- 2 tablespoon dill, chopped

Instructions:
1. Put carrot, water, salt, pepper and molasses in your instant pot, stir, cover and cook at High for 3 minutes.
2. Release the pressure, uncover the pot, add butter and dill, stir, divide among plates and serve.

Bon Appétit!

253. Tasty Braised Endives

Perp time: 10 minutes **Cooking time:** 7 minutes **Servings:** 4

Nutrition Facts:
- Calories: 80
- Fat (In grams): 3.1
- Fiber (In grams): 0.5
- Carbs (In grams): 12
- Protein: 1.2 g

Ingredients:
- 4 endives, trimmed and cut into halves
- Salt and black pepper to the taste
- One-tablespoon lemon juice
- One-tablespoon butter

Instructions:
1. Set your instant pot on Sauté mode.
2. Add butter and melt it.
3. Arrange endives in the pot, add salt and pepper and the lemon juice, cover and cook at High for 7 minutes.
4. Release the pressure naturally, arrange endives on a platter, add cooking juice all over them and serve.

Bon Appétit!

254. Quick Endives Risotto

Perp time: 10 minutes **Cooking time:** 20 minutes **Servings:** 2

Nutrition Facts:
- Calories: 260
- Fat (In grams): 5
- Fiber (In grams): 5
- Carbs (In grams): 13
- Protein: 16 g

Ingredients:
- 3/4 cup rice
- 2 Belgian endives, trimmed and cut into halves lengthwise and roughly chopped
- ½ yellow onion, chopped
- 2 tablespoons extra virgin olive oil
- ½ cup white wine
- 2 cups veggie stock
- 2 ounces parmesan, grated
- 3 tablespoons heavy cream
- Salt and black pepper to the taste

Instructions:
1. Set your instant pot on Sauté mode, add oil and heat it up.
2. Add onion, stir and sauté for 4 minutes.
3. Add endives, stir and cook for 4 minutes more.
4. Add rice, wine, salt, pepper, stock, stir, cover and cook at High for 10 minutes.
5. Release the pressure fast, uncover pot and set it on Sauté mode again.
6. Add cheese and heavy cream, stir, cook for 1 minute, transfer to plates and serve.

Bon Appétit!

255. Delicious Sautéed Endives

Perp time: 10 minutes **Cooking time:** 15 minutes **Servings:** 4

Nutrition Facts:
- Calories: 90
- Fat (In grams): 1
- Fiber (In grams): 4
- Carbs (In grams): 4
- Protein: 2 g

Ingredients:
- 8 endives, trimmed
- Salt and black pepper to the taste
- 4 tablespoon butter
- Juice of ½ lemon
- Half-cup water
- One-teaspoon Sugar
- 2 tablespoons parsley, chopped

Instructions:
1. Put the endives in your instant pot, add One-tablespoon butter, lemon juice, Half-cup water, Sugar, salt and pepper, stir gently, cover and cook at High for 10 minutes.
2. Release the pressure fast, uncover the pot and transfer endives to a plate.
3. Heat up a pan with 3 tablespoons butter over medium high heat, add endives, more salt and pepper if needed and parsley, stir and cook for 5 minutes.
4. Transfer endives to plates and serve.

Bon Appétit!

256. Smple Eggplant Dish

Perp time: 10 minutes **Cooking time:** 8 minutes **Servings:** 2

Nutrition Facts:
- Calories: 130
- Fat (In grams): 3
- Fiber (In grams): 2
- Carbs (In grams): 3
- Protein: 3 g

Ingredients:
- 4 cups eggplant, cubed
- One-tablespoon extra virgin olive oil
- 3 garlic cloves, minced
- One-tablespoon garlic powder
- Salt and black pepper to the taste
- One-cup marinara sauce
- ½ cup water

Instructions:
1. Set your instant pot on Sauté mode, add the oil and heat it up.
2. Add garlic, stir and cook for 2 minutes.
3. Add eggplant, salt, pepper, garlic powder, marinara sauce and water, stir gently, cover and cook at High for 8 minutes.
4. Release the pressure fast, uncover the pot and serve your eggplant mix right away with your favorite spaghetti.

Bon Appétit!

---

257. SPECIAL BABAGANOUSH DISH

Perp time: 10 minutes **Cooking time:** 4 minutes **Servings:** 6

Nutrition Facts:
- Calories: 70
- Fat (In grams): 2
- Fiber (In grams): 2
- Carbs (In grams): 7
- Protein: 1 g

Ingredients:
- 2 pounds eggplant, peeled and cut into medium chunks
- Salt and black pepper to the taste
- 1/4 cup extra virgin olive oil
- Half-cup water
- 4 garlic cloves
- 1/4 cup lemon juice
- 1 bunch thyme, chopped
- One-tablespoon tahini
- A drizzle of olive oil
- 3 olives, pitted and sliced

Instructions:
1. Put the eggplant pieces in your instant pot, add 1/4 cup oil, set the pot on Sauté mode and heat everything up.
2. Add garlic, water, salt and pepper, stir, cover and cook at High for 3 minutes.
3. Release the pressure, uncover the pot, transfer eggplant pieces and garlic to your blender, add lemon juice and tahini and pulse well.
4. Add thyme and blend again.
5. Transfer eggplant spread to a bowl, top with olive slices and a drizzle of oil and serve.

Bon Appétit!

---

258. YUMMY EGGPLANT RATATOUILLE

Perp time: 15 minutes **Cooking time:** 8 minutes **Servings:** 6

Nutrition Facts:
- Calories: 109
- Fat (In grams): 5
- Fiber (In grams): 3

- Carbs (In grams): 14
- Protein: 2 g

Ingredients:
- 1 big eggplant, peeled and thinly sliced
- 2 garlic cloves, minced
- 3 tablespoons extra virgin olive oil
- Salt and black pepper to the taste
- One-cup onion, chopped
- 1 green bell pepper, chopped
- 1 red bell pepper, chopped
- Half-cup water
- One-teaspoon thyme
- 14 ounces canned tomatoes, chopped
- A pinch of Sugar
- One-cup basil, chopped

Instructions:
1. Set your instant pot on Sauté mode, add oil and heat it up.
2. Add green and red bell pepper, onion and garlic, stir and cook for 3 minutes.
3. Add eggplant, water, salt, pepper, thyme, Sugar and tomatoes, cover the pot and cook at High for 4 minutes.
4. Release the pressure fast, uncover the pot, add basil, stir gently, divide among plates and serve.

Bon Appétit!

259. BRAISED FENNEL

Perp time: 10 minutes **Cooking time:** 12 minutes **Servings:** 4

Nutrition Facts:
- Calories: 70
- Fat (In grams): 1
- Fiber (In grams): 2
- Carbs (In grams): 2
- Protein: 1 g

Ingredients:
- 2 fennel bulbs, trimmed and cut into quarters
- 3 tablespoons extra virgin olive oil
- Salt and black pepper to the taste
- 1 garlic clove, chopped
- 1 dried red pepper
- 3/4 cup veggie stock
- Juice of ½ lemon
- 1/4 cup white wine
- 1/4 cup parmesan, grated

Instructions:
1. Set your instant pot on Sauté mode, add oil and heat it up.
2. Add garlic and red pepper, stir, cook for 2 minutes and discard garlic.
3. Add fennel, stir and brown it for 8 minutes.
4. Add salt, pepper, stock, wine, cover and cook at High for 4 minutes.
5. Release the pressure, uncover the pot, add lemon juice, more salt and pepper if needed and cheese.
6. Toss to coat, divide among plates and serve.

Bon Appétit!

260. Surprise Eggplant

Perp time: 10 minutes **Cooking time:** 7 minutes **Servings:** 4

Nutrition Facts:
- Calories: 140
- Fat (In grams): 3.4
- Fiber (In grams): 7
- Carbs (In grams): 20
- Protein: 5 g

Ingredients:
- 1 eggplant, roughly chopped
- 3 zucchinis, roughly chopped
- 3 tomatoes, sliced
- 2 tablespoons lemon juice
- Salt and black pepper to the taste
- One-teaspoon thyme, dried
- One-teaspoon oregano, dried
- 3 tablespoons extra virgin olive oil

Instructions:
1. Put eggplant pieces in your instant pot.
2. Add zucchinis and tomatoes.
3. In a bowl, mix lemon juice with salt, pepper, thyme, oregano and oil and stir well.
4. Pour this over veggies, toss to coat, cover the pot and cook at High for 7 minutes.
5. Release the pressure, uncover the pot, divide among plates and serve.

Bon Appétit!

261. Easy Fennel Risotto

Perp time: 10 minutes **Cooking time:** 10 minutes **Servings:** 2

Nutrition Facts:
- Calories: 200
- Fat (In grams): 10
- Fiber (In grams): 2
- Carbs (In grams): 20
- Protein: 12 g

Ingredients:
- 1 ½ cups Arborio rice
- 1 yellow onion, chopped
- 3 cups chicken stock
- 1 fennel bulb, trimmed and chopped
- 2 tablespoons butter
- One-tablespoon extra virgin olive oil
- 1/4 cup white wine
- Salt and black pepper to the taste
- Half-teaspoon thyme, dried
- 3 tablespoons tomato paste
- 1/3 cup parmesan cheese, grated

Instructions:
1. Set your instant pot on Sauté mode, add butter and melt it.
2. Add fennel and onion, stir, sauté for 4 minutes and transfer to a bowl.
3. Add oil to your pot and heat it up.
4. Add rice, stir and cook for 3 minutes.
5. Add tomato paste, stock, fennel, onions, wine, salt, pepper and thyme, stir, cover and cook at High for 8 minutes.
6. Release the pressure, uncover, add cheese, stir, divide among plates and serve.

Bon Appétit!

262. Kale With Lemon And Garlic

Perp time: 10 minutes **Cooking time:** 5 minutes **Servings:** 4

Nutrition Facts:
- Calories: 60
- Fat (In grams): 3
- Fiber (In grams): 1
- Carbs (In grams): 2.4
- Protein: 0.7 g

Ingredients:
- 3 garlic cloves, chopped
- One-tablespoon extra virgin olive oil
- 1 pound kale, trimmed
- Salt and black pepper to the taste
- Half-cup water
- Juice of ½ lemon

Instructions:
1. Set the instant pot on Sauté mode, add oil and heat it up.
2. Add garlic, stir and cook for 2 minutes.
3. Add kale and water, cover and cook at High for 5 minutes.
4. Release the pressure, uncover the pot, add salt, pepper and lemon juice, stir, divide among plates and serve.

Bon Appétit!

263. Bacon And Kale

Perp time: 10 minutes **Cooking time:** 10 minute **Servings:** 4

Nutrition Facts:
- Calories: 140
- Fat (In grams): 7
- Fiber (In grams): 1
- Carbs (In grams): 7
- Protein: 2 g

Ingredients:
- 6 bacon slices, chopped
- One-tablespoon vegetable oil
- 1 onion, thinly sliced
- 6 garlic cloves, chopped
- 1 ½ cups chicken stock
- One-tablespoon brown Sugar
- 2 tablespoons apple cider vinegar
- 10 ounces kale leaves, chopped
- One-teaspoon red chili, crushed
- One-teaspoon liquid smoke
- Salt and black pepper to the taste

Instructions:
1. Set your instant pot on Sauté mode, add oil and heat it up.
2. Add bacon, stir and cook for 1-2 minutes.
3. Add onion, stir and cook for 3 minutes.
4. Add garlic, stir and cook for 1 minute.
5. Add vinegar, stock, Sugar, liquid smoke, red chilies, salt, pepper, kale, stir, cover and cook at High for 5 minutes.
6. Release the pressure fast, uncover, divide among plates and serve.

Bon Appétit!

264. Tasty Braised Kale

Perp time: 10 minutes **Cooking time:** 10 minutes **Servings:** 2

Nutrition Facts:
- Calories: 60
- Fat (In grams): 2
- Fiber (In grams): 2
- Carbs (In grams): 4
- Protein: 1 g

Ingredients:
- 10 ounces kale, chopped
- 1 yellow onion, thinly sliced
- One-tablespoon kale
- 3 carrots, sliced
- Half-cup chicken stock
- 5 garlic cloves, chopped
- Salt and black pepper to the taste
- A splash of balsamic vinegar
- 1/4 teaspoon red pepper flakes

Instructions:
1. Set your instant pot on Sauté mode, add ghee and melt it.
2. Add carrots and onion, stir and sauté for 2 minutes.
3. Add garlic, stir and cook for 1 minute more.
4. Add kale, stock, salt and pepper, stir, cover and cook at High for 7 minutes.
5. Release the pressure, uncover the pot, add vinegar and pepper flakes, toss to coat, divide among plates and serve.

Bon Appétit!

265. Corn And Okra

Perp time: 10 minutes **Cooking time:** 17 minutes **Servings:** 6

Nutrition Facts:
- Calories: 140
- Fat (In grams): 5
- Fiber (In grams): 6
- Carbs (In grams): 22
- Protein: 4 g
- Sugar (In grams): 9

Ingredients:
- 1 pound okra, trimmed
- 6 scallions, chopped
- 3 green bell peppers, chopped
- Salt and black pepper to the taste
- 2 tablespoons vegetable oil
- One-teaspoon Sugar
- 28 ounces canned tomatoes, chopped
- One-cup corn kernels

Instructions:
1. Set your instant pot on Sauté mode, add oil and heat it up.
2. Add scallions and bell peppers, stir and cook for 5 minutes.
3. Add okra, salt, pepper, Sugar and tomatoes, stir, cover and cook at High for 10 minutes.
4. Release the pressure fast, uncover, add corn, cover pot again and cook at High for 2 minutes.
5. Release pressure again, transfer okra mix on plates and serve.

Bon Appétit!

266. Quick Steamed Leeks

Perp time: 10 minutes   **Cooking time:** 10 minutes   **Servings:** 4

Nutrition Facts:
- Calories: 70
- Fat (In grams): 4
- Fiber (In grams): 1.4
- Carbs (In grams): 10
- Protein: 1.2 g

Ingredients:
- 4 leeks, washed, roots and ends cut off
- Salt and black pepper to the taste
- 1/3 cup water
- One-tablespoon butter

Instructions:
1. Put leeks in your instant pot, add water and butter, salt and pepper to the taste, stir, cover and cook at High for 5 minutes.
2. Release the pressure fast, uncover the pot, set it on Sauté mode and cook leeks for 5 more minutes.
3. Divide among plates and serve.

Bon Appétit!

267. Mouthwatering Crispy Potatoes

Perp time: 10 minutes   **Cooking time:** 7 minutes   **Servings:** 4

Nutrition Facts:
- Calories: 132
- Fat (In grams): 1
- Fiber (In grams): 0
- Carbs (In grams): 23
- Protein: 3 g

Ingredients:
- Half-cup water
- 1-pound gold potatoes, cubed
- Salt and black pepper to the taste
- 2 tablespoons ghee
- Juice of ½ lemon
- 1/4 cup parsley leaves, chopped

Instructions:
1. Put the water in your instant pot, add potatoes in the steamer basket, cover and cook at High for 5 minutes.
2. Release the pressure naturally, uncover the pot and set it on Sauté mode.
3. Add ghee, lemon juice, parsley, salt and pepper, stir and cook for 2 minutes.
4. Transfer to plates and serve.

Bon Appétit!

268. Special Okra Pilaf

Perp time: 10 minutes   **Cooking time:** 25 minutes   **Servings:** 4

Nutrition Facts:
- Calories: 300
- Fat (In grams): 11
- Fiber (In grams): 4.2
- Carbs (In grams): 41
- Protein: 7.8 g

Ingredients:
- 2 cups okra, sliced
- 4 bacon slices, chopped
- 2 teaspoons paprika
- One-cup brown rice
- One-cup tomatoes, chopped
- 2 and 1/4 cups water
- Salt and black pepper to the taste

Instructions:
1. Set your instant pot on Sauté mode, add bacon and brown it for 2 minutes.
2. Add okra, stir and cook 5 minutes.
3. Add paprika and rice, stir and cook for 2 minutes.
4. Add salt, pepper, water and tomatoes, stir, cover and cook for 16 minutes.
5. Release the pressure, uncover pot, divide pilaf among plates and serve.

Bon Appétit!

269. HOT ROASTED POTATOES

Perp time: 10 minutes **Cooking time:** 17 minutes **Servings:** 4

Nutrition Facts:
- Calories: 50
- Fat (In grams): 1.4
- Fiber (In grams): 1
- Carbs (In grams): 7.4
- Protein: 1 g

Ingredients:
- 2 pounds baby potatoes
- 5 tablespoons vegetable oil
- Salt and black pepper to the taste
- 1 rosemary spring
- 5 garlic cloves
- Half-cup stock

Instructions:
1. Set your instant pot on Sauté mode, add oil and heat it up.
2. Add potatoes, rosemary and garlic, stir and brown them for 10 minutes.
3. Prick each potato with a knife, add stock, salt and pepper to the pot, cover and cook at High for 7 minutes.
4. Release the pressure, uncover the pot, divide potatoes among plates and serve.

Bon Appétit!

270. TOMATOES AND ZUCCHINIS

Perp time: 10 minutes **Cooking time:** 12 minutes **Servings:** 4

Nutrition Facts:
- Calories: 155
- Fat (In grams): 2
- Fiber (In grams): 4
- Carbs (In grams): 12
- Protein: 22 g

Ingredients:
- 6 zucchinis, roughly chopped
- 2 yellow onions, chopped
- One-tablespoon vegetable oil
- One-cup tomato puree
- 1-pound cherry tomatoes, cut into halves
- A drizzle of olive oil
- Salt and black pepper to the taste

- 2 garlic cloves, minced
- 1 bunch basil, chopped

Instructions:
1. Set your instant pot on Sauté mode, add vegetable oil and heat it up.
2. Add onion, stir and cook for 5 minutes.
3. Add tomatoes, tomato puree, zucchinis, salt and pepper, stir, cover and cook at High for 5 minutes.
4. Release the pressure, uncover the pot, add garlic and basil, stir and divide among plates.
5. Drizzle some olive oil at the end and serve.

Bon Appétit!

271. CARROTS AND TURNIPS

Perp time: 5 minutes **Cooking time:** 9 minutes **Servings:** 4

Nutrition Facts:
- Calories: 70
- Fat (In grams): 0
- Fiber (In grams): 1
- Carbs (In grams): 0.4
- Protein: 2 g

Ingredients:
- 2 turnips, peeled and sliced
- 3 carrots, sliced
- 1 small onion, chopped
- One-teaspoon cumin, ground
- One-tablespoon extra virgin olive oil
- One-cup water
- Salt and black pepper to the taste
- One-teaspoon lemon juice

Instructions:
1. Set your instant pot on Sauté mode, add oil and heat it up.
2. Add onion, stir and sauté for 2 minutes.
3. Add turnips, carrots, cumin and lemon juice, stir and cook for 1 minute.
4. Add salt, pepper, and water, stir, cover and cook at High for 6 minutes.
5. Release the pressure, uncover the pot, divide turnips and carrots among plates and serve.

Bon Appétit!

272. TASTY AND SPICY TURNIPS

Perp time: 10 minutes **Cooking time:** 22 minutes **Servings:** 4

Nutrition Facts:
- Calories: 80
- Fat (In grams): 2.4
- Fiber (In grams): 4
- Carbs (In grams): 12
- Protein: 3 g

Ingredients:
- 20 ounces turnips, peeled and chopped
- One-teaspoon garlic, minced
- One-teaspoon ginger, grated
- 2 yellow onions, chopped
- 2 tomatoes, chopped
- One-teaspoon Sugar
- One-teaspoon cumin powder
- One-teaspoon coriander powder
- 2 green chilies, chopped
- Half-teaspoon turmeric powder
- One-cup water
- 2 tablespoons butter

- Salt to the taste
- A handful coriander leaves, chopped

Instructions:
1. Set your instant pot on Sauté mode, add butter and melt it.
2. Add green chilies, garlic and ginger, stir and cook for 1 minute.
3. Add onions, stir and cook 3 minutes.
4. Add salt, tomatoes, turmeric, cumin and coriander powder, stir and cook 3 minutes.
5. Add turnips and water, stir, cover and cook on Low for 15 minutes.
6. Release the pressure, uncover the pot, add Sugar and coriander, stir, divide among plates and serve.

Bon Appétit!

273. DELICIOUS CORN SOUP

Perp time: 10 minutes **Cooking time:** 15 minutes **Servings:** 4

Nutrition Facts:
- Calories: 300
- Fat (In grams): 8.3
- Fiber (In grams): 8
- Carbs (In grams): 50
- Protein: 13 g

Ingredients:
- 2 leeks, chopped
- 2 tablespoons butter
- 2 garlic cloves, minced
- 6 ears of corn, kernels cut off, cobs reserved
- 2 bay leaves
- 4 tarragon sprigs, chopped
- 1-quart chicken stock
- Salt and black pepper to the taste
- A drizzle of extra virgin olive oil
- One-tablespoon chives, chopped

Instructions:
1. Set your instant pot on Sauté mode, add butter and melt it.
2. Add garlic and leeks, stir and cook for 4 minutes.
3. Add corn, corn cobs, bay leaves, tarragon and stock to cover everything, cover pot and cook at High for 15 minutes.
4. Release the pressure, uncover the pot, discard bay leaves and corn cobs and transfer everything to your blender.
5. Pulse well o obtain a smooth soup, add the rest of the stock and blend again.
6. Add salt and pepper to the taste, stir well, divide into soup bowls and serve cold with chives and olive oil on top.

Bon Appétit!

274. YUMMY STUFFED TOMATOES

Perp time: 10 minutes **Cooking time:** 10 minutes **Servings:** 4

Nutrition Facts:
- Calories: 140
- Fat (In grams): 3
- Fiber (In grams): 1.4
- Carbs (In grams): 10
- Protein: 4 g

Ingredients:
- 4 tomatoes, tops cut off and pulp scooped
- Salt and black pepper to the taste
- 1 yellow onion, chopped
- One-tablespoon butter
- 2 tablespoons celery, chopped
- Half-cup mushrooms, chopped
- 1 slice of bread, crumbled
- One-cup cottage cheese
- 1/4 teaspoon caraway seeds
- One-tablespoon parsley, chopped
- Half-cup water

Instructions:
1. Chop tomato pulp and put it in a bowl.
2. Heat up a pan with the butter over medium high heat, add onion and celery, stir and cook for 3 minutes.
3. Add tomato pulp and mushrooms, stir and cook for 1 minute more.
4. Add salt, pepper, crumbled bread, cheese, caraway seeds and parsley, stir and cook for 4 minutes more.
5. Fill each tomato with this mix and arrange them in the steamer basket of your instant pot.
6. Add the water to the pot, cover and cook at High for 2 minutes.
7. Release the pressure fast, uncover the pot, transfer stuffed potatoes to plates and serve.

Bon Appétit!

SOUPS AND STEWS RECIPES

275. Yummy Chicken Soup

Perp time: 10 minutes **Cooking time:** 17 minutes **Servings:** 4

Nutrition Facts:
- Calories: 210
- Fat (In grams): 4.4
- Fiber (In grams): 4.3
- Carbs (In grams): 18
- Protein: 26 g

Ingredients:
- 4 chicken breasts, skinless and boneless
- 2 tablespoons extra virgin olive oil
- 1 onion, chopped
- 3 garlic cloves, minced
- 16 ounces jarred chunky salsa
- 29 ounces canned tomatoes, peeled and chopped
- 29 ounces canned chicken stock
- Salt and black pepper to the taste
- 2 tablespoons parsley, dried
- One-teaspoon garlic powder
- One-tablespoon onion powder
- One-tablespoon chili powder
- 15 ounces frozen corn
- 32 ounces canned black beans, drained

Instructions:
1. Set your instant pot on Sauté mode, add oil and heat it up.
2. Add onion, stir and cook 5 minutes.
3. Add garlic, stir and cook for 1 minute more.
4. Add chicken breasts, salsa, tomatoes, stock, salt, pepper, parsley, garlic powder, onion and chili powder, stir, cover and cook at High for 8 minutes.
5. Release the pressure for 10 minutes, uncover the pot, transfer chicken breasts to a cutting board, shred with 2 forks and return to pot.
6. Add beans and corn, set the pot on Simmer mode and cook for 2-3 minutes more.
7. Divide into soup bowls and serve.

Bon Appétit!

276. Cheese And Potato Soup

Perp time: 10 minutes **Cooking time:** 10 minutes **Servings:** 6

Nutrition Facts:
- Calories: 188
- Fat (In grams): 7.14
- Fiber (In grams): 1.5
- Carbs (In grams): 22
- Protein: 9 g

Ingredients:
- 6 cups potatoes, cubed
- 2 tablespoons butter
- Half-cup yellow onion, chopped
- 28 ounces canned chicken stock
- Salt and black pepper to the taste
- 2 tablespoons parsley, dried
- 1/8 red pepper flakes
- 2 tablespoons cornstarch
- 2 tablespoons water
- 3 ounces cream cheese, cubed
- 2 cups half and half
- One-cup cheddar cheese, shredded
- One-cup corn
- 6 bacon slices, cooked and crumbled

Instructions:
1. Set your instant pot on Sauté mode, add butter and melt it.

2. Add onion, stir and cook 5 minutes
3. Add half of the stock, salt, pepper, pepper flakes and parsley and stir.
4. Put potatoes in the steamer basket, cover the pot and cook at High for 4 minutes.
5. Release the pressure fast, uncover pot and transfer potatoes to a bowl.
6. In another bowl, mix cornstarch with water and stir well.
7. Set the pot to Simmer mode, add cornstarch, cream cheese and shredded cheese and stir well.
8. Also add the rest of the stock, corn, bacon, potatoes, half and half.
9. Stir, bring to a simmer, ladle into bowls and serve.

Bon Appétit!

277. AMAZING SPLIT PEA SOUP

Perp time: 10 minutes **Cooking time:** 20 minutes **Servings:** 6

Nutrition Facts:
- Calories: 30
- Fat (In grams): 11
- Fiber (In grams): 12
- Carbs (In grams): 14
- Protein:20 g

Ingredients:
- 2 tablespoons butter
- 1 pound chicken sausage, ground
- 1 yellow onion, chopped
- Half-cup carrots, chopped
- Half-cup celery, chopped
- 2 garlic cloves, minced
- 29 ounces chicken stock
- Salt and black pepper to the taste
- 2 cups water
- 16 ounces split peas, rinsed
- Half-cup half and half
- 1/4 teaspoon red pepper flakes, dried

Instructions:
1. Set the pot on Sauté mode, add sausage, brown it on all sides and transfer to a plate.
2. Add butter to your instant pot and melt it.
3. Add celery, onions, and carrots, stir and cook 4 minutes.
4. Add garlic, stir and cook for 1 minute.
5. Add water, stock, peas and pepper flakes, stir, cover and cook at High for 10 minutes.
6. Release the pressure, puree the mix using an immersion blender and set the pot on Simmer mode.
7. Add sausage, salt, pepper and half and half, stir, bring to a simmer and ladle into soup bowls.

Bon Appétit!

278. TASTY BUTTERNUT SQUASH SOUP

Perp time: 10 minutes   **Cooking time:** 16 minutes   **Servings:** 6

Nutrition Facts:
- Calories: 130
- Fat (In grams): 2.3
- Fiber (In grams): 0.4
- Carbs (In grams): 18
- Protein: 6 g

Ingredients:
- 1 ½ pounds butternut squash, baked, peeled and cubed
- Half-cup green onions, chopped
- 3 tablespoons butter
- Half-cup carrots, chopped
- Half-cup celery, chopped
- 29 ounces canned chicken stock
- 1 garlic clove, minced
- Half-teaspoon Italian seasoning
- 15 ounces canned tomatoes and their juice, chopped
- Salt and black pepper to the taste
- 1/8 teaspoon red pepper flakes, dried
- One-cup orzo, already cooked
- 1/8 teaspoon nutmeg, grated
- 1 ½ cup half and half
- One-cup chicken meat, already cooked and shredded
- Some green onions, chopped for serving

Instructions:
1. Set your instant pot on Sauté mode, add butter and melt it.
2. Add celery, carrots and onions, stir and cook for 3 minutes.
3. Add garlic, stir and cook for 1 minute more.
4. Add squash, tomatoes, stock, Italian seasoning, salt, pepper, pepper flakes and nutmeg.
5. Stir, cover and cook at High for 10 minutes.
6. Release the pressure fast, uncover and puree everything with your immersion blender.
7. Set the pot on Simmer mode, add half and half, orzo and chicken, stir and cook for 3 minutes.
8. Divide soup into bowls, sprinkle green onions on top and serve.

Bon Appétit!

279. RICE AND BEEF SOUP

Perp time: 10 minutes   **Cooking time:** 15 minutes   **Servings:** 6

Nutrition Facts:
- Calories: 230
- Fat (In grams): 7
- Fiber (In grams): 4
- Carbs (In grams): 10
- Protein: 3 g

Ingredients:
- 1 pound beef meat, ground
- 3 garlic cloves, minced
- 1 yellow onion, chopped
- One-tablespoon vegetable oil
- 1 celery rib, chopped
- 28 ounces canned beef stock
- 14 ounces canned tomatoes, crushed
- Half-cup white rice
- 12 ounces spicy V8 juice
- 15 ounces canned garbanzo beans, rinsed
- 1 potato, cubed
- Salt and black pepper to the taste
- Half-cup frozen peas

- 2 carrots, thinly sliced

Instructions:
1. Set your instant pot on Sauté mode, add beef, stir, cook until it browns and transfer to a plate.
2. Add the oil to your pot and heat it up.
3. Add celery and onion, stir and cook for 5 minutes.
4. Add garlic, stir and cook for 1 minute more.
5. Add V8 juice, stock, tomatoes, rice, beans, carrots, potatoes, beef, salt and pepper, stir, cover and cook at High for 5 minutes.
6. Release the pressure, uncover the pot and set it on Simmer mode.
7. Add more salt and pepper if needed and peas, stir, bring to a simmer, transfer to bowls and serve hot.

Bon Appétit!

280. WILD RICE AND CHICKEN SOUP

Perp time: 10 minutes **Cooking time:** 15 minutes **Servings:** 6

Nutrition Facts:
- Calories: 200
- Fat (In grams): 7
- Fiber (In grams): 1
- Carbs (In grams): 19
- Protein: 5 g

Ingredients:
- One-cup yellow onion, chopped
- 2 tablespoons butter
- One-cup celery, chopped
- One-cup carrots, chopped
- 28 ounces chicken stock
- 2 chicken breasts, skinless and boneless and chopped
- 6 ounces wild rice
- A pinch of red pepper flakes
- Salt and black pepper to the taste
- One-tablespoon parsley, dried
- 2 tablespoons cornstarch mixed with 2 tablespoons water
- One-cup milk
- One-cup half and half
- 4 ounces cream cheese, cubed

Instructions:
1. Set your instant pot on Sauté mode, add butter and melt it.
2. Add carrot, onion and celery, stir and cook for 5 minutes.
3. Add rice, chicken, stock, parsley, salt and pepper, stir, cover and cook at High for 5 minutes.
4. Release the pressure, uncover, add cornstarch mixed with water, stir and set the pot on Simmer mode.
5. Add cheese, milk and half and half, stir, heat up, transfer to bowls and serve.

Bon Appétit!

281. CHINESE CHICKEN NOODLE SOUP

Perp time: 10 minutes **Cooking time:** 12 minutes **Servings:** 6

Nutrition Facts:
- Calories: 100
- Fat (In grams): 1
- Fiber (In grams): 1
- Carbs (In grams): 4
- Protein: 7 g

Ingredients:
- 1 yellow onion, chopped
- One-tablespoon butter
- 1 celery rib, chopped
- 4 carrots, sliced
- Salt and black pepper to the taste
- 6 cups chicken stock
- 2 cups chicken, already cooked and shredded
- Egg noodles, already cooked

Instructions:
1. Set your instant pot on Sauté mode, add butter and heat it up.
2. Add onion, stir and cook 2 minutes.
3. Add celery and carrots, stir and cook 5 minutes.
4. Add chicken, stock, stir, cover pot and cook at High for 5 minutes.
5. Release the pressure, uncover the pot, add salt and pepper to the taste and stir.
6. Divide noodles into soup bowls, add soup over them and serve.

Bon Appétit!

282. AWESOME ZUPPA TOSCANA

Perp time: 10 minutes   **Cooking time:** 17 minutes   **Servings:** 8

Nutrition Facts:
- Calories: 170
- Fat (In grams): 4
- Fiber (In grams): 2
- Carbs (In grams): 24
- Protein: 10 g

Ingredients:
- 1 pound chicken sausage, ground
- 6 bacon slices, chopped
- 3 garlic cloves, minced
- One-cup yellow onion, chopped
- One-tablespoon butter
- 40 ounces chicken stock
- Salt and black pepper to the taste
- A pinch of red pepper flakes
- 3 potatoes, cubed
- 3 tablespoons cornstarch
- 12 ounces evaporated milk
- One-cup parmesan, shredded
- 2 cup spinach, chopped

Instructions:
1. Set your instant pot on Sauté mode, add bacon, stir, cook until it's crispy and transfer to a plate.
2. Add sausage to the pot, stir, cook until it browns on all sides and also transfer to a plate.
3. Add butter to the pot and melt it.
4. Add onion, stir and cook for 5 minutes.
5. Add garlic, stir and cook for 1 minute.
6. Add 1/3 of the stock, salt, pepper and pepper flakes and stir.
7. Place potatoes in the steamer basket of the pot, cover and cook at High for 4 minutes.
8. Release the pressure fast, uncover and transfer potatoes to a bowl.
9. Add the rest of the stock to the pot, cornstarch mixed with some evaporated milk and the milk, stir and set the pot on Simmer mode.
10. Add parmesan, sausage, bacon, potatoes, spinach, more salt and pepper if needed, stir, divide into bowls and serve.

Bon Appétit!

283. HOT CREAMY TOMATO SOUP

Perp time: 10 minutes **Cooking time:** 6 minutes **Servings:** 8

Nutrition Facts:
- Calories: 280
- Fat (In grams): 8
- Fiber (In grams): 4
- Carbs (In grams): 32
- Protein: 24 g

Ingredients:
- 1 yellow onion, chopped
- 3 tablespoons butter
- 1 carrot, chopped
- 2 celery stalks, chopped
- 2 garlic cloves, minced
- 29 ounces canned chicken stock
- Salt and black pepper to the taste
- 1/4 cup basil, chopped
- 3 pounds tomatoes, peeled, cored and cut into quarters
- One-tablespoon tomato paste
- One-cup half and half
- Half-cup parmesan cheese, shredded

Instructions:
1. Set your instant pot on Sauté mode, add butter and melt it.
2. Add onion, carrots and celery, stir and cook for 3 minutes.
3. Add garlic, stir and cook for 1 minute more.
4. Add tomatoes, tomato paste, stock, basil, salt and pepper, stir, cover and cook at High for 5 minutes.
5. Release the pressure, uncover pot and puree soup using and immersion blender.
6. Add half and half and cheese, stir, set the pot on Simmer mode and heat everything up.
7. Divide into soup bowls and serve.

Bon Appétit!

284. SPECIAL MINESTRONE SOUP

Perp time: 10 minutes **Cooking time:** 15 minutes **Servings:** 8

Nutrition Facts:
- Calories: 110
- Fat (In grams): 2
- Fiber (In grams): 4
- Carbs (In grams): 18
- Protein: 5 g

Ingredients:
- One-tablespoon extra virgin olive oil
- 1 celery stalk, chopped
- 2 carrots, chopped
- 1 onion, chopped
- One-cup corn kernels
- 1 zucchini, chopped
- 3 pounds tomatoes, peeled and chopped
- 4 garlic cloves, minced
- 29 ounces canned chicken stock
- One-cup uncooked pasta
- Salt and black pepper to the taste
- One-teaspoon Italian seasoning
- 2 cups baby spinach
- 15 ounces canned kidney beans
- One-cup asiago cheese, grated
- 2 tablespoons basil, chopped

Instructions:
1. Set your instant pot on Sauté mode, ad oil and heat it up.

2. Add onion, stir and cook for 5 minutes.
3. Add carrots, garlic, celery, corn and zucchini, stir and cook 5 minutes.
4. Add tomatoes, stock, Italian seasoning, pasta, salt and pepper, stir, cover and cook at High for 4 minutes.
5. Release the pressure fast, uncover, add beans, basil and spinach.
6. Add more salt and pepper if needed, divide into bowls, add cheese on top and serve.

Bon Appétit!

285. SPECIAL TOMATO SOUP

Perp time: 10 minutes   **Cooking time:** 45 minutes   **Servings:** 6

Nutrition Facts:
- Calories: 150
- Fat (In grams): 1
- Fiber (In grams): 3
- Carbs (In grams): 3
- Protein: 4 g

Ingredients:

For the roasted tomatoes:
- 14 garlic cloves, crushed
- 3 pounds cherry tomatoes, cut into halves
- Salt and black pepper to the taste
- 2 tablespoons extra virgin olive oil
- Half-teaspoon red pepper flakes

For the soup:
- 1 yellow onion, chopped
- 2 tablespoons olive oil
- 1 red bell pepper, chopped
- 3 tablespoons tomato paste
- 2 celery ribs, chopped
- 2 cups chicken stock
- One-teaspoon garlic powder
- One-teaspoon onion powder
- Half-tablespoon basil, dried
- Half-teaspoon red pepper flakes
- Salt and black pepper to the taste
- One-cup heavy cream

For serving:
- Basil leaves, chopped
- Half-cup parmesan, grated

Instructions:
1. Place tomatoes and garlic in a baking tray, drizzle 2 tablespoons oil, season with salt, pepper and Half-teaspoons red pepper flakes, toss to coat, introduce in the oven at 425 degrees F and roast for 25 minutes.
2. Take tomatoes out of the oven and leave them aside for now.
3. Set your instant pot on Sauté mode, add 2 tablespoons oil and heat it up.
4. Add onion, bell pepper and celery and stir.
5. Also add salt, pepper, garlic powder, onion powder, dried basil and Half-teaspoon pepper flakes, stir and cook for 3 minutes.
6. Add tomato paste, roasted tomatoes and garlic and stir.
7. Add stock, cover pot and cook at High for 10 minutes.
8. Release the pressure naturally, uncover the pot and set it on Sauté mode.
9. Add heavy cream and blend everything using an immersion blender.
10. Divide in bowls, add basil leaves and cheese on top and serve.

Bon Appétit!

286. TASTY CARROT SOUP

Perp time: 10 minutes **Cooking time:** 16 minutes **Servings:** 4

Nutrition Facts:
- Calories: 60
- Fat (In grams): 1
- Fiber (In grams): 3.1
- Carbs (In grams): 12
- Protein: 2 g

Ingredients:
- One-tablespoon vegetable oil
- 1 onion, chopped
- One-tablespoon butter
- 1 garlic clove, minced
- 1 pound carrots, chopped
- 1 small ginger piece, grated
- Salt and black pepper to the taste
- 1/4 teaspoon brown Sugar
- 2 cups chicken stock
- One-tablespoon Sriracha
- 14 ounces canned coconut milk
- Cilantro leaves, chopped for serving

Instructions:
1. Set your instant pot on Sauté mode, add butter and oil and heat them up.
2. Add onion, stir and cook for 3 minutes.
3. Add ginger and garlic, stir and cook for 1 minute.
4. Add Sugar, carrots, salt and pepper, stir and cook 2 minutes more.
5. Add sriracha sauce, coconut milk, stock, stir, cover and cook at High for 6 minutes.
6. Release the pressure for 10 minutes, uncover, blend soup with an immersion blender, add more salt and pepper if needed and divide into soup bowls.
7. Add cilantro on top and serve.

Bon Appétit!

287. HEALTHY CABBAGE SOUP

Perp time: 10 minutes **Cooking time:** 10 minutes **Servings:** 4

Nutrition Facts:
- Calories: 100
- Fat (In grams): 1
- Fiber (In grams): 2
- Carbs (In grams): 10
- Protein: 10 g

Ingredients:
- 1 cabbage head, chopped
- 12 ounces baby carrots
- 3 celery stalks, chopped
- ½ onion, chopped
- 1 packet veggie soup mix
- 2 tablespoons olive oil
- 12 ounces soy burger
- 3 teaspoons garlic, minced
- 1/4 cup cilantro, chopped
- 4 cups chicken stock
- Salt and black pepper to the taste

Instructions:
1. In your instant pot, mix cabbage with celery, carrots, onion, veggie soup mix, soy burger, stock, olive oil and garlic, stir, cover and cook on High for 5 minutes.
2. Release pressure, uncover the pot, add salt, pepper and cilantro, stir again well, divide into soup bowls and serve.

Bon Appétit!

288. Healthy Cream Of Asparagus

Perp time: 10 minutes **Cooking time:** 25 minutes **Servings:** 4

Nutrition Facts:
- Calories: 80
- Fat (In grams): 8
- Fiber (In grams): 1
- Carbs (In grams): 16
- Protein: 6.3 g

Ingredients:
- 2 pounds green asparagus, trimmed, tips cut off and cut into medium pieces
- 3 tablespoons butter
- 1 yellow onion, chopped
- 6 cups chicken stock
- 1/4 teaspoon lemon juice
- Half-cup crème fraiche
- Salt and white pepper to the taste

Instructions:
1. Set your instant pot on Sauté mode, add butter and melt it.
2. Add asparagus, salt and pepper, stir and cook for 5 minutes.
3. Add 5 cups stock, cover pot and cook on Low for 15 minutes.
4. Release the pressure, uncover the pot and transfer soup to your blender.
5. Pulse very well and return to pot.
6. Set the pot on Simmer mode, add crème fraiche, the rest of the stock, salt and pepper and lemon juice, bring to a boil, divide into soup bowls and serve.

Bon Appétit!

289. Amazing Artichoke Soup

Perp time: 10 minutes **Cooking time:** 20 minutes **Servings:** 4

Nutrition Facts:
- Calories: 95
- Fat (In grams): 2
- Fiber (In grams): 4
- Carbs (In grams): 15
- Protein: 4 g

Ingredients:
- 5 artichoke hearts, washed and trimmed
- 1 leek, sliced
- 5 tablespoons butter
- 6 garlic cloves, minced
- Half-cup shallots, chopped
- 8 ounces gold potatoes, chopped
- 12 cups chicken stock
- 1 bay leaf
- 4 parsley springs
- 2 thyme springs
- 1/4 teaspoon black peppercorns, crushed
- Salt to the taste
- 1/4 cup cream

Instructions:
1. Set your instant pot on Sauté mode, add butter and melt it.
2. Add artichoke hearts, shallots, leek and garlic, stir and brown for 3-4 minutes.
3. Add potatoes, stock, bay leaf, thyme, parsley, peppercorns and salt, stir, cover and cook at High for 15 minutes.
4. Release the pressure, uncover the pot, discard herbs, blend well using an immersion blender, add salt to the taste and cream, stir well, divide into bowls and serve.

Bon Appétit!

290. Delicious Beet Soup

Perp time: 10 minutes **Cooking time:** 10 minutes **Servings:** 4

Nutrition Facts:
- Calories: 100
- Fat (In grams): 4
- Fiber (In grams): 2
- Carbs (In grams): 8
- Protein: 3 g

Ingredients:
- One-tablespoon sesame oil
- One-cup red lentils
- 1 red onion, chopped
- 2 carrots, chopped
- 3 beets, chopped
- 3 bay leaves
- 6 cups veggie stock
- Half-teaspoon thyme leaves, chopped
- 3 tablespoons dark miso
- 1 ½ tablespoons parsley, chopped
- Salt and black pepper to the taste

Instructions:
1. Set your instant pot on Sauté mode, add oil and heat it up.
2. Add onion, stir and cook for 5 minutes.
3. Add lentils, carrots, beets, thyme, bay leaves, stock, salt and pepper, stir, cover and cook at High for 5 minutes.
4. Release the pressure, uncover the pot, discard bay leaves, puree soup using an immersion blender, add miso mixed with some water, more salt and pepper if needed and parsley, stir, divide into soup bowls and serve.

Bon Appétit!

291. Yummy Cream Of Broccoli

Perp time: 10 minutes **Cooking time:** 10 minutes **Servings:** 4

Nutrition Facts:
- Calories: 180
- Fat (In grams): 11
- Fiber (In grams): 3
- Carbs (In grams): 14
- Protein: 6 g

Ingredients:
- 1 yellow onion, chopped
- 3 carrots, chopped
- 1 potato, chopped
- 1 broccoli head, florets separated and chopped
- One-tablespoons olive oil
- 2 cups chicken stock
- 5 garlic cloves, minced
- Salt and black pepper to the taste
- 2 tablespoons cream
- Cheddar cheese, grated for serving
- One-tablespoon chives, chopped

Instructions:
1. Set your instant pot on Sauté mode, add oil and heat it up.
2. Add onion and garlic, stir and cook for 2 minutes.
3. Add broccoli, carrots, potato, stock, salt and pepper, stir, cover and cook at High for 5 minutes.
4. Release the pressure, uncover the pot, set it on Simmer mode, add cream, cheese and chives, stir, heat up for 2 minutes, divide into bowls and serve.

Bon Appétit!

292. TASTY LENTILS SOUP

Perp time: 10 minutes **Cooking time:** 30 minutes **Servings:** 4

Nutrition Facts:
- Calories: 175
- Fat (In grams): 1
- Fiber (In grams): 1
- Carbs (In grams): 2
- Protein: 2 g

Ingredients:
- 2 celery stalks, chopped
- One-tablespoon olive oil
- 1 small onion, chopped
- 2 carrots, chopped
- ½ pound chicken sausage, ground
- 3 ½-cups beef stock
- 2 teaspoons garlic, minced
- One-cup lentils
- 15 ounces canned tomatoes, chopped
- Salt and black pepper to the taste
- 2 cups spinach

Instructions:
1. Set your instant pot on Sauté mode, add oil and heat it up.
2. Add celery, onion, carrots, stir and cook for 4 minutes.
3. Add chicken sausage, stir and cook 5 minutes.
4. Add stock, garlic, lentils, tomatoes, salt, pepper and spinach, stir, cover and cook at High for 25 minutes.
5. Release the pressure fast, uncover, divide into soup bowls and serve.

Bon Appétit!

293. SIMPLE CELERY SOUP

Perp time: 10 minutes **Cooking time:** 17 minutes **Servings:** 2

Nutrition Facts:
- Calories: 90
- Fat (In grams): 4
- Fiber (In grams): 4
- Carbs (In grams): 8.5
- Protein: 2 g

Ingredients:
- 1 yellow onion, chopped
- 7 celery stalks, chopped
- 3 potatoes, chopped
- One-teaspoon extra virgin olive oil
- Salt and black pepper to the taste
- 4 cups veggie stock
- One-tablespoon curry powder
- One-teaspoon celery seeds
- A handful parsley, chopped for serving

Instructions:
1. Set your instant pot on Sauté mode, add oil and heat it up.
2. Add onion, celery seeds and curry powder, stir and cook for 1 minute.
3. Add celery and potatoes, stir and cook for 5 minutes.
4. Add stock, salt, pepper stir, cover and cook at High for 10 minutes.
5. Release the pressure, uncover the pot, blend well using an immersion blender, add parsley, stir, divide into soup bowls and serve.

Bon Appétit!

294. Delicious Chestnut Soup

Perp time: 10 minutes **Cooking time:** 25 minutes **Servings:** 4

Nutrition Facts:
- Calories: 230
- Fat (In grams): 13
- Fiber (In grams): 2
- Carbs (In grams): 22
- Protein: 2.1 g

Ingredients:
- 1 pound canned chestnuts, drained and rinsed
- 1 celery stalk, chopped
- 4 tablespoons butter
- 1 yellow onion, chopped
- 1 sage spring, chopped
- Salt and white pepper to the taste
- 1 bay leaf
- 1 potato, chopped
- 4 cups chicken stock
- 2 tablespoons rum
- A pinch of nutmeg
- Whole cream for serving
- Sage leaves, chopped for serving

Instructions:
1. Set your instant pot on Sauté mode, add butter and melt it.
2. Add onion, sage, celery, salt and pepper, stir and cook for 5 minutes.
3. Add chestnuts, potato, bay leaf and stock, stir, cover and cook on Low for 20 minutes.
4. Release the pressure, uncover the pot, add nutmeg and rum, discard bay leaf and blend soup using an immersion blender.
5. Divide soup into bowls, add cream and sage leaves on top and serve.

Bon Appétit!

295. Simple Fennel Soup

Perp time: 10 minutes **Cooking time:** 15 minutes **Servings:** 3

Nutrition Facts:
- Calories: 100
- Fat (In grams): 2.2
- Fiber (In grams): 4
- Carbs (In grams): 15
- Protein: 5 g

Ingredients:
- 1 fennel bulb, chopped
- 1 bay leaf
- 1 leek, chopped
- 2 cups water
- One-tablespoon extra virgin olive oil
- ½ cube vegetable bouillon
- Salt and black pepper to the taste
- 2 teaspoons parmesan cheese, grated

Instructions:
1. In your instant pot, mix fennel with leek, bay leaf, vegetable bouillon and water.
2. Stir, cover and cook at High for 15 minutes.
3. Release the pressure, uncover the pot, add cheese, oil, salt and pepper, stir, divide into bowls and serve.

Bon Appétit!

296. HEALTHY CAULIFLOWER SOUP

Perp time: 10 minutes **Cooking time:** 10 minutes **Servings:** 6

Nutrition Facts:
- Calories: 78
- Fat (In grams): 1.2
- Fiber (In grams): 1
- Carbs (In grams): 10
- Protein: 3 g

Ingredients:
- 1 small onion, chopped
- 1 cauliflower head, florets separated and chopped
- 2 tablespoons butter
- 3 cups chicken stock
- Salt and black pepper to the taste
- One-teaspoon garlic powder
- 4 ounces cream cheese, cubed
- One-cup cheddar cheese, grated
- Half-cup half and half

Instructions:
1. Set your instant pot on Sauté mode, add butter and melt it.
2. Add onion, stir and cook for 3 minutes.
3. Add cauliflower, stock, salt, pepper and garlic powder, stir, cover and cook at High for 5 minutes.
4. Release the pressure, uncover the pot, blend everything using an immersion blender, add more salt and pepper if needed, cream cheese, grated cheese and half and half.
5. Stir, set the pot on Simmer mode, heat up for 2 minutes, divide into soup bowls and serve.

Bon Appétit!

297. SWEET POTATO AND TURKEY SOUP

Perp time: 10 minutes **Cooking time:** 12 minutes **Servings:** 4

Nutrition Facts:
- Calories: 190
- Fat (In grams): 12
- Fiber (In grams): 1
- Carbs (In grams): 2
- Protein: 5 g

Ingredients:
- 1 pound Italian turkey sausage, chopped
- 1 yellow onion, chopped
- 2 celery stalks, chopped
- 2 carrots, chopped
- 1 big sweet potato, cubed
- 5 cups turkey stock
- 2 garlic cloves, minced
- One-teaspoon red pepper flakes
- One-teaspoon basil, dried
- One-teaspoon oregano, dried
- Salt and black pepper to the taste
- One-teaspoon thyme, dried
- 5 ounces spinach, chopped
- 2 bay leaves

Instructions:
1. Set your instant pot on Sauté mode, add sausage, brown it and transfer to a plate.
2. Add onion, celery and carrots, stir and cook for 2 minutes.
3. Add potato, stir and cook 2 minutes.
4. Add stock, garlic, red pepper, salt, pepper, basil, oregano, thyme, spinach and bay leaves,
5. Stir, cover and cook at High for 4 minutes.
6. Release the pressure, uncover the pot, discard bay leaves, divide soup into bowls and serve.

298. Mouthwatering Chicken Meatball Soup

Perp time: 10 minutes **Cooking time:** 20 minutes **Servings:** 6

Nutrition Facts:
- Calories: 190
- Fat (In grams): 2.8
- Fiber (In grams): 2.3
- Carbs (In grams): 10
- Protein: 29 g

Ingredients:
- 1 ½ pounds chicken breast, ground
- Salt and black pepper to the taste
- 2 tablespoons arrowroot powder
- One-teaspoon garlic powder
- Half-teaspoon crushed red pepper
- One-teaspoon onion powder
- Half-tablespoon basil, dried
- Half-tablespoon oregano, dried
- 2 tablespoons nutritional yeast

For the soup:
- 6 cups chicken stock
- 4 celery stalks, chopped
- 3 carrots, chopped
- 2 yellow onions, chopped
- 1 bunch kale, chopped
- 2 teaspoons thyme, dried
- 2 garlic cloves, minced
- Half-teaspoon red pepper, crushed
- 2 eggs, whisked
- 2 tablespoons extra virgin olive oil

Instructions:
1. Set your instant pot on Sauté mode, add oil and heat it up.
2. Add onions, celery and carrots, stir and cook for 3 minutes.
3. Add garlic, salt, pepper, kale, stock, 2 teaspoons thyme and Half-teaspoon red pepper, stir and continue cooking.
4. Meanwhile, in a bowl mix chicken meat with arrow powder, salt, pepper, Half-teaspoon red pepper, garlic powder, onion powder, oregano, basil and yeast and stir well.
5. Shape meatballs using your hands and drop them gently into the soup.
6. Cover pot and cook at High for 15 minutes.
7. Release the pressure, uncover the pot and set it on Sauté mode again.
8. Add eggs slowly, stir and cook for 2 minutes.
9. Divide into soup bowls and serve hot.

Bon Appétit!

299. Healthy Veggie Soup

Perp time: 10 minutes **Cooking time:** 15 minutes **Servings:** 4

Nutrition Facts:
- Calories: 80
- Fat (In grams): 1
- Fiber (In grams): 2
- Carbs (In grams): 14
- Protein: 2 g

Ingredients:
- 1 brown onion, chopped
- One-tablespoon coconut oil
- Salt and black pepper to the taste
- ½ red chili, chopped
- 2 carrots, chopped
- 2 celery sticks, chopped
- 6 big mushrooms, sliced
- 4 garlic cloves, minced

- A handful dried porcini mushrooms
- 3.5 ounces kale leaves, roughly chopped
- One-cup tomatoes, chopped
- 1 zucchini, chopped
- 4 cups veggie stock
- 1 bay leaf
- One-teaspoon lemon zest
- A handful parsley, chopped

Instructions:
1. Set your instant pot on Sauté mode, add oil and heat it up.
2. Add onion, celery, carrots, salt and pepper, stir and cook for 1 minute.
3. Add chili, dried mushrooms, mushrooms, garlic, stir and cook for 2 minutes.
4. Add kale leaves, zucchini, tomatoes, bay leaf and stock, stir, cover and cook at High for 10 minutes.
5. Release the pressure naturally, uncover the pot, divide soup into bowls, add lemon zest and parsley on top and serve.

Bon Appétit!

300. Amazing Chicken Chili Soup

Perp time: 10 minutes   **Cooking time:** 30 minutes   **Servings:** 4

Nutrition Facts:
- Calories: 200
- Fat (In grams): 8
- Fiber (In grams): 6
- Carbs (In grams): 17
- Protein: 19 g

Ingredients:
- 1 white onion, chopped
- 2 tablespoons olive oil
- 1 jalapeno pepper, chopped
- 4 garlic cloves, minced
- 2 teaspoons oregano, dried
- One-teaspoon cumin
- Half-teaspoon red pepper flakes, crushed
- 3 cups chicken stock
- 1 pound chicken breast, skinless and boneless
- 30 ounces canned cannellini beans, drained
- Salt and black pepper to the taste
- Cilantro, chopped for serving
- Tortilla chips, for serving
- Lime wedges for serving

Instructions:
1. Set your instant pot on Sauté mode, add oil and heat it up.
2. Add jalapeno and onion, stir and cook for 3 minutes.
3. Add garlic, stir and cook for 1 minute.
4. Add oregano, cumin, pepper flakes, stock, chicken, beans, salt and pepper, stir, cover and cook on Low for 30 minutes.
5. Release the pressure, uncover the pot, shred meat with 2 forks, add more salt and pepper, stir and divide into soup bowls.
6. Serve with cilantro on top and with tortilla chips and lime wedges on the side.

Bon Appétit!

301. Bacon And Broccoli Soup

Perp time: 10 minutes **Cooking time:** 10 minutes **Servings:** 6

Nutrition Facts:
- Calories: 151
- Fat (In grams): 2.2
- Fiber (In grams): 7
- Carbs (In grams): 26
- Protein: 10 g

Ingredients:
- 4 bacon slices, chopped
- One-teaspoon olive oil
- 2 small broccoli heads, chopped
- 1 leek, chopped
- 1 celery rib, chopped
- 2 cups spinach, chopped
- 4 tablespoons basmati rice
- One-tablespoon parmesan, grated
- 1-quart veggie stock
- Salt and black pepper to the taste

Instructions:
1. Set your instant pot on Sauté mode, add oil and bacon, cook until it's crispy, transfer to a plate and leave aside.
2. Add broccoli, leek, celery, spinach, rice, salt, pepper and veggie stock, stir, cover and cook at High for 6 minutes.
3. Release the pressure, uncover, add more salt and pepper if needed, add bacon, divide into soup bowls and serve with parmesan on top.

Bon Appétit!

302. Chorizo, Kale And Chicken Soup

Perp time: 10 minutes **Cooking time:** 10 minutes **Servings:** 8

Nutrition Facts:
- Calories: 200
- Fat (In grams): 9
- Fiber (In grams): 2
- Carbs (In grams): 19
- Protein: 11 g

Ingredients:
- 9 ounces chorizo, casings removed
- 2 tablespoons olive oil
- 4 chicken thighs, chopped
- Salt and black pepper to the taste
- 4 garlic cloves, minced
- 2 yellow onions, chopped
- 4 cups chicken stock
- 15 ounces canned tomatoes, chopped
- 3 potatoes, chopped
- 2 bay leaves
- 5 ounces baby kale
- 14 ounces garbanzo beans, drained

Instructions:
1. Set your instant pot on Sauté mode, add oil and heat it up.
2. Add chorizo, chicken and onion, stir and cook 5 minutes.
3. Add garlic, stir and cook for 1 minute.
4. Add stock, tomatoes and bay leaves and stir again.
5. Also add, kale and potatoes, salt and pepper, stir, cover and cook at High for 4 minutes.
6. Release the pressure, uncover the pot, add beans, more salt and pepper if needed, stir, divide into bowls and serve.

Bon Appétit!

303. TASTY ENDIVE SOUP

Perp time: 10 minutes **Cooking time:** 25 minutes **Servings:** 4

Nutrition Facts:
- Calories: 207
- Fat (In grams): 9
- Fiber (In grams): 12
- Carbs (In grams): 12
- Protein: 11.5 g

Ingredients:
- One-tablespoon canola oil
- 2 teaspoons sesame oil
- 2 scallions, chopped
- 3 garlic cloves chopped
- One-tablespoon ginger, grated
- One-teaspoon chili sauce
- Half-cup uncooked rice
- 6 cups veggie stock
- 1 ½ tablespoons soy sauce
- 3 endives, trimmed and roughly chopped
- Salt and white pepper to the taste

Instructions:
1. Set your instant pot on Sauté mode, add canola and sesame oil and heat it up.
2. Add scallions and garlic, stir and cook for 4 minutes.
3. Add chili sauce and ginger, stir and cook for 1 minute.
4. Add stock and soy sauce, stir and cook for 2 minutes.
5. Add rice, stir, cover and cook at High for 15 minutes.
6. Release the pressure, uncover the pot, add salt, pepper and endives, stir, cover again and cook at High for 5 minutes.
7. Release the pressure again, uncover the pot, stir soup, divide into bowls and serve.

Bon Appétit!

304. SPECIAL CHICKEN ENCHILADA SOUP

Perp time: 10 minutes **Cooking time:** 30 minutes **Servings:** 4

Nutrition Facts:
- Calories: 400
- Fat (In grams): 23
- Fiber (In grams): 3
- Carbs (In grams): 23
- Protein: 27 g

Ingredients:
- 2 chicken breasts, boneless and skinless and chopped
- 1 and 1/4 cup jarred red enchilada sauce
- 3 cups chicken stock
- 14 ounces canned tomatoes, chopped
- 28 ounces canned black beans, drained
- 15 ounces canned corn, drained
- Salt and black pepper to the taste
- 4 ounces canned green chilies, chopped
- 2 garlic cloves, minced
- One-cup white onion, chopped
- Half-cup quinoa
- One-teaspoon cumin, ground
- One-teaspoon oregano

For serving:
- Chopped cilantro
- Chopped avocado
- Chopped red onion
- Shredded cheddar cheese

Instructions:
1. In your instant pot, mix chicken with enchilada sauce, stock, tomatoes, black beans, corn, green chilies, salt, pepper, garlic, onion, quinoa, cumin and oregano, stir, cover and cook on Medium heat for 25 minutes.
2. Release the pressure, uncover the pot, divide soup into bowls and serve with chopped cilantro, avocado and red onion on top and with shredded cheese sprinkled all over.

Bon Appétit!

---

305. BARLEY AND BEEF SOUP

Perp time: 10 minutes **Cooking time:** 25 minutes **Servings:** 4

Nutrition Facts:
- Calories: 120
- Fat (In grams): 3
- Fiber (In grams): 2
- Carbs (In grams): 11
- Protein: 5 g

Ingredients:
- 1 ½ pounds beef stew meat, chopped
- 2 tablespoons vegetable oil
- Salt and black pepper to the taste
- 10 baby bell mushrooms, cut into quarters
- 3 cups mixed onion, carrots and celery
- 8 garlic cloves, minced
- 6 cups beef stock
- 2 bay leaves
- One-cup water
- Half-teaspoon thyme, dried
- 1 potato, chopped
- 2/3 cup barley

Instructions:
1. Set your instant pot on Sauté mode, add oil and heat it up.
2. Add meat, salt and pepper, stir, cook for 3 minutes and transfer to a plate.
3. Add mushrooms, stir, brown them for 2 minutes and transfer to a plate.
4. Add mixed veggies to the pot, stir and cook for 4 minutes.
5. Return meat, mushrooms to the pot and stir everything.
6. Also add bay leaves, thyme, water, stock, salt and pepper, stir, cover and cook at High for 16 minutes.
7. Release the pressure, uncover the pot, add potatoes and barley, stir, cover and cook on Low for 1 hour.
8. Release the pressure again, stir soup, divide it into bowls and serve.

Bon Appétit!

---

306. YUMMY BEEF STEW

Perp time: 10 minutes **Cooking time:** 30 minutes **Servings:** 8

Nutrition Facts:
- Calories: 300
- Fat (In grams): 12
- Fiber (In grams): 5
- Carbs (In grams): 1
- Protein: 25 g

Ingredients:
- One-tablespoon vegetable oil
- 2 pounds beef stew, cubed

- 1 yellow onion, chopped
- 5 carrots, chopped
- 8 potatoes, cubed
- Salt and black pepper to the taste
- 2 teaspoons cornstarch
- 2 beef bouillon cubes
- 2 cups water

Instructions:
1. Set your instant pot on Sauté mode, add oil and heat it up.
2. Add beef and onion, stir and cook until it browns on all sides.
3. Add carrots, water and bouillon, stir, cover and cook on Medium for 20 minutes.
4. Put water in a pot, add some salt, bring to a boil over medium high heat, add potatoes, cook for 10 minutes and drain them.
5. Release the pressure, uncover the pot and set it on Simmer mode.
6. Add cornstarch mixed with some water, salt, pepper and potatoes, stir, bring to a boil, take off heat and divide stew among plates.

Bon Appétit!

---

307. TASTY CHICKEN STEW

Perp time: 10 minutes
Cooking time: 1 hour and 15 minutes
Servings: 6

Nutrition Facts:
- Calories: 271
- Fat (In grams): 2
- Fiber (In grams): 4
- Carbs (In grams): 18
- Protein: 15 g

Ingredients:
- 6 chicken thighs
- One-teaspoon vegetable oil
- Salt and black pepper to the taste
- 1 yellow onion, chopped
- 1/4 pound baby carrots, sliced
- 1 celery stalk, chopped
- Half-teaspoon thyme, dried
- 2 tablespoons tomato paste
- Half-cup white wine
- 2 cups chicken stock
- 15 ounces canned tomatoes, chopped
- 3/4 pound baby carrots
- 1 ½ pounds new potatoes

Instructions:
1. Set your instant pot on Sauté mode, add oil and heat it up.
2. Add chicken, salt and pepper, brown for 4 minutes on each side and transfer to a plate.
3. Add celery, onion, tomato paste, carrots, thyme, salt and pepper, stir and cook for 5 minutes.
4. Add wine, stir, bring to a boil and simmer for 3 minutes.
5. Add stock, return chicken, add tomatoes and put potatoes in the steamer basket of your pot.
6. Cover pot and cook at High for 30 minutes.
7. Release the pressure, uncover the pot, take potatoes out of the pot and put them in a bowl.
8. Transfer chicken pieces to a cutting board, leave aside to cool down for a few minutes, discard bones, shred meat and return it to the stew.
9. Add more salt and pepper if needed, stir, divide into bowls and serve hot.

Bon Appétit!

308. EASY FISH CHOWDER

Perp time: 10 minutes **Cooking time:** 10 minutes **Servings:** 4

Nutrition Facts:
- Calories: 195
- Fat (In grams): 4.4
- Fiber (In grams): 2
- Carbs (In grams): 21
- Protein: 17 g

Ingredients:
- 1 yellow onion, chopped
- 2 celery ribs, chopped
- 3/4 cup bacon, chopped
- 1 carrot, chopped
- 2 garlic cloves, chopped
- 3 cups potatoes, cubed
- 4 cups chicken stock
- 1 pound haddock fillets
- 2 tablespoons butter
- One-cup frozen corn
- Salt and white pepper to the taste
- One-tablespoon potato starch
- 2 cups heavy cream

Instructions:
1. Set your instant pot on Sauté mode, add butter and melt it.
2. Add bacon, stir and cook until it's crispy.
3. Add garlic, celery and onion, stir and cook fro 3 minutes.
4. Add salt, pepper, fish, potatoes, corn and stock, stir, cover and cook at High for 5 minutes.
5. Release the pressure naturally, uncover the pot, add heavy cream mixed with potato starch, stir well, set the pot on Simmer mode and cook everything for 3 minutes.
6. Divide into bowls and serve.

Bon Appétit!

309. TASTY QUIK BEAN STEW

Perp time: 10 minutes **Cooking time:** 25 minutes **Servings:** 4

Nutrition Facts:
- Calories: 164
- Fat (In grams): 2
- Fiber (In grams): 9
- Carbs (In grams): 28
- Protein: 8.2 g

Ingredients:
- 1 yellow onion, chopped
- 2 carrots, chopped
- 1 garlic head, halved
- 1 pound chickpeas, drained
- 22 ounces canned tomatoes, chopped
- 22 ounces water
- One-teaspoon oregano, dried
- 3 bay leaves
- 2 tablespoons olive oil
- Salt and black pepper to the taste
- Half-teaspoon red pepper flakes
- A drizzle of olive oil for serving
- 2 tablespoons parmesan cheese, grated

Instructions:
1. Put onion, carrots, garlic, chickpeas, tomatoes, water, oregano, bay leaves, 2 tablespoons olive oil, salt, and pepper in your instant pot.
2. Cover, cook at High for 25 minutes and release pressure.
3. Ladle into bowls, add parmesan, pepper flakes and a drizzle of oil on top and serve.

310. Delicious Sweet Potato Stew

Perp time: 10 minutes **Cooking time:** 20 minutes **Servings:** 4

Nutrition Facts:
- Calories: 150
- Fat (In grams): 9
- Fiber (In grams): 3
- Protein: 4 g
- Carbs (In grams): 25

Ingredients:
- 1 big onion, chopped
- 1 sweet potato, cubed
- 3 garlic cloves, chopped
- 1 celery stalk, chopped
- 2 carrots, chopped
- One-cup green lentils
- Half-cup red lentils
- 2 cups veggie stock
- 1/4 cup raisins
- 14 ounces canned tomatoes, chopped
- Salt and black pepper to the taste

For the spice blend:
- One-teaspoon cumin
- One-teaspoon turmeric
- Half-teaspoon cinnamon
- One-teaspoon paprika
- 2 teaspoons coriander
- 1/4 teaspoon ginger, grated
- A pinch of cloves
- A pinch of chili flakes

Instructions:
1. Set your instant pot on Sauté mode, add onions and brown them for 2 minutes adding some of the stock from time to time.
2. Add garlic, stir and cook for 1 minute.
3. Add carrots, raisins, celery, and sweet potatoes, stir and cook for 1 minute.
4. Add red and green lentils, stock, tomatoes, salt, pepper, turmeric, cinnamon, paprika, cumin, coriander, ginger, cloves and chili flakes, stir, cover and cook at High for 15 minutes.
5. Release the pressure, uncover the pot, stir stew one more time, add more salt and pepper if needed, ladle into bowls and serve.

Bon Appétit!

311. Healthy Spinach Stew

Perp time: 10 minutes **Cooking time:** 30 minutes **Servings:** 4

Nutrition Facts:
- Calories: 100
- Fat (In grams): 2
- Fiber (In grams): 5
- Carbs (In grams): 16
- Protein: 7 g

Ingredients:
- 1 small yellow onion, chopped
- 2 teaspoons olive oil
- 1 celery stalk, chopped
- 2 carrots, chopped
- 4 garlic cloves, minced
- One-teaspoon turmeric
- 2 teaspoons cumin
- One-teaspoon thyme
- Salt and black pepper to the taste
- One-cup brown lentils, rinsed
- 6 cups baby spinach
- 4 cups veggie stock

Instructions:
1. Set your instant pot on Sauté mode, add oil and heat it up.
2. Add onions, celery and carrots, stir and cook for 5 minutes.
3. Add garlic, turmeric, cumin, thyme, salt and pepper, stir and cook for 1 minute more.
4. Add stock and lentils, stir, cover and cook at High for 12 minutes.
5. Release the pressure for 10 minutes, uncover the pot, add spinach, more salt and pepper, stir, divide into bowls and serve.

Bon Appétit!

---

312. Amazing Oxtail Stew

Perp time: 10 minutes **Cooking time:** 40 minutes **Servings:** 4

Nutrition Facts:
- Calories: 312
- Fat (In grams): 12
- Fiber (In grams): 14
- Carbs (In grams): 15
- Protein: 14 g
- Sugar (In grams): 1

Ingredients:
- 5 pounds oxtails
- 1 yellow onion, chopped
- Salt and black pepper to the taste
- 3 carrots, chopped
- 3 celery stalks, chopped
- 1 garlic clove, chopped
- 1 parsley bunch, chopped
- 2 cups red wine, chopped
- One-cup tomatoes, chopped
- One-cup water
- Sugar (In grams): to the taste

Instructions:
1. In your instant pot, mix oxtails with salt, pepper, onion, carrots, celery, garlic, tomatoes, red wine, parsley, water and Sugar, stir, cover and cook on Medium for 40 minutes.
2. Release the pressure, uncover the pot, divide oxtail stew into bowls and serve.

Bon Appétit!

---

313. Tasty Lamb Stew

Perp time: 10 minutes **Cooking time:** 30 minutes **Servings:** 4

Nutrition Facts:
- Calories: 700
- Fat (In grams): 52
- Fiber (In grams): 4.4
- Carbs (In grams): 17
- Protein: 40 g

Ingredients:
- 2 pounds lamb shoulder, cubed
- 1/4 cup red wine vinegar
- One-tablespoon garlic, minced
- 14 ounces canned tomatoes, chopped
- 2 yellow onions, chopped
- One-tablespoon olive oil
- 2 tablespoons tomato paste
- One-teaspoon oregano, dried
- One-teaspoon basil, dried
- Salt and black pepper to the taste
- 2 bay leaves
- 1 red bell pepper, chopped
- 1 green bell pepper, chopped
- 1/3 cup parsley, chopped

Instructions:
1. Set the pot on Sauté mode, add oil and heat it up.
2. Add onions and garlic, stir and cook for 2 minutes.
3. Add vinegar, stir and cook for 2 minutes.
4. Add lamb, tomatoes, tomato paste, oregano, basil, salt, pepper and bay leaves, stir, cover pot and cook at High for 12 minutes.
5. Release the pressure for 10 minutes, uncover the pot, discard bay leaves, add green and red pepper, more salt and pepper if needed, stir, cover and cook on High for 8 more minutes.
6. Release the pressure again, uncover, add parsley, stir and divide into bowls.

Bon Appétit!

314. CLASSIC TURKEY STEW

Perp time: 10 minutes   **Cooking time:** 35 minutes   **Servings:** 4

Nutrition Facts:
- Calories: 210
- Fat (In grams): 4
- Fiber (In grams): 0
- Carbs (In grams): 15
- Protein: 28 g

Ingredients:
- One-tablespoon avocado oil
- 1 yellow onion, chopped
- 3 celery stalks, chopped
- 2 carrots, chopped
- Salt and black pepper to the taste
- 2 cups potatoes, chopped
- 3 cups turkey meat, already cooked and shredded
- 15 ounces canned tomatoes, chopped
- 5 cups turkey stock
- One-tablespoon cranberry sauce
- One-teaspoon dried garlic, minced

Instructions:
1. Set your instant pot on Sauté mode, add oil and heat it up.
2. Add carrots, celery and onions, stir and cook for 3 minutes.
3. Add potatoes, tomatoes, stock, garlic, meat and cranberry sauce, stir, cover and cook on Low for 30 minutes.
4. Release the pressure, uncover the pot, add salt and pepper, stir, divide into bowls and serve.

Bon Appétit!

315. BEEF AND MUSHROOM STEW

Perp time: 10 minutes   **Cooking time:** 25 minutes   **Servings:** 6

Nutrition Facts:
- Calories: 322
- Fat (In grams): 18
- Fiber (In grams): 3
- Carbs (In grams): 12
- Protein: 24 g

Ingredients:
- One-tablespoon olive oil
- 1 red onion, chopped
- 2 pounds beef chuck, cubed
- One-teaspoon rosemary, chopped
- 1 celery stalk, chopped
- Half-cup red wine
- One-cup beef stock
- Salt and black pepper to the taste

- 1 ounce dried porcini mushrooms, chopped
- 2 carrots, chopped
- 2 tablespoons flour
- 2 tablespoons butter

Instructions:
1. Set your instant pot on Sauté mode, add oil and beef, stir and brown for 5 minutes.
2. Add onion, celery, rosemary, salt, pepper, wine and stock and stir.
3. Add carrots and mushrooms, cover pot and cook at High for 15 minutes.
4. Release the pressure, uncover the pot and set it on Simmer mode.
5. Meanwhile, heat up a pan over medium high heat, add butter and melt it.
6. Add flour and 6 tablespoons of cooking liquid from the stew and stir well.
7. Pour this over stew, stir, cook for 5 minutes, divide into bowls and serve.

Bon Appétit!

---

316. Root Vegetables And Beef Stew

Perp time: 10 minutes **Cooking time:** 32 minutes **Servings:** 4

Nutrition Facts:
- Calories: 302
- Fat (In grams): 9
- Fiber (In grams): 6
- Carbs (In grams): 33
- Protein: 18 g

Ingredients:
- 1 pound beef meat, cubed
- 2 tablespoons olive oil
- 2 bacon slices, cooked and crumbled
- Half-cup white flour
- Salt and black pepper to the taste
- 1 rutabaga, diced
- One-cup cipollini onions, peeled
- 4 carrots, chopped
- 4 garlic cloves, minced
- 2 cups beef stock
- One-tablespoon tomato paste
- Half-cup bourbon
- A bunch of thyme, chopped
- A bunch of rosemary, chopped
- One-cup peas
- 2 bay leaves

Instructions:
1. Mix flour with salt and pepper and place on a plate.
2. Dredge meat in flour mix and leave aside.
3. Set your instant pot on Sauté mode, add oil and heat up.
4. Add meat, brown on all sides and transfer to a bowl.
5. Add garlic, bourbon, stock, thyme, rutabaga, carrots, tomato paste, rosemary and onions, stir and cook fro 2 minutes.
6. Return beef to pot, cover and cook at High for 10 minutes.
7. Release the pressure fast, uncover the pot, add bay leaves, bacon, peas, more salt and pepper, stir and cook on Low for 12 minutes.
8. Release the pressure again, uncover the pot, stir, discard bay leaves, divide into bowls and serve.

Bon Appétit!

317. Special Lamb Stew

Perp time: 10 minutes **Cooking time:** 15 minutes **Servings:** 6

Nutrition Facts:
- Calories: 236
- Fat (In grams): 8
- Fiber (In grams): 2.5
- Carbs (In grams): 22
- Protein: 19 g

Ingredients:
- 2 onions, chopped
- 3 pounds lamb shoulder, cut into medium chunks
- 2 big potatoes, roughly chopped
- Salt and black pepper to the taste
- 2 thyme springs, chopped
- 6 ounces dark beer
- 2 cups water
- 2 carrots, chopped
- 1/4 cup parsley, minced

Instructions:
1. Put onions and lamb in your instant pot.
2. Add salt, pepper, potatoes, thyme, water, beer and carrots, stir, cover and cook at High for 15 minutes.
3. Release the pressure, uncover the pot, add parsley, more salt and pepper if needed, stir, divide into bowls and serve.

Bon Appétit!

318. Amazing German Stew

Perp time: 10 minutes **Cooking time:** 10 minutes **Servings:** 4

Nutrition Facts:
- Calories: 140
- Fat (In grams): 4
- Fiber (In grams): 2
- Carbs (In grams): 11
- Protein: 12 g

Ingredients:
- 1 pound kielbasa, cut into medium pieces
- 14 ounces canned tomatoes, chopped
- 2 potatoes, cut into quarters
- 1 small jar sauerkraut
- 1 onion, cut into medium chunks

Instructions:
1. In your instant pot, add kielbasa, tomatoes, potatoes, sauerkraut and onion, stir, cover and cook at High for 10 minutes.
2. Release pressure, uncover the pot, divide stew into bowls and serve.

Bon Appétit!

319. Tasty Okra Stew

Perp time: 10 minutes **Cooking time:** 20 minutes **Servings:** 4

Nutrition Facts:
- Calories: 230
- Fat (In grams): 10
- Fiber (In grams): 8
- Carbs (In grams): 15
- Protein: 20 g

Ingredients:
- 1 yellow onion, chopped
- 1 garlic clove, minced

- 1 pound beef meat, cubed
- 1 cardamom pod
- 2 cups chicken stock
- 14 ounces frozen okra
- 12 ounces tomato sauce

For the marinade:
- Half-teaspoon onion powder
- Half-teaspoon garlic powder
- Salt and black pepper to the taste
- Half-cup parsley, chopped
- A drizzle of olive oil
- Juice of ½ lemon
- A pinch of salt
- One-tablespoon 7- spice mix

Instructions:
1. In a bowl, mix meat with 7-spice mix, a pinch of salt, onion and garlic powder, toss to coat and leave aside for now.
2. Set your instant pot on Sauté mode, add some olive oil and heat it up.
3. Add onion, stir and cook 2 minutes.
4. Add garlic and cardamom, stir and cook for 1 minute.
5. Add meat, stir and brown meat for 2 minutes.
6. Add stock, tomato sauce, okra, salt and pepper, stir, cover and cook on Low for 20 minutes.
7. Release the pressure, uncover the pot, add more salt and pepper if needed, lemon juice and parsley, stir, divide into bowls and serve.

Bon Appétit!

---

320. AMAZING ITALIAN STYLE SAUSAGE STEW

Perp time: 10 minutes **Cooking time:** 20 minutes **Servings:** 6

Nutrition Facts:
- Calories: 230
- Fat (In grams): 10
- Fiber (In grams): 1
- Carbs (In grams): 24
- Protein: 28 g

Ingredients:
- 1 pound Andouille sausage, crumbled
- ½ pound cherry tomatoes, cut into halves
- 1 sweet onion, chopped
- 1 ½ pounds gold potatoes, cubed
- 3/4 pound collard greens, thinly sliced
- One-cup chicken stock
- Salt and black pepper to the taste
- Juice of ½ lemon

Instructions:
1. Set your instant pot on Sauté mode, add sausage, stir and cook for 8 minutes.
2. Add onions and tomatoes, stir and cook 4 minutes more.
3. Add potatoes, stock, salt, pepper and collard greens, stir, cover pot and cook at High for 10 minutes.
4. Release the pressure, uncover the pot, add more salt and pepper and lemon juice, stir, divide into bowls and serve.

Bon Appétit!

BEANS AND GRAINS RECIPES

321. SPECIAL BARLEY DISH

Perp time: 10 minutes **Cooking time:** 25 minutes **Servings:** 4

Nutrition Facts:
- Calories: 170
- Fat (In grams): 6
- Fiber (In grams): 4.5
- Carbs (In grams): 30
- Protein: 8 g

Ingredients:
- One-tablespoon extra virgin olive oil
- One-tablespoon butter
- 1 white onion, chopped
- 1 garlic clove, minced
- 1 ½ cups pearl barley, rinsed
- 1 celery stalk, chopped
- 1/3 cup mushrooms, chopped
- 4 cups veggie stock
- 2 and 1/4 cups water
- Salt and black pepper to the taste
- 3 tablespoons parsley, chopped
- One-cup parmesan cheese, grated

Instructions:
1. Set your instant pot on Sauté mode, add oil and butter and heat them up.
2. Add onion and garlic, stir and cook for 4 minutes.
3. Add celery and barley and toss to coat.
4. Add mushrooms, water, stock, salt and pepper, stir, cover pot and cook at High for 18 minutes.
5. Release the pressure, uncover the pot, add cheese and parsley and more salt and pepper if needed, stir for 2 minutes, divide into bowls and serve.

Bon Appétit!

322. TASTY BARLEY SALAD

Perp time: 10 minutes **Cooking time:** 20 minutes **Servings:** 4

Nutrition Facts:
- Calories: 170
- Fat (In grams): 7
- Fiber (In grams): 7
- Carbs (In grams): 0
- Protein: 5 g

Ingredients:
- One-cup hulled barley, rinsed
- 2 ½-cups water
- 3/4 cup jarred spinach pesto
- 1 green apple, chopped
- 1/4 cup celery, chopped
- Salt and white pepper to the taste

Instructions:
1. Put barley, water, salt and pepper in your instant pot, stir, cover and cook at High for 20 minutes.
2. Release the pressure fast, uncover pot, strain barley and put in a bowl.
3. Add celery, apple, spinach pesto and more salt and pepper, toss to coat and serve right away.

Bon Appétit!

323. MUSHROOM AND BARLEY RISOTTO

Perp time: 10 minutes **Cooking time:** 30 minutes **Servings:** 4

Nutrition Facts:
- Calories: 200
- Fat (In grams): 5
- Fiber (In grams): 6.1
- Carbs (In grams): 31
- Protein: 7.6 g

Ingredients:
- 2 cups yellow onions, chopped
- One-tablespoon olive oil
- One-cup pearl barley
- One-teaspoon fennel seeds
- 2 tablespoons black barley
- 3 cups chicken stock
- 1/3 cup dry sherry
- 1 ½ cups water
- 1.5 ounce dried mushrooms
- Salt and black pepper to the taste
- 1/4 cup parmesan, grated

Instructions:
1. Set your instant pot on Sauté mode, add oil and heat it up.
2. Add fennel and onions, stir and cook for 4 minutes.
3. Add barley and black barley, sherry, mushrooms, stock, water, salt and pepper and stir well.
4. Cover the pot, cook at High for 18 minutes, release the pressure, uncover the pot and set it on Simmer mode.
5. Add more salt and pepper of needed, stir and cook for 5 more minutes.
6. Divide into bowls, add parmesan on top and serve.

Bon Appétit!

324. VEGGIES AND CRACKED WHEAT

Perp time: 10 minutes **Cooking time:** 15 minutes **Servings:** 4

Nutrition Facts:
- Calories: 145
- Fat (In grams): 2
- Fiber (In grams): 4
- Carbs (In grams): 16
- Protein: 7 g

Ingredients:
- Half-cup cracked whole wheat
- 1 ½ cups water
- 2 tomatoes, chopped
- 2 small potatoes, cubed
- 5 cauliflower florets, chopped
- Salt and black pepper to the taste
- 1/4 teaspoon mustard seeds
- 1/4 teaspoon cumin seeds
- One-teaspoon ginger, grated
- One-tablespoon chana dal
- 2 garlic cloves, minced
- 1 yellow onion, chopped
- 2 curry leaves
- 3 teaspoons vegetable oil
- 1/4 teaspoon garam masala
- A few cilantro leaves, chopped for serving

Instructions:
1. Set your instant pot on Sauté mode, add oil and heat it up.
2. Add cumin and mustard seeds, stir and cook for 1 minute.

3. Add onion, garlic, chana dal, garam masala, ginger and curry leaves, stir and cook for 2 minutes.
4. Add cauliflower, potatoes and tomatoes, stir and cook for 4 minutes.
5. Add wheat, salt, pepper and water, stir, cover and cook on High for 5 minutes.
6. Release the pressure, uncover the pot, transfer wheat and veggies to plates, sprinkle cilantro on top and serve.

Bon Appétit!

---

325. YUMMY BULGUR SALAD

Perp time: 15 minutes   **Cooking time:** 12 minutes   **Servings:** 4

Nutrition Facts:
- Calories: 232
- Fat (In grams): 7
- Fiber (In grams): 6
- Carbs (In grams): 38
- Protein:7 g

Ingredients:
- Zest from 1 orange
- Juice from 2 oranges
- 2 garlic cloves, minced
- 2 teaspoons canola oil
- 2 tablespoons ginger, grated
- One-cup bulgur, rinsed
- One-tablespoon soy sauce
- 2/3 cup scallions, chopped
- 1/3 cup almonds, chopped
- Salt to the taste
- 2 teaspoons brown Sugar
- Half-cups water

Instructions:
1. Set your instant pot on Sauté mode, add oil and heat it up.
2. Add ginger and garlic, stir and cook for 1 minutes.
3. Add bulgur, Sugar, water, and orange juice, stir, cover and cook at High for 5 minutes.
4. Release the pressure naturally, uncover the pot and leave bulgur aside for now.
5. Heat up a pan over medium heat, add almonds, stir and toast them for 3 minutes.
6. Add orange zest, salt, soy sauce and scallions, stir and cook for 1 minute.
7. Add this to bulgur mix, stir with a fork, transfer to a bowl and serve.

Bon Appétit!

---

326. SPECIAL WHEAT BERRY SALAD

Perp time: 10 minutes   **Cooking time:** 35 minutes   **Servings:** 6

Nutrition Facts:
- Calories: 240
- Fat (In grams): 11
- Fiber (In grams): 6.3
- Carbs (In grams): 31
- Protein:5 g

Ingredients:
- 1 ½ cups wheat berries
- One-tablespoon extra virgin olive oil
- Salt and black pepper to the taste
- 4 cups water

For the salad:
- One-tablespoon balsamic vinegar
- One-tablespoon olive oil
- One-cup cherry tomatoes, cut into halves
- 2 green onions, chopped
- 2 ounces feta cheese, crumbled

- Half-cup kalamata olives, pitted and chopped
- 1 handful basil leaves, chopped
- 1 handful parsley leaves, chopped

Instructions:
1. Set your instant pot on Sauté mode, add One-tablespoon oil and heat it up.
2. Add wheat berries, stir and cook for 5 minutes.
3. Add water, salt and pepper to the taste, cover pot and cook on High for 30 minutes.
4. Release the pressure for 10 minutes, uncover the pot, drain wheat berries and put them in a salad bowl.
5. Add salt and pepper, One-tablespoon oil, balsamic vinegar, tomatoes, green onions, olives, cheese, basil and parsley, toss to coat and serve right away.

Bon Appétit!

327. DELICIOUS BULGUR PILAF

Perp time: 10 minutes **Cooking time:** 21 minutes **Servings:** 6

Nutrition Facts:
- Calories: 270
- Fat (In grams): 12
- Fiber (In grams): 8
- Carbs (In grams): 38
- Protein: 7 g

Ingredients:
- 2 cups red onions, chopped
- 2 tablespoons extra virgin olive oil
- Salt and black pepper to the taste
- 2 teaspoons ginger, grated
- 1/4 cup dill, chopped
- 1 garlic clove, minced
- 1 ½ cups bulgur
- 1/4 cup mint, chopped
- 1/4 cup parsley, chopped
- 3 tablespoons lemon juice
- Half-teaspoon cumin, ground
- Half-teaspoons turmeric, ground
- 2 cups veggie stock
- 1 ½ cups carrot, chopped
- Half-cup walnuts, toasted and chopped

Instructions:
1. Set your instant pot on Sauté mode, add oil and heat it up.
2. Add onion, stir and cook on Low temperature for 12 minutes.
3. Add garlic, stir and cook for 1 minute.
4. Add cumin, turmeric and bulgur, stir and cook for 1 minute.
5. Add ginger, stock, carrots, salt and pepper, stir, cover and cook at High for 5 minutes.
6. Release the pressure, uncover the pot, add mint, dill, parsley, lemon juice and more salt and pepper if needed and stir gently.
7. Divide among plates and serve with almonds on top.

Bon Appétit!

328. YUMMY CRACKED WHEAT SURPRISE

Perp time: 5 minutes **Cooking time:** 17 minutes **Servings:** 2

Nutrition Facts:
- Calories: 120
- Fat (In grams): 1
- Fiber (In grams): 1

- Carbs (In grams): 4
- Protein: 8 g

Ingredients:
- 2 cups cracked wheat
- One-teaspoon fennel seeds
- 2 ½-cups clarified butter
- 2 cups jaggery
- 3 cloves
- One-cup milk
- A pinch of salt
- 3 cups water
- A few almonds, chopped

Instructions:
1. Set your instant pot on Sauté mode, add butter and heat it up.
2. Add cracked wheat, stir and cook for 5 minutes.
3. Add cloves and fennel seeds, stir and cook for 2 minutes.
4. Add jaggery, a pinch of salt, milk and water, stir, cover and cook at High for 10 minutes.
5. Release the pressure, uncover the pot, divide into bowls and serve with chopped almonds on top.

Bon Appétit!

329. Easy Buckwheat Porridge

Perp time: 10 minutes **Cooking time:** 6 minutes **Servings:** 4

Nutrition Facts:
- Calories: 400
- Fat (In grams): 3
- Fiber (In grams): 13
- Carbs (In grams): 30
- Protein: 13 g

Ingredients:
- 3 cups rice milk
- One-cup buckwheat groats
- 1 banana, sliced
- One-teaspoon cinnamon
- 1/4 cup raisins
- One-teaspoon cinnamon, ground
- Half-teaspoon vanilla
- Chopped nuts for serving

Instructions:
1. Put buckwheat in your instant pot, add milk, raisins, banana, vanilla and cinnamon, stir, cover and cook on High for 6 minutes.
2. Release the pressure for 15 minutes, uncover the pot, stir porridge, divide into bowls and serve with chopped nuts on top.

Bon Appétit!

330. Couscous With Veggies And Chicken

Perp time: 10 minutes **Cooking time:** 15 minutes **Servings:** 4

Nutrition Facts:
- Calories: 300
- Fat (In grams): 10
- Fiber (In grams): 3
- Carbs (In grams): 35
- Protein: 20 g

Ingredients:
- 8 chicken thighs, skinless
- 1 ½ cups mushrooms, cut into halves
- 1 ½ cups carrots, chopped
- 1 green bell pepper, chopped

- 1 yellow onion, chopped
- 2 garlic cloves, minced
- 15 ounces canned stewed tomatoes, chopped
- Salt and black pepper to the taste
- 3/4 cup couscous
- 1 zucchini, chopped
- Half-cup chicken stock
- A handful parsley, chopped

Instructions:
1. In your instant pot, mix chicken with mushrooms, carrots, bell pepper, onion, garlic, tomatoes and stock, stir, cover and cook at High for 8 minutes.
2. Release the pressure fast, uncover the pot, add couscous, zucchini, salt and pepper, stir, cover again and cook on Low for 6 minutes.
3. Release the pressure again, uncover the pot, add parsley, stir gently, divide into bowls and serve.

Bon Appétit!

331. Israeli Style Couscous

Perp time: 10 minutes **Cooking time:** 8 minutes **Servings:** 4

Nutrition Facts:
- Calories: 150
- Fat (In grams): 1
- Fiber (In grams): 5
- Carbs (In grams): 33
- Protein: 6 g

Ingredients:
- Half-cup red onion, chopped
- Half-teaspoon sesame oil
- 1/4 cup red bell pepper, chopped
- One-cup couscous, rinsed
- 1 ½ cups veggie stock
- Half-teaspoon cinnamon, ground
- 1/4 teaspoon coriander, ground
- Salt and black pepper to the taste
- 2 tablespoons red wine vinegar

Instructions:
1. Set your instant pot on Sauté mode, add oil and heat it up.
2. Add bell pepper and onion, stir and cook for 5 minutes.
3. Add couscous, coriander, stock, cinnamon, salt, pepper and vinegar, stir, cover and cook at High for 3 minutes.
4. Release the pressure, uncover the pot, divide couscous into bowls and serve.

Bon Appétit!

332. Mouthwatering Millet Dish

Perp time: 10 minutes **Cooking time:** 25 minutes **Servings:** 4

Nutrition Facts:
- Calories: 100
- Fat (In grams): 1.2
- Fiber (In grams): 7
- Carbs (In grams): 20
- Protein: 10 g

Ingredients:
- One-cup onion, chopped
- 2 garlic cloves, minced
- Half-cup oyster mushrooms, sliced
- Half-cup green lentils, rinsed

- One-cup millet
- 2 and 1/4 cups veggie stock
- Half-cup bok choy, sliced
- One-cup snow peas
- 1/4 cup parsley and chives, chopped
- One-cup asparagus, chopped
- One-tablespoon lemon juice
- Salt and black pepper to the taste

Instructions:
1. Set your instant pot on Sauté mode, add onions, garlic and mushrooms, stir and cook for 2 minutes.
2. Add millet and lentils, stir and cook for 1 minute.
3. Add stock, stir, cover and cook at High for 10 minutes.
4. Release the pressure naturally, uncover the pot, add asparagus, bok choy and peas, stir, cover and cook at High for 3 minutes.
5. Release the pressure again, uncover, add lemon juice, salt, pepper and mixed parsley and chives, stir gently, divide into bowls and serve.

Bon Appétit!

333. TASTY VEGGIES AND OATS

Perp time: 10 minutes **Cooking time:** 15 minutes **Servings:** 4

Nutrition Facts:
- Calories: 211
- Fat (In grams): 6.3
- Fiber (In grams): 5.6
- Carbs (In grams): 32
- Protein:7.5 g

Ingredients:
- One-cup steel cut oats
- 1 ½ cups water
- 1 carrots, chopped
- ½ green bell pepper, chopped
- 1 inch ginger, grated
- 1 Thai green chili, chopped
- 2 curry leaves
- 1/4 teaspoon mustard seeds
- Half-teaspoon urad dal
- A pinch of asafetida powder
- 1 ½ tablespoons canola oil
- A pinch of turmeric powder
- Salt to the taste

Instructions:
1. Put oats in your instant pot, add water, cover and cook at High for 7 minutes.
2. Heat up a pan with the oil over medium heat, add mustard seeds, urad dal, asafetida powder, turmeric, chili pepper, curry leaf, ginger, carrot and bell pepper, stir and cook for 5 minutes.
3. Release pressure from the pot, uncover, add oats to the pan, also add salt, stir, divide into bowls and serve.

Bon Appétit!

334. TASTY CREAMY MILLET DISH

Perp time: 10 minutes **Cooking time:** 20 minutes **Servings:** 4

Nutrition Facts:
- Calories: 231
- Fat (In grams): 2
- Fiber (In grams): 8
- Carbs (In grams): 41
- Protein:11 g

Ingredients:
- One-cup split mung beans
- 1 bay leaf
- One-cup carrot, chopped
- One-cup millet, chopped
- One-cup celery, chopped
- 4 cardamom pods
- 6 cups water
- 1 ½ cups fresh peas
- One-tablespoon lime juice
- 1/4 cup cilantro, chopped
- One-tablespoon ghee
- One-teaspoon coriander seeds, ground
- One-teaspoon fennel seeds, ground
- Half-teaspoon cumin seeds, ground
- Half-teaspoon turmeric powder
- Salt and black pepper to the taste
- Half-teaspoon ginger, grated

Instructions:
1. Set your instant pot on Sauté mode, add mung beans, stir and cook until they are golden.
2. Add millet, carrot, bay leaf, celery, cardamom, water, salt and pepper, stir, cover and cook at High for 10 minutes.
3. Release pressure, uncover the pot and set it on simmer mode.
4. Heat up a pan with the ghee over medium heat, add coriander, fennel, cumin, turmeric and ginger, stir and cook for 2 minutes.
5. Add this to your instant pot, stir, add more salt and pepper, peas and lime juice, simmer for 5 minutes, divide among plates, sprinkle cilantro and serve.

Bon Appétit!

335. PASTA AND CRANBERRY BEANS

Perp time: 10 minutes **Cooking time:** 20 minutes **Servings:** 8

Nutrition Facts:
- Calories: 330
- Fat (In grams): 14
- Fiber (In grams): 10
- Carbs (In grams): 32
- Protein: 18 g

Ingredients:
- 2 cups dried cranberry beans, soaked for 8 hours and drained
- 7 garlic cloves, minced
- 6 cups water
- 2 celery ribs, chopped
- 1 yellow onion, chopped
- One-teaspoon rosemary, chopped
- 1/4 teaspoon red pepper flakes
- 26 ounces canned tomatoes, chopped
- 3 teaspoons basil, dried
- Half-teaspoon smoked paprika
- 2 teaspoons oregano, dried
- Salt and black pepper to the taste
- 2 cups small pasta
- 3 tablespoons nutritional yeast
- 10 ounces kale leaves

Instructions:
1. Set your instant pot on Sauté mode, add onion, celery, garlic, pepper flakes, rosemary and a pinch of salt, stir and brown for 2 minutes.
2. Add tomatoes, basil, oregano and paprika, stir and cook for 1 minute.
3. Add beans, 6 cups water, cover pot and cook at High for 10 minutes.

4. Release the pressure, uncover the pot, add pasta, yeast, kale, salt and pepper, stir and set the pot on Sauté mode again.
5. Cook for 5 minutes more, divide into bowls and serve.

Bon Appétit!

336. VEGGIES AND QUINOA

Perp time: 10 minutes **Cooking time:** 2 minutes **Servings:** 4

Nutrition Facts:
- Calories: 249
- Fat (In grams): 7
- Fiber (In grams): 5.4
- Carbs (In grams): 20
- Protein: 7.4 g

Ingredients:
- 1 ½ cups quinoa
- 1 red bell pepper, chopped
- 3 celery stalks, chopped
- Salt to the taste
- 4 cups spinach
- 2 tomatoes, chopped
- 1 ½ cups chicken stock
- Half-cup black olives, pitted and chopped
- Half-cup feta cheese, crumbled
- 1/3 cup jarred pesto
- 1/4 cup almonds, sliced

Instructions:
1. In your instant pot, mix quinoa with bell pepper, celery, spinach, stock and salt, stir gently, cover and cook at High for 2 minutes.
2. Release the pressure for 10 minutes, uncover pot, add tomatoes, pesto and olives, stir and transfer to plates.
3. Add cheese and almonds on top, toss to coat and serve.

Bon Appétit!

337. MEXICAN STYLE CRANBERRY BEANS

Perp time: 10 minutes **Cooking time:** 20 minutes **Servings:** 6

Nutrition Facts:
- Calories: 100
- Fat (In grams): 1
- Fiber (In grams): 4
- Carbs (In grams): 10
- Protein: 6 g

Ingredients:
- 1 pound cranberry beans, soaked for 8 hours and drained
- 3 and 1/4 cups water
- 4 garlic cloves, minced
- 1 yellow onion, chopped
- 1 ½ teaspoons cumin
- 1/3 cup cilantro, chopped
- One-tablespoon chili powder
- One-teaspoon oregano, dried
- Salt and black pepper to the taste
- Cooker rice for serving

Instructions:
1. Put beans in your instant pot, add the water, garlic and onion, cover and cook at High for 20 minutes.

2. Release the pressure, uncover the pot, add cumin, cilantro, oregano, chili powder, salt and pepper, stir well, mash a bit using a potato mashes, divide among plates on top of rice and serve.

Bon Appétit!

338. Amazing Lentils Tacos

Perp time: 10 minutes   **Cooking time:** 15 minutes   **Servings:** 4

Nutrition Facts:
- Calories: 157
- Fat (In grams): 4
- Fiber (In grams): 8
- Carbs (In grams): 24
- Protein:6.4 g

Ingredients:
- 4 ounces tomato sauce
- Half-teaspoon cumin
- One-teaspoon salt
- One-teaspoon garlic powder
- One-teaspoon chili powder
- One-teaspoon onion powder
- 4 cups water
- 2 cups brown lentils
- Taco shells for serving

Instructions:
1. In your instant pot, mix lentils with water, tomato sauce, cumin, garlic powder, chili powder and onion powder, stir, cover and cook at High for 15 minutes.
2. Release the pressure, uncover the pot, divide lentils mix into taco shells and serve.

Bon Appétit!

339. Tomato Sauce And Lentils

Perp time: 10 minutes   **Cooking time:** 20 minutes   **Servings:** 4

Nutrition Facts:
- Calories: 105
- Fat (In grams): 3
- Fiber (In grams): 4.6
- Carbs (In grams): 1.7
- Protein:6 g

Ingredients:
- One-tablespoon olive oil
- 1 green bell pepper, chopped
- 1 yellow onion, chopped
- 1 celery stalk, chopped
- 1 ½ cups tomatoes, chopped
- Salt and black pepper to the taste
- One-teaspoon curry powder
- 2 cups water
- 1 ½ cups lentils

Instructions:
1. Set your instant pot on Sauté mode, add the oil and heat it up.
2. Add celery, bell pepper, onion and tomatoes, stir and cook for 4 minutes.
3. Add curry, salt, pepper, lentils and water, stir, cover and cook at High for 15 minutes.
4. Release the pressure, uncover the pot, divide lentils among bowls and serve.

Bon Appétit!

340. YUMMY CRANBERRY BEANS MIX

Perp time: 10 minutes **Cooking time:** 15 minutes **Servings:** 6

Nutrition Facts:
- Calories: 228
- Fat (In grams): 2
- Fiber (In grams): 14
- Carbs (In grams): 41
- Protein: 9 g

Ingredients:
- 1 ½ cups cranberry beans, soaked for 8 hours and drained
- 4-inch kombu piece, sliced
- 4 bacon slices, chopped
- Salt and black pepper to the taste
- 8 cups kale, chopped
- 4 ounces shiitake mushrooms, chopped
- Half-teaspoon garlic powder
- One-teaspoon extra virgin olive oil

Instructions:
1. Put beans in your instant pot, add 2 inches water, salt, pepper, kombu, cover and cook at High for 8 minutes.
2. Release the pressure uncover the pot, transfer beans and cooking liquid to a pot and leave aside for now.
3. Set your pot on Sauté mode, add oil and heat it up.
4. Add garlic powder, bacon, mushrooms, salt, pepper and 3/4 cup cooking liquid from the pot, stir well and cook for 1 minute.
5. Cover pot, cook at High for 3 minutes and release pressure.
6. Add beans and kale, stir and divide into bowls.

Bon Appétit!

341. DELICIOUS CRANBERRY BEAN CHILI

Perp time: 10 minutes **Cooking time:** 40 minutes **Servings:** 8

Nutrition Facts:
- Calories: 200
- Fat (In grams): 13
- Fiber (In grams): 4
- Carbs (In grams): 14
- Protein: 15 g

Ingredients:
- 1 pound cranberry beans, soaked in water for 7 hours and drained
- 5 cups water
- 14 ounces canned tomatoes and green chilies, chopped
- 1/4 cup millet
- Half-cup bulgur
- 1 ½ teaspoons cumin, ground
- 2 tablespoons tomato paste
- One-teaspoon chili powder
- One-teaspoon garlic, minced
- Half-teaspoon liquid smoke
- One-teaspoon oregano, dried
- Half-teaspoon ancho chili powder
- Salt and black pepper to the taste
- Hot sauce for serving
- Pickled jalapenos for serving

Instructions:
1. Put beans and 3 cups water in your instant pot, cover and cook at High for 25 minutes.

2. Release the pressure fast, add the rest of the water, tomatoes and chilies, millet, bulgur, cumin, tomato paste, chili powder, garlic, liquid smoke, oregano, ancho chili powder, salt and pepper, stir, cover and cook on High for 10 minutes more.
3. Release the pressure again, uncover, divide into bowls and serve with hot sauce on top and pickled jalapenos on the side.

Bon Appétit!

---

342. ITALIAN STYLE LENTILS DINNER

Perp time: 10 minutes **Cooking time:** 15 minutes **Servings:** 4

Nutrition Facts:
- Calories: 186
- Fat (In grams): 2
- Fiber (In grams): 3.3
- Carbs (In grams): 28
- Protein:14.4 g

Ingredients:
- Half-cup brown rice, soaked overnight and drained
- 3/4 cup green lentils, soaked overnight and drained
- 2 ½-cups chicken stock
- One-cup tomato sauce
- 3/4 cup onion, chopped
- One-cup green and red bell pepper, chopped
- 2 cups chicken, already cooked and shredded
- 3 carrots, chopped
- A handful greens
- Salt and black pepper to the taste
- 3 teaspoons Italian seasoning
- 2 garlic cloves, crushed
- One-cup mozzarella cheese, shredded

Instructions:
1. In your instant pot, mix lentils with rice, salt, pepper, stock, tomato sauce, onion, red and green pepper, chicken, carrots, greens, Italian seasoning and garlic, stir, cover and cook on High for 15 minutes.
2. Release the pressure, uncover pot, add cheese, stir, divide among bowls and serve.

Bon Appétit!

---

343. INDIAN STYLE LENTILS

Perp time: 10 minutes **Cooking time:** 20 minutes **Servings:** 4

Nutrition Facts:
- Calories: 198
- Fat (In grams): 6
- Fiber (In grams): 8.7
- Carbs (In grams): 26
- Protein:10.4 g

Ingredients:
- 3 teaspoons butter
- One-teaspoon extra virgin olive oil
- One-cup red lentils
- 1 yellow onion, chopped
- 2 teaspoons cumin
- 1/4 teaspoon coriander
- 1/4 teaspoon garlic powder
- 1/4 teaspoon turmeric
- 1/4 teaspoon Aleppo pepper
- 1/4 teaspoon red pepper flakes
- Salt and black pepper to the taste
- 3 cups chicken stock

Instructions:
1. Set your instant pot on Sauté mode, add butter and oil and heat up.
2. Add onions, stir and cook for 4 minutes.
3. Add cumin, coriander, garlic powder, turmeric, Aleppo pepper and pepper flakes, stir and cook for 2 minutes.
4. Add lentils and stock, stir, cover and cook at High for 15 minutes.
5. Release the pressure, uncover pot, divide into bowls and serve.

Bon Appétit!

344. TASTY LENTILS SALAD

Perp time: 10 minutes   **Cooking time:** 8 minutes   **Servings:** 4

Nutrition Facts:
- Calories: 165
- Fat (In grams): 5
- Fiber (In grams): 10
- Carbs (In grams): 20
- Protein: 9 g

Ingredients:
- 2 cups chicken stock
- One-cup lentils
- 1 bay leaf
- Half-teaspoon thyme, dried
- 1/4 cup red onion, chopped
- Half-cup celery, chopped
- 1/4 cup red bell pepper, chopped
- 2 tablespoons extra virgin olive oil
- One-tablespoon garlic, minced
- Half-teaspoon oregano, dried
- Juice of 1 lemon
- 2 tablespoons parsley, chopped
- Salt and black pepper to the taste

Instructions:
1. Put lentils in your instant pot.
2. Add bay leaf, stock and thyme, stir, cover and cook at High for 8 minutes.
3. Release pressure, uncover the pot, drain lentils and put them in a bowl.
4. Add celery, onion, bell pepper, garlic, parsley, oregano, lemon juice, olive oil, salt and pepper to the taste, toss to coat and serve.

Bon Appétit!

345. AMAZING KIDNEY BEANS ETOUFFEE

Perp time: 10 minutes   **Cooking time:** 30 minutes   **Servings:** 4

Nutrition Facts:
- Calories: 189
- Fat (In grams): 3
- Fiber (In grams): 10
- Carbs (In grams): 32
- Protein: 11.3 g

Ingredients:
- One-tablespoon vegetable oil
- 2 cups bell pepper, chopped
- One-cup yellow onion, chopped
- 2 teaspoons garlic, chopped
- One-cup water
- 3 bay leaves
- One-cup red kidney beans, soaked for 12 hours and drained
- 2 teaspoons smoked paprika
- 1 ½ teaspoons thyme, dried

- A pinch of cayenne pepper
- 2 teaspoons marjoram, dried
- One-teaspoon oregano, dried
- 14 ounces canned tomatoes, crushed
- Half-teaspoon liquid smoke
- Salt and black pepper to the taste
- Already cooked rice for serving

Instructions:
1. Set your instant pot on Sauté mode, add oil and heat it up.
2. Add onion, stir and cook for 5 minutes.
3. Add bell pepper and garlic, stir and cook 5 more minutes.
4. Add beans, bay leaves, water, thyme, paprika, cayenne and marjoram, stir, cover and cook on High for 15 minutes.
5. Release the pressure, uncover the pot, discard bay leaves, add oregano, tomatoes, liquid smoke, salt and pepper to the taste, stir, cover the pot again and cook at High for 3 more minutes.
6. Release the pressure naturally, uncover the pot and divide beans mix among plates on top of already cooked rice.

Bon Appétit!

---

346. Tasty Kidney Beans Curry

Perp time: 10 minutes **Cooking time:** 1 hour and 10 minutes **Servings:** 8

Nutrition Facts:
- Calories: 224
- Fat (In grams): 4
- Fiber (In grams): 7
- Carbs (In grams): 30
- Protein: 12 g

Ingredients:
- 2 cups red kidney beans, soaked for 8 hours and drained
- 1 inch piece ginger, chopped
- 1 yellow onion, chopped
- 4 garlic cloves, chopped
- 2 tablespoons vegetable oil
- 2 teaspoons ghee
- 2 red chili peppers, dried and crushed
- Salt and black pepper to the taste
- 6 cloves
- One-teaspoon cumin seeds
- One-teaspoons turmeric, ground
- One-teaspoon cumin, ground
- One-teaspoon coriander, ground
- 2 tomatoes chopped
- 2 cups water
- One-teaspoon Sugar
- One-teaspoon red pepper, ground
- 2 teaspoons garam masala
- 1/4 cup cilantro, chopped

Instructions:
1. Grind ginger, garlic and onion using a mortar and pestle and transfer paste to a bowl.
2. Set your instant pot on Sauté mode, add ghee and oil and heat it up.
3. Add red chili pepper, cloves and cumin seeds, stir and fry for 3 minutes.
4. Add onion paste, stir and cook for 3 more minutes.
5. Add coriander, cumin and turmeric, stir and cook for 30 seconds.
6. Add tomatoes, stir and cook 5 minutes.
7. Add beans, 2 cups water, salt, pepper and Sugar, stir, cover and cook at High for 40 minutes.

8. Switch instant pot to Low and cook for 10 minutes more.
9. Release the pressure, uncover the pot, add red pepper, garam masala and cilantro, stir, divide among plates and serve.

Bon Appétit!

347. YUMMY CHICKPEAS CURRY

Perp time: 10 minutes   **Cooking time:** 21 minutes   **Servings:** 6

Nutrition Facts:
- Calories: 384
- Fat (In grams): 8.3
- Fiber (In grams): 12
- Carbs (In grams): 69
- Protein: 11.5 g

Ingredients:
- 4 teaspoons cumin seeds
- 8 teaspoons olive oil
- 4 teaspoons garlic, minced
- 1 yellow onion, finely chopped
- 2 teaspoons garam masala
- 2 teaspoons coriander, ground
- 2 teaspoons turmeric, ground
- 3 cups chickpeas, already cooked, drained and rinsed
- 28 ounces canned tomatoes, chopped
- 3 potatoes, cubed
- Half-cup water
- Salt and black pepper to the taste
- Basmati rice, already cooked for serving
- Some cilantro, chopped for serving

Instructions:
1. Set your instant pot on Sauté mode, add oil and heat it up.
2. Add cumin seeds, stir and cook for 30 seconds.
3. Add onion, stir and cook for 5 minutes.
4. Add garlic, garam masala, coriander, turmeric, tomatoes, potatoes, chickpeas, water, salt and pepper, stir, cover and cook at High for 15 minutes.
5. Release the pressure, uncover the pot, divide chickpeas curry on plates and serve with rice on the side and cilantro on top.

Bon Appétit!

348. DUMPLINGS AND CHICKPEAS

Perp time: 10 minutes   **Cooking time:** 17 minutes   **Servings:** 4

Nutrition Facts:
- Calories: 300
- Fat (In grams): 5
- Fiber (In grams): 10
- Carbs (In grams): 56
- Protein: 12 g

Ingredients:
- 4 carrots, chopped
- 1 yellow onion, chopped
- 4 red baby potatoes, chopped
- 2 garlic cloves, minced
- 28 ounces veggie stock
- 1 veggie bouillon cube
- 2 cans chickpeas
- Salt and black pepper to the taste
- A pinch of cayenne pepper
- 2 green onions, chopped

- 2 celery stalks, chopped
- 1 and 3/4 teaspoons baking powder
- 3/4 cup white flour
- Half-teaspoon dill, dried
- Half-cup milk

Instructions:
1. Set your instant pot on Sauté mode, add onion and garlic and a splash of stock, stir and cook for 3 minutes.
2. Add potatoes, carrots, chickpeas, stock, bouillon cube, salt, pepper and cayenne pepper, stir, cover and cook at High for 7 minutes.
3. Release the pressure, uncover the pot, add celery and green onions, stir and leave aside.
4. Meanwhile, in a bowl, mix flour with baking powder, a pinch of salt, dill and milk and stir very well.
5. Shape 10 dumplings, heat up soup on Simmer mode, drop dumplings into the pot, cover it and cook on Steam mode for 10 minutes.
6. Uncover pot, add more salt and pepper if needed, stir, divide into bowls and serve.

Bon Appétit!

349. GARLIC AND CHICKPEAS

Perp time: 10 minutes   **Cooking time:** 35 minutes   **Servings:** 4

Nutrition Facts:
- Calories: 110
- Fat (In grams): 7
- Fiber (In grams): 0.6
- Carbs (In grams): 17
- Protein: 8 g

Ingredients:
- 2 bay leaves
- 4 garlic cloves
- 2 cups chickpeas, rinsed
- Water
- 2 tomatoes, chopped
- 2 small cucumbers, chopped
- One-teaspoon olive oil
- Salt and black pepper to the taste

Instructions:
1. Put chickpeas in your instant pot.
2. Add water, garlic and bay leaves, stir, cover and cook at High for 35 minutes.
3. Release the pressure naturally for 10 minutes, uncover pot, drain water and put chickpeas and garlic in a bowl.
4. Add cucumber, tomatoes, salt, pepper and oil, toss to coat and serve.

Bon Appétit!

350. SUCCULENT CHILI LIME BLACK BEANS

Perp time: 10 minutes   **Cooking time:** 42 minutes   **Servings:** 4

Nutrition Facts:
- Calories: 200
- Fat (In grams): 3
- Fiber (In grams): 5
- Carbs (In grams): 22
- Protein: 7 g

Ingredients:

- 2 cups black beans, soaked for 8 hours and drained
- 2 teaspoons red palm oil
- 1 yellow onion, chopped
- Salt to the taste
- 4 garlic cloves, minced
- One-tablespoon chili powder
- One-teaspoon smoked paprika
- 3 cups water
- Juice from 1 lime

Instructions:
1. Set your instant pot on Sauté mode, add oil and heat it up.
2. Add garlic and onion, stir and cook for 2 minutes.
3. Add beans, chili powder, paprika, salt and water, stir, cover and cook on High for 40 minutes.
4. Release the pressure naturally, uncover the pot, add lime juice and more salt, stir, divide into bowls and serve.

Bon Appétit!

351. PESTO AND CHICKPEA DELIGHT

Perp time: 10 minutes **Cooking time:** 20 minutes **Servings:** 4

Nutrition Facts:
- Calories: 100
- Fat (In grams): 3.5
- Fiber (In grams): 3
- Carbs (In grams): 13
- Protein:3.2 g

Ingredients:

For the pesto:
- 1/4 cup extra virgin olive oil
- 1 ½ cups basil
- 1 garlic clove, minced
- 1/4 cup parmesan cheese, grated
- One-tablespoon pine nuts, roasted

For the chickpeas:
- 12 ounces chickpeas, soaked for 8 hours
- 1 yellow onion, chopped
- 2 tablespoons extra virgin olive oil
- 2 carrots, chopped
- 14 ounces canned tomatoes
- 4 cups chicken stock
- 1/4 cup parmesan, grated

Instructions:
1. In your blender, mix basil with 1/4 cup cheese, 1 garlic clove, pine nuts, 1/4 cup oil and some salt and blend very well.
2. Transfer to a bowl and leave aside for now.
3. Set your instant pot on Sauté mode, add 2 tablespoons oil and heat it up.
4. Add onion and some salt, stir and cook for 3 minutes.
5. Add carrots, chickpeas, tomatoes, stock, salt and pepper to the taste, stir, cover and cook at High for 10 minutes.
6. Release the pressure fast, uncover the pot and transfer chickpeas mix into bowls.
7. Add pesto on top, sprinkle 1/4 cup parmesan and serve.

Bon Appétit!

352. MOUTHWATERING MARROW BEANS AND LEMON

Perp time: 10 minutes   **Cooking time:** 45 minutes   **Servings:** 4

Nutrition Facts:
- Calories: 165
- Fat (In grams): 2
- Fiber (In grams): 6
- Carbs (In grams): 28
- Protein: 9 g

Ingredients:
- 2 cusp marrow beans, soaked for 8 hours and drained
- One-cup yellow onion, chopped
- One-tablespoon extra virgin olive oil
- One-tablespoon rosemary, chopped
- 4 garlic cloves, minced
- 1 carrot, chopped
- Salt and black pepper to the taste
- 4 cups water
- 1 bay leaf
- 2 tablespoons lemon juice
- Already cooked quinoa for serving

Instructions:
1. Set your instant pot on Sauté mode, add oil and heat it up.
2. Add onion, carrot, garlic and rosemary, stir and cook for 3 minutes.
3. Add water, bay leaf, beans and some salt, stir, cover and cook at High for 45 minutes.
4. Release the pressure naturally, uncover the pot, discard bay leaf, add salt and pepper to the taste and lemon juice, stir well and divide into bowls over already cooked quinoa.

Bon Appétit!

353. SHRIMP AND WHITE BEANS

Perp time: 10 minutes   **Cooking time:** 35 minutes   **Servings:** 8

Nutrition Facts:
- Calories: 340
- Fat (In grams): 13
- Fiber (In grams): 11
- Carbs (In grams): 38
- Protein: 21 g

Ingredients:
- 1 pound white beans, soaked for 8 hours and drained
- 1 garlic clove, minced
- 2 yellow onions, chopped
- 1 green bell pepper, chopped
- 1 celery rib, chopped
- 4 parsley springs, chopped
- 2 cups seafood stock
- 2 bay leaves
- 3 tablespoons canola oil
- Creole seasoning to the taste
- 1 pound shrimp, peeled and deveined
- Cooker rice for serving
- Hot sauce for serving

Instructions:
1. Set your instant pot on Sauté mode, add oil and heat it up.
2. Add onions and Creole seasoning to the taste, stir and cook for 5 minutes.
3. Add garlic, stir and cook 5 minutes more.
4. Add bell pepper and celery, stir and cook for 5 minutes.
5. Add beans, stock and some water to cover everything in the pot.
6. Add bay leaves and parsley, stir, cover and cook at High for 15 minutes.
7. Release the pressure, uncover the pot, add shrimp, cover pot and leave it aside for 10 minutes.
8. Divide beans and shrimp among plates on top of cooked rice and serve with hot sauce.

354. Different Kidney Beans Dish

Perp time: 10 minutes **Cooking time:** 25 minutes **Servings:** 8

Nutrition Facts:
- Calories: 240
- Fat (In grams): 3
- Fiber (In grams): 4
- Carbs (In grams): 16
- Protein: 5 g

Ingredients:
- 1 pound red kidney beans, soaked for 8 hours and drained
- 2 yellow onions, chopped
- 8 ounces smoked Cajun Tasso, chopped
- 1 celery rib, chopped
- 2 tablespoons garlic, minced
- 1 green bell pepper, chopped
- 2 teaspoons thyme, dried
- 3 tablespoons extra virgin olive oil
- 2 bay leaves
- Cajun seasoning to the taste
- 4 green onions, chopped
- Hot sauce to the taste

Instructions:
1. Set your instant pot on Sauté mode, add oil and heat it up.
2. Add Tasso, stir, cook for 5 minutes and transfer to a bowl.
3. Add onions and Cajun seasoning to the pot, stir and cook for 10 minutes.
4. Add garlic, stir and cook 5 minutes.
5. Add bell pepper and celery, stir and cook 5 minutes.
6. Add beans, water to cover everything, bay leaves, thyme, cover and cook at High for 15 minutes.
7. Release the pressure fast, uncover the pot, add Tasso and leave aside for 5 minutes.
8. Divide beans and Tasso mix on plates, garnish with green onions and serve with hot sauce to the taste.

Bon Appétit!

355. Chorizo And Black Beans

Perp time: 10 minutes **Cooking time:** 45 minutes **Servings:** 6

Nutrition Facts:
- Calories: 230
- Fat (In grams): 7.7
- Fiber (In grams): 8
- Carbs (In grams): 30
- Protein: 12.5 g

Ingredients:
- One-tablespoon vegetable oil
- 6 ounces chorizo, chopped
- 1 yellow onion, cut into half
- 1 pound black beans, soaked for 8 hours and drained
- 6 garlic cloves, minced
- 2 bay leaves
- 1 orange, cut into half
- 2 quarts chicken stock
- Salt to the taste
- Chopped cilantro, chopped for serving

Instructions:
1. Set your instant pot on Sauté mode, add oil and heat it up.
2. Add chorizo, stir and cook for 2 minutes.

3. Add onion, beans, garlic, bay leaves, orange, salt and stock, stir, cover and cook at High for 40 minutes.
4. Release the pressure naturally, uncover your pot, discard bay leaves, onion and orange, add more salt and cilantro, stir, divide into bowls and serve.

Bon Appétit!

356. Spicy Tasty Black Beans

Perp time: 10 minutes **Cooking time:** 35 minutes **Servings:** 8

Nutrition Facts:
- Calories: 180
- Fat (In grams): 3
- Fiber (In grams): 7
- Carbs (In grams): 7
- Protein: 10 g

Ingredients:
- 16 ounces black beans, soaked overnight and drained
- 2 tablespoons chili powder
- 1 yellow onion, chopped
- 4 garlic cloves, minced
- 2 teaspoons cumin, ground
- One-teaspoon chipotle powder
- 2 teaspoons oregano, dried
- 8 ounces tomato paste
- 2 quarts water
- 4 tablespoons sunflower oil
- Salt to the taste

Instructions:
1. In your instant pot, mix beans with garlic, onion, chili powder, chipotle powder, cumin, oregano, tomato paste, water, oil and salt, stir, cover and cook at High for 30 minutes.
2. Release the pressure, uncover the pot and set it on Simmer mode.
3. Add more salt if needed, stir, cook for 3 minutes, divide into bowls and serve.

Bon Appétit!

357. Tasty Baked Beans

Perp time: 10 minutes **Cooking time:** 55 minutes **Servings:** 4

Nutrition Facts:
- Calories: 152
- Fat (In grams): 5.5
- Fiber (In grams): 5.4
- Carbs (In grams): 21
- Protein: 5.5 g

Ingredients:
- 1 pound white beans, soaked for 8 hours and drained
- Half-cup molasses
- 2 garlic cloves, minced
- 1 yellow onion, chopped
- Half-cup maple syrup
- One-tablespoon mustard powder
- Salt and black pepper to the taste
- 7 cups water
- 1/8 cup balsamic vinegar

Instructions:
1. Put the beans and 3 cups water in your instant pot, cover and cook at High for 10 minutes.
2. Release pressure naturally, uncover the pot, drain beans and return them to the pot.
3. Add 4 cups water, molasses, garlic, onion, maple syrup, vinegar, salt and pepper, stir, cover and cook on High for 45 minutes.
4. Release the pressure again, uncover the pot, divide into bowls and serve.

358. Yummy Creamy White Beans

Perp time: 10 minutes **Cooking time:** 35 minutes **Servings:** 8

Nutrition Facts:
- Calories: 170
- Fat (In grams): 0.6
- Fiber (In grams): 10
- Carbs (In grams): 31
- Protein: 10.5 g

Ingredients:
- 1 yellow onion, chopped
- 1 pound white beans
- 5 cups water
- 2 celery ribs, chopped
- 2 bay leaves
- 4 garlic cloves, minced
- 1 green bell pepper, chopped
- One-teaspoon oregano
- One-teaspoon thyme
- Salt and white pepper to the taste
- One-tablespoon soy sauce
- One-tablespoon Tabasco sauce

Instructions:
1. Put beans and water in your instant pot.
2. Add onion, celery, garlic, bell pepper, oregano, thyme, salt, white pepper and soy sauce, stir, cover and cook at High for 15 minutes.
3. Release the pressure naturally for 15 minutes, uncover the pot and set it on Simmer mode.
4. Add more salt and pepper to the taste and Tabasco sauce, stir and cook for 20 minutes.
5. Divide into bowls and serve.

Bon Appétit!

359. Mouthwatering Mung Beans Dish

Perp time: 10 minutes **Cooking time:** 17 minutes **Servings:** 4

Nutrition Facts:
- Calories: 180
- Fat (In grams): 1
- Fiber (In grams): 15
- Carbs (In grams): 39
- Protein: 7 g

Ingredients:
- 3/4 cup mung beans, soaked for 15 minutes and drained
- 1 small red onion, chopped
- Half-teaspoon cumin seeds
- Half-teaspoon coconut oil
- Half-cup brown rice, soaked for 15 minutes and drained
- 28 ounces canned tomatoes, crushed
- 5 garlic cloves, minced
- 1 inch ginger piece, chopped
- One-teaspoon coriander, ground
- One-teaspoon turmeric
- Half-teaspoon garam masala
- A pinch of cayenne
- Salt and black pepper to the taste
- One-teaspoon lemon juice
- 4 cups water

Instructions:
1. In your food processor, mix tomatoes with onions, ginger, garlic, coriander, turmeric, cayenne, salt, pepper and garam masala and blend well.
2. Set your instant pot on Sauté mode, add oil and heat up.
3. Add cumin seeds, stir and fry for 2 minutes.

4. Add tomatoes mix, stir and cook for 15 minutes.
5. Add beans, rice, water, salt, pepper and lemon juice, stir, cover and cook at High for 15 minutes.
6. Release the pressure for 10 minutes, uncover the pot, stir again, divide into bowls and serve.

Bon Appétit!

---

360. INDIAN MUNG BEANS DISH

Perp time: 10 minutes   **Cooking time:** 1 hour   **Servings:** 4

Nutrition Facts:
- Calories: 210
- Fat (In grams): 4.3
- Fiber (In grams): 8.7
- Carbs (In grams): 33
- Protein: 13 g

Ingredients:
- One-cup mung beans, soaked for 6 hours and drained
- One-teaspoon cumin seeds
- 2 teaspoons ghee
- A pinch of cayenne pepper
- 2 teaspoons turmeric
- Half-tablespoon coriander, ground
- One-teaspoon cumin, ground
- One-tablespoon ginger, grated
- 1 yellow onion, chopped
- 1 tomato, chopped
- 1 ½ cups water
- 4 jalapeno peppers, chopped
- 1/4 cup cilantro, chopped
- Salt and black pepper to the taste

Instructions:
1. Set your instant pot on Sauté mode, add ghee and heat it up.
2. Add cumin seeds, stir and cook for 1 minute.
3. Add cayenne, turmeric, coriander, cumin and ginger, stir and cook for 2 minutes.
4. Add jalapenos and onion, stir and cook for 4 minutes.
5. Add beans and water, salt and pepper, stir, cover and cook at High for 20 minutes.
6. Release the pressure, uncover, add tomatoes, more salt and pepper if needed and set the pot on Simmer mode.
7. Stir and simmer for 20 minutes more, add cilantro, divide into bowls and serve.

Bon Appétit!

---

361. CABBAGE AND NAVY BEANS

Perp time: 10 minutes   **Cooking time:** 40 minutes   **Servings:** 8

Nutrition Facts:
- Calories: 150
- Fat (In grams): 1
- Fiber (In grams): 9.5
- Carbs (In grams): 27
- Protein: 7 g

Ingredients:
- 6 bacon slices, chopped
- 1 yellow onion, chopped
- 1 ½ cups navy beans, soaked for 8 hours and drained
- 1/4 teaspoon cloves
- 3 cups chicken stock
- 1 bay leaf
- 1 cabbage head, chopped
- 3 tablespoons honey
- 3 tablespoons white wine vinegar

- Salt and black pepper to the taste

Instructions:
1. Set your instant pot on Sauté mode, add bacon, stir and brown it for 4 minutes.
2. Add onions, stir and cook for 4 minutes.
3. Add stock, beans, clove and bay leaf, stir, cover and cook at High for 35 minutes.
4. Release the pressure fast, uncover, add vinegar, honey and cabbage, stir, cover and cook at High for 12 minutes more.
5. Release pressure again, uncover, add salt and pepper, stir, divide into bowls and serve.

Bon Appétit!

362. DELICIOUS BLACK EYED PEA CURRY

Perp time: 10 minutes **Cooking time:** 45 minutes **Servings:** 4

Nutrition Facts:
- Calories: 200
- Fat (In grams): 6
- Fiber (In grams): 12
- Carbs (In grams): 33
- Protein: 12 g

Ingredients:
- One-cup black-eyed peas, soaked for 3 hours and drained
- Half-teaspoon cumin seeds
- 2 tablespoons avocado oil
- 1 bay leaf
- 1 yellow onion, chopped
- 6 garlic cloves, minced
- 1 inch ginger piece, minced
- One-teaspoon turmeric
- A pinch of cayenne pepper
- 2 tomatoes, chopped
- Salt and black pepper to the taste
- One-teaspoon garam masala
- 3 cups water
- Cilantro leaves, chopped for serving

Instructions:
1. Set your instant pot on Sauté mode, add oil and heat it up.
2. Add cumin seeds, stir and fry for 2 minutes.
3. Add onion and bay leaf, stir and cook 8 minutes.
4. Add ginger, garlic, turmeric, cayenne, salt, pepper and garam masala, stir and cook for 2 minutes.
5. Add peas, tomatoes and water, stir, cover and cook at High for 30 minutes.
6. Release the pressure, uncover the pot, add cilantro, more salt and pepper if needed, stir, divide into bowls and serve.

Bon Appétit!

363. YUMMY FAVA BEAN DIP

Perp time: 10 minutes **Cooking time:** 30 minutes **Servings:** 6

Nutrition Facts:
- Calories: 60
- Fat (In grams): 1
- Fiber (In grams): 0
- Carbs (In grams): 9
- Protein: 3 g

Ingredients:
- 2 cups fava beans, soaked
- 2 garlic cloves, crushed
- 3 cups water
- 2 teaspoons tahini
- 2 tablespoons vegetable oil
- 2 teaspoons cumin powder
- One-teaspoon harissa
- Zest from 1 lemon
- Juice of 1 lemon
- Salt and black pepper to the taste
- One-tablespoon olive oil
- One-teaspoon paprika

Instructions:
1. Set your instant pot on Sauté mode, add vegetable oil and heat it up.
2. Add garlic, stir and cook for 3 minutes.
3. Add fava beans, 3 cups water, stir, cover and cook at High for 12 minutes.
4. Release the pressure naturally for 10 minutes, uncover the pot, drain most of the liquid and set it on Sauté mode again.
5. Add cumin, harissa, tahini, salt and pepper and lemon zest, stir and blend everything using an immersion blender.
6. Add paprika, lemon juice and olive oil and stir gently.
7. Divide into bowls and serve.

Bon Appétit!

---

364. TASTY FAVA BEAN PUREE

Perp time: 10 minutes **Cooking time:** 25 minutes **Servings:** 6

Nutrition Facts:
- Calories: 330
- Fat (In grams): 4
- Fiber (In grams): 1
- Carbs (In grams): 30
- Protein: 10 g

Ingredients:
- 1 pound fava bean, rinsed
- One-cup yellow onion, chopped
- 4 and Half-cups water
- 1 bay leaf
- 1/4 cup extra virgin olive oil
- 1 garlic clove, minced
- 2 tablespoons lemon juice
- Salt to the taste

Instructions:
1. Put fava beans in your instant pot, add 4 cups water, some salt and bay leaf, cover and cook at High for 18 minutes.
2. Release the pressure naturally, uncover the pot, drain beans and discard bay leaf.
3. Return beans to the pot, add Half-cup water, garlic, onion and salt, stir, cover and cook 5 minutes.
4. Release the pressure again, uncover pot, transfer beans mix to your food processor, add olive oil and lemon juice and blend well.
5. Divide into bowls and serve cold.

Bon Appétit!

365. DELICIOUS FULL MUDAMMAS

Perp time: 10 minutes **Cooking time:** 25 minutes **Servings:** 2

Nutrition Facts:
- Calories: 154
- Fat (In grams): 1.4
- Fiber (In grams): 3
- Carbs (In grams): 30
- Protein: 8.6 g

Ingredients:
- 2 cups already cooked fava beans
- 4 roasted garlic cloves, chopped
- 1 small red onion, chopped
- One-tablespoon olive oil
- One-teaspoon cumin
- Half-cup water
- Salt and black pepper to the taste
- Juice from 2 lemons
- 1 egg, hard boiled, peeled and sliced
- 1 tomato, finely chopped
- 1 yellow onion, cut into thin rings
- A pinch of red chili flakes
- A pinch of paprika

Instructions:
1. Set your instant pot on Sauté mode, add oil and heat it up.
2. Add red onion, stir and cook for 3 minutes.
3. Add cumin and garlic, stir and cook for 1 minute.
4. Add beans, salt, pepper and water, stir, cover and cook at High for 15 minutes.
5. Release the pressure, uncover the pot, set it on Simmer mode and cook for 10 more minutes.
6. Transfer to a bowl, add more salt, pepper and lemon juice and mash using a potato masher.
7. Garnish with egg slices, tomato pieces, yellow onion rings, red chili flakes and paprika sprinkled on top.
8. Serve hot!

Bon Appétit!

366. TASTY PINEAPPLE AND PEA CURRY

Perp time: 10 minutes **Cooking time:** 35 minutes **Servings:** 4

Nutrition Facts:
- Calories: 333
- Fat (In grams): 11
- Fiber (In grams): 17
- Carbs (In grams): 43
- Protein: 16 g

Ingredients:
- One-cup peas, soaked in water for a few hours and drained
- 4 cups water
- 3 tablespoons extra virgin olive oil
- 1 yellow onion, chopped
- One-cup brown lentils
- One-teaspoon curry powder
- Half-teaspoon turmeric
- 1/4 teaspoon cinnamon
- Half-teaspoon cumin
- 2/3 cup canned pineapple, cut into chunks
- 1/4 cup cashew butter

Instructions:
1. In a bowl, mix cashew butter with some water, stir very well and leave aside for now.

2. Put lentils and beans in you instant pot, add 3 ½-cups water, stir, cover and cook at High for 25 minutes.
3. Release the pressure, drain peas and lentils and put them in a bowl.
4. Set your instant pot on Sauté mode, add oil and heat it up.
5. Add turmeric, cumin, curry powder and cinnamon, stir and cook for 3 minutes.
6. Add onions, stir and cook for 4 minutes.
7. Set the pot on Simmer mode, add peas and lentils, cashew butter, pineapple and Half-cup water, stir, simmer for 5 minutes, divide into bowls and serve.

Bon Appétit!

367. SIMPLE SPLIT PEA CURRY

Perp time: 10 minutes   **Cooking time:** 35 minutes   **Servings:** 4

Nutrition Facts:
- Calories: 435
- Fat (In grams): 18
- Fiber (In grams): 8
- Carbs (In grams): 47
- Protein: 16 g

Ingredients:
- 7 ounces split peas
- One-tablespoon olive oil
- 2 yellow onions, chopped
- 2 bell peppers, chopped
- 4 tablespoons curry paste
- 2 teaspoons black onion seeds
- 15 ounces canned tomatoes, chopped
- 15 ounces canned coconut milk
- A bunch of coriander leaves, chopped
- Zest and juice of 1 lime
- Salt and black pepper to the taste
- 5 ounces coconut yogurt
- Naan bread for serving

Instructions:
1. Set your instant pot on Sauté mode, add oil and heat it up.
2. Add onions and bell peppers, stir and cook for 10 minutes.
3. Add curry paste and black onion seeds, stir and cook for 1 minute.
4. Add split peas, coconut milk, tomatoes and coriander.
5. Also, add some salt and pepper, stir, cover and cook at High for 25 minutes.
6. Release pressure, uncover the pot, add more salt and pepper if needed, lime zest and juice and coconut yogurt and stir.
7. Divide into bowls and serve with naan bread on the side.

Bon Appétit!

SAUCE RECIPES

368. AMAZING APPLE SAUCE

Perp time: 10 minutes **Cooking time:** 8 minutes **Servings:** 4

Nutrition Facts:
- Calories: 70
- Fat (In grams): 1
- Fiber (In grams): 1.2
- Carbs (In grams): 17
- Protein: 0.3 g

Ingredients:
- 8 apples, cored and chopped
- 2 drops cinnamon oil
- One-cup water
- One-teaspoon cinnamon powder

Instructions:
1. Put apples in your instant pot, add the water, cover pot and cook at High for 8 minutes.
2. Release the pressure, uncover the pot, add oil and cinnamon and puree using an immersion blender.
3. Serve cold.

Bon Appétit!

369. TASTY ANCHO CHILI SAUCE

Perp time: 10 minutes **Cooking time:** 10 minutes **Servings:** 8

Nutrition Facts:
- Calories: 50
- Fat (In grams): 2
- Fiber (In grams): 0
- Carbs (In grams): 2
- Protein: 0 g

Ingredients:
- 5 ancho chilies, dried, seedless and chopped
- 2 garlic cloves, crushed
- Slat and black pepper to the taste
- 1 ½ cups water
- 1 ½teaspoons Sugar
- Half-teaspoon oregano, dried
- Half-teaspoon cumin, ground
- 2 tablespoons apple cider vinegar

Instructions:
1. In your instant pot mix water chilies, garlic, salt, pepper, Sugar, cumin and oregano, stir, cover and cook at High for 8 minutes.
2. Release the pressure for 5 minutes, uncover the pot and pour sauce into a blender.
3. Add vinegar, blend well and transfer everything to a bowl.

Bon Appétit!

370. Delicious Marinara Sauce

Perp time: 10 minutes **Cooking time:** 20 minutes **Servings:** 8

Nutrition Facts:
- Calories: 60
- Fat (In grams): 2
- Fiber (In grams): 2
- Carbs (In grams): 9
- Protein: 2 g

Ingredients:
- 56 ounces canned tomatoes, crushed
- 3 garlic cloves, minced
- Half-cup red lentils
- One-cup sweet potato, finely chopped
- Salt and black pepper to the taste
- 1 ½ cups water

Instructions:
1. Set your instant pot on Sauté mode, add lentils, sweet potatoes, salt, pepper and garlic, stir and cook them for 2 minutes.
2. Add water and tomatoes, stir, cover pot and cook at High for 13 minutes.
3. Release the pressure, uncover the pot, puree everything using an immersion blender, add more salt and pepper if needed, set the pot on Simmer mode and cook the sauce for 4 minutes more.

Bon Appétit!

371. Tasty Giblet Gravy

Perp time: 10 minutes **Cooking time:** 1 hour and 30 minutes **Servings:** 2

Nutrition Facts:
- Calories: 181
- Fat (In grams): 10
- Fiber (In grams): 1
- Carbs : 11.4 g
- Protein: 10.5 g

Ingredients:
- Turkey neck, gizzard, but and heart
- One-tablespoon vegetable oil
- Half-cup dry vermouth
- 1 yellow onion, chopped
- 1-quart turkey stock
- 1 bay leaf
- 4 tablespoons butter
- 2 thyme springs
- 4 tablespoons white flour
- Salt and black pepper to the taste

Instructions:
1. Set your instant pot on Sauté mode, add oil and heat it up.
2. Add turkey pieces and onion, stir and cook for 3 minutes.
3. Stir again and cook for 3 more minutes.
4. Add vermouth, stock, bay leaf and thyme and stir.
5. Cover pot and cook at High for 36 minutes.
6. Release the pressure for 20 minutes, strain stock, reserve turkey gizzard, and heart, leave them to cool down, remove gristle and chop it along with the heart.
7. Heat up a pan with the butter over medium heat, add flour, stir and cook for 3 minutes.
8. Add strained stock, stir well, increase heat to medium high and simmer for 20 minutes.
9. Add salt and pepper, heart and gizzard, stir well and serve.

Bon Appétit!

372. GINGER AND ORANGE SAUCE

Perp time: 5 minutes **Cooking time:** 7 minutes. **Servings:** 4

Nutrition Facts:
- Calories: 100
- Fat (In grams): 1
- Fiber (In grams): 1
- Carbs (In grams): 2
- Protein: 4 g

Ingredients:
- One-cup fish stock
- Salt and black pepper to the taste
- One-tablespoon olive oil
- 4 spring onions, chopped
- 1 inch ginger piece, chopped
- Zest and juice from 1 orange

Instructions:
1. In your instant pot, mix fish stock with salt, pepper, olive oil, spring onions, ginger, orange juice and zest and stir well.
2. Cover pot and cook at High for 7 minutes.
3. Release pressure, uncover the pot and serve your sauce.

Bon Appétit!

373. TUMMY CRANBERRY SAUCE

Perp time: 10 minutes **Cooking time:** 15 minutes **Servings:** 4

Nutrition Facts:
- Calories: 151
- Fat (In grams): 0.4
- Fiber (In grams): 1
- Carbs (In grams): 39
- Protein: 0.4 g

Ingredients:
- 2 ½-teaspoons orange zest
- 12 ounces cranberries
- 1/4 cup orange juice
- 2 tablespoons maple syrup
- A pinch of salt
- One-cup Sugar

Instructions:
1. In your instant pot, mix orange juice with maple syrup and stir well.
2. Add orange zest and almost all cranberries, stir, cover and cook at High for 2 minutes.
3. Release the pressure, uncover the pot and set it on Sauté mode.
4. Add the rest of the cranberries, a pinch of salt and the Sugar, stir and cook until Sugardissolves.
5. Serve cold.

Bon Appétit!

374. SPECIAL ZUCCHINI PESTO

Perp time: 10 minutes **Cooking time:** 10 minutes **Servings:** 4

Nutrition Facts:
- Calories: 71
- Fat (In grams): 5
- Fiber (In grams): 2.3
- Carbs (In grams): 2
- Protein: 1.2 g

Ingredients:
- 1 yellow onion, chopped
- One-tablespoon extra virgin olive oil
- 1 ½ pounds zucchini, chopped
- Salt to the taste

- Half-cup water
- 1 bunch basil, chopped
- 2 garlic cloves, minced

Instructions:
1. Set your instant pot on Sauté mode, add oil and heat it up.
2. Add onion, stir and cook 4 minutes.
3. Add zucchini, salt and water, stir, cover and cook at High for 3 minutes.
4. Release the pressure, uncover the pot, add garlic and basil and blend everything using an immersion blender.
5. Transfer to a bowl and serve.

Bon Appétit!

---

375. SPECIAL SAUCE

Perp time: 10 minutes   **Cooking time:** 20 minutes   **Servings:** 8

Nutrition Facts:
- Calories: 79
- Fat (In grams): 1
- Fiber (In grams): 0.4
- Carbs (In grams): 5
- Protein: 3 g

Ingredients:
- 1 yellow onion, chopped
- 2 tablespoons olive oil
- 5 celery ribs
- 8 carrots, chopped
- 4 beets, chopped
- 1 butternut squash, chopped
- 8 garlic cloves, minced
- One cup veggie stock
- 1/4 cup lemon juice
- 1 bunch basil, chopped
- 2 bay leaves
- Salt and black pepper to the taste

Instructions:
1. Set your instant pot on Sauté mode, add oil and heat it up.
2. Add celery, onion and carrots, stir and cook for 4 minutes.
3. Add beets, squash, garlic, stock, lemon juice, basil, bay leaves, salt and pepper, stir, cover and cook for 12 minutes at High.
4. Release the pressure, uncover the pot, discard bay leaves, puree sauce using an immersion blender, transfer to a bowl and serve.

Bon Appétit!

---

376. EASY SPAGHETTI SAUCE

Perp time: 10 minutes   **Cooking time:** 40 minutes   **Servings:** 6

Nutrition Facts:
- Calories: 281
- Fat (In grams): 16
- Fiber (In grams): 5
- Carbs (In grams): 20
- Protein: 17 g

Ingredients:
- 1 and 2/3 pounds beef, ground
- 2 carrots, chopped
- 4 garlic cloves, minced
- 2 celery ribs, chopped
- 28 ounces canned tomatoes, crushed
- 1 yellow onion, chopped

- 2 bay leaves
- One-tablespoon olive oil
- A pinch of basil, dried
- A pinch of oregano, dried
- A splash of red wine
- Salt and black pepper to the taste

For the chicken stock mix:
- One-cup chicken stock
- 2 tablespoons soy sauce
- 3 tablespoons tomato paste
- 2 tablespoons fish sauce
- One-tablespoon Worcestershire sauce

Instructions:
1. Set your instant pot on Sauté mode, add beef, salt, pepper and the oil, stir and brown for 7 minutes.
2. Transfer beef to a bowl when it's brown and leave it aside for now.
3. In a bowl, mix stock with fish sauce, soy sauce, tomato paste and Worcestershire sauce and stir well.
4. Heat up you instant pot again, add onions, garlic, bay leaves, basil and oregano, stir and cook for 5 minutes.
5. Add celery, carrots, salt and pepper, stir and cook for 3 minutes.
6. Add red wine, chicken stock mix, beef and crushed tomatoes on top.
7. Cover pot and cook at High for 10 minutes.
8. Release pressure, uncover, add more salt and pepper if needed, set the pot on Simmer mode and cook the sauce for 4 minutes more.
9. Serve with your favorite pasta.

Bon Appétit!

377. TASTY CHEESE SAUCE

Perp time: 10 minutes   **Cooking time:** 5 minutes   **Servings:** 4

Nutrition Facts:
- Calories: 110
- Fat (In grams): 8.5
- Fiber (In grams): 0.4
- Carbs (In grams): 4.3
- Protein: 4.32 g

Ingredients:
- 2 cups processed cheese, cut into chunks
- One-cup Italian sausage, cooked and chopped
- 5 ounces canned tomatoes and green chilies, finely chopped
- 4 tablespoons water

Instructions:
1. In your instant pot, mix sausage with cheese, tomatoes and chilies and water.
2. Stir, cover and cook at High for 5 minutes.
3. Release pressure, uncover pot, transfer sauce to a bowl and serve with your favorite macaroni.

Bon Appétit!

378. Delicious BBQ Sauce

Perp time: 10 minutes **Cooking time:** 10 minutes **Servings:** 8

Nutrition Facts:
- Calories: 20
- Fat (In grams): 0.4
- Fiber (In grams): 0.4
- Carbs (In grams): 3.5
- Protein: 0.1 g

Ingredients:
- One-tablespoon sesame seed oil
- Half-cup tomato puree
- 1 yellow onion, chopped
- Half-cup water
- 4 tablespoons white wine vinegar
- 4 tablespoons honey
- One-teaspoon salt
- Half-teaspoon granulated garlic
- One-teaspoon liquid smoke
- One-teaspoon Tabasco sauce
- 1/8 teaspoon cumin powder
- 1/8 teaspoon clove powder
- 5 ounces plums, dried and seedless

Instructions:
1. Set your instant pot on Sauté mode, add oil and heat it up.
2. Add onion, stir and cook for 5 minutes.
3. Add tomato puree, honey, water, vinegar, salt, garlic, Tabasco sauce, liquid smoke, cumin and clove powder and stir everything very well.
4. Add plums and stir again well.
5. Cover pot and cook at High for 10 minutes.
6. Release the pressure, uncover the pot, blend everything with an immersion blender, transfer sauce to a bowl and serve.

Bon Appétit!

379. Yummy Mushroom Sauce

Perp time: 10 minutes **Cooking time:** 35 minutes **Servings:** 6

Nutrition Facts:
- Calories: 140
- Fat (In grams): 5.7
- Fiber (In grams): 3.1
- Carbs (In grams): 13
- Protein: 7.4 g

Ingredients:
- 1 yellow onion, chopped
- 1/4 cup olive oil
- One-tablespoon flour
- Salt and black pepper to the taste
- One-tablespoon thyme, chopped
- 3 garlic cloves, minced
- 1 and 1/4 cup chicken stock
- 1/4 cup dry sherry
- 10 ounces shiitake mushrooms, chopped
- 10 ounces cremini mushrooms, chopped
- 10 ounces Portobello mushrooms, chopped
- 1-ounce parmesan cheese, grated
- Half-cup heavy cream
- One-tablespoons parsley, finely chopped

Instructions:
1. Set your instant pot on Sauté mode, add oil and heat it up.
2. Add onion, salt and pepper, stir and cook for 5 minutes.
3. Add garlic, flour and thyme, stir and cook for 1 minute.
4. Add sherry, stock and all mushrooms, stir, cover and cook at High for 25 minutes.
5. Release pressure quick, uncover the pot, add cream, cheese and parsley, stir and set the pot on Simmer mode.
6. Cook for 5 minutes, transfer to a bowl and serve.

Bon Appétit!

380. SIMPLE CAULIFLOWER SAUCE

Perp time: 10 minutes   **Cooking time:** 10 minutes   **Servings:** 6

Nutrition Facts:
- Calories: 119
- Fat (In grams): 5
- Fiber (In grams): 1
- Carbs (In grams): 10
- Protein: 8 g

Ingredients:
- 2 tablespoons butter
- 8 garlic cloves, minced
- 7 cups veggie stock
- 6 cups cauliflower florets
- Salt and black pepper to the taste
- Half-cup milk

Instructions:
1. Set your instant pot on Sauté mode, add butter and melt it.
2. Add garlic, salt and pepper, stir, cook for 5 minutes and transfer to a bowl.
3. Add stock and cauliflower to the pot, heat up, cover and cook at High for 7 minutes.
4. Release pressure, transfer cauliflower and One-cup stock to your blender, add salt, pepper, milk and garlic and puree well for a few minutes.
5. Serve right away with your favorite spaghetti.

Bon Appétit!

381. TASTY MANGO SAUCE

Perp time: 10 minutes   **Cooking time:** 30 minutes   **Servings:** 4

Nutrition Facts:
- Calories: 80
- Fat (In grams): 0.3
- Fiber (In grams): 1
- Carbs (In grams): 9
- Protein: 0.9 g

Ingredients:
- 1 shallot, chopped
- One-tablespoon vegetable oil
- 1/4 teaspoon cardamom powder
- 2 tablespoons ginger, minced
- Half-teaspoon cinnamon
- 2 mangos, chopped
- 2 red hot chilies, chopped
- 1 apple, cored and chopped
- 2 teaspoons salt
- 1/4 cup raisins
- 1 and 1/4 cup raw Sugar
- 1 and 1/4 apple cider vinegar

Instructions:
1. Set your instant pot on Sauté mode, add oil and heat it up.
2. Add ginger and shallot, stir and cook for 5 minutes.
3. Add cinnamon, hot peppers and cardamom, stir and cook for 2 minutes.
4. Add mangos, apple, raisins, Sugar and cider, stir and cook until Sugarmelts.
5. Cover the pot and cook at High for 7 minutes.
6. Release the pressure, uncover the pot, transfer to a pan and simmer on medium heat for 15 minutes more, stirring from time to time.
7. Transfer to jars and serve when needed.

Bon Appétit!

382. TASTY TABASCO SAUCE

Perp time: 10 minutes **Cooking time:** 2 minutes **Servings:** 6

Nutrition Facts:
- Calories: 12
- Fat (In grams): 0.04
- Fiber (In grams): 0
- Carbs: 0.04 g
- Protein: 0.06 g

Ingredients:
- 12 ounces hot peppers, chopped
- 2 teaspoons salt
- 1 and 1/4 cups apple cider vinegar

Instructions:
1. Put peppers in your instant pot.
2. Add vinegar and salt, stir, cover and cook at High for 2 minutes.
3. Release the pressure for 15 minutes, uncover the pot and puree everything using your immersion blender.
4. Transfer to jars and serve when needed.

383. AMAZING STRAWBERRY SAUCE

Perp time: 10 minutes **Cooking time:** 2 minutes **Servings:** 8

Nutrition Facts:
- Calories: 60
- Fat (In grams): 0
- Fiber (In grams): 0
- Carbs (In grams): 13
- Protein: 1 g

Ingredients:
- 1-ounce orange juice
- 1/8 cup Sugar
- 1 pound strawberries, cut into halves
- A pinch of ginger, ground
- Half-teaspoon vanilla extract

Instructions:
1. In your instant pot, mix strawberries with Sugar, stir and leave them aside for 10 minutes.
2. Add orange juice, stir, cover and cook at High for 2 minutes.
3. Release the pressure for 15 minutes, uncover the pot, add vanilla extract and ginger, puree a but using an immersion blender and leave aside until it's cold enough.
4. Serve your strawberry sauce with some tasty pancakes.

384. INDIAN STYLE TOMATO CHUTNEY

Perp time: 10 minutes **Cooking time:** 10 minutes **Servings:** 6

Nutrition Facts:
- Calories: 140
- Fat (In grams): 10
- Fiber (In grams): 0
- Carbs (In grams): 10
- Protein: 4 g

Ingredients:
- 3 pounds tomatoes, peeled and chopped
- One-cup red wine vinegar
- 1 and 3/4 cups Sugar
- 1 inch ginger piece, grated
- 3 garlic cloves, minced
- 2 onions, chopped
- 1/4 cup raisins
- 3/4 teaspoon cinnamon, ground
- 1/4 teaspoon cloves
- Half-teaspoon coriander, ground
- 1/4 teaspoon nutmeg
- 1/4 teaspoon ginger, ground
- 1 pinch paprika
- One-teaspoon chili powder

Instructions:
1. Mix tomatoes and grated ginger in your blender, pulse well and transfer to your instant pot.
2. Add vinegar, Sugar, garlic, onions, raisins, cinnamon, cloves, coriander, nutmeg, ground ginger, paprika and chili powder, stir, cover and cook at High for 10 minutes.
3. Release the pressure, uncover the pot, transfer to jars and serve when needed.

Bon Appétit!

385. SPECIAL TOMATO SAUCE

Perp time: 10 minutes **Cooking time:** 15 minutes **Servings:** 20

Nutrition Facts:
- Calories: 70
- Fat (In grams): 4
- Fiber (In grams): 1
- Carbs (In grams): 8
- Protein: 1.7 g

Ingredients:
- 2 pounds tomatoes, peeled and chopped
- 1 apple, cored and chopped
- 1 yellow onion, chopped
- 6 ounces sultanas, chopped
- 3 ounces dates chopped
- Salt to the taste
- 3 teaspoons whole spice
- ½ pint vinegar
- ½ pound brown Sugar

Instructions:
1. Put tomatoes in your instant pot.
2. Add apple, onion, sultanas, dates, salt, whole spice and half of the vinegar, stir, cover and cook at High for 10 minutes.
3. Release the pressure, uncover the pot, set it on Simmer mode, add the rest of the vinegar and Sugar, stir and simmer until Sugar dissolves.
4. Transfer to jars and serve when needed.

Bon Appétit!

386. Different Green Tomato Sauce

Perp time: 5 minutes **Cooking time:** 10 minutes **Servings:** 12

Nutrition Facts:
- Calories: 50
- Fat (In grams): 2
- Fiber (In grams): 2.4
- Carbs (In grams): 10
- Protein: 1.5 g

Ingredients:
- 2 pounds green tomatoes, chopped
- 1 white onion, chopped
- 1/4 cup currants
- 1 Anaheim chili pepper, chopped
- 4 red chili peppers, chopped
- 2 tablespoons ginger, grated
- 3/4 cup brown Sugar
- 3/4 cup white vinegar

Instructions:
1. In your instant pot, mix green tomatoes with onion, currants, Anaheim pepper, chili pepper, ginger, Sugar, and vinegar, stir, cover and cook at High for 10 minutes.
2. Release the pressure for 5 minutes, uncover pot, transfer sauce to jars and serve.

Bon Appétit!

387. Simple Plum Sauce

Perp time: 10 minutes **Cooking time:** 15 minutes **Servings:** 20

Nutrition Facts:
- Calories: 100
- Fat (In grams): 10
- Fiber (In grams): 3
- Carbs (In grams): 23
- Protein: 26 g

Ingredients:
- 3 pounds plumps, pitted and chopped
- 2 onions, chopped
- 2 apples, cored and chopped
- 4 tablespoons ginger, ground
- 4 tablespoons cinnamon
- 4 tablespoons allspice
- 1 ½ tablespoons salt
- 1-pint vinegar
- 3/4 pound Sugar

Instructions:
1. Put plumps, apples, and onions in your instant pot.
2. Add ginger, cinnamon, allspice, salt and almost all the vinegar, stir, cover and cook at High for 10 minutes.
3. Release the pressure, uncover the pot, set it on Simmer mode, add the rest of the vinegar and the Sugar, stir and cook until Sugar dissolves.

Bon Appétit!

388. Yummy Pineapple Sauce

Perp time: 10 minutes **Cooking time:** 3 minutes **Servings:** 4

Nutrition Facts:
- Calories: 160
- Fat (In grams): 0
- Fiber (In grams): 0
- Carbs (In grams): 23
- Protein: 0

Ingredients:
- 3 cups pineapple tidbits
- 3 tablespoons rum
- 3 tablespoons butter
- 4 tablespoons brown Sugar
- One-teaspoon cinnamon
- One-teaspoon allspice
- One-teaspoon nutmeg
- One-teaspoon ginger

Instructions:
1. Set your instant pot on sauté mode, add butter and melt it.
2. Add Sugar, pineapple tidbits, rum, allspice, nutmeg, cinnamon and ginger, stir, cover and cook at High for 3 minutes.
3. Release pressure, uncover the pot, stir sauce one more time and serve.

Bon Appétit!

389. Amazing Orange Sauce

Perp time: 10 minutes **Cooking time:** 7 minutes **Servings:** 6

Nutrition Facts:
- Calories: 80
- Fat (In grams): 7
- Fiber (In grams): 1.4
- Carbs (In grams): 5
- Protein: 13 g

Ingredients:
- 1/4 cup white wine vinegar
- One-teaspoon ginger paste
- 2 tablespoons tomato paste
- 3 tablespoons Sugar
- One-cup orange juice
- One-teaspoon garlic, finely chopped
- 2 tablespoons agave nectar
- One-teaspoon sesame oil
- One-teaspoon chili sauce
- 2 tablespoons soy sauce
- 1/4 cup veggie stock
- 2 tablespoons cornstarch

Instructions:
1. Set your instant pot on Sauté mode, add oil and heat it up.
2. Add garlic and ginger paste, stir and cook for 2 minutes.
3. Add tomato paste, Sugar, orange juice, vinegar, agave nectar, soy and chili sauce, stir, cover and cook at High for 3 minutes more.
4. Release pressure, uncover the pot, add stock and cornstarch, stir, cover again and cook at High for 4 minutes.
5. Release pressure again and serve your sauce.

Bon Appétit!

390. Delicious Bread Sauce

Perp time: 10 minutes **Cooking time:** 10 minutes **Servings:** 12

Nutrition Facts:
- Calories: 113
- Fat (In grams): 5
- Fiber (In grams): 2.4
- Carbs (In grams): 11
- Protein: 3 g

Ingredients:
- 1 yellow onion, chopped
- 2 garlic cloves, crushed
- 6 cloves
- 26 ounces milk
- 6 bread slices, torn
- 2 bay leaves
- Salt to the taste
- 2 tablespoons butter
- A splash of double cream

Instructions:
1. Set your instant pot on Simmer mode, add milk and heat it up.
2. Add garlic, cloves, onion, bay leaves and salt, stir well and cook for 3 minutes.
3. Add bread, stir, cover and cook at High for 4 minutes.
4. Release the pressure, uncover pot, transfer sauce to a blender, add butter and cream, discard bay leaf and blend well.
5. Return sauce to the pot set it on Simmer mode and simmer sauce for 3 minutes more.

Bon Appétit!

391. Easy Onion Sauce

Perp time: 10 minutes **Cooking time:** 30 minutes **Servings:** 8

Nutrition Facts:
- Calories: 100
- Fat (In grams): 0.4
- Fiber (In grams): 0
- Carbs (In grams): 9
- Protein: 0

Ingredients:
- 6 tablespoons butter
- 3 pounds yellow onion, thinly chopped
- Salt and black pepper to the taste
- Half-teaspoon baking soda

Instructions:
1. Set your instant pot on Sauté mode, add butter and heat it up.
2. Add onions and soda, stir and cook for 3 minutes.
3. Cover your pot and cook at High for 20 minutes.
4. Release the pressure, uncover the pot, set it on Sauté mode again and cook for 5 minutes more stirring often.
5. Serve when needed.

Bon Appétit!

392. SIMPLE CHILI JAM

Perp time: 10 minutes **Cooking time:** 40 minutes **Servings:** 12

Nutrition Facts:
- Calories: 20
- Fat (In grams): 0.2
- Fiber (In grams): 0.4
- Carbs (In grams): 4
- Protein: 0.2 g

Ingredients:
- 4 garlic cloves, minced
- 2 red onions, finely chopped
- 4 red chili peppers, seeded and chopped
- 17 ounces cranberries
- 4 ounces Sugar
- A drizzle of olive oil
- Salt and black pepper to the taste
- 2 tablespoons red wine vinegar
- 3 tablespoons water

Instructions:
1. Set your instant pot on Sauté mode, add oil and heat it up.
2. Add onions, garlic and chilies, stir and cook for 8 minutes.
3. Add cranberries, vinegar, water and Sugar, stir, cover pot and cook at High for 14 minutes.
4. Release the pressure, uncover the pot, mash sauce using an immersion blender, set the pot on Simmer mode and cook the sauce for 15 minutes.
5. Add salt and pepper to the taste, transfer to jars and serve when needed.

Bon Appétit!

393. AMAZING CLEMENTINE SAUCE

Perp time: 10 minutes **Cooking time:** 6 minutes **Servings:** 4

Nutrition Facts:
- Calories: 50
- Fat (In grams): 0
- Fiber (In grams): 0
- Carbs (In grams): 0.3
- Protein: 0 g

Ingredients:
- 12 ounces cranberries
- One-cup water
- Juice and peel from 1 clementine
- One-cup Sugar

Instructions:
1. In your instant pot, mix cranberries with clementine juice and peel, water and Sugar, stir, cover and cook at High for 6 minutes.
2. Release pressure, uncover the pot and serve your sauce.

Bon Appétit!

394. DELICIOUS SRIRACHA SAUCE

Perp time: 10 minutes **Cooking time:** 17 minutes **Servings:** 6

Nutrition Facts:
- Calories: 90
- Fat (In grams): 0.4
- Fiber (In grams): 0.3
- Carbs (In grams): 19
- Protein: 2.4 g

Ingredients:
- 4 ounces red chilies, seeded and chopped
- 3 tablespoons palm Sugar
- 3 ounces bird's eye chilies
- 12 garlic cloves, minced
- 5 ounces distilled vinegar
- 5 ounces water

Instructions:
1. In your instant pot, mix water with palm Sugar and stir.
2. Add all chilies and garlic, stir, cover and cook at High for 7 minutes.
3. Release pressure, uncover the pot, blend sauce using an immersion blender, add vinegar, stir, set the pot on Simmer mode and cook the sauce for 10 minutes.
4. Serve when needed.

Bon Appétit!

395. TASTY GRAPES SAUCE

Perp time: 10 minutes **Cooking time:** 10 minutes **Servings:** 6

Nutrition Facts:
- Calories: 60
- Fat (In grams): 0
- Fiber (In grams): 0.3
- Carbs (In grams): 0
- Protein: 3 g

Ingredients:
- 6 ounces black grapes
- Half-cup water
- 2 ½-tablespoons Sugar
- One-cup corn flour
- A splash of lemon juice

Instructions:
1. Put grapes in your instant pot, add water to cover, cook at High for 7 minutes, release pressure, leave mix aside to cool down, blend using an immersion blender, strain sauce and leave aside for now.
2. Heat up a pan over medium heat, add grapes mix, Sugar, the water and corn flour, stir and boil until it thickens.
3. Add lemon juice, stir, take off heat and serve.

Bon Appétit!

396. SIMPLE MUSTARD SAUCE

Perp time: 10 minutes **Cooking time:** 7 minutes **Servings:** 4

Nutrition Facts:
- Calories: 67
- Fat (In grams): 0.4
- Fiber (In grams): 0.2
- Carbs (In grams): 4
- Protein: 1 g

Ingredients:
- 6 ounces' mushrooms, chopped
- 3 tablespoon olive oil
- ounces' dry sherry
- 1 thyme spring
- 1 garlic clove, minced
- ounces' beef stock
- One-tablespoon balsamic vinegar
- One-tablespoon mustard
- 2 tablespoon crème fraiche
- 2 tablespoons parsley, finely chopped

Instructions:
1. Set your instant pot on Sauté mode, add oil and heat it up.
2. Add garlic, thyme and mushrooms, stir and cook for 5 minutes.
3. Add sherry, vinegar and stock, stir, cover and cook at High for 3 minutes.
4. Release pressure, uncover the pot, discard thyme, add crème fraiche, mustard, and parsley, stir, set the pot on Simmer mode and cook the sauce for 3 minutes.
5. Serve right away.

Bon Appétit!

397. TASTY APRICOT SAUCE

Perp time: 10 minutes **Cooking time:** 20 minutes **Servings:** 6

Nutrition Facts:
- Calories: 100
- Fat (In grams): 0.6
- Fiber (In grams): 0
- Carbs (In grams): 10
- Protein: 1 g

Ingredients:
- 3 ounces apricots, dried and cut into halves
- 2 cups water
- 2/3 cup Sugar
- One-teaspoon vanilla extract

Instructions:
1. In your instant pot mix apricots with water, Sugar and vanilla, stir, cover and cook on Medium for 20 minutes.
2. Release pressure, uncover pot, transfer sauce to your blender and pulse well.
3. Divide into jars and serve with a poultry dish.

Bon Appétit!

398. Easy Eggplant Sauce

Perp time: 10 minutes　　**Cooking time:** 20 minutes　　**Servings:** 6

Nutrition Facts:
- Calories: 142
- Fat (In grams): 11
- Fiber (In grams): 4.4
- Carbs (In grams): 10
- Protein: 2.1 g

Ingredients:
- 1 pound ground meat
- 28 ounces canned tomatoes, chopped
- 5 garlic cloves, minced
- 5 ounces canned tomato paste
- 1 sweet onion, chopped
- 1 eggplant, chopped
- Half-cup olive oil
- Half-teaspoon turmeric
- One-cup bone stock
- One-tablespoon apple cider vinegar
- Half-teaspoon dill, dried
- Salt and black pepper to the taste
- 1/4 cup parsley, chopped

Instructions:
1. Set your instant pot on Sauté mode, add meat, brown for a few minutes and transfer to a bowl.
2. Heat up the oil in your instant pot, add onion and some salt and cook for 2 minutes.
3. Add eggplant and garlic, stir and cook for 1 minute.
4. Add vinegar, stir and cook for 2 minutes.
5. Add tomato paste, tomatoes, meat, salt, pepper, parsley, dill, turmeric and stock, stir, cover and cook at High for 15 minutes.
6. Release pressure, uncover the pot, add more salt and pepper and a splash of lemon juice, stir well and serve.

Bon Appétit!

399. Delicious Pomegranate Sauce

Perp time: 10 minutes　　**Cooking time:** 25 minutes　　**Servings:** 4

Nutrition Facts:
- Calories: 136
- Fat (In grams): 0.4
- Fiber (In grams): 0.8
- Carbs (In grams): 35
- Protein: 1.2 g

Ingredients:
- 5 cups pomegranate juice
- Half-cup lemon juice
- One-cup white Sugar

Instructions:
1. In your instant pot, mix pomegranate juice with Sugar and lemon juice, stir, cover and cook at High for 25 minutes.
2. Release pressure, uncover the pot, divide sauce into jars and serve when needed.

Bon Appétit!

400. Yummy Broccoli Sauce

Perp time: 10 minutes **Cooking time:** 6 minutes **Servings:** 4

Nutrition Facts:
- Calories: 128
- Fat (In grams): 10
- Fiber (In grams): 1.4
- Carbs (In grams): 6
- Protein: 5.4 g

Ingredients:
- 6 cups water
- 3 cups broccoli florets
- 2 garlic cloves, minced
- Salt and black pepper to the taste
- 1/3 cup coconut milk
- One-tablespoon white wine vinegar
- One-tablespoons nutritional yeast
- One-tablespoon olive oil

Instructions:
1. Put the water in your instant pot.
2. Add broccoli, salt, pepper and garlic, stir, cover and cook at High for 6 minutes.
3. Release pressure, uncover pot, strain broccoli and garlic and transfer to a food processor.
4. Add coconut milk, vinegar, yeast, olive oil, salt and pepper and blend very well.
5. Serve over pasta.

Bon Appétit!

401. Tasty Carrot Sauce

Perp time: 10 minutes **Cooking time:** 15 minutes **Servings:** 6

Nutrition Facts:
- Calories: 149
- Fat (In grams): 7
- Fiber (In grams): 4
- Carbs (In grams): 19
- Protein: 2 g

Ingredients:
- 4 tablespoons butter
- 2 cups carrot juice
- A pinch of cinnamon
- Salt and black pepper to the taste
- A pinch of cayenne pepper
- One-tablespoon mixed chervil, chives and tarragon

Instructions:
1. Put carrot juice in your instant pot, set the pot on Simmer mode and bring to a boil.
2. Add butter, salt, pepper, cayenne and cinnamon, stir, cover and cook at High for 5 minutes.
3. Release pressure, uncover the pot, add mixed herbs, stir and serve.

Bon Appétit!

402. Delicious Dates Sauce

Perp time: 10 minutes   **Cooking time:** 9 minutes   **Servings:** 6

Nutrition Facts:
- Calories: 30
- Fat (In grams): 0
- Fiber (In grams): 1
- Carbs (In grams): 5
- Protein: 0 g

Ingredients:
- 2 cups apple juice
- 2 cups dates, dried
- One-tablespoon lemon juice

Instructions:
1. In your instant pot, mix apple juice with lemon juice and dates, stir, cover and cook at High for 9 minutes.
2. Release pressure, uncover the pot, blend using an immersion blender and transfer to a container.
3. Serve when needed!

Bon Appétit!

403. Tasty Pear Sauce

Perp time: 10 minutes   **Cooking time:** 15 minutes   **Servings:** 5 pints

Nutrition Facts:
- Calories: 80
- Fat (In grams): 0.1
- Fiber (In grams): 0
- Carbs (In grams): 20
- Protein: 0.1 g

Ingredients:
- 10 cups pears, sliced
- 2 teaspoons cinnamon
- One-cup pear juice
- Half-teaspoon nutmeg

Instructions:
1. Put pear pieces in your instant pot, add cinnamon, nutmeg and pear juice.
2. Stir, cover pot and cook at High for 10 minutes.
3. Release pressure, uncover the pot, blend using an immersion blender and serve when needed.

Bon Appétit!

404. Tasty Cherry Sauce

Perp time: 10 minutes   **Cooking time:** 5 minutes   **Servings:** 4

Nutrition Facts:
- Calories: 60
- Fat (In grams): 0
- Fiber (In grams): 0
- Carbs (In grams): 13
- Protein: 0

Ingredients:
- One-tablespoon lemon juice
- 1/4 cup water
- One-teaspoon kirsch
- A pinch of salt
- One-tablespoon Sugar
- 2 tablespoons cornstarch
- 2 cups cherries

Instructions:
1. In your instant pot, mix water with lemon juice, salt, Sugar, kirsch and cornstarch.
2. Add cherries, stir, cover and cook at High for 5 minutes.
3. Release pressure, uncover pot, transfer sauce to a bowl and serve after it's cold.

Bon Appétit!

405. Delicious Guava Sauce

Perp time: 10 minutes   **Cooking time:** 20 minutes   **Servings:** 6

Nutrition Facts:
- Calories: 85
- Fat (In grams): 2.3
- Fiber (In grams): 8
- Carbs (In grams): 22
- Protein: 3 g

Ingredients:
- 1 can guava shells and syrup
- 2 onions, chopped
- 1/4 cup vegetable oil
- Juice from 2 lemons
- 2 garlic cloves, chopped
- 1 inch ginger piece, minced
- Half-teaspoon nutmeg
- 2 bird chilies, chopped

Instructions:
1. Put guava shells and syrup in your blender, pulse well and leave aside.
2. Set your instant pot on Sauté mode, add oil and heat it up.
3. Add onion and garlic, stir and cook for 4 minutes.
4. Add guava mix, ginger, lemon juice, chilies and nutmeg, stir, cover and cook on High for 15 minutes.
5. Release pressure, uncover the pot and serve sauce with fish.

Bon Appétit!

406. Yummy Melon Sauce

Perp time: 5 minutes **Cooking time:** 10 minutes **Servings:** 6

Nutrition Facts:
- Calories: 68
- Fat (In grams): 0.3
- Fiber (In grams): 0.1
- Carbs (In grams): 1
- Protein: 1 g

Ingredients:
- Flesh from 1 small melon
- 1-ounce Sugar
- One-cup sweet wine
- One-tablespoon butter
- One-teaspoon starch
- Juice of 1 lemon

Instructions:
1. Put melon and sweet wine in your instant pot, cover and cook at High for 7 minutes.
2. Release pressure, transfer sauce to a blender, add lemon juice, Sugar, butter and starch and blend very well.
3. Return this sauce to your instant pot, set it on Simmer mode and cook sauce until it thickens for 3 minutes.
4. Serve right away.

Bon Appétit!

407. Tasty Fennel Sauce

Perp time: 10 minutes **Cooking time:** 10 minutes **Servings:** 6

Nutrition Facts:
- Calories: 76
- Fat (In grams): 0.6
- Fiber (In grams): 0.6
- Carbs (In grams): 4
- Protein: 5

Ingredients:
- 1 fennel bulb, cut into pieces
- 2 pints grape tomatoes, cut into halves
- 1/4 cup dry white wine
- 5 thyme springs
- 3 tablespoons olive oil
- A pinch of Sugar
- Salt and black pepper to the taste

Instructions:
1. Set your instant pot in Sauté mode, add oil and heat it up.
2. Add fennel, tomatoes, thyme, Sugar, salt and pepper, stir and sauté for 5 minutes.
3. Add white wine, cover pot and cook for 4 minutes more.
4. Release pressure, uncover, discard thyme, stir sauce well and serve.

Bon Appétit!

408. Special Elderberry Sauce

Perp time: 10 minutes **Cooking time:** 10 minutes **Servings:** 20

Nutrition Facts:
- Calories: 55
- Fat (In grams): 0
- Fiber (In grams): 0
- Carbs (In grams): 13
- Protein: 0 g

Ingredients:
- 4 cups water
- One-cup elderberries
- 1-inch ginger piece, grated
- 1 cinnamon stick
- 1 vanilla bean, split
- 5 cloves
- One-cup honey

Instructions:
1. In your instant pot, mix elderberries with water, ginger, cinnamon, vanilla and cloves, stir, cover and cook at High for 10 minutes.
2. Release pressure, strain sauce and keep in jars.

Bon Appétit!

409. Simple Peach Sauce

Perp time: 5 minutes **Cooking time:** 3 minutes **Servings:** 6

Nutrition Facts:
- Calories: 100
- Fat (In grams): 1
- Fiber (In grams): 0.6
- Carbs (In grams): 4
- Protein: 6 g

Ingredients:
- 10 ounces peaches, stoned and chopped
- 1/8 teaspoon nutmeg, ground
- 2 tablespoons cornstarch
- 3 tablespoons Sugar
- Half-cup water
- A pinch of salt
- 1/8 teaspoon cinnamon
- 1/8 teaspoon almond extract

Instructions:
1. In your instant pot, mix peaches with nutmeg, cornstarch, Sugar, cinnamon and salt, stir, cover and cook at High for 3 minutes.
2. Release pressure, uncover the pot, add almond extract, stir and serve sauce.

Bon Appétit!

410. AMAZING PEACH AND WHISKEY SAUCE

Perp time: 10 minutes **Cooking time:** 10 minutes **Servings:** 6

Nutrition Facts:
- Calories: 100
- Fat (In grams): 0.7
- Fiber (In grams): 0.6
- Carbs (In grams): 7
- Protein: 7 g

Ingredients:
- One-cup brown Sugar
- 3 cups peaches, pureed
- 6 tablespoons whiskey
- One-cup white Sugar
- 2 teaspoons lemon zest, grated

Instructions:
1. In your instant pot mix peaches with brown and white Sugar, whiskey and lemon zest, stir, cover and cook at High for 10 minutes.
2. Release pressure, uncover the pot, stir sauce and transfer it to jars.
3. Serve when needed.

Bon Appétit!

411. TASTY CORN SAUCE

Perp time: 10 minutes **Cooking time:** 6 minutes **Servings:** 4

Nutrition Facts:
- Calories: 100
- Fat (In grams): 4.5
- Fiber (In grams): 2
- Carbs (In grams): 13
- Protein: 3 g

Ingredients:
- 1 yellow onion, chopped
- One-tablespoon olive oil
- One-teaspoon white flour
- 1 and 3/4 cups chicken stock
- 1/4 cup white wine
- 1 thyme spring
- 2 cups corn kernels
- Salt and black pepper to the taste
- 2 teaspoons butter
- One-teaspoon thyme, finely chopped

Instructions:
1. Set your instant pot on Sauté mode, add oil and heat it up.
2. Add onion, stir and cook for 3 minutes.
3. Add flour, stir well and cook for 1 minute more.
4. Add wine, stir and cook for 1 minute.
5. Add thyme spring, stock and corn, stir, cover and cook at High for 1 minute.
6. Release pressure, uncover the pot, discard thyme spring, transfer corn sauce to a blender, add salt, pepper, butter and chopped thyme and blend well.
7. Return to pot set it on Sauté mode again and cook 1-2 minutes more.
8. Serve when needed.

Bon Appétit!

412. Delicious Leeks Sauce

Perp time: 5 minutes   **Cooking time:** 7 minutes   **Servings:** 8

Nutrition Facts:
- Calories: 140
- Fat (In grams): 13
- Fiber (In grams): 0.4
- Carbs (In grams): 5
- Protein: 1 g

Ingredients:
- 2 leeks, thinly sliced
- 2 tablespoons butter
- One-cup whipping cream
- 3 tablespoons lemon juice
- Salt and pepper to the taste

Instructions:
1. Set your instant pot on Sauté mode, add butter and melt it.
2. Add leeks, stir and cook for 2 minutes.
3. Add lemon juice, stir, cover and cook at High for 3 minutes.
4. Release pressure, uncover pot, transfer sauce to your blender, add whipping cream and blend everything.
5. Return sauce to the pot, set on Simmer mode, add salt and pepper to the taste, stir and cook for 2 minutes.
6. Serve with fish.

Bon Appétit!

413. Yummy Chestnut Sauce

Perp time: 10 minutes   **Cooking time:** 20 minutes   **Servings:** 6

Nutrition Facts:
- Calories: 50
- Fat (In grams): 0
- Fiber (In grams): 0
- Carbs (In grams): 10
- Protein: 0 g

Ingredients:
- 11 ounces Sugar
- 11 ounces water
- 1 ½ pounds chestnuts, cut into halves and peeled
- 1/8 cup rum liquor

Instructions:
1. In your instant pot, mix Sugar with water, rum, and chestnuts.
2. Stir, cover and cook at High for 20 minutes.
3. Release pressure for 10 minutes, uncover the pot and blend everything with an immersion blender.
4. Serve when needed.

Bon Appétit!

414. SPECIAL PARSLEY SAUCE

Perp time: 10 minutes **Cooking time:** 7 minutes **Servings:** 6

Nutrition Facts:
- Calories: 70
- Fat (In grams): 2.5
- Fiber (In grams): 0.5
- Carbs (In grams): 7.3
- Protein: 2.5 g

Ingredients:
- 2 cups chicken stock
- 1 yellow onion, finely chopped
- 2 tablespoons butter
- 2 tablespoons flour
- 3/4 cup whole milk
- 4 tablespoons parsley, chopped
- 1 egg yolk
- 1/4 cup heavy cream
- Salt and white pepper to the taste

Instructions:
1. Put stock and onion in your instant pot, set the pot on Simmer mode and bring to a boil.
2. Heat up a pan with the butter over medium heat, add flour and stir well to combine.
3. Pour this mix and whole milk over stock and stir very well.
4. Bring to a boil, add parsley, stir, cover and cook at High for 2 minutes.
5. Release pressure, uncover the pot and set it back on Simmer mode.
6. In a bowl, mix cream with egg yolk and some of the sauce from the pot.
7. Stir this well, pour over sauce and whisk.
8. Add salt and pepper to the taste, stir again, cook for a couple of minutes until it thickens and serve with chicken and some rice.

Bon Appétit!

415. AMAZING CILANTRO SAUCE

Perp time: 5 minutes **Cooking time:** 6 minutes **Servings:** 6

Nutrition Facts:
- Calories: 67
- Fat (In grams): 1
- Fiber (In grams): 0.4
- Carbs (In grams): 1
- Protein: 0.5 g

Ingredients:
- 3 garlic cloves, minced
- One-tablespoon olive oil
- 2 red chilies, minced
- 3 shallots, minced
- 1/4 cup water
- 3 scallions, chopped
- 3 tomatoes, chopped
- Salt and black pepper to the taste
- 2 tablespoons cilantro, chopped

Instructions:
1. Set your instant pot on Sauté mode, add oil and heat it up.
2. Add garlic, shallots and chilies, stir and cook for 3 minutes.
3. Add scallions, tomatoes, water, salt, pepper and cilantro, stir, cover and cook on High for 3 minutes.
4. Release the pressure, uncover the pot, blend using an immersion blender and serve.

Bon Appétit!

416. SIMPLE QUINCE SAUCE

Perp time: 10 minutes   **Cooking time:** 15 minutes   **Servings:** 6

Nutrition Facts:
- Calories: 60
- Fat (In grams): 0
- Fiber (In grams): 1
- Carbs (In grams): 16
- Protein: 1 g

Ingredients:
- 2 pounds grated quince
- Juice of 1 lemon
- 10 cloves
- 2 pounds Sugar
- 1/4 cup water

Instructions:
1. In your instant pot, mix quince with Sugar and stir well.
2. Add water and stir again.
3. Tie cloves in a cheesecloth and add to the pot as well.
4. Cover and cook at High for 10 minutes.
5. Release pressure for 10 minutes, uncover the pot, stir sauce again and transfer to jars.
6. Serve on top of cakes.

Bon Appétit!

417. DELICIOUS RHUBARB SAUCE

Perp time: 10 minutes   **Cooking time:** 13 minutes   **Servings:** 6

Nutrition Facts:
- Calories: 90
- Fat (In grams): 0
- Fiber (In grams): 1
- Carbs (In grams): 23
- Protein: 1 g

Ingredients:
- 8 ounces rhubarb, trimmed and chopped
- One-tablespoon cider vinegar
- 1 small onion, chopped
- A pinch of cardamom, ground
- 1 garlic clove, minced
- 2 jalapeno peppers, chopped
- 1/3 cup honey
- 1/4 cup raisins
- 1/4 cup water

Instructions:
1. In your instant pot, mix rhubarb with vinegar, onion, cardamom, garlic, jalapenos, honey, water, and raisins, stir, cover and cook at High for 7 minutes.
2. Release the pressure, uncover the pot, set it on Simmer mode and cook for 3 more minutes.
3. Serve when needed.

Bon Appétit!

DESSERT RECIPES

418. TASTY BANANA BREAD

Perp time: 10 minutes   **Cooking time:** 30 minutes   **Servings:** 6

Nutrition Facts:
- Calories: 325
- Fat (In grams): 2
- Fiber (In grams): 1.1
- Carbs (In grams): 44
- Protein: 4.5 g

Ingredients:
- 3/4 cup coconut Sugar
- 1/3 cup ghee, soft
- One-teaspoon vanilla
- 1 egg
- 2 bananas, mashed
- One-teaspoon baking powder
- 1 ½ cups flour
- A pinch of salt
- Half-teaspoons baking soda
- 1/3 cup cashew milk
- 1 ½ teaspoons cream of tartar
- 2 cups water
- Cooking spray

Instructions:
1. In a bowl, mix milk with cream of tartar and stir well.
2. Add Sugar, ghee, egg, vanilla and bananas and stir everything.
3. In another bowl, mix flour with salt, baking powder and soda.
4. Combine the 2 mixtures, stir well, pour this into a cake pan which you've greased with some cooking spray and arrange pan in the steamer basket of your instant pot.
5. Add the water to your pot, cover and cook at High for 30 minutes.
6. Release the pressure, uncover pot, take bread out, leave aside to cool down, slice and serve it.

Bon Appétit!

419. AMAZING APPLE BREAD

Perp time: 10 minutes   **Cooking time:** 1 hour and 10 minutes   **Servings:** 6

Nutrition Facts:
- Calories: 89
- Fat (In grams): 3
- Fiber (In grams): 1
- Carbs (In grams): 17
- Protein: 0 g

Ingredients:
- 3 cups apples, cored and cubed
- One-cup Sugar
- One-tablespoon vanilla
- 2 eggs
- One-tablespoon apple pie spice
- 2 cups white flour
- One-tablespoon baking powder
- 1 stick butter
- One-cup water

Instructions:
1. In a bowl mix egg with 1 butter stick, apple pie spice and Sugar and stir using your mixer.
2. Add apples and stir again well.
3. In another bowl, mix baking powder with flour and stir.
4. Combine the 2 mixtures, stir and pour into a spring form pan.

5. Place in the steamer basket of your instant pot, add One-cup water to the pot, cover and cook at High for 1 hour and 10 minutes.
6. Release pressure, fast, leave bread to cool down, cut and serve it.

Bon Appétit!

420. APPLE CRISP

Perp time: 10 minutes **Cooking time:** 8 minutes **Servings:** 4

Nutrition Facts:
- Calories: 180
- Fat (In grams): 7
- Fiber (In grams): 2.5
- Carbs (In grams): 30
- Protein: 1.4 g

Ingredients:
- 2 teaspoons cinnamon
- 5 apples, cored and cut into chunks
- Half-teaspoon nutmeg
- One-tablespoon maple syrup
- Half-cup water
- 4 tablespoons butter
- 1/4 cup flour
- 3/4 cup old fashioned rolled oats
- 1/4 cup brown Sugar
- A pinch of salt

Instructions:
1. Put the apples in your instant pot.
2. Add cinnamon, nutmeg, maple syrup and water.
3. In a bowl, mix butter with oats, Sugar, salt and flour and stir well.
4. Drop spoonfuls of oats mix on top of apples, cover pot and cook at High for 8 minutes.
5. Release the pressure and serve warm.

Bon Appétit!

421. DELICIOUS CHOCOLATE CHEESECAKE

Perp time: 60 minutes **Cooking time:** 50 minutes **Servings:** 12

Nutrition Facts:
- Calories: 470
- Fat (In grams): 31
- Fiber (In grams): 2
- Carbs (In grams): 45
- Protein: 8 g

Ingredients:

For the crust:
- 4 tablespoons melted butter
- 1 ½ cups chocolate cookie crumbs

For the filling:
- 24 ounces cream cheese, soft
- 2 tablespoons cornstarch
- One-cup Sugar
- 3 eggs
- One-tablespoon vanilla extract
- Cooking spray
- One-cup water
- Half-cup Greek yogurt
- 4 ounces white chocolate
- 4 ounces milk chocolate
- 4 ounces bittersweet chocolate

Instructions:
1. In a bowl mix cookie crumbs with butter and stir well.

2. Spray a spring form pan with some cooking oil, line with parchment paper, press crumbs and butter mix on the bottom and keep in the freezer for now.
3. In a bowl, mix cream cheese with cornstarch and Sugar and stir using your mixer.
4. Add eggs, yogurt, and vanilla, stir again to combine everything and divide into 3 bowls.
5. Put milk chocolate in a heatproof bowl and heat up in the microwave for 30 seconds.
6. Add this into one of the bowls with the batter you've made earlier and stir well.
7. Put dark and white chocolate in 2 heatproof bowls and heat them up in the microwave for 30 seconds.
8. Add these to the other 2 bowls with cheesecake batter, stir and introduce them all in the fridge for 30 minutes.
9. Take bowls out of the fridge and layer your cheesecake.
10. Pour the dark chocolate batter in the center of the crust.
11. Add white chocolate batter on top and spread evenly and end with milk chocolate batter.
12. Put the pan in the steamer basket of your pot, add One-cup water in the pot, cover and cook at High for 45 minutes.
13. Release pressure for 10 minutes, take the cake out of the pot, leave aside to cool down and serve.

Bon Appétit!

---

422. SIMPLE CANDIED LEMON PEEL

Perp time: 20 minutes **Cooking time:** 20 minutes **Servings:** 80 pieces

Nutrition Facts:
- Calories: 7
- Fat (In grams): 0
- Fiber (In grams): 0.2
- Carbs (In grams): 2
- Protein: 0 g

Ingredients:
- 5 big lemons
- 2 and 1/4 cups white Sugar
- 5 cups water

Instructions:
1. Wash lemons, slice them in half, reserve juice for another use, slice each half into quarters, take out the pulp and cut peel into thin strips.
2. Put strips in your instant pot, add 4 cups water, cover and cook at High for 3 minutes.
3. Release pressure fast, uncover the pot, strain peel, rinse and put in a bowl.
4. Clean your instant pot and add 2 cups Sugar and One-cup water in it.
5. Add lemon strips, stir, set pot on Simmer mode and cook for 5 minutes.
6. Cover pot, cook at High for 10 more minutes and release pressure naturally for 20 minutes
7. Strain peels again, spread them on a cutting board and leave them to cool down for 10 minutes.
8. Keep them in jars until you serve them.

Bon Appétit!

423. Yummy Baked Apples

Perp time: 10 minutes **Cooking time:** 10 minutes **Servings:** 6

Nutrition Facts:
- Calories: 188
- Fat (In grams): 0.4
- Fiber (In grams): 3.5
- Carbs (In grams): 34
- Protein: 0.5 g

Ingredients:
- 6 apples, cored
- One-cup red wine
- 1/4 cup raisins
- One-teaspoon cinnamon powder
- Half-cup raw Sugar

Instructions:
1. Put the apples in your instant pot.
2. Add wine, raisins, Sugar and cinnamon, cover pot and cook at High for 10 minutes.
3. Release pressure naturally, uncover pot, transfer apples and their cooking juice to plates and serve.

Bon Appétit!

424. Special Pumpkin Chocolate Cake

Perp time: 10 minutes **Cooking time:** 45 minutes **Servings:** 12

Nutrition Facts:
- Calories: 270
- Fat (In grams): 9
- Fiber (In grams): 1
- Carbs (In grams): 45
- Protein: 3 g

Ingredients:
- 3/4 cup white flour
- 3/4 cup whole wheat flour
- A pinch of salt
- One-teaspoon baking soda
- 3/4 teaspoon pumpkin pie spice
- 3/4 cup Sugar
- 1 banana, mashed
- Half-teaspoon baking powder
- 2 tablespoons canola oil
- Half-cup Greek yogurt
- 8 ounces canned pumpkin puree
- Cooking spray
- 1-quart water
- 1 egg
- Half-teaspoon vanilla extract
- 2/3 cup chocolate chips

Instructions:
1. In a bowl, mix white flour with whole wheat flour, salt, baking soda and powder and pumpkin spice and stir.
2. In another bowl, mix Sugar with oil, banana, yogurt, pumpkin puree, vanilla and egg and stir using a mixer.
3. Combine the 2 mixtures, add chocolate chips and mix everything.
4. Pour this into a greased Bundt pan, cover pan with paper towels and foil and place in the steamer basket of your instant pot.
5. Add 1-quart water to the pot, cover and cook at High for 35 minutes.
6. Release the pressure for 10 minutes, uncover the pot, leave the cake to cool down, before cutting and serving it.

425. Tasty Chocolate Lava Cake

Perp time: 10 minutes   **Cooking time:** 6 minutes   **Servings:** 3

Nutrition Facts:
- Calories: 200
- Fat (In grams): 5
- Fiber (In grams): 1
- Carbs (In grams): 24
- Protein: 2 g

Ingredients:
- 1 egg
- 4 tablespoons Sugar
- 2 tablespoons olive oil
- 4 tablespoons milk
- 4 tablespoons flour
- A pinch of salt
- One-tablespoon cocoa powder
- Half-teaspoon baking powder
- Half-teaspoon orange zest
- One-cup water

Instructions:
1. In a bowl, mix the egg with Sugar, oil, milk, flour, salt, cocoa powder, baking powder and orange zest and stir very well.
2. Pour this into greased ramekins and place them in the steamer basket of your instant pot.
3. Add One-cup water to the pot, cover and cook at High for 6 minutes.
4. Release pressure, uncover the pot, take lava cakes out and serve them after they cool down a bit.

Bon Appétit!

426. Amazing Chocolate Fondue

Perp time: 10 minutes   **Cooking time:** 2 minutes   **Servings:** 4

Nutrition Facts:
- Calories: 210
- Fat (In grams): 20
- Fiber (In grams): 3
- Carbs (In grams): 6.5
- Protein: 2 g

Ingredients:
- 3.5 ounces' crème fraiche
- 3.5 ounces' dark chocolate, cut into chunks
- One-teaspoon liquor
- One-teaspoon Sugar
- 2 cups water

Instructions:
1. In a heat proof container, mix chocolate chunks with Sugar, crème fraiche and liquor.
2. Put the water in your instant pot, add the container in the steamer basket, cover pot and cook at High for 2 minutes.
3. Release the pressure naturally, uncover pot, take container out, stir well your fondue and serve it right away with some fresh fruits.

Bon Appétit!

427. HOLIDAY PUDDING

Perp time: 10 minutes **Cooking time:** 40 minutes **Servings:** 4

Nutrition Facts:
- Calories: 310
- Fat (In grams): 15
- Fiber (In grams): 2
- Carbs (In grams): 27.9
- Protein: 3.6 g

Ingredients:
- 4 ounces dried cranberries, soaked in hot water for 30 minutes, drained and chopped
- A drizzle of olive oil
- 2 cups water
- 4 ounces dried apricots, chopped
- One-cup white flour
- 3 teaspoons baking powder
- One-cup raw Sugar
- One-teaspoon ginger powder
- A pinch of cinnamon powder
- A pinch of salt
- 15 tablespoons butter
- 3 tablespoons maple syrup
- 4 eggs
- 1 carrot, grated

Instructions:
1. Grease a heatproof pudding mould with a drizzle of oil and leave aside for now.
2. In a blender, mix flour with baking powder, Sugar, cinnamon, salt and ginger and pulse a few times.
3. Add butter and pulse again.
4. Add maple syrup and eggs and pulse again.
5. Add dried fruits and carrot and fold them into the batter.
6. Spread this mix into the pudding mold, place this in the steamer basket of your instant pot and add 2 cups water in the pot as well.
7. Set the pot on Sauté mode and steam your pudding for 10 minutes.
8. Cover your pot, cook pudding at High for 30 minutes.
9. Release the pressure naturally for 10 minutes, leave pot aside for another 10 minutes, uncover, take pudding out and leave it aside to cool down before serving it.

Bon Appétit!

428. AMAZING APPLE CAKE

Perp time: 10 minutes **Cooking time:** 20 minutes **Servings:** 8

Nutrition Facts:
- Calories: 241
- Fat (In grams): 10
- Fiber (In grams): 2
- Carbs (In grams): 20
- Protein: 5.8 g

Ingredients:
- 1 apple, sliced
- 1 apple, chopped
- 2 cup water
- One-cup ricotta cheese
- 1/4 cup raw Sugar
- One-tablespoon lemon juice
- 1 egg
- One-teaspoon vanilla extract
- 3 tablespoons olive oil
- One-cup white flour

- 2 teaspoons baking powder
- 1/8 teaspoon cinnamon powder
- One-teaspoon baking soda

Instructions:
1. Put chopped and sliced apple in a bowl, add lemon juice, toss to coat and leave aside for now.
2. Line a heatproof dish with some parchment paper, grease with some oil and dust with some flour.
3. Sprinkle some Sugaron the bottom and arrange sliced apple on top.
4. In a bowl, mix the egg with cheese, Sugar, vanilla extract and oil and stir well.
5. Add flour, baking powder and soda and cinnamon and stir again.
6. Add chopped apple, toss to coat and pour everything into the pan.
7. Place the pan in the steamer basket of your instant pot, add the water to the pot, cover and cook at High for 20 minutes.
8. Release the pressure, uncover the pot, turn cake on a plate and serve warm.

Bon Appétit!

---

429. Yummy Tapioca Pudding

Perp time: 10 minutes **Cooking time:** 8 minutes **Servings:** 6

Nutrition Facts:
- Calories: 180
- Fat (In grams): 2.5
- Fiber (In grams): 0.1
- Carbs (In grams): 90
- Protein: 2.5 g

Ingredients:
- 1 and 1/4 cups milk
- 1/3 cup tapioca pearls, rinsed
- Half-cup water
- Half-cup Sugar
- Zest from ½ lemon
- One-cup water

Instructions:
1. In a heat proof bowl mix tapioca with milk, Sugar, Half-cup water and lemon zest and stir well.
2. Put this in the steamer basket of your instant pot, add One-cup water to the pot, cover and cook at High for 8 minutes.
3. Release the pressure, leave it aside for 5 minutes more, uncover the pot, take pudding out and serve it warm.

Bon Appétit!

---

430. Tasty Pumpkin Pie

Perp time: 10 minutes **Cooking time:** 20 minutes **Serving:** 8

Nutrition Facts:
- Calories: 143
- Fat (In grams): 3
- Fiber (In grams): 2.1
- Carbs (In grams): 19
- Protein: 3.3 g

Ingredients:
- 2 pounds butternut squash, peeled and chopped
- 2 eggs
- 2 cups water
- One-cup whole milk
- 3/4 cup maple syrup

- One-teaspoon cinnamon powder
- Half-teaspoon powdered ginger
- 1/4 teaspoon powdered cloves
- A pinch of salt
- One-tablespoon cornstarch
- Whipped cream for serving
- Chopped pecans

Instructions:
1. Put squash cubes in the steamer basket of your instant pot, add One-cup water, cover pot, cook at High for 4 minutes, release pressure, take squash and transfer to a strainer, cool it down and mash it a bit in a bowl.
2. Add maple syrup, milk, eggs, cinnamon, ginger, cloves, salt and cloves and stir very well.
3. Pour this into ramekins, place them in the steamer basket of your pot, add One-cup water to the pot, cover and cook at High for 10 minutes.
4. Release the pressure, uncover the pot, take ramekins out, garnish with whipped cream and chopped pecans and serve.

Bon Appétit!

---

431. BROWNIE CAKE

Perp time: 10 minutes **Cooking time:** 50 minutes **Servings:** 6

Nutrition Facts:
- Calories: 164
- Fat (In grams): 7.8
- Fiber (In grams): 4
- Carbs (In grams): 24
- Protein: 4.4 g

Ingredients:
- One-cup borlotti beans, soaked for 8 hours and drained
- 4 cups water

For the cake:
- 1/8 teaspoon almond extract
- Half-cup cocoa powder
- Half-cup raw Sugar
- 3 tablespoons extra virgin olive oil
- A pinch of salt
- 2 eggs
- 2 teaspoons baking powder
- 1/4 cup almonds, sliced

Instructions:
1. Put beans and water in your instant pot, cover, cook at High for 12 minutes, release pressure, uncover pot, strain beans, transfer them to a blender and puree them.
2. Discard water from the pot and keep One-cup.
3. Grease a heatproof bowl with some olive oil and leave it aside for now.
4. Add cocoa powder, almond extract, honey, salt, eggs and oil to your blender with the beans and puree everything for 1 minute.
5. Transfer mix to greased bowl, spread, place bowl in the steamer basket of your pot, add reserved water from cooking the beans, cover and cook at High for 20 minutes.
6. Release the pressure, take cake out of the pot, leave it aside for 15 minutes, transfer to a plate, sprinkle almonds on top, slice and serve.

Bon Appétit!

432. SPECIAL DULCE DE LECHE

Perp time: 10 minutes **Cooking time:** 25 minutes **Servings:** 6

Nutrition Facts:
- Calories: 300
- Fat (In grams): 10
- Fiber (In grams): 5
- Carbs (In grams): 24
- Protein: 10 g

Ingredients:
- 16 ounces canned sweet condensed milk
- Water to cover

Instructions:
1. Put condensed milk can in the steamer basket of your instant pot, add water in the pot to cover and cook at High for 20 minutes.
2. Release the pressure naturally, uncover the pot, take can out of the pot and leave it aside to cool down.
3. Serve your dulce de leche on crackers.

Bon Appétit!

433. TASTY CRÈME BRULEE

Perp time: 1 hour **Cooking time:** 15 minutes **Servings:** 6

Nutrition Facts:
- Calories: 210
- Fat (In grams): 10
- Fiber (In grams): 3
- Carbs (In grams): 18
- Protein: 13 g

Ingredients:
- 2 cups fresh cream
- One-teaspoon cinnamon powder
- 6 egg yolks
- 5 tablespoons white Sugar
- Zest from 1 orange
- A pinch of nutmeg for serving
- 4 tablespoons raw Sugar
- 2 cups water

Instructions:
1. In a pan, mix cream with cinnamon and orange zest, stir and bring to a boil over medium high heat.
2. Take the pan off heat and leave it aside for 30 minutes.
3. In a bowl, mix egg yolks with white Sugar and whisk well.
4. Add this to cooled cream and whisk well again.
5. Strain this mix and then divide it into ramekins.
6. Cover with foil, place them in the steamer basket of your instant pot, add 2 cups water to the pot, cover and cook on Low for 10 minutes.
7. Release the pressure naturally, uncover pot, take ramekins out and leave them aside for 30 minutes.
8. Sprinkle nutmeg and raw Sugaron top of each and melt this with a culinary torch.
9. Serve right away.

Bon Appétit!

434. DELICIOUS BREAD PUDDING

Perp time: 5 minutes **Cooking time:** 25 minutes **Servings:** 4

Nutrition Facts:
- Calories: 300
- Fat (In grams): 7
- Fiber (In grams): 2
- Carbs (In grams): 46
- Protein: 11 g

Ingredients:
- 4 egg yolks
- 3 cups brioche, cubed
- 2 cups half and half
- Half-teaspoon vanilla extract
- One-cup Sugar
- 2 tablespoons butter, soft
- One-cup cranberries
- 2 cups warm water
- Half-cup raisins
- Zest from 1 lime

Instructions:
1. Grease a baking dish with some butter and leave aside for now.
2. In a bowl mix, egg yolks with half and half, cubed brioche, vanilla extract, Sugar, cranberries, raisins and lime zest and stir well
3. Pour this into greased dish, cover with some tin foil and leave aside for 10 minutes.
4. Put dish in the steamer basket of your instant pot, add warm water to the pot, cover and cook at High for 20 minutes.
5. Release the pressure naturally, uncover pot, take bread out, leave it aside to cool down, slice and serve it.

Bon Appétit!

435. DELICIOUS RICE PUDDING

Perp time: 5 minutes **Cooking time:** 15 minutes **Servings:** 6

Nutrition Facts:
- Calories: 112
- Fat (In grams): 1.2
- Fiber (In grams): 0.4
- Carbs (In grams): 21
- Protein: 3.3 g

Ingredients:
- One-tablespoon butter
- 7 ounces long grain rice
- 4 ounces water
- 16 ounces milk
- 3 ounces Sugar
- A pinch of salt
- 1 egg
- One-tablespoon cream
- One-teaspoon vanilla
- Cinnamon to the taste

Instructions:
1. Put the butter in your instant pot, set it on Sauté mode, melt it, add rice and stir.
2. Add water and milk and stir again.
3. Add salt and Sugar, stir again, cover pot and cook at High for 8 minutes.
4. Meanwhile, in a bowl, mix cream with vanilla and eggs and stir well.
5. Release pressure from the pot, uncover it, and pour some of the liquid from the pot over egg mixture and stir very well.
6. Pour this into the pot and whisk well.
7. Cover pot, cook at High for 10 minutes, release pressure, uncover the pot, pour pudding into bowls, sprinkle cinnamon on top and serve.

436. Ruby Pears

Perp time: 10 minutes **Cooking time:** 10 minutes **Servings:** 4

Nutrition Facts:
- Calories: 145
- Fat (In grams): 5.6
- Fiber (In grams): 6
- Carbs (In grams): 12
- Protein: 12 g

Ingredients:
- 4 pears
- Juice and zest of 1 lemon
- 26 ounces grape juice
- 11 ounces currant jelly
- 4 garlic cloves
- ½ vanilla bean
- 4 peppercorns
- 2 rosemary springs

Instructions:
1. Pour the jelly and grape juice in your instant pot and mix with lemon zest and juice.
2. Dip each pear in this mix, wrap them in tin foil and arrange them in the steamer basket of your pot.
3. Add garlic cloves, peppercorns, rosemary and vanilla bean to the juice mixture, cover pot and cook at High for 10 minutes.
4. Release pressure, uncover the pot, take the pears out, unwrap them, arrange them on plates and serve cold with cooking juice on top.

Bon Appétit!

437. Tasty Ricotta Cake

Perp time: 30 minutes **Cooking time:** 30 minutes **Servings:** 6

Nutrition Facts:
- Calories: 211
- Fat (In grams): 8.6
- Fiber (In grams): 0.5
- Carbs (In grams): 21
- Protein: 12 g

Ingredients:
- 1 pound ricotta
- 6 oz dates, soaked for 15 minutes and drained
- 2 ounces honey softened
- 4 eggs
- 2 ounces Sugar
- Some vanilla extract
- 17 ounces water
- Orange juice and zest from ½ orange

Instructions:
1. In a bowl, whisk ricotta until it softens.
2. In another bowl, whisk eggs well.
3. Combine the 2 mixtures and stir very well.
4. Add honey, vanilla, dates, orange zest and juice to the ricotta mixture and stir again
5. Pour the batter into a heatproof dish and cover with tin foil.
6. Place dish in the steamer basket of your instant pot, add water to the pot, cover and cook at High for 20 minutes.
7. Release pressure, uncover pot, allow cake to cool down, transfer to a platter, slice and serve.

Bon Appétit!

438. SIMPLE LEMON MARMALADE

Perp time: 10 minutes **Cooking time:** 15 minutes **Servings:** 8

Nutrition Facts:
- Calories: 100
- Fat (In grams): 2
- Fiber (In grams): 2
- Carbs (In grams): 4
- Protein: 8 g

Ingredients:
- 2 pounds lemons, washed, sliced and cut into quarters
- 4 pounds Sugar
- 2 cups water

Instructions:
1. Put lemon pieces in your instant pot, add 2 cups water, cover and cook at High for 10 minutes.
2. Release the pressure naturally, uncover pot, add Sugar, stir, set pot in Simmer mode and cook for 6 minutes, stirring all the time.
3. Divide into jars and serve when needed.

Bon Appétit!

439. EASY ORANGE MARMALADE

Perp time: 10 minutes **Cooking time:** 25 minutes **Servings:** 8

Nutrition Facts:
- Calories: 50
- Fat (In grams): 0
- Fiber (In grams): 0.1
- Carbs (In grams): 12
- Protein: 0.1 g

Ingredients:
- Juice from 2 lemons
- 3 pounds Sugar
- 1 pound oranges, cut into halves
- 1-pint water

Instructions:
1. Squeeze juice from the oranges and cut the peel into pieces.
2. Put peel in a bowl, cover with water and leave aside overnight.
3. In your instant pot, mix lemon juice with orange juice, water and peel.
4. Cover pot, cook at High for 15 minutes, release pressure, uncover, add Sugar and set the pot on Simmer mode.
5. Cook until Sugardissolves, divide into jars and serve when needed.

Bon Appétit!

440. SPECIAL PUMPKIN RICE PUDDING

Perp time: 30 minutes **Cooking time:** 35 minutes **Servings:** 6

Nutrition Facts:
- Calories: 100
- Fat (In grams): 1
- Fiber (In grams): 4
- Carbs (In grams): 21
- Protein: 4.1 g

Ingredients:
- One-cup brown rice
- Half-cup water
- 3 cups cashew milk
- Half-cup dates, chopped
- A pinch of salt
- 1 cinnamon stick
- One-cup pumpkin puree
- Half-cup maple syrup
- One-teaspoon pumpkin spice mix
- One-teaspoon vanilla extract

Instructions:
1. Put the rice in your instant pot, add boiling water to cover, leave aside for 10 minutes and drain.
2. Put the water in milk in your instant pot, add rice, cinnamon stick, dates and salt, stir, cover and cook at High for 20 minutes.
3. Release pressure, uncover pot, add maple syrup, pumpkin pie spice and pumpkin puree, stir, set the pot on Simmer mode and cook for 5 minutes.
4. Discard cinnamon stick, add vanilla, stir, transfer pudding to bowls, leave aside for 30 minutes to cool down and serve.

Bon Appétit!

441. YUMMY BERRY JAM

Perp time: 60 minutes **Cooking time:** 20 minutes **Servings:** 12

Nutrition Facts:
- Calories: 60
- Fat (In grams): 0
- Fiber (In grams): 0
- Carbs (In grams): 12
- Sugar (In grams): 12
- Protein: 0 g

Ingredients:
- 1 pound cranberries
- 1 pound strawberries
- ½ pound blueberries
- 3.5 ounces' black currant
- 2 pounds Sugar
- Zest from 1 lemon
- A pinch of salt
- 2 tablespoon water

Instructions:
1. In your instant pot, mix strawberries with cranberries, blueberries, currants, lemon zest and Sugar.
2. Stir and leave aside for 1 hour.
3. Add salt and water, set the pot on Simmer mode and bring to a boil.
4. Cover pot, cook on Low for 10 minutes and release pressure for 10 minutes.
5. Uncover pot, set it on Simmer mode again, bring to a boil and simmer for 4 minutes.
6. Divide into jars and keep in the fridge until you need it.

Bon Appétit!

442. Delicious Pears Jam

Perp time: 10 minutes **Cooking time:** 4 minutes **Servings:** 12

Nutrition Facts:
- Calories: 90
- Fat (In grams): 0
- Fiber (In grams): 1
- Carbs (In grams): 20
- Sugar (In grams): 20
- Protein: 0 g

Ingredients:
- 8 pears, cored and cut into quarters
- 2 apples, peeled, cored and cut into quarters
- 1/4 cup apple juice
- One-teaspoon cinnamon, ground

Instructions:
1. In your instant pot, mix pears with apples, cinnamon and apple juice, stir, cover and cook at High for 4 minutes.
2. Release the pressure naturally, uncover the pot, blend using an immersion blender, divide jam into jars and keep in a cold place until you serve it.

Bon Appétit!

443. Red Tomato Jam

Perp time: 10 minutes **Cooking time:** 30 minutes **Servings:** 12

Nutrition Facts:
- Calories: 239
- Fat (In grams): 0
- Fiber (In grams): 2
- Carbs (In grams): 59
- Sugar (In grams): 55
- Protein: 0 g

Ingredients:
- 1 ½ pounds tomatoes, cored and chopped
- 2 tablespoons lime juice
- One-cup white Sugar
- One-tablespoon ginger, grated
- One-teaspoon cinnamon
- One-teaspoon cumin
- 1/8 teaspoon cloves, ground
- A pinch of salt
- 1 jalapeno pepper, minced

Instructions:
1. In your instant pot mix tomatoes with Sugar, lime juice, ginger, cumin, cinnamon, cloves, salt and jalapeno pepper, stir, cover and cook at High for 30 minutes.
2. Release the pressure, uncover the pot, divide jam into jars and serve when needed.

Bon Appétit!

444. Yummy Peach Jam

Perp time: 10 minutes **Cooking time:** 5 minutes **Servings:** 6

Nutrition Facts:
- Calories: 50
- Fat (In grams): 0
- Fiber (In grams): 1
- Carbs (In grams): 3
- Protein: 0 g
- Sugar (In grams): 12

Ingredients:
- 4 and Half-cups peaches, peeled and cubed
- 6 cups Sugar
- 1/4 cup crystallized ginger, chopped
- 1 box fruit pectin

Instructions:
1. Set your instant pot on Simmer mode, add peaches, ginger, and pectin, stir and bring to a boil.
2. Add Sugar, stir, cover and cook at High for 5 minutes.
3. Release pressure, uncover pot, divide jam into jars and serve.

Bon Appétit!

445. Tasty Raspberry Curd

Perp time: 10 minutes **Cooking time:** 5 minutes **Servings:** 4

Nutrition Facts:
- Calories: 110
- Fat (In grams): 4
- Fiber (In grams): 0
- Carbs (In grams): 16
- Protein: 1 g

Ingredients:
- One-cup Sugar
- 12 ounces raspberries
- 2 egg yolks
- 2 tablespoons lemon juice
- 2 tablespoons butter

Instructions:
1. Put raspberries in your instant pot.
2. Add Sugar and lemon juice, stir, cover and cook at High for 2 minutes.
3. Release pressure for 5 minutes, uncover pot, strain raspberries and discard seeds.
4. In a bowl, mix egg yolks with raspberries and stir well.
5. Return this to your instant pot, set it on Sauté mode, simmer for 2 minutes, add butter, stir and transfer to a container.
6. Serve cold.

Bon Appétit!

446. Tasty Berry Compote

Perp time: 10 minutes **Cooking time:** 5 minutes **Servings:** 8

Nutrition Facts:
- Calories: 260
- Fat (In grams): 13
- Fiber (In grams): 3
- Carbs (In grams): 23
- Protein: 3 g

Ingredients:
- One-cup blueberries
- 2 cups strawberries, sliced

- 2 tablespoons lemon juice
- 3/4 cup Sugar
- One-tablespoon cornstarch
- One-tablespoon water

Instructions:
1. In your instant pot, mix blueberries with lemon juice and Sugar, stir, cover and cook at High for 3 minutes.
2. Release pressure naturally for 10 minutes and uncover pot.
3. In a bowl, mix cornstarch with water, stir well and add to the pot.
4. Stir, set the pot on Sauté mode and cook compote for 2 minutes more.
5. Divide into jars and keep in the fridge until you serve it.

Bon Appétit!

---

447. Yummy Key Lime Pie

Perp time: 10 minutes   **Cooking time:** 15 minutes   **Servings:** 6

Nutrition Facts:
- Calories: 400
- Fat (In grams): 21
- Fiber (In grams): 0.5
- Carbs (In grams): 34
- Protein: 7 g

Ingredients:

For the crust:
- One-tablespoon Sugar
- 3 tablespoons butter, melted
- 5 graham crackers, crumbled

For the filling:
- 4 egg yolks
- 14 ounces canned condensed milk
- Half-cup key lime juice
- 1/3 cup sour cream
- Cooking spray
- One-cup water
- 2 tablespoons key lime zest, grated

Instructions:
1. In a bowl, whisk egg yolks very well.
2. Add milk gradually and stir again well.
3. Add lime juice, sour cream and lime zest and stir again.
4. In a bowl, whisk butter with crackers and Sugar, stir well and spread on the bottom of a spring form greased with some cooking spray.
5. Cover pan with some tin foil and place it in the steamer basket of your instant pot.
6. Add One-cup water to the pot, cover and cook at High for 15 minutes.
7. Release the pressure for 10 minutes, uncover the pot, take pie out, leave aside to cool down and keep in the fridge for 4 hours before slicing and serving it.

Bon Appétit!

---

448. Tasty Stuffed Peaches

Perp time: 10 minutes   **Cooking time:** 4 minutes   **Servings:** 6

Nutrition Facts:
- Calories: 160
- Fat (In grams): 6.7
- Carbs (In grams): 12

- Fiber (In grams): 3
- Sugar (In grams): 11
- Protein: 4 g

Ingredients:
- 6 peaches, insides removed
- A pinch of salt
- 1/4 cup coconut flour
- 1/4 cup maple syrup
- 2 tablespoons coconut butter
- Half-teaspoon cinnamon powder
- One-teaspoon almond extract
- One-cup water

Instructions:
1. In a bowl, mix flour with salt, syrup, butter, cinnamon and half of the almond extract and stir well.
2. Fill peaches with this mix, place them in the steamer basket of your instant pot, add the water and the rest of the almond extract to the pot, cover and cook at High for 4 minutes.
3. Release pressure naturally, divide stuffed peaches on servings plates and serve warm.

Bon Appétit!

449. AMAZING COBBLER

Perp time: 10 minutes   **Cooking time:** 12 minutes   **Servings:** 4

Nutrition Facts:
- Calories: 170
- Fat (In grams): 4
- Carbs (In grams): 10
- Fiber (In grams): 2.4
- Protein: 3 g
- Sugar (In grams): 7

Ingredients:
- 3 apples, cored and cut into chunks
- 2 pears, cored and cut into chunks
- 1 ½ cup hot water
- 1/4 cup date syrup
- One-cup steel cut oats
- One-teaspoon cinnamon
- ice cream for serving

Instructions:
1. Put apples and pears in your instant pot and mix with hot water, date syrup, oats and cinnamon.
2. Stir, cover and cook at High for 12 minutes.
3. Release pressure naturally, transfer cobbler to bowls and serve it with ice cream on top.

Bon Appétit!

450. YUMMY PEACH COMPOTE

Perp time: 10 minutes   **Cooking time:** 3 minutes   **Servings:** 6

Nutrition Facts:
- Calories: 100
- Fat (In grams): 2
- Carbs (In grams): 11
- Fiber (In grams): 1
- Sugar (In grams): 10
- Protein: 1 g

Ingredients:
- 8 peaches, chopped
- 6 tablespoons Sugar

- One-teaspoon cinnamon, ground
- One-teaspoon vanilla extract
- 1 vanilla bean, scraped
- 2 tablespoons grape nuts cereal

Instructions:
1. Put peaches in your instant pot and mix with Sugar, cinnamon, vanilla bean and vanilla extract.
2. Stir well, cover pot and cook at High for 3 minutes.
3. Release pressure for 10 minutes, add grape nuts, stir well, transfer the compote to bowls and serve.

Bon Appétit!

451. Easy Carrot Cake

Perp time: 10 minutes   **Cooking time:** 30 minutes   **Servings:** 6

Nutrition Facts:
- Calories: 140
- Fat (In grams): 3.5
- Carbs: 23.4 g
- Fiber (In grams): 4.1
- Sugar (In grams): 5.2
- Protein: 4.3 g

Ingredients:
- 5 ounces flour
- A pinch of salt
- 3/4 teaspoon baking powder
- Half-teaspoon baking soda
- Half-teaspoon cinnamon powder
- 1/4 teaspoon nutmeg, ground
- Half-teaspoon allspice
- 1 egg
- 3 tablespoons yogurt
- Half-cup Sugar
- 1/4 cup pineapple juice
- 4 tablespoons coconut oil, melted
- 1/3 cup carrots, grated
- 1/3 cup pecans, toasted and chopped
- 1/3 cup coconut flakes
- Cooking spray
- 2 cups water

Instructions:
1. In a bowl, mix flour with baking soda and powder, salt, allspice, cinnamon and nutmeg and stir.
2. In another bowl, mix egg with yogurt, Sugar, pineapple juice, oil, carrots, pecans and coconut flakes and stir well.
3. Combine the two mixtures and stir very well everything.
4. Pour this into a spring form greased with some cooking spray, add 2 cups water in your instant pot and place the form into the steamer basket.
5. Cover the instant pot and cook at High for 32 minutes.
6. Release pressure for 10 minutes, remove cake from the pot, leave it to cool down, then cut and serve it.

Bon Appétit!

452. Amazing Zucchini Nut Bread

Perp time: 10 minutes   **Cooking time:** 25 minutes   **Servings:** 6

Nutrition Facts:
- Calories: 217
- Fat (In grams): 8
- Fiber (In grams): 2
- Carbs (In grams): 35

- Sugar (In grams): 22

Ingredients:
- One-cup applesauce
- 3 eggs, whisked
- One-tablespoon vanilla extract
- 2 cups Sugar
- 2 cups zucchini, grated
- One-teaspoon salt
- 2 ½-cups white flour
- Protein: 3 g
- Half-cup baking cocoa
- One-teaspoon baking soda
- 1/4 teaspoon baking powder
- One-teaspoon cinnamon
- Half-cup walnuts, chopped
- Half-cup chocolate chips
- 1 ½ cups water

Instructions:
1. In a bowl, mix zucchini with Sugar, vanilla, eggs and applesauce and stir well.
2. In another bowl, mix flour with salt, cocoa, baking soda, baking powder, cinnamon, chocolate chips and walnuts and stir.
3. Combine the 2 mixtures, stir, pour into a Bundt pan, place pan in the steamer basket of your instant pot, add the water to the pot, cover and cook at High for 25 minutes.
4. Release the pressure naturally, uncover the pot, transfer bread to a plate, cut and serve it.

Bon Appétit!

453. Tasty Samoa Cheesecake

Perp time: 15 minutes **Cooking time:** 1 hour **Servings:** 6

Nutrition Facts:
- Calories: 310
- Fat (In grams): 8
- Fiber (In grams): 2
- Carbs (In grams): 20
- Protein: 10 g

Ingredients:

For the crust:
- 2 tablespoons butter, melted
- Half-cup chocolate graham crackers, crumbled

For the filling:
- 1/4 cup heavy cream
- Half-cup Sugar
- 12 ounces cream cheese, soft
- 1 ½ teaspoon vanilla extract
- 1/4 cup sour cream
- One-tablespoon flour
- 1 egg yolk
- 2 eggs
- Cooking spray
- One-cup water

For the topping:
- 3 tablespoons heavy cream
- 12 caramels
- 1 ½ cups coconut, sweet and shredded
- 1/4 cup chocolate, chopped

Instructions:
1. Grease a spring form pan with some cooking spray and leave it aside.
2. In a bowl, mix crackers with butter, stir, spread in the bottom of the pan and keep in the freezer for 10 minutes.

3. Meanwhile, in another bowl, mix cheese with Sugar, heavy cream, vanilla, flour, sour cream and eggs and stir very well using a mixer.
4. Pour this into the pan on top of crust, cover with tin foil and place in the steamer basket of your instant pot.
5. Add One-cup water to the pot, cover and cook at High for 35 minutes.
6. Release the pressure for 10 minutes, uncover, take the pan, remove tin foil and leave cake to cool down in the fridge for 4 hours.
7. Spread coconut on a lined baking sheet, introduce in the oven at 300 degrees F and bake for 20 minutes, stirring often.
8. Put caramels in a heatproof bowl, introduce in the microwave for 2 minutes, stir every 20 seconds and then mix with toasted coconut.
9. Spread this on your cheesecake and leave aside for now.
10. Put chocolate in another heatproof bowl, introduce in your microwave for a few seconds until it melts and drizzles over your cake.
11. Serve right away.

Bon Appétit!

454. SPECIAL PINA COLADA PUDDING

Perp time: 10 minutes **Cooking time:** 5 minutes **Servings:** 8

Nutrition Facts:
- Calories: 113
- Fat (In grams): 3.2
- Fiber (In grams): 0.2
- Carbs (In grams): 15
- Protein: 4.2 g

Ingredients:
- One-tablespoon coconut oil
- A pinch of salt
- 1 ½ cups water
- One-cup Arborio rice
- 14 ounces canned coconut milk
- 2 eggs
- Half-cup milk
- Half-cup Sugar
- Half-teaspoon vanilla extract
- 8 ounces canned pineapple tidbits, drained and halved

Instructions:
1. In your instant pot, mix oil, water, rice and salt, stir, cover and cook at High for 3 minutes.
2. Release the pressure for 10 minutes, uncover the pot, add Sugar and coconut milk and stir well.
3. In a bowl, mix eggs with milk and vanilla, stir and pour over rice.
4. Stir, set the pot on Sauté mode and bring to a boil.
5. Add pineapple tidbits, stir, divide into dessert bowls and serve.

Bon Appétit!

455. INSTANT FLAN

Perp time: 10 minutes **Cooking time:** 15 minutes **Servings:** 6

Nutrition Facts:
- Calories: 145
- Fat (In grams): 4
- Fiber (In grams): 0
- Carbs (In grams): 23
- Sugar (In grams): 20
- Protein: 4.5 g

Ingredients:

For the caramel:
- 1/4 cup water
- 3/4 cup Sugar

For the custard:
- 2 egg yolks
- 3 eggs
- 1 ½ cups water
- A pinch of salt
- 2 cups milk
- 1/3 cup Sugar
- Half-cup whipping cream
- 2 tablespoons hazelnut syrup
- One-teaspoon vanilla extract

Instructions:
1. Heat up a pot over medium heat, add 1/4 cup water and 3/4 cup Sugar, stir, cover, bring to a boil, boil for 2 minutes, uncover and boil for a few more minutes.
2. Pour this into custard cups and coat evenly their bottoms.
3. In a bowl, mix eggs with yolks, a pinch of salt and 1/3 cup Sugar and stir using your mixer.
4. Put the milk in a pan and heat up over medium heat.
5. Add this to eggs mix and stir well.
6. Add hazelnut syrup, vanilla and cream, stir and strain this mix.
7. Pour this into custard cups, place them in the steamer basket of your instant pot, add 1 ½ cups water to the pot, cover and cook at High for 6 minutes.
8. Release pressure, uncover the pot, take custard cups and leave them to cool down.
9. Keep in the fridge for 4 hours before you serve them.

Bon Appétit!

456. AWESOME CHOCOLATE PUDDING

Perp time: 10 minutes **Cooking time:** 20 minutes **Servings:** 4

Nutrition Facts:
- Calories: 200
- Fat (In grams): 3
- Fiber (In grams): 1
- Carbs (In grams): 20
- Protein: 14 g

Ingredients:
- 6 ounces bittersweet chocolate, chopped
- Half-cup milk
- 1 ½ cups heavy cream
- 5 egg yolks
- 1/3 cup brown Sugar
- 2 teaspoons vanilla extract
- 1 ½ cups water
- 1/4 teaspoon cardamom, ground
- A pinch of salt

- Crème fraiche for serving
- Chocolate shavings for serving

Instructions:
1. Put cream and milk in a pot, bring to a simmer over medium heat, take off heat, add chocolate and whisk well.
2. In a bowl, mix egg yolks with vanilla, Sugar, cardamom and a pinch of salt, stir, strain and mix with chocolate mix.
3. Pour this into a soufflé dish, cover with tin foil, place in the steamer basket of your instant pot, add water to the pot, cover, cook on Low for 18 minutes, release pressure naturally.
4. Take pudding out of the instant pot, leave aside to cool down and keep in the fridge for 3 hours before you serve it with crème fraiche and chocolate shavings on top.

Bon Appétit!

457. TASTY STICKY PUDDING

Perp time: 15 minutes **Cooking time:** 20 minutes **Servings:** 8

Nutrition Facts:
- Calories: 260
- Fat (In grams): 14
- Fiber (In grams): 1
- Carbs (In grams): 33
- Protein: 2 g
- Sugar (In grams): 21

Ingredients:
- 2 cups water
- 1 and 1/4 cups dates, chopped
- 1/4 cup blackstrap molasses
- 3/4 cup hot water
- One-teaspoon baking powder
- 1 and 1/4 cups white flour
- A pinch of salt
- 3/4 cup brown Sugar
- 1/3 cup butter, soft
- One-teaspoon vanilla extract
- 1 egg

For the caramel sauce:
- 1/3 cup whipping cream
- 2/3 cup brown Sugar
- 1/4 cup butter
- One-teaspoon vanilla extract

Instructions:
1. In a bowl, mix dates with hot water and molasses, stir and leave aside for now.
2. In another bowl, mix baking powder with flour and salt.
3. In a third bowl, mix Sugar with butter, egg and One-teaspoon vanilla extract and stir using a mixer.
4. Add flour and dates mixtures to this bowl and stir very well.
5. Divide this mix into 8 ramekins which you've greased with some butter, cover with tin foil, place them in the steamer basket of your instant pot, add 2 cups water to the pot, cover and cook on Low for 20 minutes.
6. Meanwhile, heat up a pan with the butter for the caramel sauce over medium high heat.
7. Add cream, vanilla extract and brown Sugar, stir and bring to a boil.
8. Reduce temperature to medium-low and simmer for 5 minutes stirring often.
9. Release pressure from the pot, uncover, take ramekins out, remove foil, drizzle sauce over puddings and serve them warm.

458. EASY CHOCOLATE CAKE

Perp time: 10 minutes **Cooking time:** 40 minutes **Servings:** 6

Nutrition Facts:
- Calories: 379
- Fat (In grams): 5
- Fiber (In grams): 2
- Carbs (In grams): 53
- Protein: 5 g

Ingredients:
- 3/4 cup cocoa powder
- 3/4 cup white flour
- Half-cup butter
- One-cup water
- 1 ½ cups white Sugar
- Half-teaspoon baking powder
- 3 eggs, whites and yolks separated
- One-teaspoon vanilla extract

Instructions:
1. In a bowl, beat egg whites with your mixer.
2. In another bowl, beat egg yolks with your mixer.
3. In a third bowl, mix flour with baking powder, Sugar and cocoa powder.
4. Add egg white, egg yolks and vanilla extract and stir very well.
5. Grease a spring form pan with butter, line with parchment paper, pour cake batter, arrange pan in the steamer basket of your pot, add One-cup water to the pot, cover and cook on Low for 40 minutes.
6. Release the pressure, uncover pot, take the pan out, leave cake to cool down, transfer to a platter, cut and serve it.

Bon Appétit!

459. EASY CARROT PUDDING

Perp time: 10 minutes **Cooking time:** 1 hours **Servings:** 8

Nutrition Facts:
- Calories: 316
- Fat (In grams): 16
- Fiber (In grams): 5
- Carbs (In grams): 44
- Protein: 7 g
- Sugar (In grams): 7

Ingredients:
- 1 ½ cups water
- Cooking spray
- Half-cup brown Sugar
- 2 eggs
- 1/4 cup molasses
- Half-cup flour
- Half-teaspoon allspice
- Half-teaspoon cinnamon
- A pinch of salt
- A pinch of nutmeg
- Half-teaspoon baking soda
- 2/3 cup shortening, frozen, grated
- Half-cup pecans, chopped
- Half-cup carrots, grated
- Half-cup raisins
- One-cup bread crumbs

For the sauce:
- 4 tablespoons butter
- Half-cup brown Sugar
- 1/4 cup heavy cream
- 2 tablespoons rum
- 1/4 teaspoon cinnamon

Instructions:
1. In a bowl, mix molasses with eggs and Half-cup Sugar and stir.
2. Add flour, shortening, carrots, nuts, raisins, bread crumbs, salt, Half-teaspoon cinnamon, allspice, nutmeg and baking soda and stir everything.
3. Pour this into a Bundt pan which you've greased with some cooking spray, cover with foil, place in the steamer basket of your instant pot, add the water to the pot, cover and cook at High for 1 hour.
4. Release the pressure, uncover pot, take pudding out and leave it aside to cool down.
5. Meanwhile, heat up a pan with the butter for the sauce over medium heat.
6. Add Half-cup brown Sugar, stir and cook for 2 minutes.
7. Add cream, rum, Half-teaspoon cinnamon, stir and simmer for 2 minutes more.
8. Serve your pudding with this rum sauce.

Bon Appétit!

---

460. SIMPLE EGGNOG CHEESECAKE

Perp time: 15 minutes **Cooking time:** 20 minutes **Servings:** 6

Nutrition Facts:
- Calories: 400
- Fat (In grams): 25
- Fiber (In grams): 0
- Carbs (In grams): 30
- Protein: 6 g
- Sugar (In grams): 19

Ingredients:
- 2 cups water
- 2 teaspoons butter, melted
- Half-cup ginger cookies, crumbled
- 16 ounces cream cheese, soft
- 2 eggs
- Half-cup Sugar
- One-teaspoon rum
- Half-teaspoon vanilla
- Half-teaspoon nutmeg, ground

Instructions:
1. Grease a pan with the butter, add cookie crumbs and spread them evenly.
2. In a bowl, beat cream cheese with a mixer.
3. Add nutmeg, vanilla, rum and eggs and stir very well.
4. Pour this in the steamer basket of your instant pot, add the water to your pot, cover and cook at High for 15 minutes.
5. Release pressure, uncover pot, take cheesecake out, leave aside to cool down and keep in the fridge for 4 hours before slicing and serving it.

Bon Appétit!

---

461. DELICIOUS RHUBARB COMPOTE

Perp time: 10 minutes **Cooking time:** 30 minutes **Servings:** 8

Nutrition Facts:
- Calories: 71
- Fat (In grams): 0.1
- Fiber (In grams): 1
- Carbs (In grams): 18
- Protein: 0.5 g
- Sugar (In grams): 16

Ingredients:

- 1/3 cup water
- 2 pounds rhubarb, chopped
- 3 tablespoon honey
- Some fresh mint, torn
- 1 pound strawberries, chopped

Instructions:
1. Put rhubarb and water in your instant pot, cover, cook at High for 10 minutes, release pressure and uncover pot.
2. Add strawberries and honey, stir, set the pot on Simmer mode and cook compote for 20 minutes.
3. Add mint, stir, divide into jars and serve.

Bon Appétit!

462. Tasty Corn Pudding

Perp time: 10 minutes   **Cooking time:** 30 minutes   **Servings:** 4

Nutrition Facts:
- Calories: 200
- Fat (In grams): 5
- Fiber (In grams): 2
- Carbs (In grams): 12
- Protein: 9 g

Ingredients:
- 11 ounces canned creamed corn
- 2 cups water
- 2 cups milk
- 3 tablespoons Sugar
- 2 eggs, whisked
- 2 tablespoons flour
- A pinch of salt
- One-tablespoon butter
- Cooking spray

Instructions:
1. Put the water in your instant pot, set on Simmer mode and bring to a boil.
2. In a bowl, mix corn with eggs, milk, butter, salt, flour and Sugar and stir well.
3. Grease a baking dish with some cooking spray, pour corn mix into the pan, cover with foil and arrange in the steamer basket of your instant pot.
4. Cover and cook on High 20 minutes.
5. Release the pressure, uncover pot, take pudding out, leave it aside to cool down and serve.

Bon Appétit!

463. Amazing Lemon Crème Pots

Perp time: 30 minutes   **Cooking time:** 5 minutes   **Servings:** 4

Nutrition Facts:
- Calories: 145
- Fat (In grams): 4
- Fiber (In grams): 3
- Carbs (In grams): 10
- Protein: 1 g

Ingredients:
- One-cup whole milk
- Zest from 1 lemon
- 6 egg yolks
- One-cup fresh cream
- One-cup water
- 2/3 cup Sugar
- Blackberry syrup for serving
- Half-cup fresh blackberries

Instructions:
1. Heat up a pan over medium heat, add milk, lemon zest and cream, stir, bring to a boil, take off heat and leave aside for 30 minutes.
2. In a bowl, mix egg yolks with Sugar and cold cream mix and stir well.
3. Pour this into ramekins, cover them with tin foil, place them in the steamer basket of your instant pot, add One-cup water to the pot, cover and cook at High for 5 minutes.
4. Release the pressure for 10 minutes, uncover pot, take ramekins out, leave them to cool down and serve with blackberries and blackberry syrup on top.

Bon Appétit!

464. YUMMY POACHED FIGS

Perp time: 10 minutes **Cooking time:** 7 minutes **Servings:** 4

Nutrition Facts:
- Calories: 100
- Fat (In grams): 0
- Fiber (In grams): 1
- Carbs (In grams): 13
- Sugar (In grams): 0.6
- Protein: 0 g

Ingredients:
- One-cup red wine
- 1 pound figs
- Half-cup pine nuts, toasted
- Half-cup Sugar

For the yogurt crème:
- 2 pounds plain yogurt

Instructions:
1. Put the yogurt in a strainer, press well, transfer to a container and keep in the fridge overnight.
2. Put the wine in your instant pot, place figs in the steamer basket, cover and cook on Low for 4 minutes.
3. Release the pressure, uncover the pot, take figs out and arrange them on plates.
4. Set the pot on Simmer mode, add Sugar and stir.
5. Cook until Sugar melts and then drizzle this sauce over figs.
6. Add yogurt crème on top or the side and serve right away.

Bon Appétit!

465. SPECIAL SWEET CARROTS

Perp time: 10 minutes **Cooking time:** 16 minutes **Servings:** 4

Nutrition Facts:
- Calories: 80
- Fat (In grams): 1
- Fiber (In grams): 1
- Carbs (In grams): 3
- Protein: 4 g

Ingredients:
- One-tablespoon brown Sugar
- 2 cups baby carrots
- A pinch of salt
- Half-cup water
- Half-tablespoon butter

Instructions:
1. Set your instant pot on Sauté mode, add butter and melt it.

2. Add Sugar, water and salt, stir and cook for 1 minute.
3. Add carrots, toss to coat, cover the pot and cook at High for 15 minutes.
4. Release pressure, uncover pot, transfer carrots to plates and serve.

466. GINGER AND PINEAPPLE RISOTTO DESSERT

Perp time: 10 minutes **Cooking time:** 12 minutes **Servings:** 4

Nutrition Facts:
- Calories: 100
- Fat (In grams): 2
- Fiber (In grams): 3
- Carbs (In grams): 3
- Protein: 2 g

Ingredients:
- 1/4 cup candied ginger, chopped
- 20 ounces canned pineapple, chopped
- Half-cup coconut, shredded
- 1 and 3/4 cups risotto rice
- 4 cups milk

Instructions:
1. In your instant pot, mix milk with rice, coconut, pineapple and ginger, stir, cover and cook at High for 12 minutes.
2. Release the pressure naturally, uncover pot and serve your dessert.

Bon Appétit!

SPECIAL WEIGHT LOSS RECIPES
(LOW CARB KETOGENIC RECIPES)

"SPECIAL KETOGENIC BREAKFAST RECIPES"

467. Tasty Keto Coconut Bread

Prep Time: 6 minutes **Cook Time:** 12 minutes **Servings:** 1

Nutrition facts:
- Calories: 218g
- Total Fat: 16.5g
- Saturated Fat: 1.8g;
- Trans Fat: 0g
- Protein: 6.6g
- Net Carbs: 11.3g

Ingredients:
- 2 cups almond, flour
- 300 grams ripe banana, mashed
- 3 large eggs
- Half-cup raisins
- Half-cup walnuts, chopped
- 1/4 cup olive oil
- One-teaspoon baking soda

Instructions:
1. Mix all the first 5 ingredients in a small mixing bowl; knead the dough and form into an elongated roll that would fit a tall greased tin can or heat tempered tall glass container; cover the container with aluminum foil and place it on your steamer basket.
2. Pour a couple of cups of water in the inner pot of your pressure cooker; place the steamer basket with the dough in mug; close the lid, lock and seal the valve.
3. On STEAM setting, set the timer for 15 minutes.
4. As soon as you hear the timer beep, slide the valve open to release pressure quickly; take out the steamer basket with the mug or container and set aside to cool.
5. Remove the keto banana walnut raisin bread from the container and slice to desired thickness.

468. Delicious Keto Cabbage Onspoo Sauté

Prep Time: 5 minutes **Cook Time:** 27 minutes **Servings:** 10

Nutrition facts:
- Calories: 301
- Total Fat: 24.0.4g
- Saturated Fat: 7.2g
- Trans Fat: 0g
- Protein: 0.3g
- Net Carbs: 4.3g

Ingredients:
- 250 grams bacon
- 4 tablespoons olive oil
- 6 tablespoons onion, chopped
- One-tablespoon garlic, minced
- 3 cups cabbage, sliced in thin strips
- One-teaspoon caraway seeds
- One-teaspoon fresh ground black pepper
- One-cup sauerkraut, drained
- 100 grams frankfurters, sliced
- 100 grams provolone cheese
- Half-cup mustard, prepared

Instructions:
1. Preheat your pressure cooker to the SAUTE function; add the bacon and cook until crisp; remove from the heat onto a rack and set aside; add the olive oil.
2. When heated through, add the chopped onion, garlic and cabbage; sauté for a minute or two.
3. Stir in the caraway seeds, black pepper and sauerkraut followed by the sliced frankfurters.

4. Close and lock the lid; press cancel and shift to STEAM function on HIGH pressure and set the timer to 2 minutes. Do the Quick Release Method to let off when done.

Transfer the sautéed and steamed bacon hot dog and veggies mixture in a shallow baking dish; top with shredded Provolone cheese and pop in the microwave for a minute or two or until the cheese melts. Serve with prepared mustard on the side.

469. YUMMY KETO BERRIES AND CREAM CAKE

Prep Time: 5 minutes **Cook Time:** 15 minutes **Servings:** 4

Nutrition facts:
- Calories: 358
- Total Fat: 32.7g
- Saturated Fat: 15.6g
- Trans Fat: 0g
- Protein: 10.0g
- Net Carbs: 13.3g

Ingredients:
- 2 large eggs
- 10 grams sweetener
- 2 tbsp. ghee, melted
- 2 tbsp. cream cheese
- 1/4 cup almond, flour
- 1/4 cup mixed berries
- 1/4 cup heavy whipping cream
- ½ tbsp. brown sugar

Instructions:
1. In a blender, blend the eggs with the melted ghee, sweetener and cream cheese.
2. Transfer to a large heat-proof mug; stir in the flour and the berries.
3. Place the dish in your pressure cooker set on STEAM function on HIGH; set the timer to 5 minutes; when done, remove mug from the pressure cooker and set aside to cool.
4. Process the heavy whipping cream and brown sugar; blend until soft peaks form.
5. Top your Berries and Cream Keto Mug Cake with whipped cream and enjoy!

470. EASY CHEESY KETO SAUSAGE ROUNDING

Prep Time: 10 minutes **Cook Time:** 15 minutes **Servings:** 6

Nutrition facts:
- Calories: 452
- Total Fat: 35.9g
- Saturated Fat: 15.3g
- Trans Fat: 0g
- Protein: 28.5g
- Net Carbs: 2.8g

Ingredients:
- 2 red bell peppers
- 6 eggs
- 1 pound breakfast sausage
- 2 tablespoon coconut oil
- 1/4 teaspoon salt
- 1/4 teaspoon pepper
- 4 tablespoon shredded parmesan cheese

Instructions:
1. Slice two large bell peppers into half inch-thick rings; remove the core and seeds and set aside.
2. Prepare your pressure cooker on SAUTE function; place the inner pot and add the coconut oil.
3. Cut the sausages into ring slices and stir into the hot oil. Sauté and brown for 3 minutes before removing from heat and setting aside.
4. Arrange 4 bell pepper rings on the same inner pot of your pressure cooker.

5. Crack an egg on a small saucer and slowly slide the egg inside one of the bell pepper rings on your pressure cooker; add salt and pepper to taste.
6. Repeat cracking and sliding an egg inside each of the remaining bell pepper rings.
7. Put some sausage rings on top of the eggs.
8. Remove all cooked egg sausage bell pepper rings from the pressure cooker and transfer to individual serving plates. Sprinkle grated parmesan cheese before serving.

471. Amazing Keto Coffee Jug Chocolate Cake

Prep Time: 5 minutes **Cook Time:** 15 minutes **Servings:** 6

Nutrition facts:
- Calories: 262
- Total Fat: 24.2g
- Saturated Fat: 13.4g
- Trans Fat: 0g
- Protein: 6.2g
- Net Carbs: 7.2g

Ingredients:
- One-tablespoon cocoa powder plus 2 teaspoons
- 3 tablespoons almond flour
- Half-teaspoon salt
- One-teaspoon sweetener
- 1/4 tsp baking powder
- 3 teaspoons coconut oil
- 3 tablespoons milk, almond
- Half-teaspoon almond extract

Directions
1. Mix all the ingredients in a large coffee mug; cover the mug with aluminum foil.
2. Pour a couple of cups of water in the inner pot of your pressure cooker; and place your steamer basket; place your mug on top of the steamer basket; close the lid, lock and seal the vent valve.
3. On STEAM setting, set the timer for 15 minutes.
4. As soon as you hear the timer beep, slide the valve open to release pressure quickly; take out your Coffee Mug Keto Chocolate and enjoy with your Keto coffee.

472. Keto Garlic Butter Spread

Prep Time: 5 minutes **Cook Time:** 1 minute **Servings:** 6

Nutrition facts:
- Calories: 139
- Total Fat: 15.4g
- Saturated Fat: 9.7g
- Trans Fat: 0g
- Protein: 0.3g
- Net Carbs: 0.7g

Ingredients:
- Half-cup butter, softened
- One-teaspoon salt
- 4 cloves garlic
- 1/4 cup basil leaves
- One-tablespoon lemon juice
- 1 pinch white sugar

Instructions:
1. Preheat your pressure cooker to the STEAM function. Put 2 cups water. Mix all ingredients in a tempered glass bowl placed on a steamer basket. Put the steamer basket in your preheated pressure cooker.
2. Close and lock the lid; set the timer to ZERO minute. Do the Quick Release Method when done.

3. Transfer your butter mixture in your preferred molding container. Keep the container in the fridge until ready to spread on your Keto White Loaf.

473. DELICIOUS KETO BLUEBERRY MUFFINS

Prep Time: 10 minutes   **Cook Time:** 20 minutes   **Servings:** 6

Nutrition facts:
- Calories: 309
- Total Fat: 27.4 g
- Saturated Fat: 8.0g
- Trans Fat: 0g
- Protein: 9.3g
- Net Carbs: 6.6g

Ingredients:
- 2 cups almond, flour
- One-teaspoon baking powder
- One-cup whip cream
- 2 large eggs
- 1/4 cup butter (melted)
- 5 grams sweetener
- Half-cup blueberries
- Half-teaspoon lemon extract
- 1/4 teaspoon lemon zest

Instructions:
1. Spray the bottom and sides of your 6 silicone muffin cups with cooking oil spray.
2. In a medium size mixing bowl, combine all the ingredients and mix well.
3. Transfer the batter into the greased baking cups and evenly spread the mixture in each cup.
4. You have the option to refrigerate the batter for up to 8 hours before cooking. Remove from the fridge and set the batter in cups to reach room temperature within 25 minutes.
5. Cover each batter cup with aluminum foil.
6. Pour 2 cups of water in the inner pot of your pressure cooker; insert the trivet and arrange the batter cups over your trivet. Close the lid, lock and seal the pressure cooker valve. Set the cooker on STEAM on HIGH and set the timer to cook for 20 minutes.

When done, release the pressure with the Quick release method; transfer your steamed six Blueberry Keto Muffins Cups to a cooling rack. Serve warm or store in fridge when completely cooled.

474. YUMMY KETO CAULIFLOWER MUFFINS

Prep Time: 5 minutes   **Cook Time:** 15 minutes   **Servings:** 4

Nutrition facts:
- Calories: 318
- Total Fat: 26.4g
- Saturated Fat: 16.8g
- Trans Fat: 0g
- Protein: 15.7g
- Net Carbs: 13.3g

Ingredients:
- Half-cup coconut flour
- Half-teaspoon salt
- ½ tsp black pepper
- One-cup cheddar cheese, shredded
- One-cup mozzarella cheese, shredded
- 1 ounce parmesan cheese, grated
- One-tablespoon onion, dried flakes
- One-teaspoon baking powder
- One-teaspoon garlic powder
- 2 cups cauliflower, riced
- 2 eggs, beaten
- 2 tablespoons jalapeno, minced
- 3 tablespoons butter, melted

Instructions:
1. In a large mixing bowl, combine all the ingredients and mix well.
2. Transfer the batter to greased muffin cups.
3. Place your steamer basket in the pressure cooker filled with 2 cups of water.
4. Arrange the muffin cups over the steamer basket.
5. Cover, lock the lid and set your pressure cooker to STEAM function on HIGH pressure.
6. Set the timer to 20 minutes; when done, do the Quick Release method to let out steam pressure.
7. Take out your Cauliflower Keto Muffins and serve with your favorite Keto beverage.

---

475. TASTY KETO BANANA AND NUT LOAF

Prep Time: 10 minutes　　**Cook Time:** 15 minutes　　**Servings:** 6

Nutrition facts:
- Calories: 291
- Total Fat: 24.5g
- Saturated Fat: 2.6g
- Trans Fat: 0g
- Protein: 9.3g
- Net Carbs: 8.8g

Ingredients:
- 2 cups almond flour
- One-teaspoon baking soda
- 250 grams ripe bananas
- 3 eggs
- 1/4 cup olive oil
- Half-cup walnuts, chopped
- Oil or butter to grease loaf pan

Instructions:
1. Combine the first 5 ingredients in a medium size mixing bowl; beat until just incorporated. Add half of the chopped walnuts and give the mixture a final stir.
2. Brush the insides of a silicone loaf pan with a small amount of oil or butter.
3. Transfer the almond batter into the loaf pans and sprinkle the remaining chopped walnuts on top of the batter; cover the loaf pan with aluminum foil and place it on your steamer basket.
4. Pour 2 cups of water in the inner pot of your pressure cooker; place the steamer basket with the loaf pan; close the lid, lock and seal the valve.
5. On STEAM setting, set the timer for 15 minutes.
6. Release pressure by natural release method; take out the steamer basket with the loaf pan and set aside to cool.
7. Remove the almond banana keto loaf from the loaf pan and slice to desired thickness before serving in individual serving plates. Best served with your Olive Garlic Butter Spread.

---

476. AMAZING KETO SUNNY SIDE UP WITH BACON

Prep Time: 10 minutes　　**Cook Time:** 20 minutes　　**Servings:** 4

Nutrition facts:
- Calories: 415
- Total Fat: 30.6g
- Saturated Fat: 10.0g
- Trans Fat: 0g
- Protein: 29.3g
- Net Carbs: 2.8g

Ingredients:
- 250 g honey cured bacon slices
- 4 eggs
- 250 g cherry tomatoes
- Half-teaspoon rosemary

- 2 teaspoon garlic

Instructions:
1. Slice bacon into half inch squares; slice cherry tomatoes in half.
2. Prepare your pressure cooker on SAUTE function; set the timer to 15 minutes.
3. Place the inner pot; sauté the bacon squares until brown on the edges.
4. Push the bacon pieces to one side and crack the eggs one at time directly into the pot.
5. Toss the cherry tomatoes and rosemary in the pot, close the lid, lock and seal the pressure valve.
6. Press CANCEL and shift to MANUAL function on HIGH pressure. Set the timer to zero.
7. When done, release the pressure by Natural Release Method.

477. TASTY KETO FASHIONED SCRAMBLED EGGS

Prep Time: 10 minutes **Cook Time:** 8 minutes **Servings:** 6

Nutrition facts:
- Calories: 461
- Total Fat: 42.4g
- Saturated Fat: 23.7g
- Trans Fat: 0g
- Protein: 7.7g
- Net Carbs: 1.0g

Ingredients:
- 2 large eggs
- 2 tablespoons butter
- 1 oz. cheddar cheese
- 1 tsp. chives

Instructions:
1. Set your pressure cooker on SAUTE function on MEDIUM heat. Add the butter.
2. Beat 2 eggs, stir in the chives and any of your favorite seasoning; pour in the pressure cooker once the butter has melted.
3. Let the eggs cook for 6 minutes before adding the cheese and briskly whisking to scramble.
4. Set the pressure cooker to STEAM function, close the lid and cook for 2 minutes more.

478. TASTY KETO TOAST

Prep Time: 5 minutes **Cook Time:** 5 minutes **Servings:** 4

Nutrition facts:
- Calories: 82
- Total Fat: 5.4g
- Saturated Fat: 1.6g
- Trans Fat: 0g
- Protein: 6.7g
- Net Carbs: 1.4g

Ingredients:
- 2 slices keto bread
- 2 eggs
- Half-cup almond milk, unsweetened
- One-teaspoon cinnamon
- One-teaspoon vanilla
- Half-cup butter
- Half-cup sweetener
- Half-cup coconut milk

Instructions:
1. Preheat your pressure cooker on SAUTE function on HIGH.
2. Beat the eggs in a bowl along with the almond milk, cinnamon and vanilla.

3. Dip the Keto bread slices into the egg mixture.
4. Place the bread slices into the pressure cooker. Brown each side of the bread slices.
5. Prepare the syrup by melting butter in the pressure cooker. Whisk in the sweetener and the coconut milk. Cook until you achieve thick syrup consistency; drizzle the Keto Syrup over the Keto Toast.

479. DELICIOUS KETO EGG LOAF SPREAD

Prep Time: 5 minutes   **Cook Time:** 5 minutes   **Servings:** 6

Nutrition facts:
- Calories: 210
- Total Fat: 17.4g
- Saturated Fat: 3.5g
- Trans Fat: 0g
- Protein: 6.7g
- Net Carbs: 4.3g

Ingredients:
- 8 eggs
- Half-cup mayonnaise
- 3 tablespoons prepared mustard
- Half-cup onion, chopped
- 1/4 tsp salt
- 1/4 tsp black pepper
- 2 table spoon olive oil

Instructions:
1. You can steam a batch of 10 eggs at a time in your pressure cooker so as to save time and energy. Just store the extras for later use.
2. Prep your pressure cooker to steam eggs by pouring in 2 cups of water and placing the steamer basket in.
3. Put the eggs over the steamer basket. Close, lock the lid and seal the vent valve of your pressure cooker; set to STEAM function and set timer to 7 minutes.
4. When done, do the Quick Release method to let out steam; transfer the eggs to a bowl of ice cold water; this makes peeling the eggs easy to handle.
5. Break the eggs to crumbles with a masher or fork; the crumbled egg with the all remaining ingredients and toss well.
6. Spread a tablespoonful of your Egg Keto Loaf Spread on a slice of Keto White Loaf.

480. YUMMY KETO EGG SCRAMBLE

Prep Time: 5 minutes   **Cook Time:** 15 minutes   **Servings:** 4

Nutrition facts:
- Calories: 185
- Total Fat: 14.4g
- Saturated Fat: 7.3g
- Trans Fat: 0g
- Protein: 7.3g
- Net Carbs: 5.8g

Ingredients:
- 3 tablespoons ghee
- One-teaspoon cumin seeds
- One-tablespoon shallot, chopped
- 1 green bell pepper, coarsely chopped
- 1 jalapeno pepper, sliced into matchsticks
- 3 cloves garlic, sliced
- Half-teaspoon turmeric
- Half-teaspoon ground ginger
- Half-teaspoon salt, more to taste
- One-teaspoon ground cinnamon
- 2 tomatoes, coarsely chopped

- 4 eggs, beaten
- 100 grams cilantro, chopped

Instructions:
1. Prepare your pressure cooker to set in SAUTE function.
2. Add the ghee and stir in the cumin seeds to toast until you smell the fragrant aroma.
3. Add the shallot and continue sautéing for approximately 3 minutes more.
4. Add the jalapeno and the garlic along with the bell pepper and tomatoes.
5. Sauté for another 3 minutes.
6. Stir in the turmeric, ginger, salt, and cinnamon.
7. Add the beaten eggs and let cook without stirring for the first 30 seconds.
8. Stir in intervals until liquid has evaporated.
9. Stir in the cilantro, salt and pepper to taste.
10. Cover, lock the lid and seal the vent valve; press CANCEL and shift to MANUAL function and set the timer to 13 minutes. Do the Quick Release method to let out steam pressure.

---

481. AWESOME KETO CHEESY AND MILKY BACON MUFFIN

Prep Time: 10 minutes   **Cook Time:** 15 minutes   **Servings:** 12

Nutrition facts:
- Calories: 337
- Total Fat: 29.1g
- Saturated Fat: 12.0g
- Trans Fat: 0g
- Protein: 14.1g
- Net Carbs: 2.5g

Ingredients:
- 3 tablespoons butter
- Half-cup almond flour
- 1/4 cup flax seed meal
- One-tablespoon baking soda
- One-teaspoon baking powder
- One-teaspoon sea salt
- One-teaspoon black pepper
- 1/4 teaspoon red pepper flake
- 1/4 teaspoon garlic powder
- 10 grams green onions
- Half-cup cheddar cheese
- 250 grams bacon, crisped cooked
- 6 eggs
- 8 ounces coconut milk
- One-tablespoon lemon juice
- 2 avocados, cored and sliced to cubes

Instructions:
1. Prepare 12 silicon muffin cups by spraying the insides with non-stick cooking spray.
2. Mix all ingredients, except the avocado cubes, in a large mixing bowl until smooth texture is achieved.
3. Gently pour the batter into the greased silicone cups and arrange them on top of the steamer basket; top each muffin batter cup with avocado cubes and cover each silicone muffin cup with a sheet of foil.
4. Set your pressure cooker to STEAM function; add two cups of water. Place the steamer basket with muffin cups.
5. Close the lid and lock your pressure cooker. Set the timer to cook for 25 minutes.
6. Release the pressure the natural way; remove the muffin cups and transfer to a cooling rack; let cool for 30 minutes before removing the muffins from the cups.

482. Tasty Keto Garlic & Olive Butter Spread

Prep Time: 5 minutes   **Cook Time:** 1 minute   **Servings:** 6

Nutrition facts:
- Calories: 179
- Total Fat: 20.0g
- Saturated Fat: 10.4g
- Trans Fat: 0g
- Protein: 0.3g
- Net Carbs: 0.8g

Ingredients:
- Half-cup butter, unsalted
- Half-teaspoon salt, ground
- 1/4 teaspoon black pepper
- 2 tablespoon olive oil
- 4 cloves garlic, minced
- 2 tablespoons parsley, fresh

Instructions:
1. Preheat your pressure cooker to the STEAM function. Put 2 cups water. Mix all ingredients in a tempered glass bowl placed on a steamer basket. Put the steamer basket in your preheated pressure cooker.
2. Close and lock the lid; set the timer to 00.00 minute. (Yes, you're seeing it right)
3. Do the Natural Release Method when done.
4. Transfer your olive garlic butter mixture in your preferred molding container. Keep the container in the fridge until ready to spread on your Almond Banana Loaf or Keto Bread.

483. Amazing Keto Pumpkin Spice Almond Cake

Prep Time: 10 minutes   **Cook Time:** 20 minutes   **Servings:** 6

Nutrition facts:
- Calories: 185
- Total Fat: 15.3g
- Saturated Fat: 4.8g
- Trans Fat: 0g
- Protein: 2.1g
- Net Carbs: 6.9g

Ingredients:
- 3 tablespoon butter
- 2 tablespoon sugar
- 2 tablespoon pumpkin spice
- 2 large eggs
- One-teaspoon vanilla
- One-cup almond flour
- Half-teaspoon salt
- 1/4 teaspoon cinnamon
- 1/4 teaspoon baking soda

Instructions:
1. Spray the bottom and sides of your 6-inch round baking pan with cooking oil spray.
2. In a medium size mixing bowl, combine all the ingredients and mix well.
3. Transfer the batter into the greased baking pan and evenly spread the mixture.
4. You have the option to refrigerate the batter for up to 8 hours before cooking. Remove from the fridge and set it to reach room temperature within 25 minutes.
5. Cover the pan with aluminum foil.
6. Pour 2 cups of water in the inner pot of your pressure cooker; insert the trivet and place the baking pan over your trivet. Close the lid, lock and seal the pressure cooker valve. Set the cooker on STEAM on HIGH and set the timer to cook for 20 minutes.
7. When done, release the pressure with the Quick release method; transfer your steamed Pumpkin Spice Keto Almond Cake to a cooling rack. Serve warm or store in fridge when completely cooled.

484. EASY KETO EGG FAST

Prep Time: 5 minutes   **Cook Time:** 5 minutes   **Servings:** 4

Nutrition facts:
- Calories: 82
- Total Fat: 5.4g
- Saturated Fat: 1.6g
- Trans Fat: 0g
- Protein: 6.7g
- Net Carbs: 1.4g

Ingredients:
- 4 large eggs
- One-cup cold water
- 50 grams scallions, chopped
- One-teaspoon sesame seeds
- Half-teaspoon garlic powder
- Half-teaspoon salt
- Half-teaspoon black pepper

Instructions:
1. In a small mixing bowl, combine the eggs and water; beat and sieve the mixture with a strainer onto an oven-proof bowl.
2. Add the scallions, black pepper, salt, garlic powder sesame seeds and scallions; mix well to incorporate.
3. Pour a cup of water in the inner pot of your pressure cooker.
4. Position the steamer basket in the inner pot.
5. Set the bowl with egg mixture over the steamer basket.
6. Close the lid, lock and seal the vent valve.
7. Choose and press the MANUAL function on HIGH pressure and adjust the timer to 5 minutes.
8. When done, do the Quick Release method to let off steam.
9. Serve at once with your hot Cauliflower Keto PressuRice!

485. YUMMY KETO EGG SPINACH MUFFINS

Prep Time: 10 minutes   **Cook Time:** 20 minutes   **Servings:** 6

Nutrition facts:
- Calories: 254
- Total Fat: 19.6g
- Saturated Fat: 8.1g
- Trans Fat: 0g
- Protein: 17.3g
- Net Carbs: 2.0g

Ingredients:
- One-tablespoon butter
- 8 eggs
- 1/4 cup cream, all purpose
- 1/4 cup milk, whole
- 4 ounces bacon, crispy fried and crumbled
- 2 teaspoons dried parsley
- One-cup spinach leaves, chopped
- Half-teaspoon pepper
- 1/4 teaspoon salt
- Half-cup shredded cheese

Instructions:
1. Preheat your pressure cooker to the STEAM function. Add 2 cups of water.
2. Grease 6 muffin tin cups with butter.
3. In a mixing bowl, beat the eggs, cream and milk with a whisk.
4. Stir in the crumbled bacon chopped spinach leaves, parsley, salt and pepper.
5. Pour the egg cream mixture into each greased muffin cup.

6. Arrange the muffin tin cups in your basket strainer and insert the basket in the preheated pressure cooker; steam for 15 minutes; take out the muffin tin cups from the pressure cooker; sprinkle shredded cheese on top of each muffin and return all cups to the pressure cooker; cook for 5 minutes more or until cheese is melted.
7. Take out the muffin tin cups from the pressure cooker, transfer to cool on a cooling rack.

486. Delicious Keto Steamed Scallion Omelet

Prep Time: 15 minutes **Cook Time:** 5 minutes **Servings:** 8

Nutrition facts:
- Calories: 211
- Total Fat: 15.0g
- Saturated Fat: 6.5g;
- Trans Fat: 0.0g
- Protein: 12.5g;
- Net Carbs: 5.6g

Ingredients:
- 4 eggs, large
- 1/4 cup water, cold
- One-tablespoon butter, melted
- 8 grams scallions
- Half-teaspoon sesame seeds
- Half-teaspoon garlic, minced
- Half-teaspoon sea salt
- Half-teaspoon pepper

Instructions:
1. Beat the eggs and water in a medium size bowl. Stir in the melted butter.
2. Strain the beaten egg butter mixture over a strainer straight into a tempered glass baking dish that could fit in your pressure cooker.
3. Add the rest scallions, sesame seeds, salt and pepper; blend until well incorporated.
4. Pour 2 cups of tap water to inner pot of your pressure cooker and place the steamer basket in the pot.
5. Place the baking dish with egg mixture over the steamer basket.
6. Close the pressure cooker lid tightly along with the vent valve.
7. On MANUAL, set to HIGH and set timer to 5 minutes.
8. When the timer goes off, do a QUICK RELEASE.
9. Take out the baking dish and set on the cooling rack for about 5 minutes. Slice in serving portions and place on individual plates. Best served with Cheesy Bacon Biscuit.

487. Tasty Keto Coconut Zucchini Muffins

Prep Time: 10 minutes; **Cook Time:** 20 minutes **Servings:** 6;

Nutrition facts:
- Calories: 257
- Total Fat: 24.1 g
- Saturated Fat: 9,4g;
- Trans Fat: 0g
- Protein: 71g;
- Net Carbs: 3.7g

Ingredients:
- Half-cup zucchini, packed
- 6 tablespoons butter, melted
- 2 eggs
- One-teaspoon vanilla extract
- 1/4 cup almond, milk
- One-cup almond, flour
- 3 tablespoons coconut, flour
- 1/4 cup sweetener
- 3 tablespoons cocoa powder
- 1/4 teaspoon xanthan gum

- 1/4 teaspoon salt
- 2 tsp baking powder

Instructions:
1. Spray the bottom and sides of your 6 silicone muffin cups with cooking oil spray.
2. In a medium size mixing bowl, combine all the cake ingredients and mix well.
3. Transfer the batter into the greased baking cups and evenly spread the mixture in each cup. You have the option to refrigerate the batter for up to 8 hours before cooking. Remove from the fridge and set the batter in cups to reach room temperature within 25 minutes.
4. Cover each batter cup with aluminum foil.
5. Pour 2 cups of water in the inner pot of your pressure cooker; insert the trivet and arrange the batter cups over your trivet. Close the lid, lock and seal the pressure cooker valve. Set the cooker on STEAM on HIGH and set the timer to cook for 20 minutes.
6. When done, release the pressure with the Quick release method; transfer your steamed six Zucchini Keto Muffin Cups to a cooling rack. Serve warm or store in fridge when completely cooled.

"SPECIAL KETOGENIC LUNCH RECIPES"

488. Amazing Keto Cranberry Turkey

Prep Time: 10 minutes;   **Cook Time:** 20 minutes   **Servings:** 6;

Nutrition facts:
- Calories: 300g
- Total Fat: 13.0g
- Saturated Fat: 2.5g;
- Trans Fat: 0g
- Protein: 34.4g;
- Net Carbs: 6.5g

Ingredients:
- 1 ½ pounds turkey, breasts
- One-teaspoon salt
- One-teaspoon freshly ground pepper
- 3 tablespoons canola oil, divided
- 4 shallots, peeled and quartered
- 10 grams thyme
- One-cup chicken broth
- Cranberry Sauce
- 1 ½ cups cranberry
- 1/4 cup dried cranberry
- 2 tablespoons brown sugar
- One-tablespoon vinegar, apple cider

Instructions:
1. Rub turkey breasts with half a teaspoon of salt and half a teaspoon of pepper.
2. Set your pressure cooker to SAUTE function on High pressure; set the timer to 20 minutes.
3. Heat half of the canola oil in the pressure cooker; add the seasoned turkey and brown all sides. Add the remaining ingredients; press CANCEL and switch to POULTRY function; set the timer to 35 minutes.
4. When done, do a Quick Release method to release steam pressure.
5. Open the lid and add the cranberry sauce ingredients.
6. Press the CANCEL button and shift to MANUAL function; set the timer to 10 minutes.
7. When done, do the Natural Release method to release steam pressure.
8. Take out your Cranberry Keto Turkey and slice to serving pieces.

489. Easy Keto Squid Springs Sauté

Prep Time: 10 minutes;   **Cook Time:** 20 minutes   **Servings:** 8;

Nutrition facts:
- Calories: 200 g
- Total Fat: 0.2g
- Saturated Fat: 1.6g;
- Trans Fat: 0g
- Protein: 14.0g;
- Net Carbs: 5.7g

Ingredients:
- 2 tablespoons olive oil
- 2 grams anchovy
- 1 clove garlic, smashed
- 100 grams onion
- One-teaspoon red pepper flakes
- 400 grams tomatoes
- 2 pounds squid, sliced in rings
- Half-cup white wine
- 1 red bell pepper
- One-tablespoon lemon juice
- 1/4 teaspoon salt
- 2 tablespoons olive oil
- One-cup parsley, chopped

Instructions:
1. Set your pressure cooker to SAUTE function on HIGH pressure and put two (2) tablespoons of olive oil; stir in the anchovy, minced garlic, onion and hot pepper.
2. Stir in the squid rings and lightly brown them a bit.
3. Add the wine and let it reduce to a minimum. Lastly, add the chopped tomatoes, half a cup of parsley and a cup of water.
4. Press cancel and shift to MANUAL function on HIGH pressure and set the timer to 15 minutes. Close, lock the lid and seal the vent valve of your pressure cooker.
5. When done, release the pressure by the Quick Release method. Open the lid and stir in the juice of 1 lemon, the remaining half a cup of parsley and some olive oil. Serve at once.

490. TASTY KETO BACON CHICKEN

Prep Time: 10 minutes;   **Cook Time:** 20 minutes   **Servings:** 6;

Nutrition facts:
- Calories: 283g
- Total Fat: 24.8g
- Saturated Fat: 13.3g;
- Trans Fat: 0g
- Protein: 14.0g;
- Net Carbs: 1.1g

Ingredients:
- 1 pound chicken breast, filet
- ½-pound bacon
- 4 tablespoon coconut oil
- Half-cup heavy whipping cream
- 3 tablespoon butter
- 2 tablespoon prepared mustard

Instructions:
1. Slice the chicken breast filet into bite-sized pieces and wrap each piece with a bacon slice.
2. Spray a baking pan with non-stick cooking spray and place wrapped chicken filet in the baking pan.
3. Set the pressure cooker on SAUTE function; add the oil and brown the bacon hugged chicken tenders.
4. Cook the dipping sauce in a saucepan over your stove top in medium heat by melting the butter and whisking in the whipping cream; heat for about a minute; remove from heat and stir the mustard in; serve with your bacon-hugged chicken tenders with this dipping sauce and your Cauliflower Keto PressuRice or Keto Mashed Cauliflower.

491. YUMMY KETO CHEESY HOTDOG HUGGERS

Prep Time: 10 minutes;   **Cook Time:** 20 minutes   **Servings:** 12;

Nutrition facts:
- Calories: 350g
- Total Fat: 28.5g
- Saturated Fat: 10.6g;
- Trans Fat: 0g
- Protein: 14.0g;
- Net Carbs: 1.1g

Ingredients:
- 1 pound hot dogs
- 1 pound bacon
- 2 ounces cheddar cheese
- One-teaspoon garlic powder
- One-teaspoon onion powder
- Half-teaspoon salt
- Half-teaspoon pepper

Instructions:
1. Set your pressure cooker to SAUTE function on HIGH. Add 2 cups of water.
2. Score hotdogs with a slit in each lengthwise where the cheese can be stuffed.
3. Slice a couple of ounces of cheese into rectangular strips just about the length of your hotdogs. Insert the cheese strips in the hotdog.
4. Wrap around the hotdog a slice of bacon and seal with a wooden pick.
5. Set the wrapped hotdogs on the steamer basket. Place the steamer basket in the preheated pressure cooker.
6. Place the hotdogs on top of the steamer basket.
7. Close the lid, lock and seal the vent valve.
8. When done, do the Quick Release method to release steam pressure.

Serve with your favorited creamed or buttered vegetables.

---

492. DELICIOUS KETO TACO BEEF FRITTATA

Prep Time: 10 minutes; **Cook Time:** 20 minutes **Servings:** 10;

Nutrition facts:
- Calories: 305g
- Total Fat: 13.1g
- Saturated Fat: 6g;
- Trans Fat: 0g
- Protein: 33.1g;
- Net Carbs: 1.7g

Ingredients:
- 1 pound ground beef
- 100 grams taco seasoning
- 3/4 cup water
- 6 large eggs
- One-cup heavy whipping cream
- 2 cloves garlic, minced
- Half-teaspoon salt
- 1/4 teaspoon pepper
- One-cup shredded Cheddar cheese

Instructions:
1. Preheat pressure cooker on SAUTE function; grease a 6-inch baking dish with butter.
2. Without the lid on, brown the ground beef for 8 to 10 minutes; add the taco seasoning; stir well to incorporate. Add half a cup of water; continue cooking until sauce thickens.
3. When done, transfer the beef taco mixture to a greased 6-inch baking dish.
4. Wash the inner pot of your pressure cooker; return the pot and fill in 2 cups water.
5. Combine eggs, heavy whipping cream, garlic, salt and pepper In a large bowl; mix well and pour over beef taco mixture; sprinkle top with shredded cheddar cheese.
6. Set the pressure cooker on STEAM function on HIGH pressure and set the timer to 15 minutes.
7. Place your steamer basket and the baking dish with your beef taco egg mixture.
8. Cover, lock the lid and set the vent valve. When done, let the steam pressure out with the Natural Release method. Take out your Beef Taco Keto Frittata and top with sliced tomatoes or chopped avocado for added flavor.

493. AMAZING KETO PROVOLONE SIRLOIN STEAK

Prep Time: 5 minutes; **Cook Time:** 20 minutes **Servings:** 8;

Nutrition facts:
- Calories: 417
- Total Fat: 23.0g
- Saturated Fat: 11,6g;
- Trans Fat: 0g
- Protein: 47.4g;
- Net Carbs: 3.0g

Ingredients:
- 2 pounds beef, sirloin Steak
- 4 tablespoons mayo
- 2 tablespoons Dijon mustard
- 400 grams provolone cheese

Instructions:
1. Place a steamer base basket and a cup or two cups of water in your pressure cooker.
2. Smother your steak pieces with mayo and mustard; arrange steak pieces in a baking tray; top each piece with a slice of provolone cheese; place the baking tray on top of the steamer basket.
3. Close and lock the lid and seal the valve of your pressure cooker.
4. Set the pressure cooker on MEAT function at high; set the timer to 20 minutes.
5. When done, carefully release the pressure manually by swinging the valve pressure release quickly.
6. Open the pressure cooker lid after all steam had been released; immediately transfer the steak pieces in a serving platter or onto individual serving plates. Serve with your cauliflower rice.

494. DIFFERENT KETO CHUCK ROAST

Prep Time: 10 minutes; **Cook Time:** 20 minutes **Servings:** 10;

Nutrition facts:
- Calories: 305g
- Total Fat: 13.1g
- Saturated Fat: 6g;
- Trans Fat: 0g
- Protein: 33.1g;
- Net Carbs: 1.7g

Ingredients:
- 2 pounds chuck roast
- Half-teaspoon kosher salt
- 1/4 teaspoon black pepper
- 4 tablespoons ghee
- 20 grams onion, chopped
- 1 clove garlic, minced
- One-tablespoon tomato paste
- 2 cups broth
- 1/4 cup red wine
- One-tablespoon soy sauce
- 1 ½ pounds rutabaga
- 1 pound carrot
- 8 ounces' mushrooms
- Half-teaspoon salt
- Half-teaspoon pepper

Instructions:
1. Rub the chuck roast with pepper and salt.
2. Put the ghee in the pressure cooker; set to SAUTE function.
3. When ghee is heated up, add the chuck roast to brown all sides for approximately six (6) minutes; when browned, take out the chuck roast onto a platter and in with the onion to sauté for approximately three (3) minutes with constant stirring.

4. Add the tomato paste and garlic; continue sautéing, then stir in the broth, soy sauce and red wine; return the chuck roast and its drippings to the pressure cooker to simmer.
5. Cover, lock the lid and seal the vent valve of your pressure cooker; press CANCEL and shift to the MEAT function on HIGH pressure for 35 minutes.
6. When done, use the Quick Release method to let out the steam pressure.
7. Open and transfer the cooked chuck roast to a baking sheet; add the carrots, rutabaga and mushrooms and cover the pot; and reset to MEAT function on HIGH pressure for five (5) minutes. While vegetables are in the pot, broil the roast under 5 minutes in the oven until top is crispy. When done, do the quick-release method to let out steam; press CANCEL and switch to SAUTE until liquid is reduced to half. Serve with the cooked veggies and a bowlful of Keto Cauliflower Rice.

495. SURPRISE KETO OLIVE CHICKEN WALNUT

Prep Time: 10 minutes;   **Cook Time:** 25 minutes   **Servings:** 6;

Nutrition facts:
- Calories: 405
- Total Fat: 27.10g
- Saturated Fat: 5.6g;
- Trans Fat: 0g
- Protein: 28.2g;
- Net Carbs: 9.5g

Ingredients:
- 2 tablespoons butter
- 2 tablespoons olive oil
- 1 pound chicken legs
- One-teaspoon salt
- One-teaspoon pepper
- 1 onion, medium size sliced
- One-cup thyme, fresh
- One-cup cranberries
- One-cup walnuts, shelled
- One-cup orange juice

Instructions:
1. Pre-heat your pressure cooker on HIGH in SAUTE function without closing the lid.
2. Add the olive oil and butter to melt.
3. Brown the chicken legs putting the pieces in the pressure cooker one at a time; add salt and pepper.
4. After about 3 minutes of browning the chicken legs on both sides, take out the pieces from the pressure cooker; add the sliced onion and put back the browned chicken legs; add the walnuts, cranberries, thyme and a cup of orange juice.
5. Lock the lid onto the pressure cooker. Seal the valve and set the timer to 20 minutes. Put the heat on HIGH up to the pressure point; lower heat, count 15 minutes to cook at HIGH pressure.
6. Release the pressure by waiting for the pressure on coming down for about 10 to 20 minutes. (If you are in a hurry, release the pressure by the Quick release method)
7. Carefully transfer the chicken legs to a serving platter. Top with onions, cranberries and walnuts.
8. Reduce the remaining liquid in the pressure cooker to half and pour over the braised chicken legs when ready to serve.

496. KETO CHICKEN GREEN PAPAYA

Prep Time: 15 minutes; **Cook Time:** 20 minutes **Servings:** 8;
Nutrition facts:
- Calories: 262
- Total Fat: 15.7g
- Saturated Fat: 3.1g;
- Trans Fat: 0g
- Protein: 25.0g;
- Net Carbs: 4.4g

Ingredients:
- 4 tablespoons olive oil
- 10 grams ginger, peeled and minced
- 20 grams onion, sliced
- 500 grams chicken thighs
- One-tablespoon fish sauce
- 100 grams papaya, green – cut to bite-sized cubes
- 100 grams kale leaves

Instructions:
1. Set your pressure cooker to SAUTE function on HIGH pressure and adjust the timer to 10 minutes. Add 4 tablespoons olive oil, ginger, onion, fish sauce and the chicken thighs to brown. Flip chicken thigh pieces to the other side to brown evenly.
2. When done, add One-cup of water in your pressure cooker. Cover with the lid, lock and seal the valve. Press CANCEL and shift to the POULTRY function on HIGH. Set the timer to 15 minutes.
3. When done, do a quick release to let off steam; open the lid and add the green papaya cubes and 3 cups of water. Press cancel and shift to MANUAL function on HIGH and set the timer to 10 minutes; add the kale leaves after 10 minutes of cooking.
4. Turn the heat off in the next 5 minutes and transfer your green papaya chicken keto tinola onto individual serving soup bowls. Best served immediately while piping hot with your cauliflower rice.

497. DELICIOUS KETO SMOKED SALMON AVOCADO CAULIROLLS

Prep Time: 10 minutes; **Cook Time:** 20 minutes **Servings:** 12;
Nutrition facts:
- Calories: 134g
- Total Fat: 9.6g
- Saturated Fat: 4.0g;
- Trans Fat: 0g
- Protein: 5,2g;
- Net Carbs: 6.4g

Ingredients:
- 16 ounces' cauliflower
- 6 ounce cream cheese, softened
- One-tablespoon mirin rice vinegar
- One-tablespoon light soy sauce
- 1 cucumber, remove core and slice into strips
- ½ avocado, medium size
- 5 ounces smoked salmon
- One-cup parsley, chopped
- 1 pack seaweed sushi wrapper
- 2 tablespoons olive oil

Instructions:
1. Using a blender, grind cauliflower into corn meal size crumbs with pulse beating intervals.
2. Place the crumbled cauliflower in your pressure cooker.
3. Set to Manual mode, close, lock and seal the vent; set the timer to 5 minutes.
4. As soon as you hear the timer beep, slide the valve open to release pressure quickly.
5. Take out the cauliflower rice and transfer to a bowl.

6. Sprinkle mirin and light soy sauce over the cauliflower rice; stir gently just to incorporate
7. Slice the avocado in half, scoop out the meat and slice into strips. Slice cucumber into long thin strips along with the smoked salmon.
8. Lay a sheet of seaweed sushi wrapper on a bamboo mat or roller. Brush the nori sheet with olive oil and place a spoonful of cauliflower mixture over the nori sheet; leave an inch of open space from the top edge.
9. Arrange slices of avocado, cucumber and smoked salmon about one and a half inches from the bottom edge of your cauliflower mixture laden seaweed sushi sheet. Roll the assembly from the bottom edge tightly.
10. Slice the cauliflower keto rolls into bite size pieces and serve.

498. Yummy Keto Smoked Bacon Asparagus Spears

Prep Time: 5 minutes; **Cook Time:** 7 minutes **Servings:** 8;

Nutrition facts:
- Calories: 327
- Total Fat: 23.6g
- Saturated Fat: 7.8g;
- Trans Fat: 0g
- Protein: 23.3;
- Net Carbs: 2.8g

Ingredients:
- 2 pounds Asparagus
- 450 grams smoked bacon

Instructions:
1. Pre-heat your pressure cooker in STEAM function on HIGH pressure without closing the lid.
2. Add 1 to 2 cups of water to the inner pot.
3. Wrap each asparagus stick with a slice of smoked bacon.
4. Lay a few asparagus sticks on the steamer basket in a single layer.
5. Lay the smoked bacon wrapped asparagus keto sticks on the single layer of unwrapped asparagus sticks.
6. Repeat layering until all your wrapped keto sticks are neatly arranged in the steamer basket before lowering it in the inner pot of your pressure cooker.
7. Close and lock the lid of your pressure cooker.
8. Raise the heat on HIGH; lower the heat when pan reaches the correct pressure level; set the timer to 3 minutes cooking time on HIGH pressure.
9. When done, use the Natural Release method to open the pressure cooker.
10. Immediately take out the steamer basket and transfer the smoked bacon asparagus keto sticks to your serving platter. Best paired with mashed cauliflower.

499. Tasty Keto Chicken Chorizo Charade

Prep Time: 10 minutes; **Cook Time:** 30 minutes **Servings:** 8;

Nutrition facts:
- Calories: 382
- Total Fat: 16.1g
- Saturated Fat: 4.1g;
- Trans Fat: 0.1g
- Protein: 31.7g;
- Net Carbs: 9g

Ingredients:
- 3 tablespoons olive oil, extra-virgin
- 8 ounces sausage, sliced chorizo
- 3 cups onion, chopped
- 2 tablespoons garlic, minced

- 2 grams bell pepper
- 1 ½ pounds chicken, skinless thighs
- Half-teaspoon salt
- Half-teaspoon ground pepper
- 3 cups wine, white
- 4 cups tomatoes
- 2 cups water
- 1/4 cup parsley, flat
- 3 grams saffron

Instructions:
1. Heat the oil in the pressure cooker on SAUTÉ function without closing the lid.
2. Add the chorizo slices and cook for about 5 minutes.
3. Add the minced garlic, chopped onion, bell pepper, tomatoes, parsley and saffron and the chicken thighs.
4. Season with salt and pepper and stir in the wine and water.
5. Cook for a minute before closing and locking the lid to set to Poultry mode pressure cooking.
6. When done, release the pressure. Transfer to a serving platter and top with a sprinkling of your favorite shredded cheese.

500. TASTY KETO TUNA-BACON & STEAMED EGG SPREAD

Prep Time: 15 minutes;   **Cook Time:** 15 minutes   **Servings:** 6;

Nutrition facts:
- Calories: 260
- Total Fat: 17.2g
- Saturated Fat: 5.1g;
- Trans Fat: 0g
- Protein: 22.9g;
- Net Carbs: 1.9g

Ingredients:
- 1 large egg
- 1 can tuna flakes in olive oil
- One-tablespoon chopped onion
- 100 grams bacon, cooked and crumbled
- 2 teaspoons prepared mustard
- 1/4 teaspoon dill
- One-tablespoon mayonnaise with olive oil
- One-tablespoon sour cream
- Iceberg lettuce

Instructions:
1. Place a steamer base basket and a cup or two cups of water in your pressure cooker.
2. Place the eggs on top of the steamer basket. You can do 4 to 8 eggs in one batch cooking and just store steamed eggs in the refrigerator for later use.
3. Close and lock the lid and seal the valve of your pressure cooker.
4. On STEAM function, set the timer to 7 minutes.
5. Set the pressure cooker to LOW.
6. When done, carefully release the pressure manually by swinging the valve pressure release quickly.
7. Open the pressure cooker lid after all steam had been released; immediately transfer the eggs in a bowl filled with ice cubes and water and let them sit there for 12 minutes before transferring to the fridge until ready to crack and use.
8. For this recipe, crack one egg, chop to small pieces and place in a small mixing bowl.

9. Add the tuna flakes, chopped onion, crumbled bacon, prepared mustard, dill, mayonnaise and sour slices of almond ream. Toss well. Serve on a bed of iceberg lettuce or spread over a slice of Almond Banana Keto Loaf.

501. DELICIOUS KETO SPICED CHICKEN ROMAINE WRAP

Prep Time: 5 minutes;   **Cook Time:** 20 minutes   **Servings:** 8;

Nutrition facts:
- Calories: 171
- Total Fat: 15.7g
- Saturated Fat: 12.2g;
- Trans Fat: 0g
- Protein: 6.7g;
- Net Carbs: 0.9g

Ingredients:
- 1 pound chicken breast
- 4 tablespoons coconut oil
- 3 tablespoons apple cider vinegar
- One-teaspoon ground cumin
- One-teaspoon ground mustard
- One-teaspoon paprika
- One-teaspoon black pepper
- 6 lettuce leaves, romaine

Instructions:
1. In a small mixing bowl, combine the apple cider vinegar with coconut oil, cumin, mustard, paprika and black pepper; mix well.
2. Rub the chicken breast with the vinegar, 2 tablespoons of oil and spices mixture; marinade for at least 30 minutes.
3. Set your pressure cooker to SAUTE function on HIGH pressure and adjust the timer to 10 minutes. Add the remaining 2 tablespoons oil and the chicken breasts to brown. Flip to the other side to brown evenly.
4. Add 2 cups of water in your pressure cooker. Press CANCEL and shift to the POULTRY function on HIGH. Set the timer to 20 minutes. When done, remove the chicken breasts from the pressure cooker; shred the chicken breasts when cool enough to handle.
5. Get a piece of lettuce leaf scoop onto it about 2 tablespoons of shredded chicken; sprinkle the shredded chicken filling with leftover oil, vinegar and spices mixture before folding the lettuce leaf to wrap the shredded chicken filling. Do the same for the remainder of the shredded chicken. Best served with cauliflower rice.

"SPECIAL KETOGENIC DINNER RECIPES"

502. TASTY KETO TOMATO SAUTÉ AND GREEN BEANS

Prep Time: 10 minutes;   **Cook Time:** 20 minutes   **Servings:** 6;

Nutrition facts:
- Calories: 151g
- Total Fat: 8.6g
- Saturated Fat: 1.4g;
- Trans Fat: 0g
- Protein: 15.2g;
- Net Carbs: 2.2g

Ingredients:
- 3 tablespoons olive oil
- 300 grams chicken breast filet, sliced to strips
- 1 garlic clove, minced
- One-cup tomatoes, chopped
- Half-cup onion, sliced
- Half-teaspoon salt
- Half-teaspoon black pepper, ground
- 100 grams green beans
- 6 grams basil

Instructions:
1. Set the pressure cooker on SAUTE function.
2. Add the oil and brown the chicken filet strips.
3. When done, push the browned strips to one side of the pan and add the garlic, tomatoes and onions; sauté for a minute or two.
4. Cover, lock and seal the vent valve.
5. Press cancel and shift to MANUAL function on HIGH pressure.
6. Set the timer to 2 minutes.
7. When done, do the Natural Release method to let out steam pressure.

503. MOUTHWATERING KETO CHICKEN VEGGIES SALAD

Prep Time: 10 minutes;   **Cook Time:** 10 minutes   **Servings:** 4;

Nutrition facts:
- Calories: 203
- Total Fat: 9.7g
- Saturated Fat: 2.2g;
- Trans Fat: 0g
- Protein: 21.4g;
- Net Carbs: 3.8g

Ingredients:
- 3 pounds chicken breast
- 100 grams roasted peppers
- One-cup celery
- Half-cup sliced basil
- Half-cup scallion
- Half-cup avocado oil
- Half-cup vinegar, white wine
- One-tablespoon mustard, prepared
- 5 ounces arugula

Instructions:
1. Preheat your pressure cooker on POULTRY function. Add the chicken breasts and a cup of water.
2. Close and lock the lid of your pressure cooker; set the timer to 8 minutes.
3. When done, release the pressure with the natural depressurizing method.

4. Take out the cooked chicken breasts from your pressure cooker and shred by pulling the meat off from the chunk.
5. Place shredded chicken breasts in a medium size bowl; add the chopped red bell peppers, basil, celery, and scallions.
6. In a small bowl, mix together the avocado oil, mustard and vinegar and pour the mixture over the bowl of shredded chicken and veggies. Toss well.
7. Arrange a bed of arugula on your serving platter topped with your shredded chicken veggie salad and serve.

504. Amazing Keto Beef Burgundy Stew

Prep Time: 10 minutes; **Cook Time:** 30 minutes **Servings:** 6;

Nutrition facts:
- Calories: 432g
- Total Fat: 22.9g
- Saturated Fat: 8.0g;
- Trans Fat: 0.1g
- Protein: 36.3g;
- Net Carbs: 9.1g

Ingredients:
- 1 pound beef flank steak
- 2 tablespoons avocado oil
- 2 cloves garlic, minced
- 2 teaspoon rock salt
- 2 tablespoons thyme
- 2 tablespoons parsley
- 2 teaspoon ground black pepper
- ½ pound bacon
- 100 grams onion, slices
- 250 grams carrot, julienned
- One-cup red wine
- One-tablespoon maple syrup
- Half-cup beef broth

Instructions:
1. Set your pressure cooker to SAUTE function; add the avocado oil.
2. In a small bowl, combine salt and spices and rub this mixture on beef steaks.
3. Cut the bacon in strips; place strips in the pressure cooker to brown; add the onion and stir occasionally for 5 minutes.
4. Add the seasoned beef steaks and the remaining ingredients.
5. Close, lock and seal the vent valve of your pressure cooker.
6. Press CANCEL and shift to MEAT function on HIGH pressure.
7. Adjust the timer to desired cooking duration.
8. Do the Natural Release method to let out steam pressure.

505. Tasty Cheesy Keto Hungarian Style Meatballs

Prep Time: 10 minutes; **Cook Time:** 20 minutes **Servings:** 6;

Nutrition facts:
- Calories: 418g
- Total Fat: 34.8g
- Saturated Fat: 13.6g;
- Trans Fat: 0.1g
- Protein: 15.2g;
- Net Carbs: 2.3g

Ingredients:
- 1 pound sausage, Hungarian
- 1 large egg
- 1/4 tsp salt
- One-cup almond flour
- 8 ounces cheddar cheese
- 50 grams grated parmesan

- One-tablespoon butter
- 2 tsp baking powder

Instructions:
1. Prepare your pressure cooker in STEAM function.
2. In a bowl, combine the eggs and spices and beat well.
3. Add all other ingredients to egg mixture, mix well and make meatballs.
4. Use a cookie scoop in measuring individual servings.
5. Put the sausage balls on a greased baking dish that can fit inside your pressure cooker.
6. Cover, lock and seal the vent valve and set the timer to 15 minutes.
7. Store in a sandwich bag or covered bowl in the fridge if not ready to consume.

506. DELICIOUS KETO CAULIFLOWER PANCAKES

Prep Time: 10 minutes; **Cook Time:** 20 minutes **Servings:** 6;

Nutrition facts:
- Calories: 213g
- Total Fat: 19.8g
- Saturated Fat: 14.2g;
- Trans Fat: 0g
- Protein: 5.6g;
- Net Carbs: 5.6g

Ingredients:
- 2 cups Kale, chopped
- 1 pound cauliflower
- One-tablespoon olive oil
- 2 cloves garlic, minced
- Half-cup cheddar cheese, shredded
- One-cup mozzarella cheese, shredded
- 1 large egg
- 2 tablespoons almond, flour
- Half-teaspoon red pepper flakes
- One-teaspoon salt
- One-teaspoon ground pepper
- Half-cup coconut oil, for frying

Instructions:
1. Prepare your pressure cooker by filling in 2 cups of water; put in the steamer basket.
2. Set at STEAM function on HIGH pressure and adjust the timer for 10 minutes.
3. Place cauliflower florets over the steamer basket.
4. Cover, lock the lid and seal the vent valve.
5. When done and cool enough to handle, break the florets to smaller crumbles and squeeze out excess water.
6. Combine the cauliflower with the kale, cheeses, egg, flour, pepper flakes, salt and pepper.
7. Form meatballs out of the mixture and flatten them to resemble a pancake.
8. Discard the water from the inner pot of your pressure cooker; wipe with towel.
9. Return the inner pot to your pressure cooker and set it to SAUTE function.
10. Set the timer to fifteen (15) minutes; add oil and fry the patty for 3 minutes on each side.
11. Repeat with the remaining patties. Serve with your favorite condiment or side dish.

507. YUMMY KETO BLUE ARUGULA TOSS

Prep Time: 5 minutes; **Cook Time:** no cooking **Servings:** 8;

Nutrition facts:
- Calories: 376
- Total Fat: 15.1g
- Saturated Fat: 4.6g;
- Trans Fat: 0g
- Protein: 48.8g;
- Net Carbs: 9.6g

Ingredients:
- 2 cups blueberries
- 10 ounces arugula
- 1/4 cup olive oil
- One-tablespoon prepared mustard
- 2 tablespoons balsamic vinegar
- 2 tablespoons orange juice

Instructions:
Give your pressure cooker a break with this easy salad toss.
1. Toss all ingredients in a mixing bowl.
2. Enjoy your light dinner salad with your Keto Bacon Chicken Huggers leftovers.

508. TASTY KETO TUNA PECAN TOSS

Prep Time: 15 minutes; **Cook Time:** 20 minutes **Servings:** 8;

Nutrition facts:
- Calories: 284
- Total Fat: 15.3g
- Saturated Fat: 2.7g;
- Trans Fat: 0g
- Protein: 37.1g;
- Net Carbs: 4.8g

Ingredients:
- 2 pounds tuna
- Half-cup pecan
- Half-cup mayonnaise
- Half-cup grapes, seedless sliced in halves
- salt and pepper to taste
- dash of ginger powder
- iceberg lettuce

Instructions:
1. Cut tuna into bite size cubes and season with salt, pepper and ginger powder.
2. Place the tuna cubes in a heat tempered baking dish and cover the dish with aluminum foil.
3. Place the dish over the trivet in the inner pot of your pressure cooker filled with 2 cups of water.
4. Close the lid, lock and seal the valve.
5. Press the STEAM button on HIGH pressure and set the timer to 15 minutes.
6. Release the pressure when done with the natural release method.
7. Transfer the cooked tuna cubes to a mixing bowl and toss in all the remaining ingredients.
8. Serve on a bed of iceberg lettuce on individual salad serving bowls.

509. FAVORITE KETO TUNA BELLY ADOBO

Prep Time: 15 minutes; **Cook Time:** 25 minutes **Servings:** 6;

Nutrition facts:
- Calories: 340
- Total Fat: 24.3g
- Saturated Fat: 8.5g;
- Trans Fat: 0g
- Protein: 24.8g;
- Net Carbs: 4.7g

Ingredients:
- 1/4 cup olive oil
- 500 grams tuna belly
- One-teaspoon salt
- 1/4 cup light soy sauce
- 1/4 cup coconut vinegar
- 2 teaspoons garlic, crushed
- One-tablespoon ginger, minced

- One-teaspoon black pepper, coarsely ground
- 1/4 cup butter, melted
- 200 grams spinach

Instructions:
1. On STEAM function on HIGH pressure of your pressure cooker, set the timer to 15 minutes; pour 2 cups of water into the inner pot of the cooker.
2. Take a shallow baking tin pan, add the oil and lay the tuna belly slab skin side down over the baking pan.
3. Place the pan with tuna belly on your steamer basket; Combine the soy sauce, vinegar, salt, pepper and crushed garlic in a small mixing bowl; pour the mixture over the tuna belly; insert the steamer basket with the pan in your pressure cooker.
4. When done, do the Quick Release method by flipping the valve open to let the steam out.
5. Open the lid and add the butter and spinach; close the lid without closing the valve, press cancel and shift to MANUAL function; set the timer to 1 minute.
6. When done, transfer the tuna belly to a serving platter, arrange the spinach leaves on top and serve immediately.

510. DELICIOUS KETO GREEN BEANS AND CHEESY BEEF CASSEROLE

Prep Time: 15 minutes;   **Cook Time:** 30 minutes   **Servings:** 12;

Nutrition facts:
- Calories: 215
- Total Fat: 10.3g
- Saturated Fat: 4.1g;
- Trans Fat: 0g
- Protein: 27.2g;
- Net Carbs: 1.6g

Ingredients:
- 2 tablespoon olive oil
- 2 pounds ground beef
- Half-cup onion, chopped
- One-teaspoon salt
- One-teaspoon parsley
- One-teaspoon black pepper, ground
- One-teaspoon oregano
- Half-cup cheddar cheese
- 2 cups green beans
- 4 mozzarella sticks

Instructions:
1. On SAUTE function of your pressure cooker, brown the ground beef in olive oil; add the chopped onion, herbs, spices and salt.
2. When beef is browned, remove from pot and set aside.
3. Wash the inner pot of your pressure cooker and fill with two cups water; return the inner pot to the pressure cooker; place the trivet inside the inner pot with water.
4. In a tempered glass low baking dish, spread and arrange the green beans strips; cover with the browned ground beef; sprinkle the cheddar cheese and mozzarella sticks.
5. Cover and lock the pressure cooker's lid; Press cancel and switch to STEAMER function on High. Set the timer to 15 minutes.
6. When done, release the pressure by doing the Quick Release method.
7. Carefully take out the trivet with the baking dish and transfer to a hot pad. Best served immediately with Cauliflower Keto Rice.

511. AMAZING KETO SMOKE SPICE BEEF BRISKET

Prep Time: 10 minutes; **Cook Time:** 20 minutes **Servings:** 6;

Nutrition facts:
- Calories: 308g
- Total Fat: 15.0g
- Saturated Fat: 3.9g;
- Trans Fat: 0g
- Protein: 36.5g;
- Net Carbs: 4.4g

Ingredients:
- lb. beef brisket
- 2 tbsp. brown sugar
- 2 tsp. sea salt
- 1 tsp. black pepper
- 1 tsp. mustard, powder
- 1 tsp. onion, powder
- ½ tsp. paprika, smoked
- 2 c. broth
- 20 grams thyme sprigs
- 3 tablespoons coconut oil

Instructions:
1. In a small mixing bowl, combine the spices with brown sugar; mix well
2. Rub the beef brisket with the sugar and spice blend.
3. Set your pressure cooker to SAUTÉ; add coconut oil.
4. Brown the beef brisket on all sides taking care not to burn the meat.
5. Add the remaining ingredients and cover the pot, lock the lid and seal the vent valve.
6. Press CANCEL and switch to MANUAL function; set the timer to fifty (50) minutes.
7. When done, do the Natural Release method to let out steam pressure.
8. Take out the cooked meat and cover with aluminum foil.
9. Press CANCEL and switch to SAUTE function once more; set the timer to 10 minutes.
10. With the lid off, stir constantly to reduce and thicken the remaining liquid.
11. Slice your Smoke n' Spice Keto Beef Brisket and serve with your favorite Keto Mashed Cauliflower with a generous sprinkling of the reduced drippings.

512. YUMMY KETO SAUTÉED BEEF BROCCOLI MUSHROOM ENSEMBLE

Prep Time: 15 minutes; **Cook Time:** 20 minutes **Servings:** 6;

Nutrition facts:
- Calories: 263
- Total Fat: 7.6g
- Saturated Fat: 2.7g;
- Trans Fat: 0g
- Protein: 37.1g;
- Net Carbs: 6.0g

Ingredients:
- 1 ½ pounds ground beef
- Half-cup red wine
- 150 grams sliced mushrooms
- 135 grams broccoli
- 75 grams spinach, raw
- 2 tablespoons soy sauce
- 2 teaspoons garlic
- 2 teaspoons minced ginger
- One-tablespoon five spice
- One-tablespoon pepper
- One-teaspoon salt
- 2 teaspoons cumin
- One-teaspoon cayenne pepper
- Half-teaspoon onion powder
- 3 tablespoons ketchup

Instructions:
1. Peel the ginger and garlic and mince together; break broccoli into florets and chop the stalk.

2. Brown ground beef in pressure cooker on high heat at SAUTE setting. Add the minced garlic and ginger. Sauté the beef mixture for about 6 minutes or until the beef is browned. Stir in the broccoli with the soy sauce and all the spices. Stir in the red wine and add the mushrooms.
3. Lower the heat and continue to sauté for another 10 minutes. Add the spinach and continue to sauté for 4 minutes more. Remove from heat; transfer to a serving platter; add some ketchup and immediately serve.

513. MOUTHWATERING KETO TUNA EGG SALAD SANDWICH

Prep Time: 5 minutes; **Cook Time:** 10 minutes **Servings:** 2;

Nutrition facts:
- Calories: 376
- Total Fat: 34.5g
- Saturated Fat: 10.3g;
- Trans Fat: 0g
- Protein: 45.9g;
- Net Carbs: 3.7g

Ingredients:
- 1 tuna in can
- 1 steamed egg, chopped
- 100 grams bacon, crisp crumbled
- One-tablespoon onion, chopped
- One-tablespoon sour cream
- One-tablespoon mayonnaise
- 2 teaspoons prepared mustard
- Half-teaspoon dill
- Lettuce leaf, shredded

Instructions:
1. Prepare your pressure cooker by setting the function to SAUTE and set the timer to 10 minutes.
2. Sauté the bacon strips until crispy; when done, remove from heat and when cool enough to handle, crumble to pieces.
3. In a medium size bowl, combine half of the crumbled bacon, the chopped steamed egg (see How to Steam Eggs in Pressure Cooker), onion, sour cream, mayonnaise, mustard and dill; mix well.
4. Take a slice of Keto Bread, place a couple of spoonful of prepared Tuna Egg Salad and sprinkle bacon crumbles. Serve open face or cover with another slice of Keto Bread.

514. TASTY KETO CREAMY SPINACH BACON DISH

Prep Time: 10 minutes; **Cook Time:** 10 minutes **Servings:** 6;

Nutrition facts:
- Calories: 375
- Total Fat: 29.7g
- Saturated Fat: 13.9g;
- Trans Fat: 0g
- Protein: 23.4g;
- Net Carbs: 2.9g

Ingredients:
- 5 ounces bacon, sliced to bite size pieces
- ½ pound spinach leaves
- 8 eggs, large
- One-cup whip cream
- 5 ounces cheese, shredded
- 2 tablespoons butter
- Salt and pepper to taste

Instructions:
1. Preheat your pressure cooker on STEAM function on HIGH.
2. Place the steamer basket in the inner pot and pour 2 cups of water.
3. Place a glass baking dish on top of the steamer basket.

4. Add the butter and bacon to fry; Stir in the spinach.
5. Mix the eggs and cream in a medium size mixing bowl; transfer the mixture to the baking dish with bacon and spinach.
6. Sprinkle shredded cheese on top of the mixture.
7. Lock the lid of the pressure cooker and seal the vent. Set the timer to 10 minutes.
8. Do a Quick Release when done.

515. TASTY KETO TOMATO BASE SPICY BEEF STEW

Prep Time: 10 minutes; **Cook Time:** 30 minutes **Servings:** 8;

Nutrition facts:
- Calories: 260
- Total Fat: 16.6 g
- Saturated Fat: 6.0g;
- Trans Fat: 0g
- Protein: 19.4g;
- Net Carbs: 6.9g

Ingredients:
- 1 pound beef shank
- 4 tablespoons olive oil
- 4 tablespoons butter
- One-tablespoon soy sauce
- 2 cloves garlic, chopped
- 100 grams onion, chopped
- 1oo grams bell pepper, sliced
- One-teaspoon sea salt
- One-teaspoon cayenne
- One-teaspoon black pepper, ground
- One-tablespoon hot sauce, Sirach
- 2 cups tomato sauce
- One-cup water
- 100 grams carrots
- 100 grams green peas

Instructions:
1. Set the pressure cooker on SAUTE function; brown the steaks in olive oil.
2. When steaks are browned, press cancel and switch to MEAT function on HIGH pressure.
3. Add the rest of the ingredients except for the carrots and green peas, simmer for 10 minutes, before closing the lid, locking and sealing the vent valve. Switch to LOW pressure and set the timer for 30 minutes. When done, do the Quick Release method to let off steam; open the lid and stir in the carrots and green peas.
4. Press CANCEL and switch to MANUAL mode; set the timer to 5 minutes; cover, lock and seal the lid and vent valve. When done, transfer your delish Tomato Base Keto Spicy Beef Stew in your serving platter along with your Keto Mashed Cauliflower.

516. AMAZING KETO SALMON STEAMED FILET

Prep Time: 10 minutes; **Cook Time:** 20 minutes **Servings:** 8;

Nutrition facts:
- Calories: 227
- Total Fat: 10.4g
- Saturated Fat: 1.5g;
- Trans Fat: 0g
- Protein: 19.4g;
- Net Carbs: 3.7

Ingredients:
- 10 grams garlic, minced
- 20 grams ginger, crushed
- One-teaspoon fish sauce
- One-teaspoon lemon, juice
- 2 pounds salmon, filet
- One-cup, sour cream

- One-tablespoon mayo
- Half-teaspoon, dill weed
- 1/4 teaspoon, garlic powder
- 1/4 teaspoon, onion powder

Instructions:
1. In a small bowl, combine the first four ingredients; rub the mixture over all sides of the salmon filet.
2. Apply non-stick cooking spray to your steamer basket and place it inside your pressure cooker filled with 2 cups of water.
3. Put the seasoned salmon filet over the steamer basket, skin side down; set the pressure cooker on STEAM function on HIGH pressure and the timer to 20 minutes;
4. When done, open the vent valve to do a Quick Release to let the steam pressure out.
5. In a small bowl, combine the ingredients of your dipping sauce and serve with steamed salmon filet along with your Keto Mashed Cauliflower.

517. DIFFERENT KETO GREEN MANGO SALMON STRIPS

Prep Time: 10 minutes; **Cook Time:** 17 minutes **Servings:** 8;

Nutrition facts:
- Calories: 278
- Total Fat: 18.0g
- Saturated Fat: 6.8g;
- Trans Fat: 0g
- Protein: 18.8g;
- Net Carbs: 9.6g

Ingredients:
- 1/4 cup coconut oil
- 500 grams salmon fillet strips, with skin on
- One-teaspoon salt
- One-teaspoon fish sauce
- 1/4 cup vinegar, coconut
- 2 tablespoons ginger, crushed
- Half-cup tomatoes, sliced
- Half-cup onion, sliced
- One-teaspoon black pepper, coarsely ground
- 5 cups water
- 30 grams green mango, powder soup base
- 200 grams mustard, leaves

Instructions:
1. Place all the ingredients except the mustard leaves in your pressure cooker. Close, lock and seal the pressure valve. Press the SOUP function on HIGH pressure, set the timer to 15 minutes.
2. When done, do the Quick Release method by flipping the valve open to let the steam out.
3. Open the lid and add the mustard leaves; press cancel and shift to MANUAL function; adjust the timer to 2 minutes.

518. DELICIOUS KETO CHUCK EYE ROAST STEW

Prep Time: 15 minutes; **Cook Time:** 45 minutes **Servings:** 12;

Nutrition facts:
- Calories: 405
- Total Fat: 25.8g
- Saturated Fat: 12.3g;
- Trans Fat: 0g
- Protein: 35.7g;
- Net Carbs: 5.6g

Ingredients:
- 3 tablespoons olive oil
- 2 pounds beef, chuck eye roast
- 10 grams onion, sliced
- 2 teaspoons garlic
- 4 teaspoons rosemary
- One-teaspoons thyme

- 2 tablespoons soy sauce
- 8 tablespoons butter
- 100 grams sweet potatoes
- Half-cup broccoli, florets chopped
- Half-cup carrots, chopped
- 3 tablespoons tomato paste
- 1/4 cup coconut milk

Instructions:
1. On SAUTE function on HIGH pressure of your pressure cooker, set the timer to 15 minutes; brown the beef in olive oil; add the onions and garlic followed by rosemary, thyme and soy sauce; add a cup of water.
2. Cover, lock and seal the valve; press cancel and shift to the MEAT function on HIGH pressure, set the timer to 20 minutes.
3. Do the quick release method when done; open the cooker and add the butter, sweet potato, broccoli and carrots.
4. Reset the timer to cook for 15 minutes; cover, lock and seal the valve. Do the Quick release method to release the pressure when done.
5. Open the lid and pour in the tomato paste and coconut milk; replace the lid and press cancel; shift to MANUAL mode. Set the timer to 5 minutes. Cover, lock and seal the pressure valve.

519. Yummy Keto Lemon, Honey And Salmon Steamed Filets

Prep Time: 10 minutes;   **Cook Time:** 10 minutes   **Servings:** 4;

Nutrition facts:
- Calories: 252
- Total Fat: 12.2g
- Saturated Fat: 21.8g;
- Trans Fat: 0g
- Protein: 27.3g;
- Net Carbs: 5.4g

Ingredients:
- One-tablespoon olive oil
- 1.2 pounds salmon fillet
- One-tablespoon honey
- One-teaspoon salt
- One-teaspoon pepper
- 1 onion, sliced in rings
- 1 lemon, sliced
- 3 grams thyme leaves
- 10 grams parsley sprigs

Instructions:
1. Measure the width of your pressure cooker to determine the size of parchment paper to use before assembling your packets.
2. Coat your salmon fillets with olive oil, honey, salt and pepper
3. Lay the parchment paper on your work table and begin layering your ingredients - 1 salmon fillet, onion rings and a slice of lemon.
4. Fold up the paper packet. Cut a piece of aluminum foil enough to wrap your paper packet.
5. Pour a couple of cups of water in your pressure cooker. Put your steamer basket inside the pressure cooker. Arrange two salmon fillets packets in steamer basket.
6. Lock the pressure cooker lid. Set the pressure to HIGH on STEAM function; when the instant pot reaches the right pressure, turn down the heat to the lowest pressure maintenance level.
7. Cook for ten (10) minutes on HIGH pressure. Release the pressure when done.

8. Remove the packets from the pressure cooker. Gently remove the aluminum foil and set the fillet packets on individual plates. Tear the parchment paper just before serving.

520. TASTY KETO CREAMY MUSHROOM SAUCE WITH COD FISH

Prep Time: 10 minutes; **Cook Time:** 20 minutes **Servings:** 6;
Nutrition facts:
- Calories: 340g
- Total Fat: 26.9g
- Saturated Fat: 13.3g;
- Trans Fat: 0g
- Protein: 20.7g;
- Net Carbs: 3.9g

Ingredients:
- 1 pound mushrooms
- 3 ounces butter
- One-teaspoon salt
- 10 grams ginger
- 2 tablespoons fresh parsley
- 2 cups heavy whipping cream
- 3 tablespoons Dijon mustard
- ½-pound shredded cheese
- 1 ½ pounds cod
- 1 ½ pounds cauliflowers florets
- 3 ounces olive oil

Instructions:
1. Set the pressure cooker to SAUTE function on HIGH; add the butter.
2. Slice the mushrooms and stir fry in butter; season with the herbs, salt and pepper.
3. Stir in the mustard and heavy whipping cream; switch to LOW mode. Simmer uncovered for about 5-10 minutes to infuse sauce reduction.
4. Season cod fish with pepper and salt; carefully arrange the pieces in the pot; sprinkle half of the cheese and scoop out cream sauce to pour over the cod fish pieces and top with the remainder of the cheese.
5. Cover, lock the lid and seal the vent valve. Shift to MANUAL function and set the timer to 15 minutes.
6. When done, do the Quick Release method to release steam pressure.

"SPECIAL KETOGENIC SNACKS RECIPES"

521. YUMMY KETO RAZIL NUTS SNACKS

Prep Time: 10 minutes;   **Cook Time:** 20 minutes   **Servings:** 16;
Nutrition facts:
- Calories: 204
- Total Fat: 20.4g
- Saturated Fat: 10.2g;
- Trans Fat: 0g
- Protein: 5.1g;
- Net Carbs: 1.8g

Ingredients:
- Half-cup coconut oil
- 1/4 cup butter, unsalted
- 2 teaspoons maple syrup
- One-teaspoon almond extract
- 1/4 teaspoon sea salt.
- 62 grams whey protein
- 250 grams Brazil nuts, roasted

Instructions:
1. Spread a thick layer of sea salt at the bottom of the inner pot of your pressure cooker; place your trivet and steamer basket on top of the layer of sea salt.
2. Preheat the pressure cooker on SAUTE function for 10 minutes.
3. In a medium size bowl, mix all the ingredients and knead to make small balls.
4. Spray a 6-inch wide low baking pan with non-stick cooking spray.
5. Arrange and flatten the cookie balls about half an inch apart on the low baking pan.
6. Place the low baking pan in the pressure cooker atop the trivet and steamer basket.
7. Raise the heat to HIGH and set the timer to 20 minutes.
8. Loosely cover the pressure cooker with the lid.
9. When done, transfer the cookies to a cooling rack.

When completely cooled, store the cookies in a jar.

522. AMAZING KETO BROCCOLI AND ALMOND MUFFINS

Prep Time: 10 minutes;   **Cook Time:** 20 minutes   **Servings:** 4;
Nutrition facts:
- Calories: 307
- Total Fat: 29.3g
- Saturated Fat: 15.2g;
- Trans Fat: 0.0g
- Protein: 5.6g;
- Net Carbs: 8.1g

Ingredients:
- 2 cups broccoli
- 6 eggs
- 2 tablespoons coconut oil
- Half-cup almond flour
- 1/4 teaspoon baking soda
- Half-teaspoon salt
- Half-teaspoon baking powder
- Butter for greasing muffin cups

Instructions:
1. Preheat your pressure cooker to the STEAM function. Add 2 cups of water.
2. Place broccoli florets on a steamer basket and put in the pressure cooker.
3. Close and lock the lid; set the timer to five (5) minutes.
4. When done, take out the broccoli florets and break into coarse crumbles
5. Grease four (4) muffin tin cups with butter.

6. In a mixing bowl, beat the eggs; stir in the broccoli crumbles and coconut oil.
7. In another bowl, combine the almond flour, baking soda, salt and baking powder; fold in the broccoli-egg mixture.
8. Pour the broccoli-egg-almond flour mixture into each greased muffin cup.
9. Arrange the muffin tin cups in your basket strainer and insert the basket in the preheated pressure cooker.
10. Set the timer for 15 minutes; when done, take out the muffin tin cups from the pressure cooker; transfer to cool on a cooling rack.

523. AWESOME KETO BANANA NUT MUFFINS

Prep Time: 10 minutes;   **Cook Time:** 20 minutes   **Servings:** 4;

Nutrition facts:
- Calories: 307
- Total Fat: 29.3g
- Saturated Fat: 15.2g;
- Trans Fat: 0.0g
- Protein: 5.6g;
- Net Carbs: 8.1g

Ingredients:
- Half-cup almond, flour
- Half-cup butter
- 1 medium banana
- 3 tablespoons milk, almond
- 1/8 teaspoon salt,
- 2 grams sweetener
- One-teaspoon cinnamon
- Cheddar cheese

Instructions:
1. Preheat your pressure cooker to the STEAM function. Add 2 cups of water.
2. Grease 4 muffin tin cups with butter.
3. In a mixing bowl, combine all the ingredients and mix well.
4. Pour the egg cream mixture into each greased muffin cup.
5. Arrange the muffin tin cups in your basket strainer and insert the steamer basket in the preheated pressure cooker; steam for 15 minutes; take out the muffin tin cups from the oven; sprinkle shredded cheese on top of each muffin and return all cups to the pressure cooker; cook for 5 minutes more or until cheese is melted.
6. Take out the muffin tin cups from the pressure cooker, transfer to cool on a cooling rack.

524. AMAZING KETO CREAM CHEESE CELERY BACON DIP

Prep Time: 5 minutes;   **Cook Time:** 10 minutes   **Servings:** 8;

Nutrition facts:
- Calories: 229
- Total Fat: 21.8g
- Saturated Fat: 13.1g;
- Trans Fat: 0g
- Protein: 6.3g;
- Net Carbs: 2.1g

Ingredients:
- 8 ounces' cream cheese
- 1 pound bacon
- 8 celery stalks

Instructions:
1. Set your pressure cooker to the SAUTE function.
2. Arrange bacon slices in inner pot and cook occasionally turning over the slices.
3. When done, remove cooked bacon from the inner pot.
4. Put the cream cheese in a small bowl and add in the bacon drippings from the inner pot.
5. Chop the bacon slices and stir it into the cream cheese bacon drippings mixture.
6. Wash and cut celery stalks to serving size pieces and serve with your prepared cream cheese celery bacon keto dip.

525. DELICIOUS KETO ARUZMAT PIZZA

Prep Time: 20 minutes; **Cook Time:** 45 minutes **Servings:** 8;

Nutrition facts:
- Calories: 120
- Total Fat: 8.7g
- Saturated Fat: 3.9g;
- Trans Fat: 0g
- Protein: 6.8g;
- Net Carbs: 3.1g

Ingredients:
- One-tablespoon of olive oil
- 2 tablespoons butter
- 1.5 ounces onion, minced
- 1 head cauliflower, chopped
- 1/4 cup of water
- 3 eggs
- 2 cups mozzarella, chopped
- One-teaspoon fennel seed
- 2 teaspoons Italian seasoning
- 1/4 cup grated parmesan

Instructions:
1. Preheat your oven to 375°C. Brush a cookie sheet with some olive oil.
2. Set your pressure cooker in SAUTE function and melt the butter; add the onion and cauliflower.
3. Add half a cup of water; cover and set to STEAM function to cook for 10 minutes before removing the cooked cauliflower from the heat. Set aside to cool.
4. When cooled, scoop out 3 cups of cauliflower and process to puree in a food processor
5. In a mixing bowl, transfer the pureed cauliflower and stir in eggs, the 2 cheeses, and spices.
6. With a spatula, distribute the cauliflower mixture on the greased cookie sheet.
7. Bake the cauliflower pizza bed in the pre-heated oven for approximately 20 minutes
8. Take out the cauliflower pizza bed on your work table and start arranging all the toppings after spreading pizza sauce.
9. You can add Italian sausage, pepperoni and vegetables, sprinkle cheese generously, and return the filled-up cauliflower pizza bed to the oven and continue baking for 20 additional minutes.

526. EASY CHEESY KETO BACON BISCUIT

Prep Time: 5 minutes; **Cook Time:** 10 minutes **Servings:** 8;

Nutrition facts:
- Calories: 619
- Total Fat: 48.3g
- Saturated Fat: 24.2g;
- Trans Fat: 0g
- Protein: 26.0g;
- Net Carbs: 19.7g

Ingredients:
- 1 egg
- 2 tablespoons butter
- 3 tablespoons flour, almond
- Half-teaspoon baking powder
- 3 slices bacon, cooked and crumbled
- One-tablespoon cheese, white cheddar shredded
- One-tablespoon chive
- Half-teaspoon salt
- 1/4 teaspoon pepper

Instructions:
1. In a mixing bowl, blend all ingredients together.
2. Transfer the mixture to a ramekin or heatproof mug.
3. Set your pressure cooker to STEAM function; pour in 2 cups of water.
4. Place the steamer rack and set the ramekin or mug on top of it.
5. Close the lid and seal the vent valve.
6. Steam on HIGH for 10 minutes.
7. When done, do the Quick Release method to let out steam pressure.
8. Let cool for some time before digging into it.

527. TASTY KETO PEANUT BUTTER COCONUT COOKIES

Prep Time: 10 minutes; **Cook Time:** 20 minutes **Servings:** 12;

Nutrition facts:
- Calories: 220
- Total Fat: 16.5g
- Saturated Fat: 4.3g;
- Trans Fat: 0g
- Protein: 8.3g;
- Net Carbs: 10.4g

Ingredients:
- 350 grams peanut butter
- 2 eggs
- Half-cup coconut, shredded (unsweetened)
- Half-cup brown sugar
- One-tablespoon of vanilla extract

Instructions:
1. Spread a thick layer of sea salt at the bottom of the inner pot of your pressure cooker; place your trivet and steamer basket on top of the layer of sea salt.
2. Preheat the pressure cooker on SAUTE function for 10 minutes.
3. In a medium size bowl, mix all the ingredients and knead to make small balls.
4. Spray a 6-inch wide low baking pan with non-stick cooking spray.
5. Arrange and flatten the cookie balls about half an inch apart on the low baking pan.
6. Place the low baking pan in the pressure cooker atop the trivet and steamer basket.
7. Raise the heat to HIGH and set the timer to 20 minutes.
8. Loosely cover the pressure cooker with the lid.
9. When done, transfer the cookies to a cooling rack.
10. When completely cooled, store the cookies in a jar.

528. DIFFERENT KETO COCONUT BREAD

Prep Time: 6 minutes;   **Cook Time:** 12 minutes   **Servings:** 1;

Nutrition facts:
- Calories: 469g
- Total Fat: 40.2g
- Saturated Fat: 14.3g;
- Trans Fat: 0g
- Protein: 20.9g;
- Net Carbs: 3.7g

Ingredients:
- 2 eggs
- 2 tablespoons almond flour
- 2 tablespoons coconut flour
- Half-teaspoon baking powder
- One-tablespoon butter
- peanut butter
- guava jelly

Instructions:
1. Mix all the first 5 ingredients in a small mixing bowl; knead the dough and form into an elongated roll that would fit a tall greased mug or heat tempered tall glass container; cover the mug or container with aluminum foil and place it on your steamer basket.
2. Pour a couple of cups of water in the inner pot of your pressure cooker; place the steamer basket with the dough in mug; close the lid, lock and seal the valve.
3. On STEAM setting, set the timer for 15 minutes.
4. As soon as you hear the timer beep, slide the valve open to release pressure quickly; take out the steamer basket with the mug or container and set aside to cool.
5. Remove the keto bread from the mug or container and slice to desired thickness.
6. Spread your favorite peanut butter and guava jelly on each keto bread slice.

529. DELICIOUS KETO DARK CHOCOLATE BUTTER COOKIES

Prep Time: 10 minutes;   **Cook Time:** 20 minutes   **Servings:** 8;

Nutrition facts:
- Calories: 379
- Total Fat: 16.0g
- Saturated Fat: 6.5g;
- Trans Fat: 0g
- Protein: 49.5g;
- Net Carbs: 4.9g

Ingredients:
- 2 tablespoons almond butter
- One-tablespoon coconut oil
- 1/4 cup coconut milk
- 2 tablespoon coconut syrup
- 2 large eggs
- Half-teaspoon baking powder
- Half-teaspoon tsp salt
- 2 tablespoon sweetener
- 1Half-cups coconut, dried
- Half-cup flax meal
- 20 grams dark chocolate
- 18 almonds

Instructions:
1. In a small bowl, combine the pie crust ingredients and mix until well incorporated. Scoop out crust mixture to individual silicone cups and arrange the cups on a steamer basket.
2. Put 2 cups of water in the pressure cooker and insert the steamer basket with the pie crust cups; set the pressure cooker to STEAM function on HIGH pressure and set the timer to cook for 15 minutes.

3. Close the lid and seal the vent valve. When done, take out the pie crust cups on a cooling rack before putting them in the fridge to chill for at least an hour.
4. Crack the eggs in a medium size mixing bowl; add the remaining filling ingredients and mix thoroughly; pour this mixture in a saucepan and simmer over low heat, with constant stirring until a thick pudding-like texture is achieved; fill the chilled pie crust cups with the cooked filling.
5. Cover your Lemon Asparagus Keto Pancetta Cups with a plastic wrap and serve or store in your fridge for when future cravings attack.

530. YUMMY KETO CHEESE AUBERGINES SPINACH LAYERS

Prep Time: 30 minutes; **Cook Time:** 5 minutes **Servings:** 4;

Nutrition facts:
- Calories: 293
- Total Fat: 22.3g
- Saturated Fat: 8.0g;
- Trans Fat: 0g
- Protein: 6.3g;
- Net Carbs: 15.6g

Ingredients:
- 1 ½ pounds aubergines
- One-cup Marinara sauce
- 300 g spinach, fresh leaves
- 1 1/4 cup feta cheese
- One-cup mozzarella cheese, grated
- 100 grams Parmesan cheese, grated
- 6 eggs, large
- 85 grams ghee
- ½ tsp salt
- 10 grams oregano, fresh leaves
- 10 grams basil

Instructions:
1. Place two (2) cups of water into the inner pot of the pressure cooker,
2. Preheat the pressure cooker on STEAM function on High,
3. Slice the aubergines or eggplants into half inch slices; place the aubergines or eggplant slices on a baking dish greased with a quarter of melted ghee; adjust the taste of eggplants or aubergines with salt and pepper and arrange the slices in a glass tempered baking dish.
4. Place the dish in the pressure cooker. Close and lock the lid and set timer to cook for 10 minutes. Do a quick release method when done. Remove the aubergines or eggplants from the pressure cooker, slice and set aside.
5. Blanch the spinach by boiling water and dipping the spinach in it for at least 58 seconds. Transfer blanched spinach leaves to a bowl of cold water; drain excess water after 5 minutes.
6. Beat the eggs in a small bowl and cook over a stove top with your fry pan to do some thin omelet spread.
7. You can now start your lasagna assembly. Put two (2) omelets at the bottom of a baking sheet.
8. Spread some Marinara sauce over the omelets. Do the layers alternately using a layer of all the ingredients - eggplant slices, mozzarella cheese, spinach leaves and half of the crumbled feta cheese.
9. Place the baking dish in the pressure cooker; close the lid and lock; set the timer to 15 minutes and set the function to STEAM. Use the Quick release method when done.

531. AMAZING KETO AVOCADO CHOCOLATE CAKE

Prep Time: 10 minutes;   **Cook Time:** 20 minutes   **Servings:** 6;

Nutrition facts:
- Calories: 173
- Total Fat: 12.8g
- Saturated Fat: 3.0g;
- Trans Fat: 0.0g
- Protein: 5.6g;
- Net Carbs: 7.8g

Ingredients:
- One-cup almond, flour
- ½ tsp baking soda
- ½ tsp salt
- 1/4 cup sweetener
- 6 tablespoons cocoa powder, unsweetened
- One-cup water
- 1/4 cup yogurt
- 60 grams avocado, mashed
- 2 teaspoons pure vanilla extract
- 1/4 cup chocolate chips

Instructions:
1. Preheat the pressure cooker in STEAM function, pour 2 cups of water and turn on the timer for 5 minutes; brush the insides of a Bundt pan with coconut oil.
2. Mix all dry ingredients in a medium size mixing bowl; add the water, yogurt and mashed avocado; beat until incorporated.
3. Transfer the batter in a tempered glass 6-inch round baking dish; cover the dish with aluminum foil and place the dish on top of your trivet; insert the trivet in your preheated pressure cooker. Close the lid, lock and seal the vent valve. Cook on HIGH for 20 minutes.
4. Do the Quick Release method to let out the steam pressure.
5. Take out your Avocado Keto Chocolate Cake to cool on a cooling rack.
6. Serve plain or top with your favorite healthy cream cheese frosting.

532. TASTY KETO MANGO MACADAMIA AVOCADO TOSS

Prep Time: 10 minutes;   **Cook Time:** 10 minutes   **Servings:** 6;

Nutrition facts:
- Calories: 214
- Total Fat: 17.8g
- Saturated Fat: 5.3g;
- Trans Fat: 0g
- Protein: 2.1g;
- Net Carbs: 9.2g

Ingredients:
- 400 grams avocado, seeds removed and sliced in halves
- One-cup mango, cut to cubes
- 2 tablespoons coconut, shredded
- 4 tablespoons coconut, oil
- 2 tablespoons macadamia nuts, chopped
- One-teaspoon olive oil
- Iceberg lettuce, torn to bite size pieces

Instructions:
1. Set your steamer basket in the inner pot of your pressure cooker; pour 2 cups water.
2. Arrange the avocado halves skin side down over the steamer basket and cover with a paper towel.
3. Turn the pressure cooker on and set to STEAM function; set the timer to ten (10) minutes.
4. When done, do a Quick Release to let out steam pressure; take out the steamed avocado halves and scoop out the flesh; cut avocado flesh into bite size cubes.

5. In a medium size mixing bowl combine the ripe mango cubes with shredded coconut and coconut oil.
6. Toss in the steamed avocado cubes and lettuce; sprinkle the chopped macadamia nuts and some olive oil.
7. Give it one good toss and dig in.

---

533. EASY KETO COCONUT LOCO BREAD

Prep Time: 15 minutes; **Cook Time:** 20 minutes **Servings:** 8;

Nutrition facts:
- Calories: 237
- Total Fat: 17.6g
- Saturated Fat: 12.4g;
- Trans Fat: 0g
- Protein: 7.3g;
- Net Carbs: 10.8g

Ingredients:
- 8 eggs
- Half-teaspoon vanilla
- 1 ½ cups canned coconut, milk
- 1/4 teaspoon baking soda
- One-cup coconut, flour
- 1/4 teaspoon salt
- 200 grams pears, diced
- Half-cup dark chocolate, chips
- One-tablespoon coconut oil

Instructions:
1. Preheat the pressure cooker in STEAM function on HIGH pressure. Place the steamer rack inside the pressure cooker and fill in 2 cups of water.
2. Whisk together the eggs, vanilla, and coconut milk. In a separate bowl, sift together the coconut flour, baking soda, and salt.
3. Fold egg mixture slowly into the flour blend.
4. Add the diced pears and chocolate chips into the batter.
5. Brush the bread baking pans with coconut oil. Pour enough batter in each pan. Place in the baking pan over the steamer basket.
6. Cover, lock the lid and seal the vent valve; reset the timer to 20 minutes.
7. 7.When done, use the Quick Release method to let steam pressure out.

---

534. TASTY KETO WHITE LOAF

Prep Time: 10 minutes; **Cook Time:** 20 minutes **Servings:** 6;

Nutrition facts:
- Calories: 170
- Total Fat: 12.9g
- Saturated Fat: 1.4g;
- Trans Fat: 0g
- Protein: 7.2g;
- Net Carbs: 4.8g

Ingredients:
- 2 cups almond, flour
- Half-teaspoon baking soda
- One-teaspoon salt
- One-teaspoon olive oil
- 1 1/4 cup yogurt

Instructions:
1. Prepare the pressure cooker with the trivet.

2. Spray cooking oil on the bottom and sides of a cylindrical heat tempered 1-liter capacity container.
3. In a mixing bowl, combine the almond flour with salt and baking soda; stir in the yoghurt and mix well.
4. On a floured work board, lightly knead the flour mixture to form a cylindrical dough log; add a little bit of water if the mixture does not stick well after kneading.
5. Put the dough log in your greased cylindrical container; spray the top of the dough log and cover the container with aluminum foil.
6. Put the covered container over the trivet in the pressure cooker; pour 3-4 cups of hot tap water into the pressure cooker to cover half the height of your cylindrical container.
7. Close, lock the lid and pressure valve; set in STEAM function on HIGH pressure to cook for up to 20 minutes.
8. When done, use the Natural release method to let the pressure out for about 10 minutes; unplug the cooker and remove the cylindrical container and transfer to a cooling rack. Let stand for 15-20 minutes before taking out your Keto White Bread from the container and slicing it to desired thickness.
9. Best served with your favorite Basil Garlic Keto Butter Spread.

535. TASTY KETO TUNA TOSS

Prep Time: 10 minutes; **Cook Time:** 10 minutes **Servings:** 4;

Nutrition facts:
- Calories: 158
- Total Fat: 10.0g
- Saturated Fat: 2.4g;
- Trans Fat: 0g
- Protein: 13.5g;
- Net Carbs: 1.8g

Ingredients:
- 100 grams avocados
- 5-ounce tuna
- 1 stalk celery, minced
- One-tablespoon mayonnaise
- 1/4 tsp salt
- 1/4 tsp black pepper
- 2 ounces shredded cheddar
- 10 grams chives

Instructions:
1. Set your steamer basket in the inner pot of your pressure cooker; pour 2 cups water.
2. Arrange the avocado halves skin side down over the steamer basket and cover with a paper towel.
3. Turn the pressure cooker on and set to STEAM function; set the timer to ten (10) minutes.
4. When done, do a Quick Release to let out steam pressure; take out the steamed avocado halves and scoop out the flesh; cut avocado flesh into bite size cubes.
5. In a medium size mixing bowl combine the tuna with minced celery, mayonnaise, salt and pepper; toss in the steamed avocado cubes and sprinkle shredded cheddar cheese and chives.

536. YUMMY KETO JAMANA GRAPEFRUIT AVOCADO TOSS

Prep Time: 10 minutes; **Cook Time:** 10 minutes **Servings:** 6;

Nutrition facts:
- Calories: 130
- Total Fat: 12.6g
- Saturated Fat: 2.0g;
- Trans Fat: 0g
- Protein: 0.6g;
- Net Carbs: 2.5g

Ingredients:
- 100 grams avocado, seeds removed and sliced in halves
- 100 grams jicama
- 100 grams grapefruit
- Half-cup apple cider vinegar
- 2 grams sweetener
- 4 tablespoons olive oil

Instructions:
1. Set your steamer basket in the inner pot of your pressure cooker; pour 2 cups of water.
2. Arrange the avocado halves skin side down over the steamer basket and cover with a paper towel.
3. Turn the pressure cooker on and set to STEAM function; set the timer to ten (10) minutes.
4. When done, do a Quick Release to let out steam pressure; take out the steamed avocado halves and scoop out the flesh; cut avocado flesh into bite size cubes.
5. In a medium size mixing bowl combine the jicama with grapefruit, apple cider, sweetener and olive oil; toss in the steamed avocado cubes.

537. DELICIOUS KETO CREAMY CAULIFLOWER MASHED

Prep Time: 5 minutes; **Cook Time:** 10 minutes **Servings:** 4;

Nutrition facts:
- Calories: 205
- Total Fat: 18.8g
- Saturated Fat: 11.6g;
- Trans Fat: 0g
- Protein: 6.3g;
- Net Carbs: 5.2g

Ingredients:
- 1 pound cauliflower
- 2 cups water mixed with One-tablespoon salt
- 4 ounces parmesan cheese
- 4 ounces butter
- 1 fruit lemon, juice and zest
- One-teaspoon olive oil
- 1/4 cup sour cream
- 3 tablespoons heavy whipping cream
- 1/4 teaspoon garlic powder
- 2 tablespoon chives, chopped
- salt and pepper to taste

Instructions:
1. Place your cauliflower over your steamer basket in the pressure cooker; add 2 cups of salted water.
2. Set your pressure cooker to STEAM function, close the lid and seal the vent valve.
3. Set the timer to 15 minutes. When done, do the Quick Release to let off steam.

4. Break the steamed cauliflower into florets, place in a medium size bowl and mash florets with a masher or fork; stir in the rest of the ingredients and mix well. Serve immediately or store in the refrigerator until ready to serve.

"SPECIAL KETOGENIC DESSERT RECIPES"

538. AWESOME KETO CHEESECAKE WITH MARMALADE

Prep Time: 10 minutes;   **Cook Time:** 20 minutes   **Servings:** 8;

Nutrition facts:
- Calories: 276
- Total Fat: 21.1g
- Saturated Fat: 12.8g;
- Trans Fat: 0g
- Protein: 6.0g;
- Net Carbs: 5.4g

Ingredients:
- 16 ounces cream cheese
- 2 large eggs
- 2 teaspoons vanilla extract
- Half-cup sugar
- One-cup blueberry marmalade

Instructions:
1. Put all the ingredients except the blueberry marmalade in a blender. Beat until smooth in texture.
2. Transfer the mixture to a seven-inch spring-form pan; cover the pan with aluminum foil.
3. Place two (2) cups of water into the inner pot of the pressure cooker; place the steamer basket in and gently place the tin pan on top of the steamer basket.
4. Steam pressure for 20 minutes on HIGH.
5. Use the natural depressurizing technique. Remove the tin pan from the pressure cooker and transfer to a cooling; let stand for 45 minutes

Place in the fridge for at least an hour before serving topped with blueberry marmalade.

539. TASTY KETO FROSTED ALMOND COCONUT CUPCAKES

Prep Time: 20 minutes;   **Cook Time:** 15 minutes   **Servings:** 14;

Nutrition facts:
- Calories: 386
- Total Fat: 33.9g
- Saturated Fat: 20.5g;
- Trans Fat: 0g
- Protein: 7.4g;
- Net Carbs: 10.3g

Ingredients:

Cupcake
- One-cup flour, coconut
- One-cup milk, almond
- 8 eggs
- Half-cup butter. unsalted
- One-tablespoon baking powder
- 3 teaspoons vanilla extract
- Half-teaspoon salt
- Half-cup sweetener
- ½ tsp stevia

Frosting
- 16 ounces cream cheese
- 26 fresh red raspberries
- One-cup butter, melted
- One-tablespoon pure vanilla extract
- 1/4 cup sweetener
- Half-teaspoon liquid stevia

Instructions:
1. Mix all cupcake ingredients in a large mixing bowl until smooth texture is achieved.

2. Gently pour the mixture into the greased silicone cups and arrange them on top of the steamer basket; cover each silicone cup with a sheet of foil.
3. Set your pressure cooker to STEAM function; add two cups water. Place the steamer basket with cupcake tins.
4. Close the lid and lock your pressure cooker. Set the timer to cook for 25 minutes.
5. Release the pressure the natural way; remove the cupcake tins and transfer to a cooling rack; let cool for 30 minutes before removing the cupcakes from the tins.
6. In a small bowl, whisk together the frosting ingredients until fluffy. Spread frosting on each cooled cupcake.

540. YUMMY KETO COCOA MACADAMIA BOOSTERS

Prep Time: 15 minutes; **Cook Time:** 10 minutes **Servings:** 8;

Nutrition facts:
- Calories: 208
- Total Fat: 23.2g
- Saturated Fat: 17.1g;
- Trans Fat: 0g
- Protein: 10.8g;
- Net Carbs: 7.9g

Ingredients:
- 150 grams coconut oil
- 30 grams cocoa powder, unsweetened
- 2 grams sweetener, granules
- 42 grams macadamia nuts, chopped

Instructions:
1. Heat coconut oil in the pressure cooker on SAUTE function on NORMAL pressure setting.
2. Stir in the cocoa powder and sweetener; remove from heat after 5 minutes.
3. Spoon the cocoa mixture into candy molds or ice cube trays.
4. Place the trays in the fridge for at least an hour or more until mixture starts to get thick like gel.
5. Top each cocoa mold with chopped macadamia nuts.
6. Return the tray mold in the fridge until the fat bombs harden.
7. Serve or let sit in the refrigerator until the next craving bout.

541. DELICIOUS KETO PEANUT BUTTER COOKIES

Prep Time: 14 minutes; **Cook Time:** 19 minutes **Servings:** 15;

Nutrition facts:
- Calories: 242g
- Total Fat: 17.9g
- Saturated Fat: 3.8g;
- Trans Fat: 0g
- Protein: 9.3g;
- Net Carbs: 12.8g

Ingredients:
- 2 eggs
- One-cups confectioner's sugar
- One-teaspoon almond extract
- 2 cups peanut butter

Instructions:
1. Spread a thick layer of sea salt at the bottom of the inner pot of your pressure cooker; place your trivet and steamer basket on top of the layer of sea salt.
2. Preheat the pressure cooker on STEAM function for 10 minutes.
3. In a medium size bowl, mix all the ingredients and knead to make small balls.
4. Spray a 6-inch wide low baking pan with non-stick cooking spray.
5. Arrange and flatten the cookie balls about half an inch apart on the low baking pan.

6. Place the low baking pan in the pressure cooker atop the trivet and steamer basket.
7. Close, lock and seal the valve.
8. Raise the heat to HIGH and set the timer to 10 minutes.
9. Loosely cover the pressure cooker with the lid.
10. When done, transfer the cookies to a cooling rack.
11. When completely cooled, store the almond peanut butter keto cookies in a jar.

542. TASTY KETO TORCHED CREAMY EGG CUSTARD

Prep Time: 20 minutes; **Cook Time:** 15 minutes **Servings:** 3;

Nutrition facts:
- Calories: 228
- Total Fat: 17.9g
- Saturated Fat: 8.8g;
- Trans Fat: 0g
- Protein: 6.7g;
- Net Carbs: 8.1g

Ingredients:
- 6 egg yolks
- 4 grams sugar, raw
- 2 cups cream, fresh
- One-tablespoon vanilla extract

Instructions:
1. Mix the egg yolks, sugar, cream and vanilla in a medium sized mixing bowl.
2. Gently pour the mixture into the ramekins through a sieve.
3. Cover the ramekins with foil.
4. Set your pressure cooker to STEAM function. Add two cups water. Place the steamer basket and on it, arrange the ramekins.
5. Close the lid and lock your pressure cooker. Set the time to cook for 15 minutes.
6. Release the pressure the natural way; remove the ramekins and transfer to a cooling rack. Take off the tin foil and let cool for 30 minutes before transferring to the fridge to completely chill for a minimum of 5 hours.
7. Before serving, sprinkle raw sugar on top of each cooled custard and torch to caramelize.

543. MOUTHWATERING KETO CARAMEL GLAZED CHEESECAKE CUPS

Prep Time: 15 minutes; **Cook Time:** 30 minutes **Servings:** 10;

Nutrition facts:
- Calories: 181
- Total Fat: 17.3g
- Saturated Fat: 9.1g;
- Trans Fat: 0g
- Protein: 3.0g;
- Net Carbs: 9.8g

Ingredients:
- 6 tablespoon butter
- Half-cup sweetener
- Half-cup almond, flour
- Half-cup coconut, meat
- ½ tsp baking powder
- 8 ounces cream, heavy whip
- Half-cup sweetener
- 1 egg
- Salted Caramel Sauce
- 100 grams brown sugar
- 2 tablespoon sweetener
- 1/4 cup almond, flour
- Pinch of salt

Instructions:

1. In a small bowl, combine butter with sweetener; stir in the flour, shredded coconut, and baking powder and mix until well incorporated. Scoop about 2 tablespoon of the batter into silicone baking cups; place the cups over a steamer basket.
2. Put 2 cups of water in the pressure cooker and insert the steamer basket with the silicone cups; set the pressure cooker to STEAM function on HIGH pressure and set the timer to cook for 15 minutes.
3. Close the lid and seal the vent valve. When done, take out the cups on a cooling rack.
4. In a small bowl, combine the heavy whipping cream, half a cup of sweetener and the egg; beat and top each silicone cups with the heavy whipping cream mixture.
5. Put all filled cups back to the pressure cooker; cover and seal the vent valve; press cancel and set function to MANUAL; set the timer cooker to five (5) minutes; when done, do the Natural Release method to let off the pressure steam. Take out the cream cheesecake to cool in a cooling rack; place in the refrigerator when cool enough to handle.
6. Prepare the salted caramel sauce by cooking all ingredients in a sauce pan over low heat, stirring constantly. When done, pour a layer of the salted caramel sauce on top of each cheesecake cup; put them back in the refrigerator to set for 2 hours.

---

544. AMAZING KETO NUTTY CHEESECAKE OVERLOAD

Prep Time: 15 minutes; **Cook Time:** 10 minutes **Servings:** 4;

Nutrition facts:

- Calories: 420
- Total Fat: 38.6g
- Saturated Fat: 20.1g;
- Trans Fat: 0g
- Protein: 10.8g;
- Net Carbs: 7.9g

Ingredients:

Base Crust

- 2 tablespoon butter, softened
- 2 tablespoon cocoa powder
- 2 tablespoon almond flour
- 2 tablespoon sweetener
- 2 eggs
- One-teaspoon almond extract
- One-tablespoon pecans, chopped finely
- One-tablespoon walnuts, chopped finely

Filling

- 8 ounces cream cheese, softened
- 2 tablespoon sweetener
- 2 tablespoon sour cream, full fat
- One-teaspoon vanilla extract

Glaze

- 1 ounce dark chocolate, shaved
- One-tablespoon peanut butter

Instructions:

1. Preheat the pressure cooker on STEAM function on HIGH pressure; brush a 6-inch cheesecake pan with butter; combine the butter with almond flour, cocoa powder, and sweetener in a medium size bowl until smooth; beat an egg in a small bowl; add the almond extract and beat

well; stir in the chopped nuts and pour the mixture in prepared baking pan; cover with aluminum foil.
2. Place the pan on top of a steamer basket and insert the same inside the pressure cooker.
3. Cover, lock the lid and seal the vent valve; set the timer to 5 minutes; when done, do the Quick Release method to release steam pressure.
4. In a medium size bowl, beat the cream cheese; add the sweetener and beat in the remaining egg, sour cream, and vanilla extract; Pour this mixture into the cooled base crust.
5. Return the base crust to the pressure cooker. Cover, close the lock and seal the vent valve. Reset the time to 20 minutes. Do the natural release method to let out steam pressure.
6. Remove your Keto Cheesecake and refrigerate for two (2) hours or until set.
7. Prepare the ganache topping by melting the chocolate and butter over high heat; constantly stir until smooth. Drizzle a couple of spoonfuls over each serving and indulge!

545. Yummy Keto Dark Chocolate Brownies

Prep Time: 15 minutes;   **Cook Time:** 30 minutes   **Servings:** 12;
Nutrition facts:
- Calories: 183
- Total Fat: 13.5g
- Saturated Fat: 4.3g;
- Trans Fat: 0g
- Protein: 5.3g;
- Net Carbs: 10.6g

Ingredients:
- One cup almond, flour
- 1/4 teaspoon salt
- 1/4 teaspoon baking powder
- Half-cup cocoa, natural powder
- 2 teaspoon stevia powder
- 1/4 cup butter, melted
- 1 egg
- 2 eggs, egg whites
- 2 teaspoons vanilla extract
- 100 grams marshmallows, cut to tidbits
- Half-cup walnuts, chopped coarsely
- 1/4 cup chocolate, dark chips

Instructions:
1. Spray the bottom and sides of your 6-inch round baking pan with cooking oil spray.
2. In a medium size mixing bowl, combine the almond flour, salt, cocoa, stevia, and baking powder.
3. In a separate bowl, mix the melted butter with, egg, egg whites and vanilla.
4. Pour the butter mixture into the almond flour mixture and whisk until just incorporated.
5. Transfer the batter into the greased baking pan and evenly spread the mixture.
6. You have the option to refrigerate the batter for up to 8 hours before cooking if you have the luxury of time to savor the best tasting brownies ever.
7. Remove from the fridge and set it to reach room temperature within 25 minutes.
8. Top the chilled batter with marshmallow tidbits and chopped walnuts; cover the pan with aluminum foil.
9. Pour 2 cups of water in the inner pot of your pressure cooker; insert the trivet and place the baking pan over your trivet. Close the lid, lock and seal the pressure cooker valve. Cook on HIGH for 20 minutes.

10. When done, release the pressure with the Quick release method; transfer your baked brownies to a cooling rack. Serve warm or store in fridge when completely cooled.

546. DELICIOUS KETO COCO WALNUT SNOWBALL

Prep Time: 10 minutes; **Cook Time:** 15 minutes **Servings:** 18;

Nutrition facts:
- Calories: 197
- Total Fat: 15.0g
- Saturated Fat: 4.1g;
- Trans Fat: 0g
- Protein: 4.3g;
- Net Carbs: 12.0g

Ingredients:
- 2 cups almond flour
- One-cup walnuts
- 2 tablespoon coconut flour
- One-teaspoon baking powder
- One-teaspoon cardamom
- 1/4 teaspoon salt
- Half-cup butter, softened
- Half-cup sugar
- 1 large egg
- One-teaspoon vanilla extract
- 1/4 cup powdered Stevia

Instructions:
1. Spread a thick layer of sea salt at the bottom of the inner pot of your pressure cooker; place your trivet and steamer basket on top of the layer of sea salt.
2. Preheat the pressure cooker on SAUTE function for 15 minutes.
3. In a medium size bowl, mix all the ingredients except the powdered Stevia and knead to make small balls.
4. Spray a 6-inch wide low baking pan with non-stick cooking spray.
5. Arrange and flatten the cookie balls about half an inch apart on the low baking pan.
6. Place the low baking pan in the pressure cooker atop the trivet and steamer basket.
7. Raise the heat to HIGH and set the timer to 20 minutes.
8. Loosely cover the pressure cooker with the lid.
9. When done, transfer the snowballs to a cooling rack; sprinkle powdered Stevia over the cookie balls.
10. When completely cooled, store your Coco-Walnut Coco Snowballs in a cookie jar.

547. TASTY KETO TORCHED COCO AVOCADO CUSTARD

Prep Time: 15 minutes; **Cook Time:** 10 minutes **Servings:** 36;

Nutrition facts:
- Calories: 323
- Total Fat: 25.9g
- Saturated Fat: 6.4g;
- Trans Fat: 0g
- Protein: 6.3g;
- Net Carbs: 14.4g

Ingredients:
- 120 grams avocado
- Half-cup milk, coconut
- Half-teaspoon almond extract
- 1/8 teaspoon salt
- 5 grams sweetener
- One-teaspoon brown sugar

Instructions:

1. Preheat the pressure cooker in STEAM mode, pour 2 cups of water and turn on the timer for 5 minutes.
2. In a blender, puree the avocado with the coconut milk and all ingredients except brown sugar.
3. Pour the pureed mixture in ramekins; cover the ramekins with aluminum foil
4. Place the ramekins on top of your trivet and insert in pressure cooker.
5. Close the lid, lock and seal the pressure cooker valve. Cook on HIGH for 10 minutes. Do the Quick Release method to let out steam pressure.
6. Refrigerate each ramekin for at least an hour up to five hours to achieve the desired thickness.
7. Before serving, sprinkle one half (½) teaspoon brown sugar on top of each ramekin.
8. Use your blow torch to brown the sugar or broil for five (5) minutes.

548. YUMMY KETO CINNAMON VANILLA COOKIES

Prep Time: 14 minutes; **Cook Time:** 19 minutes **Servings:** 15;

Nutrition facts:
- Calories: 219g
- Total Fat: 20.4g
- Saturated Fat: 6.0g;
- Trans Fat: 0g
- Protein: 6.1g;
- Net Carbs: 2.4g

Ingredients:
- 1 ½ cups almond, flour
- Half-teaspoon baking soda
- Half-teaspoon cream of tartar
- 1/4 teaspoon cinnamon (in a small bowl)
- 4 tablespoon butter
- 1 large egg
- Half-teaspoon vanilla
- 1/4 cup stevia
- 10 ml stevia

Instructions:
1. Spread a thick layer of sea salt at the bottom of the inner pot of your pressure cooker; place your trivet and steamer basket on top of the layer of sea salt.
2. Preheat the pressure cooker on STEAM function for 10 minutes.
3. In a medium size bowl, mix all the ingredients and knead to make small balls.
4. Spray a 6-inch wide low baking pan with non-stick cooking spray.
5. Arrange and flatten the cookie balls about half an inch apart on the low baking pan.
6. Place the low baking pan in the pressure cooker atop the trivet and steamer basket.
7. Close, lock and seal the valve.
8. Raise the heat to HIGH and set the timer to 10 minutes.
9. Loosely cover the pressure cooker with the lid.
10. When done, transfer the cookies to a cooling rack.
11. When completely cooled, store the almond cinnamon keto cookies in a jar.

549. AMAZING KETO BUTTERNUT SQUASH CUPCAKE

Prep Time: 30 minutes; **Cook Time:** 10 minutes **Servings:** 4;

Nutrition facts:
- Calories: 289
- Total Fat: 24.3g
- Saturated Fat: 15.0g;
- Trans Fat: 0g
- Protein: 3.1g;
- Net Carbs: 14.6g

Ingredients:

- 10 grams flour, coconut
- 500 grams butternut squash
- 1 egg
- Half-cup butter
- One-teaspoon vanilla extract
- Half-teaspoon baking powder
- Half-teaspoon pumpkin pie spice

Instructions:
1. Preheat your pressure cooker on STEAM function. Add the butternut squash and a cup of water.
2. Close and lock the lid of your pressure cooker; set the timer to 5 minutes.
3. When done, release the pressure with the natural release method.
4. Take out the cooked butternut squash from your pressure cooker and mash with a fork.
5. Place mashed butternut squash in a medium size bowl; add the egg, melted butter, baking powder, and pumpkin pie spice. Mix well.
6. Preheat your pressure cooker on STEAMER function. Add 2 cups of water to the inner pot.
7. With an ice cream scoop, place a scoopful of mashed butternut squash mixture into greased muffin cups; arrange the filled muffin cups on the steamer basket and place the basket in the pressure cooker inner pot filled with 2 cups water
8. Close and lock the lid of your pressure cooker; set the timer to 10 minutes.
9. When done, do the Quick release method to release pressure.
10. Take out the muffin cups from the pressure cooker and set on a cooling rack to cool.

550. Delicious Keto Dark Chocolate Truffles

Prep Time: 15 minutes; **Cook Time:** 20 minutes **Servings:** 36;

Nutrition facts:
- Calories: 247
- Total Fat: 25.4g
- Saturated Fat: 17.9g;
- Trans Fat: 0g
- Protein: 23.9g;
- Net Carbs: 4.9g

Ingredients:
- 2 pounds macadamia nuts
- Half-cup (125 ml) liquor, rum liquor
- 150 grams butter
- Half-cup sugar
- One-cup hazelnuts (or almonds), unshelled
- 1/4 cup dark chocolate, powder

Instructions:
1. Place the macadamia nuts in your pressure co0ker with One-cup water. Close, lock the lid and seal the vent valve of your pressure cooker.
2. Set the pressure on HIGH; when pressure cooker is up to the standard level of pressure, lower the heat to the required minimum.
3. Cook for 8 minutes at high pressure. When done, release the pressure with the natural release method.
4. Transfer the macadamia nuts to a mixing bowl; stir in the liquor, butter, and sugar and mash. Let it sit for at least an hour to let the nuts absorb excess liquid.
5. Form small bite size balls using your hand; tuck in a whole hazelnut in the center of each ball.
6. Place the little balls on a plate dusted with cocoa to keep them from sticking.
7. Drizzle a little cocoa powder on top; repeat rolling into a compact ball.

You can do this in batches, Chill in the fridge for at least an hour to maximize highlights in your itinerary before serving.

551. MOUTHWATERING KETO MACADAMIA LACED CAKE

Prep Time: 14 minutes; **Cook Time:** 19 minutes **Servings:** 12;

Nutrition facts:
- Calories: 154g
- Total Fat: 14.4g
- Saturated Fat: 3.7g;
- Trans Fat: 0g
- Protein: 3.5g;
- Net Carbs: 2.8g

Ingredients:
- 1 large egg
- 4 tablespoons butter
- 2 tablespoons brown sugar
- 1 ½ cups almond, flour
- Half-teaspoon baking soda
- Half-cup macadamia nuts, chopped

Instructions:
1. Spray the bottom and sides of your 6-inch round baking pan with cooking oil spray.
2. In a medium size mixing bowl, combine all the ingredients except the chopped macadamia nuts.
3. Transfer the batter into the greased baking pan and evenly spread the mixture.
4. You have the option to refrigerate the batter for up to 8 hours before cooking. Remove from the fridge and set it to reach room temperature within 25 minutes.
5. Top the chilled batter with chopped macadamia nuts; cover the pan with aluminum foil.
6. Pour 2 cups of water in the inner pot of your pressure cooker; insert the trivet and place the baking pan over your trivet. Close the lid, lock and seal the pressure cooker valve. Set the cooker on STEAM on HIGH and cook for 20 minutes.
7. When done, release the pressure with the Quick release method; transfer your steamed macadamia-laced cake to a cooling rack. Serve warm or store in fridge when completely cooled.

CONCLUSION

If you enjoyed this book or found it useful I'd be very grateful if you'd post a short review on Amazon. Your support really does make a difference and I read all the reviews personally so I can get your feedback and make this book even better.

Made in the USA
Middletown, DE
02 December 2017